BUSINESS BASICS

A study guide for degree students

Accounting

BPP

PUBLISHING

Second edition October 2000

ISBN 0 7517 2125 5
(previous edition 0 7517 2116 6)

British Library Cataloguing-in-Publication Data

A catalogue record for this book
is available from the British Library

BPP Publishing Limited
Aldine House, Aldine Place
London W12 8AW

www.bpp.com

Printed in Great Britain by W M Print
45 – 47 Frederick Street
Walsall
West Midlands
WS2 9NE

All our rights reserved. No part of this publication may be reproduced, stored in a retrieval system or transmitted, in any form or by any means, electronic, mechanical, photocopying, recording or otherwise, without the prior written permission of BPP Publishing Limited.

BPP Publishing would like to thank the following:

Raymond Taylor for authorial input

Genesys Editorial for editorial and production input

We are grateful to the Chartered Institute of Management Accountants and the Association of Chartered Certified Accountants for permission to reproduce past examination questions in this text, the suggested answers to which have been prepared by BPP Publishing.

©

BPP Publishing Limited

2000

CONTENTS

PREFACE

BUSINESS BASICS are targeted specifically at the needs of:

- Students taking business studies degrees
- Students taking business-related modules of other degrees
- Students on courses at a comparable level
- Others requiring business information at this level

This *Accounting* text has been written with two key goals in mind.

- To present a substantial and useful body of knowledge on Accounting at degree level. This is not just a set of revision notes – it explains the subject in detail and does not assume prior knowledge.

- To make learning and revision as easy as possible. Therefore each chapter:
    - Starts with an introduction and clear objectives
    - Contains numerous activities
    - Includes a chapter roundup summarising the points made
    - Ends with a quick quiz

And at the back of the book you will find:
    - Multiple choice questions and answers
    - Exam style questions and answers

The philosophy of the series is thus to combine techniques which actively promote learning with a no-nonsense, systematic approach to the necessary factual content of the course.

BPP Publishing have for many years been the leading providers of targeted texts for students of professional qualifications. We know that our customers need to study effectively in order to pass their exams, and that they cannot afford to waste time. They expect clear, concise and highly focused study material. As university and college education becomes more market driven, students rightly demand the same high standards of efficiency in their learning material. The BUSINESS BASICS series meets those demands.

BPP Publishing
October 2000

Titles in this series:

Accounting
Law
Quantitative Methods
Information Technology
Economics
Marketing
Human Resource Management
Organisational Behaviour

> You may order other titles in the series using the form at the end of this book. If you would like to send in your comments on this book, please turn to the review form following the order form.

HOW TO USE THIS BOOK

This book can simply be read straight through from beginning to end, but you will get far more out of it if you keep a pen and paper to hand. The most effective form of learning is *active learning*, and we have therefore filled the text with exercises for you to try as you go along. We have also provided objectives, a chapter roundup and a quick quiz for each chapter. Here is a suggested approach to enable you to get the most out of this book.

(a) Select a chapter to study, and read the introduction and objectives at the start of the chapter.

(b) Next read the chapter roundup at the end of the chapter (before the quick quiz and the answers to activities). Do not expect this brief summary to mean too much at this stage, but see whether you can relate some of the points made in it to some of the objectives.

(c) Next read the chapter itself. Do attempt each activity as you come to it. You will derive the greatest benefit from the activity if you write down your answers before checking them against the answers at the end of the chapter.

(d) As you read, make use of the 'notes' column to add your own comments, references to other material and so on. Do try to formulate your own views. In economics, many things are matters of interpretation and there is often scope for alternative views. The more you engage in a dialogue with the book, the more you will get out of your study.

(e) When you reach the end of the chapter, read the chapter roundup again. Then go back to the objectives at the start of the chapter, and ask yourself whether you have achieved them.

(f) Finally, consolidate your knowledge by writing down your answers to the quick quiz. You can check your answers by going back to the text. The very act of going back and searching the text for relevant details will further improve your grasp of the subject.

(g) You can then try the multiple choice questions at the end of the book and the exam level question, to which you are referred at the end of the chapter. Alternatively, you could wait to do these until you have started your revision – it's up to you.

Further reading

While we are confident that the BUSINESS BASICS books offer excellent range and depth of subject coverage, we are aware that you will be encouraged to follow up particular points in books other than your main textbook, in order to get alternative points of view and more detail on key topics. We recommend the following books as a starting point for your further reading on Accounting.

Gee, *Book-keeping and Accounts*, Butterworths

Alexander and Britten, *Financial Reporting*, International Thomson Press

Hussey and Bishop, *Corporate Reports – A Guide for Preparers and Users*, Woodhead Faulkner

Blake and Arnat, *Interpreting Accounts*, International Thomson Business Press

Rickwood and Thomas, *An Introduction to Financial Accounting*, McGraw-Hill

Drury, *Management and Cost Accounting*, Chapman & Hall

Lucey, *Costing*, DP Publications

Chapter 1 :
THE NATURE AND OBJECTIVES OF ACCOUNTING

Introduction

Most people encounter accounting information of some sort during their lives. Wider share ownership means that many small shareholders now receive company reports; workers will often be presented with informal accounting information about the business they work for, and so on. It is to your advantage in real life, not just as a student, to grasp the basic concepts and facts underlying accounting. This chapter acts as a basic introduction to accounting. Remember that the more 'real' sets of accounts you look at the better you will understand them.

Your objectives

After completing this chapter you should:

(a)   Understand the main uses of accounting information

(b)   Understand the different information needs of the various people who use accounts

(c)   Be aware of the scope of accounting information – what it covers, and what it excludes

(d)   Be aware of the two main financial statements – the profit and loss account and the balance sheet

BPP PUBLISHING

1 THE OBJECTIVES OF ACCOUNTING

1.1 Accounting Definitions

In this book you are encouraged to approach the subject interactively. Attempt the following activity to assess what you already know about accounting. The solutions are found at the end of each chapter.

Activity 1

(a) You will often meet with the terms 'an accounting statement' or 'a set of accounts'.

Do you know what is meant by these terms?

(b) Who do you think has the task of preparing accounting statements? In an organisation of a reasonable size, would it be one person? One department? Several different departments?

(c) Who are the users of accounting information?

(d) What is the purpose of accounting?

Let us look at a few definitions.

Definitions

Accounting could be defined as the process of collecting, recording, summarising and communicating financial information.

Accounts are the records in which this information is recorded.

Bookkeeping is keeping the most basic records.

The *accountancy* profession is the profession responsible for summarising and communicating of financial information.

1.2 Why keep accounts?

Accounts have been kept for thousands of years because they help to keep track of money, by showing where it came from and how it has been spent.

The production of accounting information can itself play an important role in the efficient running of a business. For example, a business needs to pay bills in respect of the goods and services it purchases. It must, therefore, keep a record of such bills so that the correct amounts can be paid at the correct times. Similarly a business needs to keep track of cash and cheques received from customers. Such records form one part of a basic accounting system. Additionally, keeping records of a business's assets (for example its motor vehicles or computers) makes it easier to keep them secure.

Another reason for keeping accounts arises from the complexity of most modern businesses. Centuries ago, a business enterprise might consist of a single venture with a limited life. For example, a merchant might charter a ship to purchase goods from abroad for sale in his own country. In such cases it was easy to ascertain the merchant's

PUBLISHING

profit: it was simply the amount of cash he had left at the end of the venture. Similarly, a small shop needs to generate enough money to pay for all its proprietor's personal expenses and occasional large purchases (for example a replacement till or van). The proprietor can quite easily check that this aim is being met by counting the cash in the till.

However, modern businesses are often much more complicated. They seldom have a single owner. Some very large enterprises, such as British Telecom, may be owned by millions of shareholders. Frequently the owners are not involved in the day-to-day running of the business but appoint managers to act on their behalf. In addition, there are too many activities and assets for the managers to keep track of simply from personal knowledge and an occasional glance at the bank statement. It is therefore desirable that businesses should produce accounts which will indicate how successfully the managers are performing.

In 1975 a committee established by the UK accountancy bodies published a discussion paper called *The Corporate Report*. (A corporate report is a report, including accounts, prepared by a business enterprise.) One of the questions which the committee attempted to answer was why businesses produce accounts. They concluded that the fundamental objective of a corporate report is:

... to communicate economic measurements of, and information about, the resources and performance of the reporting entity useful to those having reasonable rights to such information.

In other words, a business should produce information about its activities because there are various groups of people who want or need to know that information. This sounds rather vague: to make it clearer, we should look more closely at the classes of people who might need information about a business. We need also to think about what information in particular is of interest to the members of each class. Because large businesses are usually of interest to a greater variety of people than small businesses we will consider the case of a large public company whose shares can be bought and sold on the Stock Exchange.

1.3 Users of accounting information

The people who might be interested in financial information about a large public company may be classified as follows.

(a) *Managers of the company*. These are people appointed by the company's owners to supervise the day-to-day activities of the company. They need information about the company's current financial situation and what it is expected to be in the future. This enables them to manage the business efficiently and to take effective control and planning decisions.

(b) *Shareholders of the company*, ie the company's owners. They will want to assess how effectively management is performing its stewardship function. They will want to know how profitably management is running the company's operations and how much profit they can afford to withdraw from the business for their own use.

(c) *Trade contacts*, including suppliers who provide goods to the company on credit and customers who purchase the goods or services provided by the company. Suppliers will want to know about the company's ability to pay its debts. Customers need to know that the company is a secure source of supply and is in no danger of having to close down.

PUBLISHING

(d) *Providers of finance to the company.* These might include a bank which provides the company with an overdraft, or longer-term loan finance. The bank will want to ensure that the company is able to keep up with interest payments, and eventually to repay the amounts advanced.

(e) *The Inland Revenue*, who will want to know about business profits in order to assess the tax payable by the company.

(f) *Employees of the company.* They should have a right to information about the company's financial situation, because their future careers and the level of their wages and salaries depend on it.

(g) *Financial analysts and advisers* need information for their clients or audience. For example, stockbrokers will need information to advise investors in stocks and shares; credit agencies will want information to advise potential suppliers of goods to the company; and journalists need information for their reading public.

Activity 2

It is easy to see how 'internal' people get hold of accounting information. A manager, for example, can just go along to the accounts department and ask the staff there to prepare whatever accounting statements he or she needs. But external users of accounts cannot do this. How, in practice, can a business contact or a financial analyst access accounting information about a company?

2 NATURE OF ACCOUNTING

2.1 Management accounting and financial accounting

To a greater or lesser extent, accountants aim to satisfy the information needs of all the different groups mentioned above. Managers of a business need the most information, to help them take their planning and control decisions; and they obviously have 'special' access to information about the business, because they are in a position to organise the provision of whatever internally produced statements they require. When managers want a large amount of information about the costs and profitability of individual products, or different parts of their business, they can arrange to obtain it through a system of *cost and management accounting*. The preparation of accounting reports for external use is called *financial accounting*. Bookkeeping and costing are the bases of financial and management accounting respectively.

Management accounting systems produce detailed information often split between different departments within an organisation (sales, production, finance and so on). Although much of the information necessarily deals with past events and decisions, management accountants are also responsible for preparing budgets, helping to set price levels and other decisions about the future activities of a business.

Financial accountants are usually solely concerned with summarising historical data. Often they use the same basic records as management accountants, but in a different way. This difference arises partly because external users have different interests from management and have neither the time nor the need for very detailed information. In addition, financial statements are prepared under constraints which do not apply to management accounts produced for internal use.

These constraints apply particularly to the accounts of limited companies. The owners of a limited company (the shareholders or members of the company) enjoy limited liability, which means that as individuals they are not personally liable to pay the company's debts. If the company's own assets are not sufficient to do so, the company may have to cease trading, but the shareholders are not obliged to make up any shortfall from their own private assets.

Clearly this system is open to abuse, and one of the safeguards is that limited companies must follow a number of accounting regulations that do not apply to other forms of organisation. For example, they are required by law to prepare financial accounts annually, the minimum content of such accounts being laid down by detailed legal regulations.

In addition, their annual accounts must be audited (ie checked) by an independent person with defined qualifications. The auditor must make a report on the accounts, and will highlight any material areas where they do not comply either with the legal regulations or with other regulations laid down by the accounting profession.

Different types of financial statements are produced for each external user group. Use the following activity to develop your understanding of the statements received by the user groups.

Activity 3

Mark the following statements as true or false.

1   Shareholders receive annual accounts as prepared in accordance with legal and professional requirements.

2   The accounts of limited companies are sometimes filed with the Registrar of Companies.

3   Employees always receive the company's accounts and an employee report.

4   The Inland Revenue will receive the published accounts and as much supplementary detail as the Inspector of Taxes needs to assess the corporation tax payable on profits.

5   Banks frequently require more information than is supplied in the published accounts when considering applications for loans and overdraft facilities.

Activity 4

We have already mentioned that a company's auditor must possess a suitable qualification. In practice this means that an auditor will be a member of one or other of the professional accountancy bodies in the United Kingdom and Ireland. Do you know the names of these bodies? They are often mentioned in the financial press.

2.2 The scope of accounting information

Accounting statements are presented in monetary terms. It follows that they will only include items to which a monetary value can be attributed. For example, in the balance sheet of a business monetary values can be attributed to such assets as machinery (for example the original cost of the machinery, or the amount it would cost to replace it); whereas the flair of a good manager, or the loyalty and commitment of a dedicated workforce, cannot be evaluated in monetary terms and therefore do not appear in the accounts.

Similarly, there are important factors in the successful running of a business which are non-financial by nature. A manager in a manufacturing business will need a detailed knowledge of his machinery's capabilities, the skills of his production staff and the characteristics of his raw materials. All of these things are important in planning production, but none of them would appear in a set of accounts.

Subject to these limitations, the range of accounting information which can be prepared is very wide. Accounting statements may cover:

(a)   The profit earned by a business, or by each of its departments or divisions, in a period

(b)   The assets and liabilities of a business at a particular date

(c)   The cost of producing and/or selling a particular product or range of products

(d)   The cost of running a particular department or division

(e)   The quantity of a product which must be sold in order for it to pay its way (break even)

(f)   The amount of cash coming into and leaving a business over a defined period

(g)   The expected overdraft requirement of a business at defined intervals in the future

The list is far from exhaustive. To ensure you understand the difference between financial and management accountancy, mark each of the above as financial or management statements.

(a)   You could have classified this as both financial and management information. Generally the profit earned by the whole business, included in a historical statement (for example for the past 12 months), will be financial accounting. Forecast information, or information relating to parts of the business, for example departments or divisions is management accounting.

(b)   This usually falls within the scope of financial accounting, although it may be used as an input to management accounting, for example as a basis for a forecast.

(c)   Management accounting.

(d)   Management accounting.

(e)   Management accounting.

(f)   Cash flow accounting is financial information when it is a historical statement and usually management accounting when it is a forecast or budget.

(g)   Management accounting.

> **Activity 5**
>
> Try to think of two or three other areas that an accounting statement might cover.

2.3 The main financial statements

We end this chapter by looking briefly at the two principal financial statements drawn up by accountants: the balance sheet and the profit and loss account.

Definition

> The *balance sheet* is simply a list of all the assets owned by a business and all the liabilities owed by a business as at a particular date. It is a snapshot of the financial position of the business at a particular moment.

Assets are the business's resources so, for example, a business may buy buildings to operate from, plant and machinery, stock to sell and cars for its employees. These are all resources which it uses in its operations. Additionally, it may have bank balances, cash and amounts of money owed to it. These provide the funds it needs to carry out its operations, and are also assets. On the other hand, it may owe money to the bank or to suppliers. These are liabilities.

Definition

> A *profit and loss account* is a record of income generated and expenditure incurred over a given period.

The period chosen will depend on the purpose for which the statement is produced. The profit and loss account which forms part of the published annual accounts of a limited company will be made up for the period of a year, commencing from the date of the previous year's accounts. On the other hand, management might want to keep a closer eye on a company's profitability by making up quarterly or monthly profit and loss accounts. The profit and loss account shows whether the business has had more income than expenditure (a profit) or vice versa (a loss). Organisations which are not run for profit (for example, charities) produce a similar statement called an income and expenditure account which shows the surplus of income over expenditure (or a deficit where expenditure exceeds income).

It is very important to grasp the principle, which is applied in nearly all businesses' accounts, that accounts are not prepared on a cash basis but on an accruals (or earnings) basis. That is, a sale or purchase is dealt with in the year in which it is made, even if cash changes hands in a later year. This is important because most businesses, even if they do not sell on credit, make purchases on credit. If cash accounting is used, then accounts do not present a true picture of the business's activities in any given period. Accountants call this convention an application of the *accruals concept*. We will look at this in more detail in Chapter 2, but in the meantime let us cover it briefly by means of the example below.

EXAMPLE: ACCRUALS

Brenda has a business importing and selling model Corgi dogs. In May 20X6 she makes the following purchases and sales.

Invoice date	Numbers	Amount	Date paid
Purchases	bought/sold	£	
7.5.X6	20	100	1.6.X6
Sales			
8.5.X6	4	40	1.6.X6
12.5.X6	6	60	1.6.X6
23.5.X6	10	100	1.7.X6

What is Brenda's profit for May?

ANSWER

	£
Cash basis	
Sales	0
Purchases	0
Profit/loss	0
Accruals basis	
Sales (£40 + £60 + £100)	200
Purchases	100
Profit	100

Obviously, the accruals basis gives a truer picture than the cash basis. Brenda has no cash to show for her efforts until June but her customers are legally bound to pay her and she is legally bound to pay for her purchases.

Her balance sheet as at 31 May 20X6 would therefore show her assets and liabilities as follows.

	£
Assets	
Debtors (£40 + £60 + £100)	200
Liabilities	
Creditors	100
Net assets	100
Proprietor's capital	100

Capital is a special form of liability, representing the amount owed by the business to its proprietor(s). In Brenda's case it represents the profit earned in May, which she, as sole proprietor of the business, is entitled to in full. Usually, however, capital will also include the proprietor's initial capital, introduced as cash and perhaps equipment or other assets.

For example, if Brenda had begun her business on 30 April 20X6 by opening a business bank account and paying in £100, her balance sheet immediately after this transaction would look like this.

	£
Assets	
Bank	<u>100</u>
Proprietor's capital	<u>100</u>

On 31 May 20X6 the balance sheet would look like this.

	£
Assets	
Debtors	200
Bank	<u>100</u>
	300
Liabilities	
Creditors	<u>100</u>
Net assets	<u>200</u>
Proprietor's capital	
Brought forward	100
Profit for the period	<u>100</u>
Carried forward	<u>200</u>

This simple example shows that both the balance sheet and the profit and loss account are summaries of a great many transactions. In later chapters we will look in detail at the ways in which these transactions are recorded and financial statements prepared.

Activity 6

By looking at the example of Brenda, you may be able to see that there is a simple arithmetical relationship linking capital at the beginning of a period, capital at the end of the period, and profit earned during the period. Can you formulate the relationship?

Chapter roundup

You should now have an understanding of accounting and its main uses.

- Accounting is the process of collecting, recording, summarising and communicating financial information.

- Accounting information is essential to the efficient running of a business. It helps managers to control the use of resources, keep track of the assets and liabilities of the business and plan effectively for the future.

- Accounting information is required by a wide range of interested parties both within and outside the organisation.

- The scope of accounting information is very wide, but it does not embrace every aspect of an organisation's affairs. Even within its own province, the scope of accounting is limited by its restriction to items which have a monetary value.

- The two most important financial statements prepared by accountants are the profit and loss account and the balance sheet. Both are prepared on an accruals basis, not a cash basis.

In Chapter 2 we will develop your understanding of accountancy by considering the concepts, conventions and regulations used in preparing accounts.

Quick quiz

1   How has the increasing complexity of modern business contributed to the development of accounting?   (see para 1.2)

2   List five categories of people who might want accounting information about a business. How do their information needs differ?   (1.3)

3   Explain the distinction between financial accounting and management accounting.   (2.1)

4   What safeguards are in place to prevent the abuse of limited liability?
                                                                          (2.1)

5   What limitations are there on the scope of accounting information?   (2.2)

6   Explain briefly:

    (a)   What a balance sheet is

    (b)   What a profit and loss account is   (2.3)

7   In what sense is the capital of a business a liability of the business? (2.3)

Answers to activities

1   (a)   An accounting statement is any collection of related accounting information. It might be, for example, a profit and loss account or a balance sheet. A set of accounts is a number of accounting statements presented together with the intention of showing an overall view of an organisation's income, expenditure, assets and liabilities.

(b) Most organisations of reasonable size will have at least one dedicated accounts department. This is staffed by people with detailed knowledge of accounting systems and theory, perhaps gained while acquiring a professional qualification in accountancy. In large organisations there may be several departments, or groups, responsible for preparing accounting information of many different kinds to meet the needs of accounts users.

(c) The users of accounts, as explained in the text of this chapter, include a variety of people and organisations, both internal and external. The extent of their information needs of course varies widely.

(d) There are many purposes of accounting. You may have thought of: control over the use of resources; knowledge of what the business owes and owns; calculation of profits and losses; effective financial planning.

2   Limited companies (though not other forms of business such as partnerships) are required to make certain accounting information public. They do so by sending copies of the required information to the Registrar of Companies at Companies House. The information filed at Companies House is available, at a fee, to any member of the public who asks for it. Other sources include financial comment in the press and company brochures.

3   True:

1.   Yes, and, in addition, companies listed on the Stock Exchange have to comply with the regulations in the Stock Exchange's 'Yellow Book'.

4.

5.   Yes, banks may require cash flow and profit forecasts and budgets prepared to show management's estimates of future activity in the business.

False:

2.   The accounts of limited companies MUST be filed with the Registrar of Companies and be available for public inspection. In addition, the company itself will often distribute these accounts on request to potential shareholders, the bank and financial analysts. These accounts are all that is usually available to suppliers and customers.

3.   Employees will not necessarily receive company accounts (unless they are shareholders for example). However, many companies do distribute the accounts to employees as a matter of policy. Some companies produce employee reports which summarise and expand on matters which are covered in the annual accounts and are of particular interest to them.

4   The auditor of a company will usually be either a chartered accountant (a member of the Institute of Chartered Accountants in England and Wales (ICAEW), the Institute of Chartered Accountants in Ireland (ICAI), or the Institute of Chartered Accountants of Scotland (ICAS), or a certified accountant (a member of the Association of Chartered Certified Accountants, the ACCA). The auditors of some public sector organisations, such as local authorities, are members of the Chartered Institute of Public Finance and Accountancy (CIPFA). Qualified

management accountants are usually members of the Chartered Institute of Management Accountants (CIMA). CIMA members however are not authorised to conduct audits. The six organisations are jointly responsible for developing detailed accounting regulations known as Financial Reporting Standards (previously Statements of Standard Accounting Practice).

5   There are many possibilities. Two that you may have heard of in connection with limited companies' financial accounts are a cash flow statement and a five-year summary of key accounting statistics. Other management accounting examples you might suggest are a forecast of sales revenue (perhaps analysed by product, or by geographical area), or an aged debtors analysis. This shows the sums of money owed to the business by its customers and the length of time they have been outstanding.

6   The relationship is: opening capital + profit = closing capital. In more complicated examples it would be necessary to make adjustments for new capital introduced during the period, and for any capital withdrawn during the period.

Further question practice

Now try the following practice questions at the end of this text

Multiple choice questions: **1 and 2**

Exam style question: **1**

Chapter 2 :
PREPARING ACCOUNTS: CONCEPTS, CONVENTIONS AND REGULATIONS

Introduction

The purpose of this chapter is to encourage you to think deeply about the assumptions on which financial accounts are prepared. The specific regulations governing partnership accounts and the accounts of limited companies are covered in Chapters 7 and 8 respectively. You can appreciate the role of the regulatory authorities more fully by reading the financial press.

Accounting practice has developed gradually over a period of centuries. Many of its procedures are operated automatically by people who have never questioned whether alternative methods exist which have equal validity. However, the procedures in common use imply the acceptance of certain concepts which are by no means self-evident; nor are they the only possible concepts which could be used to build up an accounting framework.

Our next step is to look at some of the more important concepts which are taken for granted in preparing accounts.

Your objectives

After completing this chapter you should:

(a) Know about the more widely accepted concepts underlying the preparation of accounts

(b) Understand some of the main conventions applied in the preparation of accounts

(c) Be aware of the main regulations governing the way in which accounts are prepared

1 CONCEPTS AND CONVENTIONS

1.1 Accounting concepts

A statement of standard accounting practice (SSAP 2 Disclosure of accounting policies) describes four concepts as fundamental accounting concepts. They are going concern, prudence, accruals and consistency. These four are also identified as fundamental by companies legislation (the Companies Act 1985), which adds a fifth to the list (the separate valuation principle). But there is no universally agreed list of fundamental concepts, and others besides these have been described as fundamental by various authors.

In this chapter we shall single out the following concepts for discussion:

(a)   The entity concept

(b)   The money measurement concept

(c)   The going concern concept

(d)   The prudence concept

(e)   The accruals or matching concept

(f)   The consistency concept

(g)   The separate valuation principle

(h)   The materiality concept

The entity concept

We will discuss this concept more fully in the next chapter. Briefly, the concept is that accountants regard a business as a separate entity, distinct from its owners or managers. The concept applies whether the business is a limited company (which is recognised in law as a separate entity) or a sole proprietorship or partnership. These types of business are not separately recognised by the law. So, in the example of Brenda in the previous chapter, the money she transferred to her business bank account becomes, in accounting terms, a business asset (but legally remains a personal asset).

Acceptance of this concept has important practical consequences. Particularly in the case of a small business run by a single individual, the owner's personal affairs and business affairs may appear to be inextricably linked. Brenda may conduct her business from home. But in preparing the business accounts it is essential to distinguish her private transactions and keep them separate.

Suppose that Brenda withdraws a number of Corgis from her stock to give to friends, how would this be reflected in her accounts? Write your answer here.

The correct accounting treatment is to regard her as having purchased the goods from the business, which is a completely separate entity. The subsequent gift to her friends is then a private transaction and is not recorded anywhere in the books of the business. Brenda should pay for the Corgis by taking money from her own purse and putting it into the till, or she should regard the withdrawal as a repayment of capital. Otherwise, the business accounts will give a misleading picture.

The money measurement concept

In Chapter 1, we stated that accounts deal only with items to which a monetary value can be attributed. This is the money measurement concept. We distinguished between an asset such as a machine (which might, for example, be valued at its original purchase cost or its replacement cost) and an asset such as the flair of a manager or the dedication of the workforce.

Although these latter assets are very hard to quantify in monetary terms, they can be of enormous significance to the success of a business. Recognising their importance, accountants in recent years have tried to suggest ways of 'bringing them on to the balance sheet' by attributing values to them. These methods of 'human resource accounting' are beyond the scope of this book, but you should be aware at least of the problems they attempt to address.

> **Activity 1**
>
> Perhaps it is too glib to say that monetary values can never be attributed to the skill of the workforce. There is at least one high-profile industry where such valuations are commonplace. Can you think of it? And do you know what the accounting consequences are in that industry?

The going concern concept

The going concern concept implies that the business will continue in operational existence for the foreseeable future, and that there is no intention to put the company into liquidation or to make drastic cutbacks to the scale of operations.

The main significance of the going concern concept is that the assets of the business should not be valued at their 'break-up' value, which is the amount that they would sell for if they were sold off piecemeal and the business were thus broken up.

Suppose, for example, that Brenda acquires a Corgi-making machine at a cost of £60,000. The asset has an estimated life of six years, and it is normal to write off the cost of the asset to the profit and loss account over this time. In this case a *depreciation cost* of £10,000 per annum will be charged. (This topic will be covered in more detail in later chapters.)

Using the going concern concept, it would be presumed that the business will continue its operations and so the asset will live out its full six years in use. A depreciation charge of £10,000 will be made each year, and the value of the asset in the balance sheet will be its cost less the accumulated amount of depreciation charged to date. After one year, the *net book value* of the asset would therefore be £(60,000 – 10,000) = £50,000, after two years it would be £40,000, after three years £30,000 and so on, until it has been written down to a value of 0 after six years.

Now suppose that this asset has no other operational use outside the business, and in a forced sale it would only sell for scrap. After one year of operation, its scrap value might be, say, £8,000. What would the net book value be after one year?

BPP PUBLISHING

The net book value of the asset, applying the going concern concept, would be £50,000 after one year, but its immediate sell-off value only £8,000. It might be argued that the asset is over-valued at £50,000 and that it should be written down to its break-up value (ie in the balance sheet it should be shown at £8,000 and the balance of its cost should be treated as an expense). However, provided that the going concern concept is valid, so that the asset will continue to be used and will not be sold, it is appropriate accounting practice to value the asset at its net book value.

Activity 2

A retailer commences business on 1 January and buys a stock of 20 washing machines, each costing £100. During the year he sells 17 machines at £150 each. How should the remaining machines be valued at 31 December if:

(a)   He is forced to close down his business at the end of the year and the remaining machines will realise only £60 each in a forced sale?

(b)   He intends to continue his business into the next year?

The prudence concept

This is the concept that where alternative procedures, or alternative valuations, are possible, the one selected should be the one which gives the most cautious presentation of the business's financial position or results. For example, you may have wondered why the three washing machines in Activity 2 were stated in the balance sheet at their cost (£100 each) rather than their selling price (£150 each). This is simply an aspect of the prudence concept: to value the machines at £150 would be to anticipate making a profit before the profit had been *realised*.

The other aspect of the prudence concept is that where a loss is foreseen, it should be anticipated and taken into account immediately. If a business purchases stock for £1,200 but because of a sudden slump in the market only £900 is likely to be realised when the stock is sold, the prudence concept dictates that the stock should be valued at £900. It is not enough to wait until the stock is sold, and then recognise the £300 loss; it must be recognised as soon as it is foreseen.

A profit can be considered to be a *realised profit* when it is in the form of:

(a)   Cash, or

(b)   Another asset which has a reasonably certain cash value. This includes amounts owing from debtors, provided that there is a reasonable certainty that the debtors will eventually pay up what they owe.

SSAP 2 describes the prudence concept as follows.

Revenue and profits are not anticipated, but are recognised by inclusion in the profit and loss account only when realised in the form either of cash or of other assets the ultimate cash realisation of which can be assessed with reasonable certainty; provision is made for all known ... expenses and losses whether the amount of these is known with certainty or is a best estimate in the light of the information available.

Try the next activity to help you to understand how the prudence concept is applied in practice.

Activity 3

(a)   A company begins trading on 1 January 20X6 and sells goods worth £100,000 during the year to 31 December. At 31 December there are debts of £15,000 owed to the business by customers. Of these, the company is now doubtful whether £6,000 will ever be paid. What is the effect of this on the company's balance sheet and profit and loss account?

(b)   Samson Feeble trades as a carpenter. He has undertaken to make a range of kitchen furniture for a customer at an agreed price of £1,000. At the end of Samson's accounting year the job is unfinished (being two thirds complete) and the following data has been assembled.

	£
Costs incurred in making the furniture to date	800
Further estimated cost to completion of the job	400
Total cost	1,200

The incomplete job represents work in progress at the end of the year which is an asset, like stock. Its cost to date is £800, but by the time the job is completed Samson will have made a loss of £200. What is the effect of this on Samson's balance sheet and profit and loss account?

It is important to understand the relationship – sometimes a conflict – between the *accruals concept* and the *prudence concept*.

- How should we value an asset? If you refer back to our discussion of the going concern concept, you will see that assets are commonly valued at amounts in excess of their realisable value. Is this prudent?

- When should we recognise a sale as having been made? According to the accruals concept (see Chapter 1) Brenda shows sales revenue in her profit and loss account in the period when she sells goods to a customer. But is this prudent, given that the customer has purchased on credit and has not yet paid Brenda the cash?

The first problem is covered in our earlier discussion. For the second case, the generally accepted rules are as follows.

Sales revenue should only be 'realised' and so 'recognised' in the trading, profit and loss account when:

(a)   The sale transaction is for a specific quantity of goods at a known price, so that the sales value of the transaction is known for certain

(b)   The sale transaction has been completed, or else it is certain that it will be completed (for example in the case of long-term contract work, when the job is well under way but not yet completed by the end of an accounting period)

(c)   The *critical event* in the sale transaction has occurred. The critical event is the event after which either:

(i)   It becomes virtually certain that cash will eventually be received from the customer, or

(ii)   Cash is actually received.

Usually, revenue is 'recognised' either:

(a)   When a cash sale is made, or

(b)   When the customer promises to pay on or before a specified future date, and the debt is legally enforceable.

The prudence concept is applied here in the sense that revenue should not be anticipated, and included in the trading, profit and loss account, before it is reasonably certain to 'happen'.

Activity 4

Given that prudence is the main consideration, consider under what circumstances, if any, revenue might be recognised at the following stages of a sale.

(a)   Goods have been acquired by the business which it confidently expects to resell very quickly.

(b)   A customer places a firm order for goods.

(c)   Goods are delivered to the customer.

(d)   The customer is invoiced for goods.

(e)   The customer pays for the goods.

(f)   The customer's cheque in payment for the goods has been cleared by the bank.

The accruals concept or matching concept

This concept states that, in computing profit, revenue earned must be matched against the expenditure incurred in earning it. This is illustrated in the example of Brenda; profit of £100 was computed by matching the revenue (£200) earned from the sale of 20 Corgis against the cost (£100) of acquiring them.

If, however, Brenda had only sold 18 Corgis, it would have been incorrect to charge her profit and loss account with the cost of 20 Corgis, as she still has two Corgis in stock. If she intends to sell them in June she is likely to make a profit on the sale. Therefore, only the purchase cost of 18 Corgis (£90) should be matched with her sales revenue, leaving her with a profit of £90.

Her balance sheet would therefore look like this.

	£
Assets	
Stock (at cost, ie 2 × £5)	10
Debtors (18 × £10)	180
	190
Liabilities	
Creditors	100
Net assets	90
Proprietor's capital (profit for the period)	90

In this example, the concepts of going concern and matching are linked. Because the business is assumed to be a going concern it is possible to carry forward the cost of the unsold Corgis as a charge against profits of the next period.

If Brenda decided to give up selling Corgis, how would the two Corgis in the balance sheet be valued? Write your answer here.

If Brenda decided to give up selling Corgis, then the going concern concept would no longer apply and the value of the two Corgis in the balance sheet would be a break-up valuation rather than cost. Similarly, if the two unsold Corgis were now unlikely to be sold at more than their cost of £5 each (say, because of damage or a fall in demand) then they should be recorded on the balance sheet at their net realisable value (ie the likely eventual sales price less any expenses to be incurred to make them saleable, for example paint) rather than cost. This shows the application of the prudence concept.

The accruals concept defined

The 'accruals' or 'matching' concept is described in SSAP 2 as follows.

Revenues and costs are accrued (that is, recognised as they are earned or incurred, not as money is received or paid), matched with one another so far as their relationship can be established or justifiably assumed, and dealt with in the profit and loss account of the period to which they relate ... Revenue and profits dealt with in the profit and loss account of the period are matched with associated costs and expenses by including in the same account the costs incurred in earning them (so far as these are material and identifiable).

Company legislation gives legal recognition to the accruals concept, stating that: 'all income and charges relating to the financial year to which the accounts relate shall be taken into account, without regard to the date of receipt or payment.' This has the effect, as we have seen, of requiring businesses to take account of sales and purchases when made, rather than when paid for, and also to carry unsold stock forward in the balance sheet rather than to deduct its cost from profit for the period.

The consistency concept

Accounting is not an exact science. There are many areas in which judgement must be exercised in attributing money values to items appearing in accounts. Over the years certain procedures and principles have come to be recognised as good accounting practice, but within these limits there are often various acceptable methods of accounting for similar items.

The consistency concept states that in preparing accounts consistency should be observed in two respects.

(a) Similar items within a single set of accounts should be given similar accounting treatment.

(b)   The same treatment should be applied from one period to another in accounting for similar items. This enables valid comparisons to be made from one period to the next.

The separate valuation principle

Company law recognises the same four fundamental accounting concepts as SSAP 2, although it describes them not as concepts but as accounting principles. The Act also mentions a fifth principle, which may be called the separate valuation principle. Although it is not described by SSAP 2 as a fundamental accounting concept it has long been recognised as good accounting practice.

The separate valuation principle states that, in determining the amount to be attributed to an asset or liability in the balance sheet, each component item of the asset or liability must be valued separately. These separate valuations must then be aggregated to arrive at the balance sheet figure. For example, if a company's stock comprises 50 separate items, a valuation must (in theory) be arrived at for each item separately; the 50 figures must then be aggregated and the total is the stock figure which should appear in the balance sheet.

Activity 5

The following true/false activity will allow you to ensure that you have understood the concepts and conventions covered so far in this chapter.

Mark the following statements as true or false.

1   The entity concept is that accountants regard a business as a separate legal entity, distinct from its owners or managers.

2   Accounts deal only with items to which a monetary value can be attributed.

3   Where the prudence and accruals concepts conflict, preparers of accounts may follow either.

4   The accruals, prudence, going concern and consistency concepts are contained in SSAP 2.

The materiality concept

As we stated above in discussing the consistency concept, accounts preparation is not an exact science. Apart from the possibility of downright error, there will be many areas where two different accountants would come up with different figures for the same item. The materiality concept is relevant in this context.

An error which is too trivial to affect anyone's understanding of the accounts is referred to as immaterial. In preparing accounts it is important to assess what is material and what is not, so that time and money are not wasted in the pursuit of excessive detail.

Determining whether or not an item is material is a very subjective exercise. There is no absolute measure of materiality. It is common to apply a convenient rule of thumb (for example to define material items as those with a value greater than 5% of the net profit disclosed by the accounts). But some items disclosed in accounts are regarded as particularly sensitive and even a very small misstatement of such an item would be regarded as a material error. An example in the accounts of a limited company might be the amount of remuneration paid to directors of the company.

The assessment of an item as material or immaterial may affect its treatment in the accounts. For example, the profit and loss account of a business will show the expenses incurred by the business grouped under suitable captions (heating and lighting expenses, rent and rates expenses and so on); but in the case of very small expenses it may be appropriate to lump them together under a caption such as 'sundry expenses', because a more detailed breakdown would be inappropriate for such immaterial amounts.

In assessing whether or not an item is material, it is not only the amount of the item which needs to be considered. The context is also important.

(a)   If a balance sheet shows fixed assets of £2 million and stocks of £30,000, an error of £20,000 in the fixed asset valuation might not be regarded as material, whereas an error of £20,000 in the stock valuation would be. In other words, the total of which the erroneous item forms a part must be considered.

(b)   If a business has a bank loan of £50,000 and a £55,000 balance on bank deposit account, it might well be regarded as a material misstatement if these two amounts were displayed on the balance sheet as 'cash at bank £5,000'. In other words, incorrect presentation may amount to material misstatement even if there is no monetary error.

Activity 6

(a)   You depreciate your office equipment by 20% each year because it has a useful life, on average, of five years. This year your profitability is down and you think you can squeeze an extra year's life out of your equipment. Is it acceptable not to charge any depreciation this year?

(b)   You have recently paid £4.95 for a waste paper bin which should have a useful life of about five years. Should you treat it as a fixed asset?

1.2   Conventions of accounting

Costs and values

Accounting concepts are a part of the theoretical framework on which accounting practice is based. Before we proceed to the chapters which discuss accounting practice in detail, it is worth looking at one further general point, the problem of attributing monetary values to the items which appear in accounts.

A basic principle of accounting (some writers include it in the list of fundamental accounting concepts) is that resources are normally stated in accounts at historical cost, ie at the amount which the business paid to acquire them. An important advantage of this procedure is that the objectivity of accounts is maximised: there is usually objective, documentary evidence to prove the amount paid to purchase an asset or pay an expense.

In general, accountants prefer to deal with costs, rather than with 'values'. This is because valuations tend to be subjective and to vary according to what the valuation is for. For example, suppose that a company acquires a machine to manufacture its products. The machine has an expected useful life of four years. At the end of two years

PUBLISHING

the company is preparing a balance sheet and has to decide what monetary amount to attribute to the asset. Suggest three possible amounts. Write your answer here.

Numerous possibilities might be considered.

(a)   The original cost (historical cost) of the machine

(b)   Half of the historical cost, on the ground that half of its useful life has expired

(c)   The amount the machine might fetch on the secondhand market

(d)   The amount it would cost to replace the machine with an identical machine

(e)   The amount it would cost to replace the machine with a more modern machine incorporating the technological advances of the previous two years

(f)   The machine's economic value, ie the amount of the profits it is expected to generate for the company during its remaining life

All of these valuations have something to commend them, but the great advantage of the first two is that they are based on a figure (the machine's historical cost) which is objectively verifiable. (Some authors regard objectivity as an accounting concept in its own right.) The subjective judgement involved in the other valuations, particularly (f), is so great as to lessen the reliability of any accounts in which they are used. As we will see in later chapters, method (b), or a variation of it, is the one which would normally be used.

The method chosen has important consequences for the measurement of profit, as the following example will show.

EXAMPLE: COSTS AND VALUES

Brian sets up in business on 1 January 20X6 selling accountancy textbooks. He buys 100 books for £5 each and by 31 December 20X6 he manages to sell his entire stock, all for cash, at a price of £8 each. On 1 January 20X7 he replaces his stock by purchasing another 100 books; by this time the cost of the books has risen to £6 each. Calculate the profit earned by Brian in 20X6.

ANSWER

In conventional historical cost accounting, Brian's profit would be computed as follows.

	£
Sale of 100 books (@ £8 each)	800
Cost of 100 books (@ £5 each)	500
Profit for the year	300

The purchase of the books is stated at their historical cost. Although this is accepted accounting practice, and is the method we will be using almost invariably throughout this book, it involves an anomaly which can be seen if we look at how well off the business is.

On 1 January 20X6 the assets of the business consist of the 100 books which Brian has purchased as stock. On 1 January 20X7 the business has an identical stock of 100 books, and also has cash of £200 (ie £800 received from customers, less the £600 cost of replacing stock). So despite making a profit of £300, measured in the conventional way, the business appears to be only £200 better off.

This anomaly could be removed if an alternative accounting convention were used. Suppose that profit was measured as the difference between the selling price of goods and the cost of replacing the goods sold. Brian's profit would then be computed as follows.

	£
Sale of 100 books	800
Cost of replacing 100 books sold	600
Profit for the year	200

Now the profit for the year is exactly matched by the increase in the company's assets over the year.

Capital maintenance

The example above leads us on to the important concept of *capital maintenance*. The capital of a business (also called its net worth) represents the excess of its assets over its liabilities, and, as we saw in the example of Brenda in Chapter 1, represents the proprietor's interest in the business. One way of measuring profit would be to measure how well off a business is at the beginning of a period, and compare it with how well off it is at the end of the period; the difference (after allowing for withdrawals of capital and injections of new capital) would be the profit or loss for the period. On this basis, measurement of profit depends on the methods we use to value the assets and liabilities of the business at the beginning and end of the period.

It is worth looking again at the example of Brian. Using historical cost as our basis of valuation, the value of his business at 1 January 20X6 and 1 January 20X7 is as follows.

	20X6	*20X7*
	£	£
Stocks (at historical cost)	500	600
Cash	0	200
	500	800

The value of the business has risen by £300 over the year and this is the amount of profit we calculated on the historical cost basis. We can say that the original capital of the business, £500, has been *maintained* and an addition to capital of £300 has been created.

Instead of using historical costs, it is theoretically possible to measure capital in physical terms. Brian's physical capital was originally 100 books; on 1 January 20X7, it consists of an identical 100 books plus £200 cash. We can say that Brian's original physical capital has been maintained and an addition to capital of £200 has been created. This is equivalent to the profit we computed on a replacement cost basis.

A system of accounting based principally on replacement costs, and measuring profit as the increase in physical capital, was used in the UK for some years. It is called *current cost accounting*. The main accounting system has always been, and will continue to be, historical cost accounting but current cost accounting was developed as a possible solution to certain problems which arise in periods of rising prices. Theoretical and practical objections to the current cost accounting system led to its withdrawal in the UK.

Accounting in periods of rising prices

In periods of *inflation*, businessmen and accountants face a number of problems.

For businessmen the major difficulty is in decision making. Successful decisions depend on correct estimates of future events and this is complicated when future costs and prices are affected by inflation. The difficulty is more acute when the effects of the decision extend over a long period, but even short-term decisions such as price increases are affected.

Another difficulty is that businessmen rely on accounts to show the profit earned by a business, and this is at least partly so that an assessment can be made of how much profit can safely be withdrawn from the business by its owners. But when prices are rising, some at least of the profit shown by historical cost accounts must be ploughed back into the business just to maintain its previous capacity.

The job of the accountant is also complicated by inflation. The accounts he or she prepares must be expressed in terms of a monetary unit (for example in the UK the £). In times of rising prices the value of the unit is not constant and comparisons between the accounts of the current year with those of previous years may be misleading. Suggest how inflation creates problems for the accountant. Write your answer here.

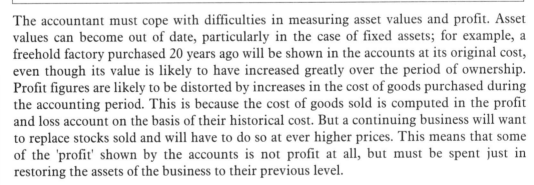

The accountant must cope with difficulties in measuring asset values and profit. Asset values can become out of date, particularly in the case of fixed assets; for example, a freehold factory purchased 20 years ago will be shown in the accounts at its original cost, even though its value is likely to have increased greatly over the period of ownership. Profit figures are likely to be distorted by increases in the cost of goods purchased during the accounting period. This is because the cost of goods sold is computed in the profit and loss account on the basis of their historical cost. But a continuing business will want to replace stocks sold and will have to do so at ever higher prices. This means that some of the 'profit' shown by the accounts is not profit at all, but must be spent just in restoring the assets of the business to their previous level.

Attempts to get round the problems of inflation have a long history in the UK and abroad. One step which has long been common in practice is to prepare *modified* historical cost accounts. This usually means that up-to-date valuations are included in the historical cost balance sheet for some or all of a company's fixed assets, without any other adjustments being made. No attempt is made to tackle the difficulties of profit measurement.

More active measures have been taken to find alternatives to the historical cost convention. The two alternative systems which have found favour, at different times, in the UK are *current cost accounting* (CCA) and *current purchasing power accounting* (CPP). CCA has already been briefly described. CPP tackles the problems of inflation by attempting to express accounting values in terms of a stable monetary unit.

BPP
PUBLISHING

For the foreseeable future, historical cost accounting is likely to be the most important system in the UK, despite its inability to reflect the effects of inflation.

Activity 7

To try and get your mind around the concept of capital maintenance, try to work out the answer to this question. In a period when prices are rising, the profit shown under the historical cost convention will differ from that shown under the current cost convention. In the case of a retail trading company, which of the two profit figures will be higher?

---

2 REGULATIONS

2.1 The regulatory framework of accounts

We have already seen that there is a wide range of accounting concepts in use, not all of them by any means self-evident and for the most part accorded different levels of importance and priority by accounting theorists. There are also different conventions under which accounts can be prepared. It may seem as though almost anything goes. What rules are there to guide us on how accounts should be prepared?

One important point to grasp is that the answer to this question is very different for a limited company compared with almost any other organisation. As we have already noted, the activities of limited companies, including the way they prepare their accounts, are closely regulated. For an unincorporated business, any form of accounting information is adequate if it gives the owner(s) of the business a basis for planning and control, and satisfies the requirements of external users such as the Inland Revenue.

As far as limited companies are concerned, the regulations on accounts come from four main sources.

(a) Company law enacted by the UK Parliament.

(b) Statements of accounting practice issued by the professional accountancy bodies in the UK and Ireland.

(c) International accounting standards.

(d) The requirements of the Stock Exchange. These of course only apply to 'listed' companies, being those large companies whose shares are bought and sold on the Stock Exchange.

Company law

Limited companies are required by law to prepare accounts annually for distribution to their shareholders. A copy of these accounts must be lodged with the Registrar of Companies and is available for inspection by any member of the public. For this reason a company's statutory annual accounts are often referred to as its published accounts.

In 1985, all existing companies legislation was brought together in a number of consolidating Acts, of which by far the most important is the Companies Act 1985 (CA 1985). This was substantially amended on the enactment of the Companies Act 1989 (CA 1989). The 1989 Act repealed parts of the 1985 Act and inserted new sections. This book reflects the 1985 Act *as amended by the 1989 Act*; unless otherwise stated, all statutory references are to the amended Companies Act 1985. Occasionally, where there is no parallel provision, a section number is followed by 'CA 1989' to indicate a section of the new Act itself.

There are many differences between accounting systems found in the various European Union (EU) member states. For example, in the UK a 'true and fair view' is sought, whereas in Germany a more 'legal and correct view' is observed. Taxation and accounting principles differ and consolidation practices (for *groups* of companies) vary.

Since the United Kingdom became a member of the EU it has been obliged to comply with legal requirements decided on by the EU. It does this by enacting UK laws to implement EU directives. For example, the CA 1989 was enacted in part to implement the provisions of the seventh and eighth EU directives, which deal with consolidated accounts and auditors.

As far as the preparation of accounts is concerned, the overriding requirement of companies legislation is that accounts should show a 'true and fair view'. This is a slippery phrase which is nowhere defined in the Companies Acts. What it certainly does *not* mean is that company accounts are to be exact to the penny in every respect. For one thing, as we shall see later, many of the figures appearing in a set of accounts are arrived at, at least partly by the exercise of judgement. For another, the amount of time and effort that such a requirement would cost would be out of all proportion to the advantages derived from it: see the discussion earlier in this chapter of the *materiality concept*.

The legislation also requires that the accounts of a limited company must be audited. An audit, for this purpose, may be defined as an 'independent examination of, and expression of opinion on, the financial statements of an enterprise'. As explained in Chapter 1, this means in practice that a limited company must engage a firm of chartered or certified accountants to conduct an examination of its accounting records and its financial statements in order to form an opinion as to whether the accounts present a 'true and fair view'. At the conclusion of their audit work, the auditors issue a report (addressed to the owners of the company, ie its *members* or *shareholders*) which is published as part of the accounts.

Non-statutory regulation

Apart from company law, the main regulations affecting accounts in the UK derive from pronouncements issued by the professional accounting bodies (though later we will look briefly at *international* accounting regulations and the regulations of the Stock Exchange).

Six accountancy bodies in the UK are represented on the Consultative Committee of Accountancy Bodies (CCAB). They are as follows.

(a)   The Institute of Chartered Accountants in England and Wales (ICAEW)

(b)   The Institute of Chartered Accountants of Scotland (ICAS)

(c)   The Institute of Chartered Accountants in Ireland (ICAI)

(d)   The Association of Chartered Certified Accountants (ACCA)

(e)   The Chartered Institute of Management Accountants (CIMA)

(f)   The Chartered Institute of Public Finance and Accountancy (CIPFA)

Through a number of operating arms the CCAB is a major influence on the way in which accounts are prepared. Our main interest at this stage will be in the accounting standards published to lay down prescribed accounting treatments in areas where a variety of approaches might be taken. Clearly the value of accounts would be reduced if users were not able to count on a measure of comparability between them; the aim of accounting standards is to ensure that such comparability exists.

The Accounting Standards Committee (ASC) and the Accounting Standards Board (ASB)

The ASC was set up in January 1970 with the aim of publishing accounting standards in order to crack down on manipulation of published accounts. This was the beginning of a long line of attempts to protect investors in the wake of accounting scandals.

Activity 8   **(15 minutes)**

You will be aware from your reading that such attempts have not yet been entirely successful. For fun, list a few of the more recent accounting scandals you can think of.

The procedure of the ASC was to publish an *Exposure Draft* (ED), outlining its proposed accounting treatment for the area under consideration. Comments were invited from interested parties, and in the light of such comments a final document was issued in the form of a *Statement of Standard Accounting Practice* (SSAP). Under the Companies Act 1989, large companies are required to state that their accounts have been prepared in accordance with applicable accounting standards. The ASC issued 25 SSAPs before it was replaced by a successor body on 1 August 1990.

In response to criticisms of the ASC's ineffectiveness, the CCAB appointed a committee under the chairmanship of Sir Ron Dearing to review and make recommendations on the process by which accounting standards are issued. The Committee reported in 1988 and as a result of its recommendations a new standard-setting process was introduced. Under the new system, there are four bodies you need to know about.

    (a)   The Financial Reporting Council (FRC)

    (b)   The Accounting Standards Board (ASB)

    (c)   The Financial Reporting Review Panel (FRRP)

    (d)   The Urgent Issues Task Force (UITF)

The Financial Reporting Council. The FRC draws its membership from a wide spectrum of accounts preparers and users. Its chairman is appointed by the Government.

The Accounting Standards Board. The FRC operates through two arms: the FRRP (see below) and the ASB. The ASB is, in effect, the successor body to the ASC and is responsible for the issue of accounting standards. Accounting standards issued by the ASB are called *Financial Reporting Standards* (FRSs). Prior to publication, the ASB circulates its proposals in the form of a *Financial Reporting Exposure Draft* (inevitably referred to as a FRED) and invites comments. To avoid chaos, the ASB has 'adopted' those SSAPs still extant, and they therefore remain in force until replaced by new FRSs.

The *Financial Reporting Review Panel.* The FRRP is the second operating arm of the FRC. Its task is to examine accounts published by companies if it appears that Companies Act requirements have been breached – in particular, the requirement that accounts should show a true and fair view. The panel has legal backing: if a public company departs from an accounting standard, the panel may apply to the courts, which may in turn instruct the company to prepare revised accounts.

The Urgent Issues Task Force. The UITF is an offshoot of the ASB. Its role is to assist the ASB in areas where an accounting standard or Companies Act provision already exists, but where unsatisfactory or conflicting interpretations have developed. As its name suggests, the UITF is designed to act quickly (more quickly than the full standard-setting process is capable of) when an authoritative ruling is urgently needed.

International accounting standards

The International Accounting Standards Committee (IASC) was set up in June 1973 in an attempt to co-ordinate the development of international accounting standards. It includes representatives from many countries throughout the world, including the USA and the UK.

International standards are not intended to override local regulations. In the UK, however, the ASC expressed their support for international standards by incorporating them within the UK standards. Not every IAS has so far been incorporated in this way. The ASB has also stated support for international standards.

The Stock Exchange regulations

The Stock Exchange is a market for stocks and shares, and a company whose securities are traded in this market is known as a 'quoted' or 'listed' company.

When a share is granted a quotation on The Stock Exchange, it appears on the 'Official List' which is published in London for each business day. The Official List shows the 'official quotation' or price for the share for that particular day; it is drawn up by the Quotations Department of The Stock Exchange, which derives its prices from those actually ruling in this market.

In order to receive a quotation for its securities, a company must conform with Stock Exchange regulations contained in the 'Yellow Book' issued by the Council of The Stock Exchange. The company commits itself to certain procedures and standards, including matters concerning the disclosure of accounting information, which are more extensive than the disclosure requirements of the Companies Acts. The detail of these requirements is beyond the scope of this book, but some of the more important ones will be mentioned when we come to look in detail at the content of company accounts.

To ensure you understand which regulations apply to which type of business, fill in the table below with a 'yes' where compliance is required and 'no' where it is not.

Type Of Business	Companies Act	FRSs/SSAPs	IASs	Stock Exchange Yellow Book
Public Listed Company				
Private Limited Company				
Sole Tradership				

Your table should look like this.

Type Of Business	Companies Act	FRSs/SSAPs	IASs	Stock Exchange Yellow Book
Public Listed Company	YES	YES	NO	YES
Private Limited Company	YES	YES	NO	NO
Sole Tradership	NO	NO	NO	NO

Activity 9

One of the Stock Exchange's accounting requirements is that listed companies give financial information regularly. How long do you think a listed company can go without providing some sort of accounts?

Chapter roundup

Having completed this chapter you should have achieved the objectives and understand the following points.

- A large number of accounting concepts are at work in the preparation of a set of accounts. To some extent the selection of concepts is an arbitrary exercise, but in fact a large measure of consensus exists among practising accountants.

- Different accounting conventions can lead to different reported results. Of the various possible conventions that could be adopted, the historical cost convention is the only one enjoying wide currency at present. However, you should also be aware of the current cost and current purchasing power conventions.

- Order in this apparent chaos is provided by a comprehensive regulatory framework, based on UK company legislation, accounting standards (both UK and international) and Stock Exchange requirements.

Next we will consider the nature of assets and liabilities.

Quick quiz

1 List the four accounting concepts identified as fundamental by SSAP 2. (see para 1.1)

2 Briefly re-cap what is meant by: the entity concept; the money measurement concept; the going concern concept; the prudence concept; the accruals concept; the consistency concept; the separate valuation principle; and the materiality concept. (1.1)

3 At what stage is it normal to recognise the revenue arising from a credit sale? (1.1)

4 The separate valuation principle is a provision of SSAP 2. True or false? (1.1)

5   List six possible values that might be attributed in the accounts to a piece of machinery. (1.2)

6   What is the concept of capital maintenance that underlies:

(a)   The historical cost convention?

(b)   The current cost convention? (1.2)

7   What is meant by modified historical cost accounts? (1.2)

8   What is the main statute governing the content of limited company accounts in the UK? (1.2)

9   Name the four bodies now responsible for the issue and enforcement of accounting regulations in the UK. (2.1)

Answers to activities

1   The industry referred to is of course the world of sport, particularly football, where transfer fees appear to provide an objective valuation of a player's worth. Many football clubs are run as substantial businesses, some of them with shares quoted on the Stock Exchange. As such, their accounting practices are widely publicised and discussed. In almost all cases, however, they make no attempt to include the value of players on their balance sheet, presumably because such values fluctuate wildly with the form and fitness of the players concerned. Almost invariably transfer fees are therefore shown simply as a cost in the profit and loss account.

2   (a)   If the business is to be closed down, the remaining three machines must be valued at the amount they will realise in a forced sale, ie $3 \times £60 = £180$.

(b)   If the business is regarded as a going concern, the stock unsold at 31 December will be carried forward into the following year, when the cost of the three machines will be matched against the eventual sale proceeds in computing that year's profits. The three machines will therefore appear in the balance sheet at 31 December at cost, $3 \times £100 = £300$.

3   (a)   The company should make a provision for doubtful debts of £6,000. Sales for 1996 will be shown in the profit and loss account at their full value of £100,000, but the provision for doubtful debts would be a cost of £6,000. Because there is some uncertainty that the sales will be realised in the form of cash, the prudence concept dictates that the £6,000 should not be included in the profit for the year. Debtors in the balance sheet will be shown at a valuation of £9,000.

(b)   The full £200 loss should be charged against profits of the current year. The value of work in progress at the year end should be its net realisable value, which is lower than its cost. The net realisable value can be calculated in either of two ways:

(i)

	£
Eventual sales value	1,000
Less further costs to completion	
in order to make the sale	400
Net realisable value	600

(ii)

	£
Work in progress at cost	800
Less loss foreseen	200
	600

4 (a) A sale must never be recognised before the goods have even been ordered. There is no certainty about the value of the sale, nor when it will take place, even if it is virtually certain that goods will be sold.

(b) A sale must never be recognised when the customer places an order. Even though the order will be for a specific quantity of goods at a specific price, it is not yet certain that the sale transaction will go through. The customer may cancel the order, or the supplier might be unable to deliver the goods as ordered.

(c) A sale will be recognised when delivery of the goods is made only when:

(i) The sale is for cash, and so the cash is received at the same time, or

(ii) The sale is on credit and the customer accepts delivery (for example by signing a delivery note).

(d) The critical event for a credit sale is usually the despatch of an invoice to the customer. There is then a legally enforceable debt, payable on specified terms, for a completed sale transaction.

(e) The critical event for a cash sale is when delivery takes place and when cash is received; both take place at the same time.

It would be too cautious or 'prudent' to await cash payment for a credit sale transaction before recognising the sale, unless the customer is a high credit risk and there is a serious doubt about his ability or intention to pay.

(f) It would again be over-cautious to wait for clearance of the customer's cheques before recognising sales revenue. Such a precaution would only be justified in cases where there is a very high risk of the bank refusing to honour the cheque.

5 True:

2.

4. Yes. Company law also recognises them as principles and adds a fifth, the separate valuation principle.

False:

1. No. Although it is certainly true that the entity concept is that accountants regard a business as a separate entity, it is not always a legal difference. For example, legally a sole trader is not separate from his business.

3. Where the prudence and accruals concepts conflict, prudence overrides accruals.

6 (a) No, because of the consistency concept. Once the depreciation policy has been established, it should not be changed without good cause.

(b)   No, because of the materiality concept. The cost of the bin is very small. Rather than cluttering up the balance sheet for five years, treat the £4.95 as an expense in this year's profit and loss account.

7   The profit shown under the historical cost convention will be higher. This is because the value of the resources consumed by the business is measured by their cost at the time they were purchased. Under the current cost convention, the value of these resources is measured by their cost at the (later) time when they were replaced. Given that prices are rising, this cost will be higher and so reported profits will be less.

8   The list is almost endless, but among the most recent you will certainly have thought of Polly Peck, BCCI and the Maxwell empire.

9   Six months. Listed companies are required to publish interim accounts covering the first half of each year as well as accounts covering the whole year. It is common to see statements of six-monthly profit (or loss) figures published by leading companies in the pages of the quality newspapers.

Further question practice

Now try the following practice questions at the end of this text

Multiple choice questions: **3 to 10**

Exam style question: **2**

Chapter 3 :
ASSETS AND LIABILITIES

Introduction

The terms 'asset' and 'liability' should be familiar to you in a day-to-day context, and indeed their accounting meaning is not far removed from that in common speech. The accounting and business equations discussed in this chapter are fundamental to your understanding of the balance sheet in Chapter 4, so do not rush this chapter – make sure you understand its contents.

Your objectives

After completing this chapter you should:

(a) Understand that a business is an entity with assets and liabilities in its own name

(b) Be aware of the main items included in the terms 'assets' and 'liabilities'

(c) Understand how the mix of assets and liabilities in a business changes over time

(d) Understand the relationship between assets, liabilities, capital and profits

1 THE NATURE OF A BUSINESS: ASSETS AND LIABILITIES

Up until now, we have used the terms 'business', 'assets' and 'liabilities' without looking too closely at their meaning. This has been possible because the terms are common in everyday speech. From now on we will be examining accounting practice in more detail and it is important to have a thorough understanding of how these terms are used in an accounting context.

Activity 1

You may already be familiar with the more technical uses of these terms. Can you distinguish, for example, between the terms 'an enterprise', 'a business', 'a company' and 'a firm'?

1.1 What is a business?

There are a number of different ways of looking at a business. Suggest three.

1.

2.

3.

Some ideas are listed below.

(a) A business is a commercial or industrial concern which exists to deal in the manufacture, re-sale or supply of goods and services.

(b) A business is an organisation which uses economic resources to create goods or services which customers will buy.

(c) A business is an organisation providing jobs for people to work in.

(d) A business invests money in resources (for example it buys buildings or machinery, it pays employees) in order to make even more money for its owners.

This last definition introduces the important idea of profit which was briefly discussed in the last chapter. Business enterprises vary in character, size and complexity. They range from very small businesses (the local shopkeeper or plumber) to very large ones (ICI). But the objective of earning profit is common to all of them.

Profit is the excess of income over expenditure. When expenditure exceeds income, the business is running at a loss. One of the jobs of an accountant is to measure income, expenditure and profit. It is not such a straightforward problem as it may seem and in later chapters we will look at some of the theoretical and practical difficulties involved.

There are some organisations which do not have a profit motive – suggest two.

1.

2.

You could have selected two of the following.

(a) Charities exist to provide help to the needy. However, a charity must keep its expenditure within the level of its income or it could not continue in operation.

(b) Public sector organisations exist to serve the community rather than to make profits. Such organisations include government departments and services (for example the fire service, police force or the national health service). But even though their purpose is not primarily to make a profit, they can only spend the money allowed to them by the Government. Like charities, they must be cost-conscious.

(c) Certain clubs and associations exist to provide services to their members. Profit is not their primary objective, but to maintain and improve the services they offer they must ensure that their income is at least as great as their expenditure.

1.2 Assets and liabilities

An asset is something valuable which a business owns or has the use of. Examples of assets are factories, office buildings, warehouses, delivery vans, lorries, plant and machinery, computer equipment, office furniture, cash and also goods held in store awaiting sale to customers, and raw materials and components held in store by a manufacturing business for use in production.

Some assets are held and used in operations for a long time. An office building might be occupied by administrative staff for years; similarly, a machine might have a productive life of many years before it wears out. Other assets are held for only a short time. The owner of a newsagent's shop, for example, will have to sell his newspapers on the same day that he gets them, and weekly newspapers and monthly magazines also have a short shelf life. The more quickly a business can sell the goods it has in store, the more profit it is likely to make.

A liability is something which is owed to somebody else. 'Liabilities' is the accounting term for the debts of a business. Here are some examples of liabilities.

(a) *A bank loan or bank overdraft.* The liability is the amount which must eventually be repaid to the bank.

(b) *Amounts owed to suppliers* for goods purchased but not yet paid for. For example, a boat builder might buy some timber on credit from a timber merchant, which means that the boat builder does not have to pay for the timber until some time after it has been delivered. Until the boat builder pays what he owes, the timber merchant will be his creditor for the amount owed.

(c) *Taxation owed to the government.* A business pays tax on its profits but there is a gap in time between when a company declares its profits and becomes liable to pay tax and the time when the tax bill must eventually be paid.

Activity 2

Attempt to classify the following items as long-term assets ('fixed assets'), short-term assets ('current assets') or liabilities.

(a)   A personal computer used in the accounts department of a retail store

(b)   A personal computer on sale in an office equipment shop

(c)   Wages due to be paid to staff at the end of the week

(d)   A van for sale in a motor dealer's showroom

(e)   A delivery van used in a grocer's business

(f)   An amount owing to a leasing company for the acquisition of a van

---

2 THE ACCOUNTING EQUATION AND THE BUSINESS EQUATION

2.1 The business as a separate entity

So far we have spoken of assets and liabilities 'of a business'. In the previous chapter, it was pointed out that in accounting terms, a business is always a separate entity; but there are two aspects to this question: the strict legal position and the convention adopted by accountants.

Many businesses are carried on in the form of *limited companies*. The owners of a limited company are its shareholders, who may be few in number (as with a small, family-owned company) or very numerous (for example in the case of a large public company whose shares are quoted on the Stock Exchange).

The law recognises a company as a legal entity, quite separate from its owners. A company may, in its own name, acquire assets, incur debts, and enter into contracts. If a company's assets become insufficient to meet its liabilities, the company as a separate entity might become 'bankrupt', but the owners of the company could not usually be required to pay the debts from their own private resources: the debts are not debts of the shareholders, but of the company. This is *limited liability*: the liability of shareholders to the company is *limited* to the amount the company asks for their shares on issue.

The case is different, in law, when a business is carried on not by a company, but by an individual (a sole trader) or by a group of individuals (a partnership). Suppose that Rodney Quiff sets himself up in business as a hairdresser trading under the business name 'Quiff's Hair Salon'. The law recognises no distinction between Rodney Quiff, the individual, and the business known as 'Quiff's Hair Salon'. Any debts of the business which cannot be met from business assets must be met from Rodney's private resources.

Activity 3

Fill in the missing words to make sure you understand the entity concept and how the law differs from accounting practice.

The entity concept regards a business as a _____ entity, distinct from its _____ . The concept applies to _____ businesses. However, the law only recognises a _____ as a legal entity separate from its _____ . The liability of shareholders to the company is _____ to the amount the company asks them to pay for their shares.

The crucial point which must be understood at the outset is that the convention adopted in preparing accounts (the *entity concept*) is always to treat a business as a separate entity from its owner(s). This applies whether or not the business is recognised in law as a separate entity, so it applies whether the business is carried on by a company or by a sole trader.

This is an idea which at first sight seems illogical and unrealistic; students often have difficulty in understanding it. Nevertheless, it is an idea which you must try to appreciate. It is the basis of a fundamental rule of accounting, which is that the assets and liabilities of a business must always be equal. A simple example may clarify the idea of a business as a separate entity from its owners.

2.2 The accounting equation

EXAMPLE: THE ACCOUNTING EQUATION

On 1 July 20X6, Liza Doolittle decided to open up a flower stall in the market, to sell flowers and potted plants. She had saved up some money in her building society, and had £2,500 to put into her business.

When the business is set up, an 'accountant's picture' can be drawn of what it owns and what it owes.

The business begins by owning the cash that Liza has put into it, £2,500. But does it owe anything? The answer is yes.

The business is a separate entity in accounting terms. It has obtained its assets, in this example cash, from its owner, Liza Doolittle. It therefore owes this amount of money to its owner. If Liza changed her mind and decided not to go into business after all, the business would be dissolved by the 'repayment' of the cash by the business to Liza.

The money put into a business by its owners is capital. In accounting, capital is an investment of money (funds) with the intention of earning a return. A business proprietor invests capital with the intention of earning profit. As long as that money is invested, accountants will treat the capital as money owed to the proprietor by the business.

When Liza Doolittle sets up her business:

$$\begin{aligned}
\text{Capital invested} &= £2,500 \\
\text{Cash} &- £2,500
\end{aligned}$$

Capital invested is a form of liability, because it is an amount owed by the business to its owner(s). Adapting this to the idea that liabilities and assets are always equal amounts, we can state the accounting equation as follows.

$$\text{Assets} = \text{Capital} + \text{Liabilities}$$

For Liza Doolittle, as at 1 July 20X6:

$$£2,500 \text{ (cash)} = £2,500 + £0$$

NOTES

Activity 4

Suppose that the original £2,500 in Liza's business had been provided only part by herself (£1,750), the balance being provided by a loan of £750 from Professor Higgins. What are the implications of this for the accounting equation we have drawn up?

Hint. The answer is not necessarily clear cut. There are different ways of looking at the Professor's investment.

EXAMPLE CONTINUED

Liza Doolittle uses some of the money invested to purchase a market stall from Len Turnip, who is retiring from his fruit and vegetables business. The cost of the stall is £1,800.

She also purchases some flowers and potted plants from a trader in the New Covent Garden wholesale market, at a cost of £650.

This leaves £50 in cash, after paying for the stall and goods for resale, out of the original £2,500. Liza kept £30 in the bank and drew out £20 in small change. She was now ready for her first day of market trading on 3 July 20X6.

The assets and liabilities of the business have now altered, and at 3 July, before trading begins, the state of her business is as follows.

Assets	£	=	Capital	+	Liabilities
Stall	1,800	=	£2,500	+	£0
Flowers and plants	650				
Cash at bank	30				
Cash in hand	20				
	2,500				

Profit introduced into the accounting equation

Let us now suppose that on 3 July Liza has a very successful day. She is able to sell all of her flowers and plants, for £900. All of her sales are for cash.

Since Liza has sold goods costing £650 to earn revenue of £900, we can say that she has earned a profit of £250 on the day's trading.

Profits belong to the owners of a business. In this case, the £250 belongs to Liza Doolittle. However, so long as the business retains the profits, and does not pay anything out to its owners, the retained profits are accounted for as an addition to the proprietor's capital.

Assets		=	Capital		+ Liabilities
	£			£	
Stall	1,800	=	Original		
Flower and plants	0		investment	2,500	
Cash in hand and			Retained profit	250	
at bank					
(30 + 20 + 900)	950				
	2,750			2,750	+ £0

Increase in net assets

We can re-arrange the accounting equation to help us to calculate the capital balance.

> Assets – liabilities = Capital, which is the same as
>
> Net assets = Capital

At the beginning and then at the end of 3 July 20X6 Liza Doolittle's financial position was as follows.

		Net assets	*Capital*
(a)	At the beginning of the day:	£(2,500 – 0) = £2,500 =	£2,500
(b)	At the end of the day:	£(2,750 – 0) = £2,750 =	£2,750

There has been an increase of £250 in net assets, which is the amount of profits earned during the day.

Drawings

Drawings are amounts of money taken out of a business by its owner.

Since Liza Doolittle has made a profit of £250 from her first day's work, she might well feel fully justified in drawing some of the profits out of the business. After all, business owners, like everyone else, need income for living expenses. We will suppose that Liza decides to pay herself £180, in 'wages'.

The payment of £180 is probably regarded by Liza as a fair reward for her day's work, and she might think of the sum as being in the nature of wages. However, the £180 is not an expense to be deducted before the figure of net profit is arrived at. In other words, it would be incorrect to calculate the net profit earned by the business as follows.

	£
Profit on sale of flowers etc	250
Less 'wages' paid to Liza	180
Net profit earned by business (incorrect)	70

This is because any amounts paid by a business to its proprietor are treated by accountants as withdrawals of profit, and not as expenses incurred by the business. In the case of Liza's business, the true position is that the net profit earned is the £250 surplus on sale of flowers.

	£
Net profit earned by business	250
Less profit withdrawn by Liza	180
Net profit retained in the business	70

Profits are capital as long as they are retained in the business. When they are paid out, the business suffers a reduction in capital.

The drawings are taken in cash, and so the business loses £180 of its cash assets. After the drawings have been made, the accounting equation would be restated.

(a) *Assets*   = *Capital*   + *Liabilities*

		£		£	
	Stall	1,800	Original investment	2,500	
	Flower and plants	0	Retained profit	70	
	Cash (950 – 180)	770			
		2,750		2,750	+ £0

(b) Alternatively   *Net assets*   *Capital*

   £(2,570 – 0)   =   £2,570

The increase in net assets since trading operations began is now only £(2,570 – 2,500) = £70, which is the amount of the retained profits.

These examples have illustrated that the basic equation (assets = capital + liabilities) always holds good. Any transaction affecting the business has a dual effect: if an asset is reduced, then either another asset must be increased or there must be a reduction in capital or in a liability; similarly, if capital is increased, then either assets increase as well or liabilities reduce. Try to reinforce your grasp of this by attempting the following activity.

Activity 5

Try to explain the dual effects of each of the following transactions.

(a) A business receives a loan of £5,000 from its bank.

(b) A business pays £800 cash to purchase a stock of goods for resale.

(c) The proprietor of a business removes £50 from the till to buy her husband a birthday present.

(d) A business sells goods costing £300 at a profit of £140.

(e) A business repays a £5,000 bank loan, plus interest of £270.

2.3   The business equation

The business equation gives a definition of profits earned. The preceding example has attempted to show that the amount of profit earned can be related to the increase in the net assets of the business, and the drawings of profits by the proprietor.

This relationship is sometimes referred to as the *business equation*. It can be expressed mathematically as follows.

$$P = I + D - C_i$$

where

P   represents profit

I   represents the increase in net assets, after drawings have been taken out by the proprietor

D   represents drawings

C_i represents the amount of extra capital introduced into the business during the period. This is a negative figure in the equation, because when a business is given new capital, perhaps in the form of extra money paid in by the proprietor himself, there will be an increase in the net assets of the business without any profits being earned. This means, say, that if a proprietor puts an extra £5,000 into his business the profit from the transaction, according to the business equation, would be P = £5,000 + 0 – £5,000 = £0.

In our example of Liza Doolittle's business on 3 July 20X6, after drawings have been taken:

Profit   =   £70 + £180 – £0

          =   £250

To develop your understanding of this concept, we proceed with the example of Liza Doolittle.

EXAMPLE: BUSINESS EQUATION

The next market day is on 10 July, and Liza gets ready by purchasing more flowers and plants for cash, at a cost of £740. She was not feeling well, however, because of a heavy cold, and so she decided to accept the offer of help for the day from her cousin Ethel. Ethel would be paid a wage of £40 at the end of the day.

Trading on 10 July was again very brisk, and Liza and Ethel sold all their goods for £1,100 cash. Liza paid Ethel her wage of £40 and drew out £200 for herself.

The accounting equation before trading begins on 10 July, and after trading ends on 10 July, can be set out as follows.

(a)   **Before trading begins**

Assets		=	*Capital*	+	*Liabilities*
	£				
Stall	1,800				
Goods	740				
Cash (770 – 740)	30				
	2,750	=	£2,570	+	£0

(b) **After trading ends**

On 10 July, all the goods are sold for £1,100 cash, and Ethel is paid £40. The profit for the day is £320, computed as follows.

	£	£
Sales		1,100
Less cost of goods sold	740	
Ethel's wage	40	
		780
Profit		320

Liza withdraws £200 of this profit for her personal use.

Assets		=	*Capital*		+ *Liabilities*
	£			£	
Stall	1,800		At beginning of		
Goods	0		10 July	2,570	
Cash (30 + 1,100			Profits retained on		
− 40 − 2000)	890		10 July (320 − 200)	120	
	2,690			2,690	+ £0

Activity 6

By using the business equation, confirm the profit figure calculated above.

Creditors and debtors

A *creditor* is a person to whom a business owes money.

A trade creditor is a person to whom a business owes money for debts incurred in the course of trading operations. The term might refer to debts still outstanding which arise from the purchase from suppliers of materials, components or goods for resale.

A business does not always pay immediately for goods or services it buys. It is a common business practice to make purchases on credit, with a promise to pay within 30 days, or two months or three months of the date of the bill or 'invoice' for the goods. For example, if A buys goods costing £2,000 on credit from B, B might send A an invoice for £2,000, dated say 1 March, with credit terms that payment must be made within 30 days. If A then delays payment until 31 March, B will be a creditor of A between 1 and 31 March, for £2,000.

A creditor is a liability of a business.

Just as a business might buy goods on credit, so too might it sell goods to customers on credit. A customer who buys goods without paying cash for them straight away is a *debtor*. For example, suppose that C sells goods on credit to D for £6,000 on terms that the debt must be settled within two months of the invoice date, 1 October. If D does not pay the £6,000 until 30 November, D will be a debtor of C for £6,000 from 1 October until 30 November.

A debtor is an asset of a business. When the debt is finally paid, the debtor 'disappears' as an asset, to be replaced by 'cash'.

Activity 7

The following descriptions are of creditors, debtors and cash. Match each item to its correct description.

1   This is an asset, highly liquid and vital to the survival of the business.

2   This is a person to whom the business owes money.

3   When this person settles, this asset will disappear and will be replaced by another.

The example of Liza Doolittle's market stall will be continued further, by looking at the consequences of the following transactions in the week to 17 July 20X6.

EXAMPLE: LIZA DOOLITTLE – FURTHER TRANSACTIONS

(a)   Liza Doolittle realises that she is going to need more money in the business and so she makes the following arrangements.

      •   She invests immediately a further £250 of her own capital.

      •   She persuades her Uncle Henry to lend her £500 immediately. Uncle Henry tells her that she can repay the loan whenever she likes, but in the meantime she must pay him interest of £5 per week each week at the end of the market day. They agree that it will probably be quite a long time before the loan is eventually repaid.

(b)   She is very pleased with the progress of her business, and decides that she can afford to buy a secondhand van to pick up flowers and plants from her supplier and bring them to her stall in the market. She finds a car dealer, Laurie Loader, who agrees to sell her a van on credit for £700. Liza agrees to pay for the van after 30 days' trial use.

(c)   During the week before the next market day (which is on 17 July), Liza's Uncle George telephones her to ask whether she would be interested in selling him some garden gnomes and furniture for his garden. Liza tells him that she will look for a supplier. After some investigations, she buys what Uncle George has asked for, paying £300 in cash to the supplier. Uncle George accepts delivery of the goods and agrees to pay £350.

(d)   The next market day approaches, and Liza buys flowers and plants costing £800. Of these purchases £750 are paid in cash, with the remaining £50 on seven days' credit. Liza decides to use Ethel's services again as an assistant on market day, at an agreed wage of £40.

(e)   For the third market day running, on 17 July, Liza succeeds in selling all her goods, earning revenue of £1,250 (all in cash). She decides to take out drawings of £240 for her week's work. She also pays Ethel £40 in cash. She decides to make the interest payment to her Uncle Henry the next time she sees him.

NOTES

(f)   We shall ignore any van expenses for the week, for the sake of relative simplicity.

Required

(a)   State the accounting equation:

(i)   After Liza and Uncle Henry have put more money into the business

(ii)   After the purchase of the van

(iii)   After the sale of goods to Uncle George

(iv)   After the purchase of goods for the weekly market

(v)   At the end of the day's trading on 17 July, and after drawings have been appropriated out of profit

(b)   State the business equation showing profit earned during the week ended 17 July.

ANSWER

There are a number of different transactions to account for here. This solution deals with them one at a time in chronological order. (In practice, it would be possible to do one set of calculations which combines the results of all the transactions, but we shall defer such 'shortcut' methods until later.)

(a)   (i)   The addition of Liza's extra capital and Uncle Henry's loan.

An investment analyst might define the loan of Uncle Henry as a capital investment on the grounds that it will probably be for the long term. Uncle Henry is not the owner of the business, however, even though he has made an investment of a loan in it. He would only become an owner if Liza offered him a partnership in the business, and she has not done so. To the business, Uncle Henry is a long-term creditor, and it is more appropriate to define his investment as a liability of the business and not as business capital.

The accounting equation after £(250 + 500) = £750 cash is put into the business will be:

Assets	£	=	Capital	£	+ Liabilities	£
Stall	1,800		As at end		Loan	500
Goods	0		of 10 July	2,690		
Cash			Additional			
(890 + 750)	1,640		capital	250		
	3,440	=		2,940	+	500

(ii)   The purchase of the van (cost £700) is on credit:

Assets	£	=	Capital	£	+ Liabilities	£
Stall	1,800		As at end			
Van	700		of 10 July	2,690	Loan	500
Cash (890			Additional			
+ 750)	1,640		capital	250	Creditor	700
	4,140	=		2,940	+	1,200

 BPP PUBLISHING

(iii)   The sale of goods to Uncle George on credit (£350) which cost the business £300 (cash paid):

Assets		=	*Capital*		+ *Liabilities*	
	£			£		£
			As at end			
Stall	1,800		of 10 July	2,690	Loan	500
			Additional			
Van	700		capital	250	Creditor	700
Debtors	350		Profit on sale to			
Cash (1,640			Uncle George			
– 300)	1,340			50		
	4,190	=		2,990	+	1,200

(iv)   After the purchase of goods for the weekly market (£750 paid in cash and £50 of purchases on credit):

Assets		=	*Capital*		+ *Liabilities*	
	£			£		£
			As at end			
Stall	1,800		of 10 July	2,690	Loan	500
			Additional			
Van	700		capital	250	Creditor	
Goods	800		Profit on sale to		for van	700
Debtors	350		Uncle George		Creditor	
Cash (1,340				50	for goods	50
– 750)	590					
	4,240	=		2,990	+	1,250

(v)   After market trading on 17 July. Sales of goods costing £800 earned revenues of £1,250. Ethel's wages were £40 (paid), Uncle Henry's interest charge is £5 (not paid yet) and drawings out of profits were £240 (paid). The profit for 17 July may be calculated as follows, taking the full £5 of interest as a cost on that day.

	£	£
Sales		1,250
Cost of goods sold	800	
Wages	40	
Interest	5	
		845
Profits earned on 17 July		405
Profit on sale of goods to Uncle George		50
Profit for the week		455
Drawings appropriated out of profits		240
Retained profit		215

	Assets	=	Capital		+ Liabilities	
	£		£		£
Stall	1,800		As at end of		Loan	500
			10 July	2,690	Creditor	
Van	700		Additional		for van	700
Goods	0		capital	250	Creditor	
Debtors	350		Profit		for goods	50
Cash			retained	215	Creditor for	
(590 + 1,250					interest	
− 40 − 240)					payments	5
	1,560					
	4,410	=		3,155	+	1,255

The increase in the net assets of the business during the week was as follows.

	£
Net assets as at the end of 17 July £(4,410 − 1,255)	3,155
Net assets as at the end of 10 July	2,690
Increase in net assets	465

The business equation for the week ended 17 July is as follows.
(Remember that extra capital of £250 was invested by the proprietor.)

$$P = I + D - C_i$$
$$= £465 + £240 - £250$$
$$= £455$$

This confirms the calculation of profit.

Activity 8 (15 minutes)

Calculate the profit of a business for the year ended 31 December 20X6 from the following information.

	1 January 20X6		31 December 20X6	
	£	£	£	£
Assets				
Property	20,000		20,000	
Machinery	6,000		9,000	
Debtors	4,000		8,000	
Cash	1,000		1,500	
		31,000		38,500
Liabilities				
Overdraft	6,000		9,000	
Creditors	5,000		3,000	
		(11,000)		(12,000)
Net assets		20,000		26,500
Drawings during the year				4,500
Additional capital introduced by				
the proprietor during the year				5,000

Chapter roundup

You should by now fully understand the following.

- A business owns assets and owes liabilities. It is important to keep business assets and liabilities separate from the personal assets and liabilities of the proprietor(s).

- Assets are items belonging to a business and used in the running of the business. They may be fixed (such as machinery or office premises), or current (such as stock, debtors and cash).

- Liabilities are sums of money owed by a business to outsiders such as a bank or a trade creditor.

- The assets of a business are always equal to its liabilities (including capital).

We will next look at how assets and liabilities are included in the balance sheet.

Quick quiz

1 What is meant by profit? (see para 1.1)

2 List as many organisations as you can which do not have profit as their main objective. (1.1)

3 Briefly explain the legal distinction between a sole trader and a limited company. (2.1)

4 In what sense can a proprietor's capital be regarded as a liability of a business? (2.1)

5 How is retained profit accounted for within the accounting equation? (2.2)

6 Explain the distinction between an expense of the business and a withdrawal of profit. (2.2)

7 Write out the business equation in its mathematical form and explain precisely how each term is defined. (2.3)

8 Creditors owe you money, while you owe money to debtors. Or is it the other way round? (2.3)

Answers to activities

1 An 'enterprise' is the most general term, referring to just about any organisation in which people join together to achieve a common end. In the context of accounting it can refer to a multinational conglomerate, a small club, a local authority and so on *ad infinitum*.

A 'business' is also a very general term, but it does not extend as widely as the term 'enterprise': for example, it would not include a charity or a local authority. But any organisation existing to trade and make a profit could be called a business.

A 'company' is an enterprise constituted in a particular legal form, usually involving limited liability for its members. Companies need not be businesses; for example, many charities are constituted as companies.

47

NOTES

A 'firm' is a much vaguer term. It is sometimes used loosely in the sense of a business or a company. Some writers, more usefully, try to restrict its meaning to that of an unincorporated business (ie a business not constituted as a company, for example a partnership).

2   (a)   Fixed asset

     (b)   Current asset

     (c)   Liability

     (d)   Current asset

     (e)   Fixed asset

     (f)   Liability

Note that the same item can be categorised differently in different businesses.

3   The missing words are:

separate; owners; all; company; owners; limited.

4   We have assets of £2,500 (cash) as before, balanced by liabilities of £2,500 (the amounts owed by the business to Liza and the Professor). The £1,750 owed to Liza clearly falls into the special category of liability labelled 'capital', because it is a sum owed to a (or the) proprietor of the business. To classify the £750 owed to the Professor, we would need to know more about the terms of his agreement with Liza. If they have effectively gone into partnership, sharing the risks and rewards of the business, then the Professor is a proprietor too and the £750 is 'capital' in the sense that Liza's £1,750 is; but if the professor has no share in the profits of the business, and can expect only a repayment of his loan plus some interest, the amount of £750 should be classified under 'liabilities'.

5   (a)   Assets (cash) increase by £5,000; liabilities (amount owed to the bank) increase by £5,000.

     (b)   Assets (cash) decrease by £800; assets (stock) increase by £800.

     (c)   Assets (cash) decrease by £50; capital decreases by £50. (The proprietor has taken £50 for her personal use. In effect, the business has repaid her part of the amount it owed.)

     (d)   Assets (cash) increase by £440; assets (stock) decrease by £300; capital (the profit earned for the proprietor) increases by £140.

     (e)   Assets (cash) decrease by £5,270; liabilities (the bank loan) decrease by £5,000; capital decreases by £270. (The proprietor has made a 'loss' of £270 on the transaction.)

6
		£
Net assets at end of 10 July		2,690
Net assets at beginning of 10 July		2,570
Increase in net assets (I)		120

We also have $D = £200$, $C_i = 0$

$$\therefore P = £120 + £200 - £0$$

$$= £320$$

7   You should have matched

1. to cash,

 BPP PUBLISHING

2. to creditors and

3. to debtors.

8   The increase in net assets during the year was £(26,500 − 20,000) = £6,500.

$$P = I + D - C_i$$

$$= £6,500 + £4,500 - £5,000$$

$$= £6,000$$

Further question practice

Now try the following practice questions at the end of this text

Multiple choice questions: **11 to 17**

Exam style question: **3**

Chapter 4 :
THE BALANCE SHEET

Introduction

This chapter introduces the topic of 'double entry bookkeeping'. This is a topic which not all students will need to know about in detail. We will look at it in much more detail in the next chapter.

In an earlier chapter it was stated that the most important financial statements are the balance sheet and the profit and loss account (more generally, the income statement). In this chapter we look at the balance sheet and examine the main items that appear on it. In the next chapter we will cover the income statement.

To begin with, it is worth explaining the meaning of the term 'balance sheet'. Our discussion will help to bring out the way in which many transactions of different kinds are grouped together in the accounting records of a business and eventually totalled and summarised in the form of financial statements.

Your objectives

After completing this chapter you should:

    (a)   Understand what a balance sheet is and how it is compiled

    (b)   Be aware of the standard layout of a balance sheet

    (c)   Understand the categories of assets and liabilities found in a typical balance sheet

1 LEDGER ACCOUNTS

1.1 The nominal ledger

In Chapter 3 we saw how every financial transaction entered into by a business has a dual aspect: an increase in one asset is balanced by a corresponding decrease in another, or alternatively by an increase in capital or liabilities. This duality of financial transactions has given rise to a system of *double entry bookkeeping* which is the basic method of recording accounting information in all businesses, however large or small.

The term bookkeeping, with its suggestion of bound ledgers, may be misleading. Although many businesses continue to use 'books of account', literally so called, accounts are increasingly maintained nowadays on computer. This of course has a dramatic effect on the practicalities of logging accounting transactions and preparing summaries, but it has no impact whatsoever on the underlying principles involved. In the discussion which follows, we will use the traditional terminology.

Activity 1

You may have come across computerised accounting packages. If not, do a little research (for example look at the advertisements in computer magazines or, better, accountancy magazines) to find out the kind of accounting tasks which computers can cope with.

The main accounting record of a business is its nominal ledger (sometimes called the general ledger). This is a book containing pages ruled off in a form known as 'T' accounts. The format is illustrated below.

Folio A123

Debit	Debtors control account	Credit
£	£	

Note the following points.

- Each page has a title. The page illustrated is called the 'Debtors control account', which means that it is an account for recording transactions with trade debtors (amounts charged to them for the goods they purchase, cash payments received from them, and so on).

- Each page has a folio number. This is just a reference number enabling a user of the ledger to find the account he is interested in quickly. Different businesses will have different systems of numbering their accounts.

- Each page has a debit side (on the left) and a credit side (on the right).

The point of double entry bookkeeping is that every financial transaction entered into by a business is entered in the ledger twice: once as a credit entry, and once as a debit. For example, if cash is received from a debtor this is recorded both in the debtors control account (to reflect the fact that the asset 'debtors' is reduced), and in the cash account (to reflect the fact that the asset 'cash' has increased). The entry in the debtors control account is on the credit side; the entry in the cash account is on the debit side.

It should be clear that the total of credit entries appearing in the ledger at any time will be equal to the total of the debit entries at that time. To check on this (and for other reasons) it is usual to 'strike a balance' on each account periodically (ie to total the debit and credit entries on each account and to express their net effect as a single figure, debit or credit). The total of the debit balances may then be compared with the total of the credit balances, and they should of course be equal.

A balance sheet is so called because in essence it is simply a listing of the balances which appear in the ledger of a business on a particular day. This is a somewhat simplified statement, however, in that any business other than the very smallest will require many ledger accounts to record its transactions. It would not be very informative to list several hundred balances and leave the reader to plough through them. To avoid this, ledger accounts are categorised under a limited number of headings and the balances on accounts within a particular category are totalled to provide a single figure on the balance sheet.

To emphasise the point that a balance sheet is a listing of balances 'on a particular day' (more accurately, 'at a particular moment'), it is sometimes compared to a kind of snapshot of a business. It captures on paper a still image, frozen at a single moment of time, of something which is dynamic and continually changing. Typically, a balance sheet is prepared to show the liabilities, capital and assets of a business at the end of the accounting period to which the accounts relate.

As you should readily appreciate, a balance sheet is therefore very similar to the accounting equation. In fact, the only differences between a balance sheet and an accounting equation are:

(a)   The manner or format in which the liabilities and assets are presented

(b)   The extra detail which a balance sheet usually goes into

---

Activity 2

Answer the following questions to make sure you are familiar with the purpose of the balance sheet.

1   In one sentence describe the balance sheet.

2   How does the balance sheet differ from the profit and loss account?

3   Is the balance sheet included in financial or management accounts?

---

2   BALANCE SHEET

2.1   Details in the balance sheet

A balance sheet is divided into two halves, usually showing capital in one half and net assets (ie assets less liabilities) in the other.

NAME OF BUSINESS
BALANCE SHEET AS AT (DATE)   £

Assets	X
Less liabilities	X
Net assets	X
Capital	X

The total value on one side of the balance sheet will equal the total value on the other side. You should readily understand this from the accounting equation.

For many businesses, the way in which assets and liabilities are categorised and presented in a balance sheet is a matter of choice, and you may come across different formats. For limited companies, the form of the balance sheet is closely defined by the Companies Act 1985. The format below, with specimen figures, should help you see how a typical balance sheet is compiled. It is a somewhat simplified version of the format prescribed for limited companies.

PARADIGM LIMITED
BALANCE SHEET AS AT 31 DECEMBER 20X6

	£	£
Fixed assets		
Land and buildings	50,000	
Plant and machinery	28,000	
Fixtures and fittings	7,500	
		85,500
Current assets	6,200	
Stocks	7,100	
Debtors	2,500	
Cash at bank and in hand	15,800	
Creditors: amounts falling due within one year		
Bank overdraft	1,700	
Trade creditors	4,900	
	6,600	
Net current assets		9,200
Total assets less current liabilities		94,700
Capital		
Share capital		30,000
Retained profits		64,700
		94,700

Activity 3   **(15 minutes)**

Using the figures in the balance sheet above, check that the accounting equation holds good in the form: Assets = Capital + Liabilities.

Business Basics: Accounting

2.2 Fixed assets

Assets in the balance sheet are divided into *fixed* and *current* assets.

Definition

> A *fixed asset* is an asset acquired for use within the business (rather than for selling to a customer), with a view to earning income or making profits from its use, either directly or indirectly.

(a) In a manufacturing industry, a production machine would be a fixed asset, because it makes goods which are then sold.

(b) In a service industry, equipment used by employees giving service to customers would be classed as fixed assets (for example the equipment used in a garage, and furniture in a hotel).

These are only ideas. You may well have included other assets such as factory premises, office furniture, computer equipment, company cars, delivery vans or pallets in a warehouse.

To be classed as a fixed asset in the balance sheet of a business, an item must satisfy two further conditions.

(a) Clearly, it must be used by the business. For example, the proprietor's own house would not normally appear on the business balance sheet.

(b) The asset must have a 'life' in use of more than one year (strictly, more than one 'accounting period' which might be more or less than one year).

A *tangible* fixed asset is a physical asset, ie one that can be touched. It has a real, 'solid' existence. All of the examples of fixed assets mentioned above are tangible.

An *intangible* fixed asset is an asset which does not have a physical existence. It cannot be 'touched'. The expense of acquiring patent rights or developing a new product would be classified as an intangible fixed asset.

An *investment* might also be a fixed asset. Investments are commonly found in the published accounts of large limited companies. A large company A might invest in another company B by purchasing some of the shares of B. This investment would earn income for A in the form of dividends paid out by B. If the shares are purchased by A with a view to holding on to them for more than one year, they would be classified as a fixed asset of A.

In this chapter, we shall restrict our attention to tangible fixed assets.

2.3 Fixed assets and depreciation

Fixed assets might be held and used by a business for a number of years, but they wear out or lose their usefulness in the course of time. Every tangible fixed asset has a limited life. The only exception is land held freehold.

The accounts of a business try to recognise that the cost of a fixed asset is gradually consumed as the asset wears out. This is done by gradually writing off the asset's cost in the profit and loss account over several accounting periods. For example, in the case of a machine costing £1,000 and expected to wear out after ten years, it might be appropriate to reduce the balance sheet value by £100 each year. This process is known as depreciation.

If a balance sheet were drawn up four years, say, after the asset was purchased, the amount of depreciation which would have accumulated would be 4 × £100 = £400. The machine would then appear in the balance sheet as follows.

	£
Machine at original cost	1,000
Less accumulated depreciation	400
Net book value*	600

* The value of the asset in the books of account, net of depreciation. After ten years the asset would be fully depreciated and would appear in the balance sheet with a net book value of zero.

Activity 4

Depreciation is discussed in a later chapter, but in the meantime here is a little test which brings in the concept of *residual value*. Suppose a business buys a car for £10,000. It expects to keep the car for three years and then to trade it in at an estimated value of £3,400. How much depreciation should be accounted for in each year of the car's useful life?

2.4 Current assets

Current assets are either:

(a) Items owned by the business with the intention of turning them into cash within one year, or

(b) Cash, including money in the bank, owned by the business

These assets are 'current' in the sense that they are continually flowing through the business.

The definition in (a) above needs explaining further. Let us suppose that a trader, Chris Rhodes, runs a business selling motor cars, and purchases a showroom which he stocks with cars for sale. We will also suppose that he obtains the cars from a manufacturer, and pays for them in cash on delivery.

(a) If he sells a car in a cash sale, the goods are immediately converted into cash. The cash might then be used to buy more cars for re-sale.

(b) If he sells a car in a credit sale, the car will be given to the customer, who then becomes a debtor of the business. Eventually, the debtor will pay what he owes, and Chris Rhodes will receive cash. Once again, the cash might then be used to buy more cars for sale.

In this example the cars, debtors and cash are all current assets. Why?

(a) The cars (goods) held in stock for re-sale are current assets, because Chris Rhodes intends to sell them within one year, in the normal course of trade.

(b) Any debtors are current assets, if they are expected to pay what they owe within one year.

(c) Cash is a current asset.

BPP
PUBLISHING

The transactions described above could be shown as a *cash cycle*.

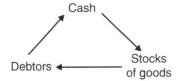

Cash is used to buy goods which are sold. Sales on credit create debtors, but eventually cash is earned from the sales. Some, perhaps most, of the cash will then be used to replenish stocks.

The main items of current assets are therefore:

(a)   Stocks

(b)   Debtors

(c)   Cash

Activity 5

This activity should ensure you understand asset classification. You should decide which of the following assets falls into the 'fixed' category and which should be treated as 'current'.

ASSET	BUSINESS	CURRENT OR FIXED
VAN	DELIVERY FIRM	
MACHINE	MANUFACTURING COMPANY	
CAR	CAR TRADER	
INVESTMENT	ANY	

There are some other categories of current assets.

(a)   *Short-term investments*. These are stocks and shares of other businesses, currently owned, but with the intention of selling them in the near future. For example, if a business has a lot of spare cash for a short time, its managers might decide to 'have a flutter' on The Stock Exchange, and buy shares in, say, Marks and Spencer, ICI or GEC. The shares will later be sold when the business needs the cash again. If share prices rise in the meantime, the business will make a profit from its short-term investment.

(b)   *Prepayments*. These are amounts of money already paid by the business for benefits which have not yet been enjoyed but will be enjoyed within the next accounting period. Suppose, for example, that a business pays an annual insurance premium of £240 to insure its premises against fire and that the premium is payable annually in advance on 1 December. Now, if the business has an accounting year end of 31 December it will pay £240 on 1 December, but only enjoy one month's insurance cover by the end of the year. The remaining 11 months' cover (£220 cost, at £20 per month) will be enjoyed in the next year. The prepayment of £220 would therefore be shown in the balance sheet of the business, at 31 December, as a current asset.

A prepayment might be thought of as a form of debtor. In the example above, at 31 December the insurance company still owes the business 11 months' worth of insurance cover.

2.5 Trade debtors and other debtors

Although it is convenient to think of debtors as customers who buy goods on credit, it is more accurate to say that a debtor is anyone who owes the business money. Continuing the example of an insurance policy, if a business makes an insurance claim for fire damage, the insurance company would be a debtor for the money payable on the claim.

A distinction can be made between:

(a)   Trade debtors, ie customers who still owe money for goods or services bought on credit in the course of the trading activities of the business

(b)   Other debtors, ie anyone else owing money to the business

2.6 The value of current assets in the balance sheet

Current assets must never be valued at more than their *net realisable value*, which is the amount of cash they will eventually earn the business when they are sold, minus the further costs required to get them into a condition for sale and to sell them.

Activity 6

How would you value debtors and stocks in the balance sheet?

Activity 7

The asset structure of a business is heavily dependent on the nature of its trading activities. Try to imagine what the main assets might be in the accounts of:

(a)   A steel manufacturing company

(b)   A bank

2.7 Liabilities

The various liabilities should be itemised separately. In addition, a distinction is made between:

(a)   Current liabilities

(b)   Long-term liabilities

Definition

Current liabilities are debts of the business that must be paid within a fairly short period of time (by convention, within one year).

In the accounts of limited companies, the Companies Act 1985 requires use of the term 'creditors: amounts falling due within one year' rather than 'current liabilities' although they mean the same thing.

Activity 8

Suggest three examples of current liabilities.

It is often argued that a bank overdraft is not a current liability, because a business is usually able to negotiate an overdraft facility for a long period of time. If an overdraft thus becomes a more permanent source of borrowing, it is really a long-term liability. However, you should normally expect to account for an overdraft as a current liability, since banks reserve the right to demand repayment at short notice.

Definition

Long-term liabilities (or *deferred liabilities*) are debts which are not payable within the 'short term' and so any liability which is not current must be long-term.

Just as 'short-term' by convention means one year or less, 'long-term' means more than one year. In the accounts of limited companies, the Companies Act 1985 requires use of the term: 'Creditors: amounts falling due after more than one year'.

Activity 9

Think of two examples of long-term liabilities.

The 'capital' section of the balance sheet will vary, depending on the nature of the entity. It will include amounts invested by the owner(s) in the business, plus profits earned by the business and not yet paid out. In the case of a limited company, amounts invested by the owners are in the form of 'share capital': this means that each investor contributes a sum of money to purchase a share in the overall ownership of the company.

Activity 10

You are required to prepare a balance sheet for the Sunken Arches Shoes and Boots Shop as at 31 December 20X6, given the information below.

	£
Capital as at 1 January 20X6	47,600
Profit for the year to 31 December 20X6	8,000
Freehold premises, net book value at 31 December 20X6	50,000
Motor vehicles, net book value at 31 December 20X6	9,000
Fixtures and fittings, net book value at 31 December 20X6	8,000
Long-term loan (mortgage)	25,000
Bank overdraft *	2,000
Goods held in stock for resale	16,000
Debtors	500
Cash in hand*	100
Creditors	1,200
Taxation payable	3,500
Drawings	4,000
Accrued costs of rent	600
Prepayment of insurance	300

*A shop might have cash in its cash registers, but an overdraft at the bank. See the specimen balance sheet of Paradigm Ltd earlier in this chapter.

Chapter roundup

By now you should understand the following points.

- A balance sheet is a statement of the financial position of a business at a given moment. It is called a balance sheet because it is a list of the balances in a company's nominal ledger at a moment in time. The balances are grouped, totalled and presented in a logical and informative format.

- A standard layout for the balance sheet is prescribed for limited companies, but other entities may adopt other formats.

- The main groupings to remember are: fixed assets; current assets; current liabilities; long-term liabilities; capital.

In the next chapter we will build on your understanding of accounts by looking at double entry bookkeeping before introducing the income statement in Chapter 6.

Quick quiz

1 What is a nominal ledger? (see para 1.1)
2 Describe the main features of a ledger account. (1.1)
3 What do you understand by the term 'double entry bookkeeping'? (1.1)
4 Why is a balance sheet so called? (1.2)

NOTES

5   List three main categories of fixed assets.   (2.2)

6   What is meant by depreciation?   (2.3)

7   What is a prepayment?   (2.4)

8   Give three examples of current liabilities.   (2.7)

Answers to activities

1   Computers can cope with virtually any accounting task. Packages are available for single applications (for example payroll or sales ledger); for integrated systems (in which all classes of transactions are logged and reports generated); for preparation of final accounts; and for advanced accounting applications such as spreadsheet work.

2   Your solutions should have covered the following points.

    1.   A balance sheet is a listing of asset and liability balances on a certain date.

    2.   The balance sheet gives a 'snapshot' of the net worth of the company at a single point in time, whereas the profit and loss account covers revenue and expenditure over a period of time, typically one year.

    3.   Both. A balance sheet will be included in financial accounts, showing the position at the year end. A forecast balance sheet may also be used in management decision making.

3
Assets	=	Capital	+ Liabilities
£(85,500 + 15,800)	=	£94,700	+ £6,600
£101,300	=	£101,300	

4   The point in this case is that the car has a residual value of £3,400. It would be inappropriate to account for depreciation in such a way as to write off the asset completely over three years; the aim should be to account only for its loss of value (£10,000 − £3,400 = £6,600), which suggests depreciation of £2,200 per annum.

5
ASSET	BUSINESS	CURRENT OR FIXED
VAN	DELIVERY FIRM	FIXED
MACHINE	MANUFACTURING COMPANY	FIXED
CAR	CAR TRADER	CURRENT
INVESTMENT	ANY	EITHER*

*The classification of the investment will depend on the purpose for which it is held. If the intention is to make a long term investment it will be a fixed asset, but if it is a short term way of investing spare cash it will be a current asset.

6   (a)   Debtors are valued at the cash value of the debt − ie at their realisable value.

    (b)   Stocks of goods are usually valued at historical cost. However, if the net realisable value (NRV) of stocks is less than their cost, the stocks will be valued at NRV instead of cost. In other words, stocks of goods are valued at the lower of their cost and net realisable value. In normal circumstances, the lower of the two amounts is cost.

BPP PUBLISHING

7   A steel manufacturing company would have a high proportion of its asset values locked up in fixed assets (factory premises, heavy machinery). It might also hold large stocks of raw materials and finished goods, and the value of debtors might be significant too.

A bank's main asset is its debtors, namely the people to whom it lends money by way of loan or overdraft. Curiously enough, cash holdings may be much smaller than debtor balances, because banks aim to use cash (ie lend it or invest it) rather than merely sitting on it. In the case of a bank with a large number of branches, land and buildings will also be a significant item.

8   Some examples of current liabilities are:

a)   Loans repayable within one year

(b)   A bank overdraft

(c)   Trade creditors

(d)   Taxation payable

(e)   'Accrued charges'. These are expenses already incurred by the business, for which no bill has yet been received.

9   Examples of long-term liabilities are:

(a)   Loans which are not repayable for more than one year, such as a bank loan, or a loan from an individual to a business.

(b)   A mortgage loan, which is a loan specifically secured against a freehold property. (If the business fails to repay the loan, the lender then has 'first claim' on the property, and is entitled to repayment out of the proceeds from the enforced sale of the property).

(c)   Debentures or debenture loans. These are usually found in larger limited companies' accounts. Debentures are securities issued by a company at a fixed rate of interest. They are repayable on agreed terms by a specified date in the future. Holders of debentures are therefore lenders of money to a company. Their interests, including security for the loan, are protected by the terms of a trust deed.

NOTES

10   SUNKEN ARCHES BALANCE SHEET
     AS AT 31 DECEMBER 20X6

	£	£
Fixed assets at net book value		
Freehold premises		50,000
Fixtures and fittings		8,000
Motor vehicles		9,000
		67,000
Current assets		
Stocks	16,000	
Debtors	500	
Prepayment	300	
Cash	100	
	16,900	
Current liabilities		
Bank overdraft	2,000	
Creditors	1,200	
Taxation payable	3,500	
Accrued costs	600	
	7,300	
		9,600
Net current assets		76,600
Long-term liabilities		
Loan		(25,000)
		51,600
Capital		
Capital as at 1 January 20X6		47,600
Profit for the year		8,000
		55,600
Less drawings		(4,000)
Capital as at 31 December 20X6		51,600

Further question practice

Now try the following practice questions at the end of this text

Multiple choice questions: **18 to 22**

Exam style question: **4**

Chapter 5 :
DOUBLE ENTRY BOOKKEEPING AND PREPARATION OF ACCOUNTS

Introduction

This very long chapter covers the major aspects of accounting records, basic double entry bookkeeping and ledger accounting, and the preparation of the profit and loss account and the balance sheet from a trial balance.

The chapter begins by looking at source documents and how transactions are recorded in the books of prime entry, including the cash book. Ledger accounting and double entry bookkeeping were described briefly at the beginning of the last chapter. Here we go further, describing the nominal ledger in detail, and the rules of double entry bookkeeping. The use of the journal is described, along with day book analysis, the use of a petty cash imprest system and the sales and purchases ledgers.

The chapter ends with a description of the trial balance and the preparation of the profit and loss account and balance sheet. Finally there is a brief look at the adjustments which may be necessary on the trial balance.

Your objectives

After completing this chapter you should:

(a)   Understand the role and function of source documents and the books of prime entry

(b)   Understand the ledger system of accounting

(c)   Know how to perform basic double entry bookkeeping

(d)   Be able to prepare a simple balance sheet and profit and loss account from a trial balance

(e)   Know how to adjust various items in the trial balance

1 SOURCE DOCUMENTS

1.1 The role of source documents

Whenever a business transaction takes place, involving sales or purchases, receiving or paying money, or owing or being owed money, it is usual for the transaction to be recorded on a document. These documents are the source of all the information recorded by a business.

Documents used to record the business transactions in the 'books of account' of the business include the following.

(a) *Sales order.* A customer writes out an order or signs an order for goods or services he wishes to buy.

(b) *Purchase order.* A business makes an order from another business for the purchase of goods or services, such as material supplies.

(c) *Invoices* and *credit notes*. These are discussed further below.

An *invoice* relates to a sales order or a purchase order.

(a) When a business sells goods or services on credit to a customer, it sends out an invoice. The details on the invoice should match up with the details on the sales order. The invoice is a request for the customer to pay what he owes.

(b) When a business buys goods or services on credit it receives an invoice from the supplier. The details on the invoice should match up with the details on the purchase order.

The invoice is primarily a demand for payment, but it is used for other purposes as well, as we shall see. Because it has several uses, an invoice is often produced on multi-part stationery, or photocopied, or carbon-copied. The top copy will go to the customer and other copies will be used by various people within the business.

What does an invoice show?

Most invoices are numbered, so that the business can keep track of all the invoices it sends out. Information usually shown on an invoice includes the following.

(a) Name and address of the seller and the purchaser.

(b) Date of the sale.

(c) Description of what is being sold.

(d) Quantity and unit price of what has been sold (for example 20 pairs of shoes at £25 a pair).

(e) Details of trade discount, if any (for example 10% reduction in cost if buying over 100 pairs of shoes).

(f) Total amount of the invoice including (in the UK) any details of VAT.

(g) Sometimes, the date by which payment is due, and other terms of sale.

The credit note

Suppose that Student Supplies sent out its invoice for 450 rulers, but the typist accidentally typed in a total of £162.10, instead of £62.10. The county council has been *overcharged* by £100. What is Student Supplies to do?

Alternatively, suppose that when the primary school received the rulers, it found that they had all been broken in the post and that it was going to send them back. Although the county council has received an invoice for £62.10, it has no intention of paying it, because the rulers were useless. Again, what is Student Supplies to do?

The answer is that the supplier (in this case, Student Supplies) sends out a *credit note*. A credit note is sometimes printed in red to distinguish it from an invoice. Otherwise, it will be made out in much the same way as an invoice, but with less detail and 'Credit Note Number' instead of 'Invoice Number'.

Other documents sometimes used in connection with sales and purchases are:

(a) Debit notes

(b) Goods received notes

A *debit note* might be issued instead of raising an invoice to adjust an invoice already issued. This is also commonly achieved by issuing a revised invoice after raising a credit or debit note purely for internal purposes (ie to keep the records straight). More commonly, a debit note is issued to a supplier as a means of formally requesting a credit note.

Goods received notes (GRNs) are filled in to record a receipt of goods, most commonly in a warehouse. They may be used in addition to suppliers' advice notes. Often the accounts department will require to see the relevant GRN before paying a supplier's invoice. Even where GRNs are not routinely used, the details of a consignment from a supplier which arrives without an advice note must always be recorded.

2   BOOKS OF ACCOUNT

2.1   The need for books of prime entry

We have seen that in the course of business source documents are created. The details on these source documents need to be summarised, as otherwise the business might forget to ask for some money, or forget to pay some, or even accidentally pay something twice. In other words, it needs to keep records of source documents – of transactions – so that it can keep tabs on what is going on.

Such records are made in *books of prime entry*. The main books of prime entry which we need to look at are:

(a) The sales day book

(b) The purchase day book

(c) The sales returns day book

(d) The purchases returns day book

(e) The journal

(f) The cash book

(g) The petty cash book

It is worth bearing in mind that, for convenience, this text describes books of prime entry as if they are actual books. Nowadays, books of prime entry are often not books at all, but rather files in the memory of a computer. However, the principles remain the same whether they are manual or computerised.

Activity 1

State which books of prime entry the following transactions would be entered into.

(a)   Your business pays A Brown (a supplier) £450.

(b)   You send D Smith (a customer) an invoice for £650.

(c)   Your accounts manager asks you for £12 urgently in order to buy some envelopes.

(d)   You receive an invoice from A Brown for £300.

(e)   You pay D Smith £500.

(f)   F Jones (a customer) returns goods to the value of £250.

(g)   You return goods to J Green to the value of £504.

(h)   F Jones pays you £500.

2.2   Sales and purchase day books

The sales day book

The *sales day book* is used to keep a list of all invoices sent out to customers each day. An extract from a sales day book might look like this.

SALES DAY BOOK

Date	Invoice	Customer	Sales ledger folio	Total amount invoiced
20X7				£
Jan 10	247	Jones & Co	SL14	105.00
	248	Smith Ltd	SL 8	86.40
	249	Alex & Co	SL 6	31.80
	250	Enor College	SL 9	1,264.60
				1,487.80

The column called 'sales ledger folio' is a reference to the sales ledger. It means, for example, that the sale to Jones & Co for £105 is also recorded on page 14 of the sales ledger.

Most businesses 'analyse' their sales. For example, suppose that the business sells boots and shoes, and that the sale to Smith was entirely boots, the sale to Alex was entirely shoes, and the other two sales were a mixture of both. Then the sales day book might look like this.

SALES DAY BOOK

Date	Invoice	Customer	Sales ledger folio	Total amount invoiced	Boot sales	Shoe sales
20X7				£	£	£
Jan 10	247	Jones & Co	SL14	105.00	60.00	45.00
	248	Smith Ltd	SL 8	86.40	86.40	
	249	Alex & Co	SL 6	31.80		31.80
	250	Enor College	SL 9	1,264.60	800.30	464.30
				1,487.80	946.70	541.10

This sort of analysis gives the managers of the business useful information which helps them to decide how best to run the business.

The purchase day book

A business also keeps a record in the purchase day book of all the invoices it receives. An extract from a purchase day book might look like this.

PURCHASE DAY BOOK

Date 20X7	Supplier	Purchase ledger folio	Total amount invoiced £	Purchases £	Electricity etc £
Mar 15	Cook & Co	PL 31	315.00	315.00	
	W Butler	PL 46	29.40	29.40	
	EEB	PL 42	116.80		116.80
	Show Fair Ltd	PL 12	100.00	100.00	
			561.20	444.40	116.80

You should note the following points.

(a) The 'purchase ledger folio' is a reference to the purchase ledger just as the sales ledger folio was to the sales ledger. Again, we will see the purpose of this later in the chapter.

(b) There is no 'invoice number' column, because the purchase day book records other people's invoices, which have all sorts of different numbers.

(c) Like the sales day book, the purchase day book analyses the invoices which have been sent in. In this example, three of the invoices related to goods which the business intends to re-sell (called simply 'purchases') and the fourth invoice was an electricity bill.

The sales returns day book

When customers return goods for some reason, the returns are recorded in the sales return day book. An extract from the sales returns day book might look like this.

SALES RETURNS DAY BOOK

Date 20X7	Customer and goods	Sales ledger folio	Amount £
30 April	Owen Plenty 3 pairs 'Texas' boots	SL 82	135.00

Not all sales returns day books analyse what goods were returned, but it makes sense to keep as complete a record as possible.

The purchase returns day book

There are no prizes for guessing that the purchase returns day book is kept to record goods which the business sends back to its suppliers. The business might expect a cash refund from the supplier. In the meantime, however, it might issue a debit note to the supplier, indicating the amount by which the business expects its total debt to the supplier to be reduced.

An extract from the purchase returns day book might look like this.

PURCHASE RETURNS DAY BOOK

Date 20X7	Supplier and goods	Purchase ledger folio	Amount £
29 April	Boxes Ltd 300 cardboard boxes	PL 123	46.60

2.3 Cash books

The cash book

The cash book is also a day book, which is used to keep a cumulative record of money received and money paid out by the business. The cash book deals with money paid into and out of the business *bank* account. This could be money received on the business premises in notes, coins and cheques. There are also receipts and payments made by bank transfer, standing order, direct debit and, in the case of bank interest and charges, directly by the bank.

Some cash, in notes and coins, is usually kept on the business premises in order to make occasional payments for odd items of expense. This cash is usually accounted for separately in a *petty cash book* (which we will look at shortly).

One part of the cash book is used to record receipts of cash, and another part is used to record payments. The best way to see how the cash book works is to follow through an example.

EXAMPLE: CASH BOOK

At the beginning of 1 September, Robin Plenty had £900 in the bank. During 1 September 20X6, Robin Plenty had the following receipts and payments.

- (a)   Cash sale – receipt of £80.
- (b)   Payment from credit customer Hay £400 less discount allowed £20.
- (c)   Payment from credit customer Been £720.
- (d)   Payment from credit customer Seed £150 less discount allowed £10.
- (e)   Cheque received for cash to provide a short-term loan from Len Dinger £1,800.
- (f)   Second cash sale – receipts of £150.
- (g)   Cash received for sale of machine £200.
- (h)   Payment to supplier Kew £120.
- (i)   Payment to supplier Hare £310.
- (j)   Payment of telephone bill £400.
- (k)   Payment of gas bill £280.
- (l)   £100 in cash withdrawn from bank for petty cash.
- (m)   Payment of £1,500 to Hess for new plant and machinery.

If you look through these transactions, you will see that seven of them are receipts and six of them are payments.

The receipts part of the cash book for 1 September would look like this.

[CASH BOOK (RECEIPTS)]

Date	Narrative	Folio	Total
20X6			£
1 Sept	Balance b/d★		900
	Cash sale		80
	Debtor: Hay		380
	Debtor: Been		720
	Debtor: Seed		140
	Loan: Len Dinger		1,800
	Cash sale		150
	Sale of fixed asset		200
			4,370
2 Sept	Balance b/d★		1,660

★ 'b/d' = brought down (ie brought forward)

You should note the following points.

(a)   There is space on the right hand side of the cash book so that the receipts can be analysed under various headings – for example, 'receipts from debtors', 'cash sales' and 'other receipts'.

(b)   The cash received in the day amounted to £3,470. Added to the £900 at the start of the day, this comes to £4,370. But this is not, of course, the amount to be carried forward to the next day, because first we have to subtract all the payments made during 1 September.

The payments part of the cash book for 1 September would look like this.

[CASH BOOK (PAYMENTS)]

Date	Narrative	Folio	Total
20X6			£
1 Sept	Creditor: Kew		120
	Creditor: Hare		310
	Telephone		400
	Gas bill		280
	Petty cash		100
	Machinery purchase		1,500
	Balance c/d		1,660
			4,370

As you can see, this is very similar to the receipts part of the cash book. The only points to note are as follows.

(a)   The analysis on the right would be under headings like 'payments to creditors', 'payments into petty cash', 'wages' and 'other payments'.

(b)   Payments during 1 September totalled £2,710. We know that the total of receipts was £4,370. That means that there is a balance of £4,370 – £2,710 = £1,660 to be 'carried down' to the start of the next day. As you can see this

NOTES

'balance carried down' is noted at the end of the payments column, so that the receipts and payments totals show the same figure of £4,370 at the end of 1 September. And if you look to the receipts part of this example, you can see that £1,660 has been brought down ready for the next day.

With analysis columns completed, the cash book given in the examples above might appear as follows.

[CASH BOOK (RECEIPTS)]

Date	Narrative	Folio	Total	Debtors	Cash sales	Other
20X6			£	£	£	£
1 Sept	Balance b/d		900			
	Cash sale		80		80	
	Debtor– Hay		380	380		
	Debtor – Been		720	720		
	Debtor – Seed		140	140		
	Loan – Len Dinger		1,800			1,800
	Cash sale		150		150	
	Sale of fixed asset		200			200
			4,370	1,240	230	2,000

[CASH BOOK (PAYMENTS)]

Date	Narrative	Folio	Total	Creditors	Petty cash	Wages	Other
20X6			£	£	£	£	£
1 Sept	Creditor – Kew		120	120			
	Creditor – Hare		310	310			
	Telephone		400				400
	Gas bill		280				280
	Petty cash		100		100		
	Machinery purchase		1,500				1,500
	Balance c/d		1,660				
			4,370	430	100	0	2,180

Bank statements

Weekly or monthly, a business will receive a bank statement. Bank statements should be used to check that the amount shown as a balance in the cash book agrees with the amount on the bank statement, and that no cash has 'gone missing'.

Petty cash book

Most businesses keep a small amount of cash on the premises to make occasional small payments in cash – to pay the milkman, buy a few postage stamps, pay the office cleaner, pay for some bus or taxi fares and so on. This is often called the cash float or petty cash account. The cash float can also be the resting place for occasional small receipts, such as cash paid by a visitor to make a phone call, or to take some photocopies.

There are usually more payments than receipts, and petty cash must be 'topped-up' from time to time with cash from the business bank account.

Definition

> Under what is called the *imprest system*, the amount of money in petty cash is kept at an agreed sum or 'float' (say £100).

Expense items are recorded on vouchers as they occur, so that at any time:

	£
Cash still held in petty cash	X
Plus voucher payments	X
Must equal the agreed sum or float	X

The total float is made up regularly (to £100, or whatever the agreed sum is) by means of a cash payment from the bank account into petty cash. The amount of the 'top-up' into petty cash will be the total of the voucher payments since the previous top-up. The imprest system is examined in more detail later in this chapter.

The format of a petty cash book is much the same as for the cash book, with analysis columns (chiefly for expenditure items, such as travel, postage or cleaning).

2.4 The nominal ledger

As we saw in Chapter 4, the nominal ledger is an accounting record which summarises the financial affairs of a business. It contains details of assets, liabilities and capital, income and expenditure and so profit and loss. It consists of a large number of different accounts, each account having its own purpose or 'name' and an identity or code. There may be various subdivisions, whether for convenience, ease of handling, confidentiality, security, or to meet the needs of computer software design.

The nominal ledger is sometimes called the 'general ledger'.

Examples of accounts in the nominal ledger include:

(a)   Plant and machinery at cost (fixed asset)

(b)   Motor vehicles at cost (fixed asset)

(c)   Plant and machinery, provision for depreciation (liability)

(d)   Motor vehicles, provision for depreciation (liability)

(e)   Proprietor's capital (liability)

(f)   Stocks – raw materials (current asset)

(g)   Stocks – finished goods (current asset)

(h)   Total debtors (current asset)

(i)   Total creditors (current liability)

(j)   Wages and salaries (expense item)

(k)   Rent and rates (expense item)

(l)   Advertising expenses (expense item)

(m)   Bank charges (expense item)

(n)   Motor expenses (expense item)

    (o)   Telephone expenses (expense item)

    (p)   Sales (income)

    (q)   Total cash or bank overdraft (current asset or liability)

The format of a ledger account

If a ledger account were to be kept in an actual book rather than as a computer record, its format might be as follows.

ADVERTISING EXPENSES

Date	Narrative	Folio	£	Date	Narrative	Folio	£
20X7 15 April	JFK Agency for quarter to 31 March	PL 348	2,500				

Only one entry in the account is shown here, because the example is introduced simply to illustrate the general format of a ledger account.

There are two sides to the account, and an account heading on top, and so it is convenient to think in terms of 'T' accounts:

    (a)   On top of the account is its name

    (b)   There is a left hand side, or debit side

    (c)   There is a right hand side, or credit side

NAME OF ACCOUNT

DEBIT SIDE	£	CREDIT SIDE	£

2.5 Double entry bookkeeping

As we have seen, since the total of liabilities plus capital is always equal to total assets, any transaction which changes the amount of total assets must also change the total liabilities plus capital, and vice versa. Alternatively, a transaction might use up assets of a certain value to obtain other assets of the same value. For example, if a business pays £50 in cash for some goods, its total assets will be unchanged, but as the amount of cash falls by £50, the value of goods in stocks rises by the same amount.

Ledger accounts, with their debit and credit side, are kept in a way which allows the two-sided nature of business transactions to be recorded. This system of accounting is known as the 'double entry' system of bookkeeping, so called because every transaction is recorded twice in the accounts. This is sometimes referred to as the concept of *duality*.

Double entry bookkeeping is not entirely standardised, and there are some variations found in practice in the way that business transactions are recorded. In this text, double entry bookkeeping will be explained according to a given set of well practised 'rules'. Variations in these rules that are made in accounting systems of some businesses might be mentioned from time to time. However, if you learn the system as described here, you should be able to adapt your knowledge to any (minor) differences which either might appear in an examination question, or you might come across in your practical experience.

The rules of double entry bookkeeping

The basic rule which must always be observed is that every financial transaction gives rise to two accounting entries, one a debit and the other a credit. The total value of debit entries in the nominal ledger is therefore always equal at any time to the total value of credit entries. Which account receives the credit entry and which receives the debit depends on the nature of the transaction.

(a)   An increase in an expense (for example a purchase of stationery) or an increase in an asset (for example a purchase of office furniture) is a *debit*.

(b)   An increase in income (for example a sale) or an increase in a liability (for example buying goods on credit) is a *credit*.

(c)   A decrease in an asset (for example making a cash payment) is a *credit*.

(d)   A decrease in a liability (for example paying a creditor) is a *debit*.

Students coming to the subject for the first time often have difficulty in knowing where to begin. A good starting point is the cash account, ie the nominal ledger account in which receipts and payments of cash are recorded. The rule to remember about the cash account is as follows.

(a)   A cash *payment* is a *credit* entry in the cash account. Here the asset is decreasing. This is because it is a decrease in the cash asset. Cash may be paid out, for example, to pay an expense (such as rates) or to purchase an asset (such as a machine). The matching debit entry is therefore made in the appropriate expense account or asset account.

(b)   A cash *receipt* is a *debit* entry in the cash account. Here the asset is increasing. Cash might be received, for example, by a retailer who makes a cash sale. The credit entry would then be made in the sales account.

EXAMPLE: DOUBLE ENTRY FOR CASH TRANSACTIONS

In the cash book of a business, the following transactions have been recorded.

(a)   A cash sale (ie a receipt) of £2

(b)   Payment of a rent bill totalling £150

(c)   Buying some goods for cash at £100

(d)   Buying some shelves for cash at £200

How would these four transactions be posted to the ledger accounts? For that matter, which ledger accounts should they be posted to? Don't forget that each transaction will be posted twice, in accordance with the rule of double entry.

ANSWER

(a)   The two sides of the transaction are:

(i)   Cash is received (debit entry in the cash account)

(ii)   Sales increase by £2 (credit entry in the sales account)

NOTES

CASH ACCOUNT

	£		£
Sales a/c	2		

SALES ACCOUNT

	£		£
		Cash a/c	2

(Note how the entry in the cash account is cross-referenced to the sales account and vice versa. This enables a person looking at one of the accounts to trace where the other half of the double entry can be found.)

(b) The two sides of the transaction are:

(i) Cash is paid (credit entry in the cash account)

(ii) Rent expense increases by £150 (debit entry in the rent account)

CASH ACCOUNT

	£		£
		Rent a/c	150

RENT ACCOUNT

	£		£
Cash a/c	150		

(c) The two sides of the transaction are:

(i) Cash is paid (credit entry in the cash account)

(ii) Purchases increase by £100 (debit entry in the purchases account)

CASH ACCOUNT

	£		£
		Purchase a/c	100

PURCHASE ACCOUNT

	£		£
Cash a/c	100		

(d) The two sides of the transaction are:

(i) Cash is paid (credit entry in the cash account)

(ii) Assets – in this case, shelves – increase by £200 (debit entry in shelves account)

CASH ACCOUNT

	£		£
		Shelves a/c	200

SHELVES (ASSET) ACCOUNT

	£		£
Cash a/c	200		

74

If all four of these transactions related to the same business, the cash account of that business would end up looking as follows.

CASH ACCOUNT

	£		£
Sales a/c	2	Rent a/c	150
		Purchases a/c	100
		Shelves a/c	200

Credit transactions

Not all transactions are settled immediately in cash. A business might purchase goods or fixed assets from its suppliers on credit terms, so that the suppliers would be creditors of the business until settlement was made in cash. Equally, the business might grant credit terms to its customers who would then be debtors of the business. Clearly no entries can be made in the cash book when a credit transaction occurs, because initially no cash has been received or paid. Where then can the details of the transactions be entered?

The solution to this problem is to use debtors and creditors accounts. When a business acquires goods or services on credit, the credit entry is made in an account designated 'creditors' instead of in the cash account. The debit entry is made in the appropriate expense or asset account, exactly as in the case of cash transactions. Similarly, when a sale is made to a credit customer the entries made are a debit to the total debtors account (instead of cash account) and a credit to sales account.

EXAMPLE: CREDIT TRANSACTIONS

Recorded in the sales day book and the purchase day book are the following transactions.

   (a)   The business sells goods on credit to a customer Mr A for £2,000.

   (b)   The business buys goods on credit from a supplier B Ltd for £100.

How and where are these transactions posted in the ledger accounts?

ANSWER

(a)

DEBTORS ACCOUNT

	£		£
Sales a/c	2,000		

SALES ACCOUNT

	£		£
		Debtors a/c	2,000

(b)

CREDITORS ACCOUNT

	£		£
		Purchases a/c	100

PURCHASES ACCOUNT

	£		£
Creditors a/c	100		

When cash is paid to creditors or by debtors

What happens when a credit transaction is eventually settled in cash? Suppose that, in the example above, the business paid £100 to B Ltd one month after the goods were acquired. The two sides of this new transaction are:

(a)   Cash is paid (credit entry in the cash account)

(b)   The amount owing to creditors is reduced (debit entry in the creditors account)

CASH ACCOUNT

	£		£
		Creditors a/c (B Ltd)	100

CREDITORS ACCOUNT

	£		£
Cash a/c	100		

If we now bring together the two parts of this example, the original purchase of goods on credit and the eventual settlement in cash, we find that the accounts appear as follows.

CREDITORS ACCOUNT

	£		£
Cash a/c	100	Purchases a/c	100

PURCHASES ACCOUNT

	£		£
Creditors a/c	100		

CASH ACCOUNT

	£		£
		Creditors a/c	100

The two entries in the creditors account cancel each other out, indicating that no money is owing to creditors any more. We are left with a credit entry of £100 in the cash account and a debit entry of £100 in the purchases account. These are exactly the entries which would have been made to record a *cash* purchase of £100 (compare example above). This is what we would expect: after the business has paid off its creditors it is in exactly the position of a business which has made cash purchases of £100, and the accounting records reflect this similarity.

Similar reasoning applies when a customer settles his debt. In the example above when Mr A pays his debt of £2,000 the two sides of the transaction are:

(a)   Cash is received (debit entry in the cash account)

(b)   The amount owed by debtors is reduced (credit entry in the debtors account)

CASH ACCOUNT

	£		£
Debtors a/c	2,000		

DEBTORS ACCOUNT

	£		£
		Cash a/c	2,000

The accounts recording this sale to, and payment by, Mr A now appear as follows.

CASH ACCOUNT

	£		£
Debtors a/c	2,000		

SALES ACCOUNT

	£		£
		Debtors a/c	2,000

DEBTORS ACCOUNT

	£		£
Sales a/c	2,000	Cash a/c	2,000

The two entries in the debtors account cancel each other out; while the entries in the cash account and sales account reflect the same position as if the sale had been made for cash (see above).

Activity 2

Identify the debit and credit entries in the following transactions.

(a) Bought a machine on credit from A, cost £8,000.
(b) Bought goods on credit from B, cost £500.
(c) Sold goods on credit to C, value £1,200.
(d) Paid D (a creditor) £300.
(e) Collected £180 from E, a debtor.
(f) Paid wages £4,000.
(g) Received rent bill of £700 from landlord G.
(h) Paid rent of £700 to landlord G.
(i) Paid insurance premium £90.

Activity 3

Record the ledger entries for the following transactions. Ron Knuckle set up a business selling keep fit equipment, trading under the name of Buy Your Biceps Shop. He put £7,000 of his own money into a business bank account (transaction A) and in his first period of trading, the following transactions occurred.

	Transaction	£
B	Paid rent of shop for the period	3,500
C	Purchased equipment (stocks) on credit	5,000
D	Raised loan from bank	1,000
E	Purchase of shop fittings (for cash)	2,000
F	Sales of equipment: cash	10,000
G	Sales of equipment: on credit	2,500
H	Payments to trade creditors	5,000
I	Payments from debtors	2,500
J	Interest on loan (paid)	100
K	Other expenses (all paid in cash)	1,900
L	Drawings	1,500

All stocks purchased during the period was sold, and so there were no closing stocks of equipment.

2.6 The journal

You should remember that one of the books of prime entry is the *journal*. The journal keeps a record of unusual movement between accounts. It is used to record any double entries made which do not arise from the other books of prime entry. For example, journal entries are made when errors are discovered and need to be corrected.

Whatever type of transaction is being recorded, the format of a journal entry is:

Date	Folio	Debit £	Credit £
Account to be debited		X	
Account to be credited			X
(Narrative to explain the transaction)			

(Remember: in due course, the ledger accounts will be written up to include the transactions listed in the journal.)

A narrative explanation must accompany each journal entry. It is required for audit and control, to indicate the purpose and authority of every transaction which is not first recorded in a book of prime entry.

EXAMPLES: JOURNAL ENTRIES

Some examples might help to illustrate the format. Note that an examination question might ask you to 'journalise' transactions which would not in practice be recorded in the journal at all. If you are faced with such a problem, you should simply record the debit and credit entries for every transaction you can recognise, giving some supporting narrative to each transaction.

The following is a summary of the transactions of Yve's hairdressing business of which Paul Brown is the sole proprietor.

1 January	Put in cash of £2,000 as capital Purchased brushes and combs for cash £50 Purchased hair driers from Z Ltd on credit £150
30 January	Paid three months' rent to 31 March £300 Collected and paid in takings £600
31 January	Gave Mrs X a perm, highlights etc on credit £80.

Show the transactions by means of journal entries.

ANSWER

JOURNAL

			£	£
1 January	DEBIT	Cash	2,000	
	CREDIT	Fred Brown – capital account		2,000
	Initial capital introduced			
1 January	DEBIT	Brushes and combs account	50	
	CREDIT	Cash		50
	The purchase for cash of brushes and combs as fixed assets			

JOURNAL cont.

			£	£
1 January	DEBIT	Hair dryer account	150	
	CREDIT	Sundry creditors account*		150
		The purchase on credit of hair driers as fixed assets		
30 January	DEBIT	Rent account	300	
	CREDIT	Cash		300
		The payment of rent to 31 March		
30 January	DEBIT	Cash	600	
	CREDIT	Sales (or takings account)		600
		Cash takings		
31 January	DEBIT	Debtors account	80	
	CREDIT	Sales account (or takings account)		80
		The provision of a hair-do on credit		

*Note. Creditors who have supplied fixed assets are included amongst sundry creditors, as distinct from creditors who have supplied raw materials or goods for resale, who are trade creditors. It is quite common to have separate 'total creditors' accounts, one for trade creditors and another for sundry other creditors.

The correction of errors

The journal is most commonly used to record corrections to errors that have been made in writing up the nominal ledger accounts. Errors corrected by the journal must be capable of correction by means of a double entry in the ledger accounts. When errors are made which break the rule of double entry, that debits and credits must be equal, the initial step in identifying and correcting the error is to open up a suspense account, to restore equality between total debits and total credits. Errors leading to the creation of a suspense account are corrected initially by making a record in the journal.

2.7 Day book analysis

Earlier in this chapter, we used the following example of four transactions entered into the sales day book.

SALES DAY BOOK

Date 20X7	Invoice	Customer	Sales ledger folios	Total amount invoiced £	Boot sales £	Shoe sales £
Jan 10	247	Jones & Co	SL 14	105.00	60.00	45.00
	248	Smith Ltd	SL 8	86.40	86.40	
	249	Alex & Co	SL 6	31.80		31.80
	250	Enor College	SL 9	1,264.60	800.30	464.30
				1,487.80	946.70	541.10

NOTES

In theory these transactions are posted to the ledger accounts as follows.

DEBIT   Total debtors account   £1,487.80
CREDIT   Sales account   £1,487.80

But a total sales account is not very informative, particularly if the business sells lots of different products. So, using our example, the business might open up a 'sale of shoes' account and a 'sale of boots' account, then at the end of the day, the ledger account postings are:

		£	£
DEBIT	Debtors account	1,487.80	
CREDIT	Sale of shoes account		541.10
	Sale of boots account		946.70

That is why the analysis of sales is kept. Exactly the same reasoning lies behind the analyses kept in other books of prime entry.

2.8 The imprest system

The petty cash book is used to operate the imprest system for petty cash. It is now time to see how the double entry works in the imprest system.

Suppose a business starts off a cash float on 1.3.20X7 with £250. This will be a payment from cash at bank to petty cash, ie:

DEBIT   Petty cash   £250
CREDIT   Cash at bank   £250

Suppose further that five payments were made out of petty cash during March 20X7. The petty cash book might look as follows.

Receipts	Date	Narrative	Total	Payments Postage	Travel
£			£	£	£
250.00	1.3.X7	Cash			
	2.3.X7	Stamps	12.00	12.00	
	8.3.X7	Stamps	10.00	10.00	
	19.3.X7	Travel	16.00		16.00
	23.3.X7	Travel	5.00		5.00
	28.3.X7	Stamps	11.50	11.50	
250.00			54.50	33.50	21.00

At the end of each month (or at any other suitable interval) the total credits in the petty cash book are posted to ledger accounts. For March 20X7, £33.50 would be debited to postage account, and £21.00 to travel account. The cash float would need to be topped up by a payment of £54.50 from the main cash book, ie:

DEBIT   Petty cash   £54.50
CREDIT   Cash   £54.50

So the rules of double entry have been satisfied, and the petty cash book for the month of March 20X7 will look like this.

Receipts	Date	Narrative	Payments Total	Postage	Travel
£			£	£	£
250.00	1.3.X7	Cash			
	2.3.X7	Stamps	12.00	12.00	
	8.3.X7	Stamps	10.00	10.00	
	19.3.X7	Travel	16.00		16.00
	23.3.X7	Travel	5.00		5.00
	28.3.X7	Stamps	11.50	11.50	
	31.3.X7	Balance c/d	195.50		
250.00			250.50	33.50	21.00
195.50	1.4.X7	Balance b/d			
54.50	1.4.X7	Cash			

As you can see, the cash float is back up to £250 on 1.4.X7, ready for more payments to be made.

2.9 The sales and purchase ledgers

Impersonal accounts and personal accounts

The accounts in the nominal ledger (ledger accounts) relate to types of income, expense, asset, liability – rent, rates, sales, debtors, creditors and so on, rather than to the person to whom the money is paid or from whom it is received. They are therefore called *impersonal* accounts. However, there is also a need for *personal* accounts, most commonly for debtors and creditors, and these are contained in the sales ledger and purchase ledger.

Personal accounts include details of transactions which have already been summarised in ledger accounts (for example sales invoices are recorded in sales and total debtors, payments to creditors in the cash and creditors accounts). The personal accounts do not therefore form part of the double entry system, as otherwise transactions would be recorded twice over (ie two debits and two credits for each transaction). They are *memorandum* accounts only.

The sales ledger

The sales day book provides a chronological record of invoices sent out by a business to credit customers. For many businesses, this might involve very large numbers of invoices per day or per week. The same customer might appear in several different places in the sales day book, for purchases he has made on credit at different times. So at any point in time, a customer may owe money on several unpaid invoices.

In addition to keeping a chronological record of invoices, a business should also keep a record of how much money each individual credit customer owes, and what this total debt consists of. The need for a *personal account* for each customer is a practical one.

(a) A customer might telephone, and ask how much he currently owes. Staff must be able to tell him.

(b) It is a common practice to send out statements to credit customers at the end of each month, showing how much they still owe, and itemising new invoices sent out and payments received during the month.

(c) The managers of the business will want to keep a check on the credit position of an individual customer, and to ensure that no customer is exceeding his credit limit by purchasing more goods.

(d) Most important is the need to match payments received against debts owed. If a customer makes a payment, the business must be able to set off the payment against the customer's debt and establish how much he still owes on balance.

Sales ledger accounts are written up as follows.

(a) When entries are made in the sales day book (invoices sent out), they are subsequently also made in the *debit side* of the relevant customer account in the sales ledger.

(b) Similarly, when entries are made in the cash book (payments received), or in the sales returns day book, they are also made in the credit side of the relevant customer account.

Each customer account is given a reference or code number, and it is that reference which is the 'sales ledger folio' in the *sales day book*. We say that amounts are *posted* from the sales day book to the sales ledger.

EXAMPLE: SALES LEDGER

Here is an example of how a sales ledger account is laid out.

ENOR COLLEGE

A/c no: SL 9

		£			£
10.1.X7	Balance b/f	250.00			
10.1.X7	Sales – SDB 48				
	(invoice no 250)	1,264.60	11.1.X7	Balance c/d	1,514.60
		1,514.60			1,514.60
11.1.97	Balance b/d	1,514.60			

The debit side of this personal account, then, shows amounts owed by Enor College. When Enor pays some of the money it owes it will be entered into the cash book (receipts) and subsequently 'posted' to the credit side of the personal account. For example, if the college paid £250 on 10.1.20X7, it would appear as follows.

ENOR COLLEGE

A/c no: SL 9

		£			£
10.1.X7	Balance b/f	250.00	10.1.X7	Cash	250.00
10.1.X7	Sales – SDB 48				
	(invoice no 250)	1,264.60	11.1.X7	Balance c/d	1,264.60
		1,514.60			1,514.60
11.1.97	Balance b/d	514.60			

The opening balance owed by Enor College on 11.1.X7 is now £1,264.60 instead of £1,514.60, because of the £250 receipt which came in on 10.1.X7.

The purchase ledger (bought ledger)

The purchase ledger, like the sales ledger, consists of a number of personal accounts. These are separate accounts for each individual supplier, and they enable a business to keep a continuous record of how much it owes each supplier at any time.

After entries are made in the purchase day book, cash book, or purchase returns day book – ie after entries are made in the books of prime entry – they are also made in the relevant supplier account in the purchase ledger. Again we say that the entries in the purchase day book are *posted* to the suppliers' personal accounts in the purchase ledger.

Here is an example of how a purchase ledger account is laid out.

COOK & CO

A/c no: SL 31

		£			£
16.3.X7	Balance c/d	515.00	15.3.X7	Balance b/f	200.00
			15.3.X7	Invoice received PDB 37	315.00
		515.00			515.00
			16.3.X7	Balance b/d	515.00

The credit side of this personal account, then, shows amounts owing to Cook & Co. If the business paid Cook & Co some money, it would be entered into the cash book (payments) and subsequently be posted to the debit side of the personal account. For example, if the business paid Cook & Co £100 on 15 March 20X7, it would appear as follows.

COOK & CO

A/c no: SL 31

		£			£
15.3.X7	Cash	100.00	15.3.X7	Balance b/f	200.00
16.3.X7	Balance c/d	415.00	15.3.X7	Invoice received PDB 37	315.00
		515.00			515.00
			16.3.X7	Balance b/d	415.00

The opening balance owed to Cook & Co on 16.3.X7 is now £415.00 instead of £515.00 because of the £100 payment made during 15.3.X7.

The roles of the sales day book and purchases day book are very similar, with one book dealing with invoices sent out and the other with invoices received. The sales ledger and purchases ledger also serve similar purposes, with one consisting of personal accounts for credit customers and the other consisting of personal accounts for creditors.

3 THE TRIAL BALANCE

Imagine that an examination question has given you a list of transactions, and has asked you to post them to the relevant ledger accounts. You do it as quickly as possible and find that you have a little time left over at the end of the examination. How do you check that you have posted all the debit and credit entries properly?

There is no foolproof method, but a technique which shows up the more obvious mistakes is to prepare a *trial balance*.

3.1 The first step

Before you draw up a trial balance, you must have a collection of ledger accounts. For the sake of convenience, we will use the accounts of Ron Knuckle, the sole trader introduced in Activity 3 above. A solution is given at the end of this chapter which goes into further detail, but the ledger entries which you should have shown are as follows.

CASH

	£		£
Capital – Ron Knuckle (A)	7,000	Rent	3,500
Bank loan	1,000	Shop fittings	2,000
Sales	10,000	Trade creditors	5,000
Debtors	2,500	Bank loan interest	100
		Incidental expenses	1,900
		Drawings	1,500
			14,000
		Balancing figure – the amount of cash left over after payments have been made	6,500
	20,500		20,500

CAPITAL (RON KNUCKLE)

	£		£
		Cash	7,000

BANK LOAN

	£		£
		Cash	1,000

PURCHASES

	£		£
Trade creditors	5,000		

TRADE CREDITORS

	£		£
Cash	5,000	Purchases	5,000

RENT

	£		£
Cash	3,500		

SHOP FITTINGS

	£		£
Cash	2,000		

SALES

	£		£
		Cash	10,000
		Debtors	2,500
			12,500

DEBTORS

	£		£
Sales	2,500	Cash	2,500

BANK LOAN INTEREST

	£		£
Cash	100		

OTHER EXPENSES

	£		£
Cash	1,900		

DRAWINGS ACCOUNT

	£		£
Cash	1,500		

The next step is to 'balance' each account.

3.2 Balancing ledger accounts

At the end of an accounting period, a balance is struck on each account in turn. This means that all the debits on the account are totalled and so are all the credits. If the total debits exceed the total credits there is said to be a debit balance on the account. If the credits exceed the debits then the account has a credit balance.

In our simple example, there is very little balancing to do.

(a)   Both the trade creditors' account and the debtors' account balance off to zero.

(b)   The cash account has a debit balance of £6,500.

(c)   The total on the sales account is £12,500, which is a credit balance.

Otherwise, the accounts have only one entry each, so there is no totalling to do to arrive at the balance on each account.

3.3 Collecting the balances

If the basic principle of double entry has been correctly applied throughout the period it will be found that the credit balances equal the debit balances in total. This can be illustrated by collecting together the balances on Ron Knuckle's accounts.

	Debit £	Credit £
Cash	6,500	
Capital		7,000
Bank loan		1,000
Purchases	5,000	
Trade creditors	0	0
Rent	3,500	
Shop fittings	2,000	
Sales		12,500
Debtors	0	0
Bank loan interest	100	
Other expenses	1,900	
Drawings	1,500	
	20,500	20,500

This list of balances is called the trial balance. It does not matter in what order the various accounts are listed, because the trial balance is not a document that a company *has* to prepare. It is just a method used to test the accuracy of the double entry bookkeeping methods.

3.4 What if the trial balance shows unequal debit and credit balances?

If the two columns of the trial balance are not equal, there must be an error in recording the transactions in the accounts. A trial balance, however, will not disclose the following types of errors.

(a) The complete omission of a transaction, because neither a debit nor a credit is made.

(b) The posting of a debit or credit to the correct side of the ledger, but to a wrong account.

(c) Compensating errors (for example an error of £100 is exactly cancelled by another £100 error elsewhere).

(d) Errors of principle, for example cash received from debtors being debited to the debtors account and credited to cash instead of the other way round.

EXAMPLE: TRIAL BALANCE

As at 30 March 20X6, your business has the following balances on its ledger accounts.

Accounts	Balance £
Bank loan	12,000
Cash	11,700
Capital	13,000
Rates	1,880
Trade creditors	11,200
Purchases	12,400
Sales	14,600

Accounts	Balance
	£
Sundry creditors	1,620
Debtors	12,000
Bank loan interest	1,400
Other expenses	11,020
Vehicles	2,020

During the year the business made the following transactions.

(a) Bought materials for £1,000, half for cash and half on credit.

(b) Made £1,040 sales, £800 of which was for credit.

(c) Paid wages to shop assistants of £260 in cash.

You are required to draw up a trial balance showing the balances as at the end of 31 March 20X6.

ANSWER

First it is necessary to put the original balances into a trial balance – ie decide which are debit and which are credit balances.

Account	Debit	Credit
	£	£
Bank loan		12,000
Cash	11,700	
Capital		13,000
Rates	1,880	
Trade creditors		11,200
Purchases	12,400	
Sales		14,600
Sundry creditors		1,620
Debtors	12,000	
Bank loan interest	1,400	
Other expenses	11,020	
Vehicles	2,020	
	52,420	52,420

Now we must take account of the effects of the three transactions which took place on 31 March 20X6.

			£	£
(a)	DEBIT	Purchases	1,000	
	CREDIT	Cash		500
		Trade creditors		500
(b)	DEBIT	Cash	240	
		Debtors	800	
	CREDIT	Sales		1,040
(c)	DEBIT	Other expenses	260	
	CREDIT	Cash		260

When these figures are included in the trial balance, it becomes:

Account	Debit £	Credit £
Bank loan		12,000
Cash	11,180	
Capital		13,000
Rates	1,880	
Trade creditors		11,700
Purchases	13,400	
Sales		15,640
Sundry creditors		1,620
Debtors	12,800	
Bank loan interest	1,400	
Other expenses	11,280	
Vehicles	2,020	
	53,960	53,960

4 FINAL ACCOUNTS

4.1 The trading, profit and loss account

The first step in the process of preparing the financial statements is to open up another ledger account, called the trading, profit and loss account.

Definition

In a trading, profit and loss account a business summarises its results for the period by gathering together all the ledger account balances relating to income and expenses.

This account is still part of the double entry system, so the basic rule of double entry still applies: every debit must have an equal and opposite credit entry.

This trading, profit and loss account we have opened up is not the financial statement we are aiming for, even though it has the same name. The difference between the two is not very great, because they contain the same information. However, the financial statement lays it out differently and may be much less detailed.

So what do we do with this new ledger account? The first step is to look through the ledger accounts and identify which ones relate to income and expenses. In the case of Ron Knuckle, the income and expense accounts consist of purchases, rent, sales, bank loan interest, and other expenses.

The balances on these accounts are transferred to the new trading, profit and loss account. For example, the balance on the purchases account is £5,000 DR. To balance this to zero, we write in £5,000 CR. But to comply with the rule of double entry, there has to be a debit entry somewhere, so we write £5,000 DR in the trading, profit and loss account. Now the balance on the purchases account has been moved to the trading, profit and loss account.

If we do the same thing with all the income and expense accounts of Ron Knuckle, the result is:

PURCHASES

	£		£
Trade creditors	5,000	Trading, P & L a/c	5,000

RENT

	£		£
Cash	3,500	Trading, P & L a/c	3,500

SALES

	£		£
Trading, P & L a/c	12,500	Cash	10,000
		Debtors	2,500
	12,500		12,500

BANK LOAN INTEREST

	£		£
Cash	100	Trading, P & L a/c	100

OTHER EXPENSES

	£		£
Cash	1,900	Trading, P & L a/c	1,900

TRADING, PROFIT AND LOSS ACCOUNT

	£		£
Purchases	5,000	Sales	12,500
Rent	3,500		
Bank loan interest	100		
Other expenses	1,900		

(Note that the trading, profit and loss account has not yet been balanced off but we will return to that later.)

If you look at the items we have gathered together in the trading, profit and loss account, they should strike a chord in your memory. They are the same items that we need to draw up the trading, profit and loss account in the form of a financial statement. With a little rearrangement they could be presented as follows.

RON KNUCKLE: TRADING, PROFIT AND LOSS ACCOUNT

	£	£
Sales		12,500
Cost of sales (= purchases in this case)		(5,000)
Gross profit		7,500
Expenses		
Rent	3,500	
Bank loan interest	100	
Other expenses	1,900	
		(5,500)
Net profit		2,000

4.2 The balance sheet

Look back at the ledger accounts of Ron Knuckle. Now that we have dealt with those relating to income and expenses, which ones are left? The answer is that we still have to find out what to do with cash, capital, bank loan, trade creditors, shop fittings, debtors and the drawings account.

Are these the only ledger accounts left? No: don't forget there is still the last one we opened up, called the trading, profit and loss account. The balance on this account represents the profit earned by the business, and if you go through the arithmetic, you will find that it has a credit balance – a profit – of £2,000. (Not surprisingly, this is the figure that is shown in the trading, profit and loss account financial statement.)

These remaining accounts must also be balanced and ruled off, but since they represent assets and liabilities of the business (not income and expenses) their balances are not transferred to the trading profit and loss account. Instead they are *carried down* in the books of the business. This means that they become opening balances for the next accounting period and indicate the value of the assets and liabilities at the end of one period and the beginning of the next.

The conventional method of ruling off a ledger account at the end of an accounting period is illustrated by the bank loan account in Ron Knuckle's books.

BANK LOAN ACCOUNT

	£		£
Balance carried down (c/d)	1,000	Cash	1,000
		Balance brought down (b/d)	1,000

Ron Knuckle therefore begins the new accounting period with a credit balance of £1,000 on this account. A credit balance brought down denotes a liability. An asset would be represented by a debit balance brought down.

One further point is worth noting before we move on to complete this example. You will remember that a proprietor's capital comprises any cash introduced by him, plus any profits made by the business, less any drawings made by him. At the stage we have now reached these three elements are contained in different ledger accounts: cash introduced of £7,000 appears in the capital account; drawings of £1,500 appear in the drawings account; and the profit made by the business is represented by the £2,000 credit balance on the trading profit and loss account. It is convenient to gather together all these amounts into one capital account, in the same way as we earlier gathered together income and expense accounts into one trading and profit and loss account.

BPP
PUBLISHING

If we go ahead and gather the three amounts together, the results are as follows.

DRAWINGS

	£		£
Cash	1,500	Capital a/c	1,500

TRADING, PROFIT AND LOSS ACCOUNT

	£		£
Purchases	5,000	Sales	12,500
Rent	3,500		
Bank loan interest	100		
Other expenses	1,900		
Capital a/c	2,000		
	12,500		12,500

CAPITAL PURCHASES

	£		£
Drawings	1,500	Cash	7,000
Balance c/d	7,500	Trading, P & L a/c	2,000
	9,000		9,000
		Balance b/d	7,500

A re-arrangement of these balances will complete Ron Knuckle's simple balance sheet.

RON KNUCKLE
BALANCE SHEET AT END OF FIRST TRADING PERIOD

	£
Fixed assets	
Shop fittings	2,000
Current assets	
Cash	6,500
Total assets	8,500
Liabilities	
Bank loan	(1,000)
Net assets	7,500
Proprietor's capital	7,500

When a balance sheet is drawn up for an accounting period which is not the first one, then it ought to show the capital at the start of the accounting period and the capital at the end of the accounting period. This will be illustrated in the next example.

In an examination question, you might not be given the ledger accounts – you might have to draw them up in the first place.

Activity 4

A business is established with capital of £2,000, and this amount is paid into a business bank account by the proprietor. During the first year's trading, the following transactions occurred.

	£
Purchases of goods for resale, on credit	4,300
Payments to trade creditors	3,600
Sales, all on credit	5,800
Payments to debtors	3,200
Fixed assets purchased for cash	1,500
Other expenses, all paid in cash	900

The bank has provided an overdraft facility of up to £3,000.

Prepare the ledger accounts, a trading, profit and loss account for the year and a balance sheet as at the end of the year.

4.3 Adjusting the trial balance

When preparing financial statements from a trial balance, in simple cases, it is sufficient to take the balances on each ledger account and enter them as appropriate into a trading, profit and loss account or a balance sheet. In practice, however, things are rarely so straightforward. For a number of reasons, the ledger account balances are unlikely to reflect all the information needed to prepare financial statements.

In this section we will describe how to tackle situations where a trial balance needs to be adjusted in the light of other information, before the final accounts can be prepared. The adjustments we will look at fall under the following headings.

    (a)   The correction of errors

    (b)   Accruals and prepayments

    (c)   Depreciation

    (d)   The disposal of fixed assets

    (e)   Bad and doubtful debts

    (f)   Opening and closing stock

The correction of errors

There are many different errors which may be made in writing up the nominal ledger accounts of a business. Such errors are often discovered during the process of preparing accounts from a trial balance.

Suppose a company makes a payment of £1,000 in respect of staff wages. The amount is correctly recorded as a credit entry in the cash book, but the debit entry is made by mistake in the purchases account instead of in the wages account. The adjustment would consist of a £1,000 credit entry to purchases (to remove the debit entry wrongly entered in the ledger account) and a £1,000 debit to wages (to insert the debit where it properly belongs). The adjustment will be noted in the journal and then posted to the ledger accounts.

For examination purposes, however, all that is necessary is to mark on your question paper ' – £1,000' against purchases and '+ £1,000' against wages, showing the same adjustment in your answer like this:

	£
Wages (£X – £1,000)	X

Accruals and prepayments

Accruals and prepayments can be described as follows.

(a)   An accrual is a liability at the year end (a creditor in the balance sheet). It is an expense which has not yet been entered in an expense account because no invoice has yet been received at the year end.

(b)   A prepayment is similar to a debtor and is a current asset in the balance sheet. It is an expense which has already been entered in an expense account (because an invoice has been received) but which is not a part of expenditure relating to the current year.

In adjusting the trial balance, an accrual is dealt with as follows. Ensure that you show the total for accruals under the 'current liabilities' heading in your balance sheet. This ensures that you have made the *credit entries*. Then make a note on your question paper to add the accrued expenses as at the end of the year to the relevant balances in the trial balance, to make the debit entries.

If there are any accruals brought forward, then these should be *deducted* from the relevant expenses, so that they are not charged against profit in two consecutive years. (This is a credit entry; the debit entry eliminates the creditor balance from the balance sheet.) So if you were told that accrued sundry expenses at the start of the year were £1,000 and at the end of the year £2,000, you would amend the trial balance figure (say £10,000) in your profit and loss account like this:

	£
Sundry expenses (£10,000 – £1,000 + £2,000)	11,000

For a prepayment, the procedure is simply reversed: ensure that the total prepayments are shown in the balance sheet as an asset; while a credit adjustment must be made to the relevant expense account, so reducing the amount to be charged to the profit and loss account. Again, if there were prepayments brought forward *add* them to the relevant expenses so that they are charged against profit this year.

Depreciation

In the nominal ledger a separate account will be maintained for each category of fixed asset and for the accumulated depreciation on each category. The balances on all these accounts will be listed in the trial balance at the end of each accounting period. In examination questions, the balance on the accumulated depreciation account is usually the balance brought forward at the *beginning* of the accounting period, plus additions in the year. It will be necessary to calculate the depreciation charge for the current period in order to arrive at the year-end balance. Do this as a working on a separate sheet of paper.

(a)   In the profit and loss account the depreciation charge for the year for each class of fixed asset is shown. Cross-reference the caption to your working.

(b)   Don't forget to increase the 'accumulated depreciation' balance. Again, clearly cross-reference the balance sheet figures to your workings.

The disposal of fixed assets

Fixed assets are not purchased by a business with the intention of reselling them in the normal course of trade. However, they will probably be sold off at some stage during their life and there will be a profit or loss on disposal. These gains or losses are reported in the profit and loss account of the business (and not as a trading profit in the trading account). They are commonly referred to as 'profit on disposal of fixed assets' or 'loss on disposal'. The profit or loss on the disposal of a fixed asset is the difference between:

(a)   The net book value of the asset at the time of its sale

(b)   Its net sale price, which is the price minus any costs of making the sale

A profit is made when the sale price exceeds the net book value, and a loss is made when the sale price is less than the net book value.

EXAMPLE: DISPOSAL OF A FIXED ASSET

A business purchased a fixed asset on 1 January 20X4 for £25,000. It had an estimated life of six years and an estimated residual value of £7,000. The asset was eventually sold after three years on 31 December 20X6 to another trader who paid £17,500 for it.

What was the profit or loss on disposal, assuming that the business uses the straight line method for depreciation?

ANSWER

$$\text{Annual depreciation} = \frac{£25,000 - 7,000}{6 \text{ years}} = £3,000 \text{ per annum}$$

	£
Cost of asset	25,000
Less accumulated depreciation (three years)	9,000
Net book value at date of disposal	16,000
Sale price	17,500
Profit on disposal	1,500

This profit will be shown in the profit and loss account of the business where it will be an item of other income added to the gross profit brought down from the trading account. If the asset had been sold for, say, £14,000, there would have been a loss on disposal of £2,000. This would be shown in the profit and loss account as an expense item, alongside depreciation.

There are three accounts involved in recording the disposal of a fixed asset.

(a)   The account for *fixed assets at cost* must be reduced by the cost of the asset disposed of. This means that the original debit balance on the account must be altered by means of a credit adjustment.

(b)   The account for *accumulated depreciation* must be reduced by the amount of depreciation accumulated on the asset to the date of its disposal. This means that the original credit balance on the account must be altered by means of a debit adjustment.

(c)   The *fixed assets disposal account* must be used to complete the double entry of (a) and (b) above. In other words, it must contain a debit adjustment in respect of the asset's cost, and a credit adjustment in respect of the asset's accumulated depreciation. The cash received on disposal should already have been credited to this account before the trial balance was extracted. The net effect of all these entries is the profit or loss on disposal which must be taken to the profit and loss account.

Bad and doubtful debts

When a business decides that a particular debt is unlikely ever to be repaid, the amount of the debt should be 'written off' as an expense in the profit and loss account. For example, if Alfred's Mini-Cab Service sends an invoice for £300 to a customer who subsequently does a 'moonlight flit' from his office premises, never to be seen or heard of again, the debt of £300 must be written off. It might seem sensible to record the business transaction as:

Sales £(300 – 300) = £0

However, bad debts written off are actually accounted for as follows.

(a)   Sales are shown at their invoice value in the trading account. The sale has been made, and gross profit should be earned. The subsequent failure to collect the debt is a separate matter, which is reported in the P & L account.

(b)   Bad debts written off are shown as an expense in the profit and loss account.

In our example of Alfred's Mini-Cab Service:

	£
Sales (invoice in the trading account)	300
Bad debts written off (expenses in the P & L account)	300
Net value of sales	0

Obviously, when a debt is written off, the value of the debtor as a current asset falls to zero. If the debt is expected to be uncollectable, its 'net realisable value' is nil, and so it has a zero balance sheet value. If Alfred's Mini-Cab Service had total debtors before writing off bad debts of £55,200, then the adjustments needed in preparing the final accounts are as follows.

(a)   Against the caption 'debtors' in the question paper the bad debt write '– £300'. On the balance sheet write:

Debtors £(55,200 – 300)   £54,900

(b)   The expense of the bad debt is shown in the profit and loss account.

When bad debts are written off, specific debts owed to the business are identified as unlikely ever to be collected. Suppose that a business commences operations on 1 July 20X6, and in the 12 months to 30 June 20X7 makes sales of £300,000 (all on credit) and writes off bad debts amounting to £6,000. Cash received from customers during the year is £244,000, so that at 30 June 20X7 the business has outstanding debtors of £50,000. Now, some of these outstanding debts might turn out to be bad. The business does not know on 30 June 20X7 which specific debts in the total £50,000 owed will be bad, but it might guess (from experience perhaps) that 5% of debts will eventually be found to be bad.

When a business expects bad debts amongst its current debtors, but does not yet know which specific debts will be bad, it can make a *provision for doubtful debts*.

(a)   When a provision is first made, the amount of this initial provision is charged as an expense in the profit and loss account of the business, for the period in which the provision is created.

(b)   When a provision already exists, but is subsequently increased in size, the amount of the *increase* in provision is charged as an expense in the profit and loss account, for the period in which the increased provision is made.

(c)   When a provision already exists, but is subsequently reduced in size, the amount of the *decrease* in provision is recorded as an item of 'income' in the profit and loss account, for the period in which the reduction in provision is made.

EXAMPLE: PROVIDING FOR DOUBTFUL DEBTS

As at 30 June 20X5, X Ltd has total debtors of £156,000 after writing off bad debts. The accountant thinks a doubtful debt provision of 2% should be made. No such provision has been made before. As at 30 June 20X6, another 2% provision is thought to be sufficient, but debtors are only £142,000. As at 30 June 20X7, a provision of 2½% is required on debtors of £168,000. For all three years, show the ledger account for the doubtful debt provision, the entry to be made in the profit and loss account and the balance to be shown against the caption 'Trade debtors' in the balance sheet.

ANSWER

PROVISION FOR DOUBTFUL DEBTS

		£			£
30.6.X5	Balance c/d	3,120	30.6.X5	Bad and doubtful debts (£156,000 × 2%)	3,120
30.6.X6	Balance c/d (£142,000 × 2%)	2,840	1.7.X5	Balance b/d	3,120
	Bad and doubtful debts expense (£3,120 – £2,840)	280			
		3,120			3,120
30.6.X7	Balance c/d (£168,000 × 2.5%)	4,200	1.7.X6	Balance b/d	2,840
			30.6.X7	Bad and doubtful debts expense (£4,200 – £2,840)	1,360
		4,200			4,200

PROFIT AND LOSS ACCOUNTS FOR THE YEARS
ENDED 30 JUNE 20X5, 20X6 AND 20X7 (extracts)

	20X7 £	20X6 £	20X5 £
Increase/(decrease) in provision for doubtful debts	1,360	(280)	3,120

BALANCE SHEETS AS AT
30 JUNE 20X5, 20X6 AND 20X7 (extracts)

	20X7 £	20X6 £	20X5 £
Trade debtors	163,800	139,160	152,880

Note that businesses do not show in their final accounts how much the provision is as this is sensitive information.

Opening and closing stocks

At the end of an accounting period a business will need to place a value on the goods it holds in stock. There are many theoretical and practical difficulties involved in this valuation process, which are beyond the scope of this text, but here our concern is only with the accounting entries necessary once the valuation has been arrived at.

In the final accounts of a business, stock appears in three places.

(a) Opening stock is one element in the cost of sales shown in the trading account.

(b) Closing stock also appears in the trading account, as a reduction in the cost of sales.

(c) The same figure of closing stock appears as an asset in the balance sheet.

To illustrate this, consider a business with opening stock of £26,000 and closing stock of £29,500. The journal entries at the end of the year are as follows.

DEBIT	Trading account	£26,000	
CREDIT	Stock		£26,000
DEBIT	Stock	£29,500	
CREDIT	Trading account		£29,500

Being elimination of opening stock balance and adjustment to record closing stock balance.

All you need do to produce the right result is to write out the trading account as follows.

	£	£
Sales		X
Opening stock	X	
Purchases	X	
	X	
Less closing stock	(X)	
Cost of goods sold		X
Gross profit		X

Also, ensure that you use the closing stock figure in the balance sheet and not the opening stock figure given in the trial balance.

Chapter roundup

You should now fully understand the following.

- Business transactions are recorded on source documents. These include: sales orders; purchase orders; invoices; credit notes.

- These transactions are recorded in books of prime entry of which there are seven.

  (i) The sales day book

  (ii) The sales returns day book

  (iii) The purchase day book

  (iv) The purchase returns day book

  (v) The cash book

  (vi) The petty cash book

  (vii) The journal

- Most businesses keep petty cash on the premises which is topped up from the main bank account. Under the imprest system the petty cash is kept at an agreed sum.

- Double entry bookkeeping is based on the same idea as the accounting equation. Every accounting transaction alters the make-up of a business's assets and liabilities.

- In a system of double entry bookkeeping every accounting event must be entered in ledger accounts both as a debit and as an equal but opposite credit. The principal accounts are contained in a ledger called the nominal ledger.

- Some accounts in the nominal ledger represent the total of very many smaller balances, for example the debtors account.

- To keep track of individual customer and supplier balances, it is common to maintain subsidiary ledgers (called the sales ledger and the purchase ledger respectively).

- The rules of double entry bookkeeping are best learnt by considering the cash book. In the cash book a *credit* entry indicates a payment made by the business; the matching debit entry is then made in an account denoting an expense paid, an asset purchased or a liability settled. A *debit* entry in the cash book indicates cash received by the business; the matching credit entry is then made in an account denoting revenue received, a liability created or an asset sold.

- At suitable intervals, the entries in each ledger accounts are totalled and a balance is struck. Balances are usually collected in a trial balance which is then used as a basis for preparing a profit and loss account and a balance sheet.

- A profit and loss ledger account is opened up to gather all items relating to income and expenses. When rearranged, the items make up the profit and loss account financial statement.

- The balances on all remaining ledger accounts (including the profit and loss account) can be listed and rearranged to form the balance sheet.

Quick quiz

1   Name four pieces of information normally shown on an invoice.

                                                                    (see para 1.1)

2   What information is summarised in the sales day book?   (2.2)

3   What is the purchase returns day book used for?   (2.2)

4   What is the difference between the cash book and the petty cash book?

                                                                              (2.3)

5   Describe how the imprest system works.   (2.3)

6   What is the double entry to record a cash sale of £50?   (2.5)

7   What is the double entry to record a credit sale?   (2.5)

8   Name one reason for making a journal entry.   (2.6)

9   What is the difference between the creditors account in the nominal
     ledger and the purchase ledger?   (2.9)

10   What is the purpose of a trial balance?   (3.1)

11   Give four circumstances in which a trial balance might balance although
     some of the balances are wrong.   (3.4)

12   What is the difference between balancing off an expense account and
     balancing off a liability account?   (4.1)

13   How is an accrued expense accounted for?   (4.3)

14   What are the three accounts involved in recording a disposal of fixed
     assets?   (4.3)

15   An increase in a provision for doubtful debts is recorded as an item of
     income in the profit and loss account. True or false?   (4.3)

Answers to activities

1   (a)   Cash book

     (b)   Sales day book

     (c)   Petty cash book

     (d)   Purchases day book

     (e)   Cash book

     (f)   Sales returns day book

     (g)   Purchase returns day book

     (h)   Cash book

2   £   £

     (a)   DEBIT   Machine account (fixed asset)   8,000
           CREDIT   Creditors (A)   8,000

     (b)   DEBIT   Purchases account   500
           CREDIT   Creditors (B)   500

     (c)   DEBIT   Debtors (C)   1,200
           CREDIT   Sales   1,200

     (d)   DEBIT   Creditors (D)   300
           CREDIT   Cash   300

     (e)   DEBIT   Cash   180
           CREDIT   Debtors (E)   180

			£	£
(f)	DEBIT	Wages account	4,000	
	CREDIT	Cash		4,000
(g)	DEBIT	Rent account	700	
	CREDIT	Creditors (G)		700
(h)	DEBIT	Creditors (G)	700	
	CREDIT	Cash		700
(i)	DEBIT	Insurance costs	90	
	CREDIT	Cash		90

3   Clearly, there should be an account for cash, debtors, creditors, purchases, a shop fittings account, sales, a loan account and a proprietor's capital account. It is also useful to keep a separate *drawings* account until the end of each accounting period. Other accounts should be set up as they seem appropriate and in this activity, accounts for rent, bank interest and other expenses would seem appropriate.

It has been suggested to you that the cash account is a good place to start, if possible. You should notice that cash transactions include the initial input of capital by Ron Knuckle, subsequent drawings, the payment of rent, the loan from the bank, the interest, some cash sales and cash purchases, and payments to creditors and by debtors. (The transactions are identified below by their reference, to help you to find them.)

CASH

	£		£
Capital –			
Ron Knuckle (A)	7,000	Rent (B)	3,500
Bank loan (D)	1,000	Shop fittings (E)	2,000
Sales (F)	10,000	Trade creditors (H)	5,000
Debtors (I)	2,500	Bank loan interest (J)	100
		Incidental expenses (K)	1,900
		Drawings (L)	1,500
			14,000
		Balancing figure – the amount of cash left over after payments have been made	6,500
	20,500		20,500

CAPITAL (RON KNUCKLE)

	£		£
		Cash (A)	7,000

BANK LOAN

	£		£
		Cash (D)	1,000

PURCHASES

	£		£
Trade creditors (C)	5,000		

TRADE CREDITORS

	£		£
Cash (H)	5,000	Purchases (C)	5,000

RENT

	£		£
Cash (B)	3,500		

SHOP FITTINGS

	£		£
Cash (E)	2,000		

SALES

	£		£
		Cash (F)	10,000
		Debtors (G)	2,500
			12,500

DEBTORS

	£		£
Sales (G)	2,500	Cash (I)	2,500

BANK LOAN INTEREST

	£		£
Cash (J)	100		

OTHER EXPENSES

	£		£
Cash (K)	1,900		

DRAWINGS ACCOUNT

	£		£
Cash (L)	1,500		

If you want to make sure that this solution is complete, you should go through the transactions A to L and tick off each of them twice in the ledger accounts, once as a debit and once as a credit. When you have finished, all transactions in the 'T' account should be ticked, with only totals left over.

4   The first thing to do is to open ledger accounts so that the transactions can be entered up. The relevant accounts which we need for this example are: cash; capital; trade creditors; purchases; fixed assets; sales and debtors.

The next step is to work out the double entry bookkeeping for each transaction. Normally you would write them straight into the accounts, but to make this example easier to follow, they are first listed below.

(a)	Establishing business (£2,000)	DR	Cash	CR	Capital
(b)	Purchases (£4,300)	DR	Purchases	CR	Creditors
(c)	Payments to creditors (£3,600)	DR	Creditors	CR	Cash
(d)	Sales (£5,800)	DR	Debtors	CR	Sales
(e)	Payments by debtors (£3,200)	DR	Cash	CR	Debtors
(f)	Fixed assets (£1,500)	DR	Fixed assets	CR	Cash
(g)	Other (cash) expenses (£900)	DR	Other expenses	CR	Cash

So far, the ledger accounts will look like this.

CASH

	£		£
Capital	2,000	Creditors	3,600
Debtors	3,200	Fixed assets	1,500
		Other expenses	900

CAPITAL

	£		£
		Cash	2,000

CREDITORS

	£		£
Cash	3,600	Purchases	4,300

PURCHASES

	£		£
Creditors	4,300		

FIXED ASSETS

	£		£
Cash	1,500		

SALES

	£		£
		Debtors	5,800

DEBTORS

	£		£
Sales	5,800	Cash	3,200

OTHER EXPENSES

	£		£
Cash	900		

The next thing to do is to balance all these accounts. It is at this stage that you could, if you wanted to, draw up a trial balance to make sure the double entries are accurate. There is not very much point in this simple example, but if you did draw up a trial balance, it would look like this.

	Debit	Credit
	£	£
Cash		800
Capital		2,000
Creditors		700
Purchases	4,300	
Fixed assets	1,500	
Sales		5,800
Debtors	2,600	
Other expenses	900	
	9,300	9,300

After balancing the accounts, the trading, profit and loss account should be opened. Into it should be transferred all the balances relating to income and expenses (ie purchases, other expenses, and sales). At this point, the ledger accounts will be:

CASH

	£		£
Capital	2,000	Trade creditors	3, 600
Debtors	3,200	Fixed assets	1,500
Balance c/d	800	Other expenses	900
	6,000		6,000
		Balance b/d	800*

* A credit balance b/d means that this cash item is a liability, not an asset. This indicates a bank overdraft of £800, with cash income of £5,200 falling short of payments of £6,000 by this amount.

CAPITAL

	£		£
Balance c/d	2,600	Cash	2,000
		P & L a/c	600
	2,600		2,600

NOTES

TRADE CREDITORS

	£		£
Cash	3,600	Stores (purchases)	4,300
Balance c/d	700		
	4,300		4,300
		Balance b/d	700

PURCHASES ACCOUNT

	£		£
Trade creditors	4,300	Trading a/c	4,300

FIXED ASSETS

	£		£
Cash	1,500	Balance c/d	1,500
Balance b/d	1,500		

SALES

	£		£
Trading a/c	5,800		5,800

DEBTORS

	£		£
Sales	5,800	Cash	3,200
		Balance c/d	2,600
	5,800		5,800
Balance b/d	2,600		

OTHER EXPENSES

	£		£
Cash	900	P & L a/c	900

TRADING, PROFIT AND LOSS ACCOUNT

	£		£
Purchases account	4,300	Sales	5,800
Gross profit c/d	1,500		
	5,800		5,800
Other expenses	900	Gross profit b/d	1,500
Net profit (transferred to			
capital account)	600		
	1,500		1,500

So the trading, profit and loss account financial statement will be as follows.

TRADING, PROFIT AND LOSS ACCOUNT
FOR THE ACCOUNTING PERIOD

	£
Sales	5,800
Cost of sales (purchases)	(4,300)
Gross profit	1,500
Expenses	900
Net profit	600

Listing and then rearranging the balances on the ledger accounts gives the balance sheet as follows.

BALANCE SHEET AS AT THE END OF THE PERIOD

	£	£
Fixed assets		1,500
Current assets		
Debtors	2,600	
Current liabilities		
Bank overdraft	800	
Trade creditors	700	
	1,500	
Net current assets		1,100
		2,600
Capital		
At start of period		2,000
Net profit for period		600
At end of period		2,600

Further question practice

Now try the following practice questions at the end of this text

Multiple choice questions: **23 to 36**

Exam style question. **5**

Chapter 6 :
THE INCOME STATEMENT

Introduction

This chapter covers the second important component of any set of accounts: the income statement, or the profit and loss account in some circumstances.

The chapter goes on to look at the important distinctions between which items appear in the balance sheet and which items appear in the income statement.

Your objectives

After completing this chapter you should:

(a)   Understand what an income statement is and how it is compiled

(b)   Be aware of how a profit and loss account is usually presented

(c)   Understand the meaning of the main items appearing in a profit and loss account

(d)   Understand the difference between capital and revenue items

1 INCOME

Any organisation will generate income (or revenue) from one or more sources. A business will sell its goods or services to customers in exchange for cash. A charity will raise money through donations, charitable events and perhaps trading activities. A police force will be granted funds from local or central government, and may also charge for providing its services (for example at sporting events).

The income generated will be used to finance the activities of the organisation: purchasing raw materials for use in manufacturing goods, purchasing ready-made goods for onward sale, purchasing equipment, paying expenses such as staff salaries, stationery, lighting and heating, rent and so on.

Periodically the organisation will prepare an accounting statement showing the income generated and the amounts spent (the 'expenditure' of the organisation). Such a statement is referred to very generally as an income statement, though more specific terms are usually used to describe the income statements of particular forms of organisation.

For businesses, the income statement is referred to as a profit and loss account. The total income earned during a period is compared with the expenditure incurred in earning it, and the difference is either a profit or a loss.

Many businesses try to distinguish between a *gross profit* earned on trading, and a *net profit*. They prepare a statement called a 'trading and profit and loss account'. In the first part of the statement (the trading account) revenue from selling goods is compared with direct costs of acquiring or producing the goods sold to arrive at a gross profit figure. From this, deductions are made in the second half of the statement (the profit and loss account) in respect of indirect costs (overheads).

The trading and profit and loss account is a statement showing in detail how the profit (or loss) of a period has been made. The owners and managers of a business obviously want to know how much profit or loss has been made, but there is only a limited information value in the profit figure alone. In order to exercise financial control effectively, managers need to know how much income has been earned, what various items of costs have been and whether the performance of sales or the control of costs appears to be satisfactory. This is the basic reason for preparing the trading, profit and loss account.

As with the balance sheet in the previous chapter, it may help you to focus on the content of the income statement if you have an example in front of you. The specimen below is based on a format prescribed for limited companies; as usual, other entities have greater flexibility in presentation.

PARADIGM LIMITED
TRADING AND PROFIT AND LOSS ACCOUNT
FOR THE YEAR ENDED 31 DECEMBER 20X6

	£	£
Turnover*		475,000
Cost of sales		218,000
Gross profit		257,000
Selling costs	50,000	
Distribution costs	47,000	
Administrative expenses	74,000	
		171,000
		86,000
Other operating income		4,000
		90,000
Interest payable		6,000
Profit before tax		84,000
Taxation		43,000
Profit after tax retained for the year		41,000
Profits retained from previous year		23,700
Retained profits carried forward		64,700

*This is the usual term to describe the revenue earned from selling goods or services to customers.

Activity 1

Refer back to the balance sheet of Paradigm Ltd in Chapter 4. Can you see how the profit and loss account is linked to the balance sheet through retained profits?

2 FINANCIAL STATEMENTS

2.1 Details in the trading and profit and loss account

The two parts of the statement may be examined in more detail.

The trading account shows the gross profit for the accounting period. Gross profit is the difference between:

(a) The value of sales (excluding value added tax), and

(b) The purchase cost or production cost of the goods sold.

In a retail business, the cost of the goods sold is their purchase cost from the suppliers. In a manufacturing business, the production cost of goods sold is the cost of raw materials in the finished goods, plus the cost of the labour required to make the goods, and often plus an amount of production 'overhead' costs.

The profit and loss account shows the net profit of the business. The net profit is:

(a) The gross profit

(b) Plus any other income from sources other than the sale of goods

(c) Minus other expenses of the business which are not included in the cost of goods sold

Selling costs might include any or all of the following.

(a) Salaries of a sales director and sales management

(b) Salaries and commissions of salesmen

(c) Travelling and entertainment expenses of salesmen

(d) Marketing costs (for example advertising and sales promotion expenses)

(e) Discounts allowed to customers for early payment of their debts. For example, a business might sell goods to a customer for £100 and offer a discount of 5% for payment in cash. If the customer takes the discount, the accounts of the business would not record the sales value at £95; they would instead record sales at the full £100, with a cost for discounts allowed of £5

(f) Bad debts written off. Sometimes debtors fail to pay what they owe, and a business might have to decide at some stage of chasing after payment that there is now no prospect of ever being paid. The debt has to be written off as 'bad'. The amount of the debt written off is charged as an expense in the profit and loss account

Activity 2 **(15 minutes)**

Apart from encouraging early payment, why else might a business allow a discount to its customers?

Distribution costs are the costs of getting goods to customers, for example the costs of running and maintaining delivery vans.

Administrative expenses are the expenses of providing management and administration for the business.

Activity 3 **(15 minutes)**

Suggest three items which might be included in administrative expenses.

Other operating income. A company might have other sources of income in addition to what it earns from selling goods and services to customers. For example, the company might sell an item of machinery and make a profit on the sale. The profit might be shown as 'other operating income'.

Interest payable. The company might have a bank loan or overdraft on which interest must be paid; or it might have debentures in issue (see Chapter 4).

The company will also have to pay taxation based on the level of its profits.

In the example of Paradigm Ltd, the profit after tax is retained in the business and goes to boost the profits retained from previous years. But of course not all profits have to be retained. It might seem appropriate to pay out some of the profits to the proprietor(s). In the case of a limited company such a payout would take the form of a *dividend* to shareholders.

An example will show how a trading and profit and loss account is compiled.

EXAMPLE: TRADING AND PROFIT AND LOSS ACCOUNT

On 1 June 20X6, Jock Heiss commenced trading as an ice-cream salesman, selling ice-creams from a van which he drove around the streets of his town.

(a) He rented the van at a cost of £1,000 for three months. Running expenses for the van averaged £300 per month.

(b) He hired a part-time helper at a cost of £100 per month.

(c) He borrowed £2,000 from his bank, and the interest cost of the loan was £25 per month.

(d) His main business was to sell ice-cream to customers in the street, but he also did some special catering arrangements for business customers, supplying ice-creams for office parties. Sales to these customers were usually on credit.

(e) For the three months to 31 August 20X6, his total sales were:

(i) Cash sales £8,900

(ii) Credit sales £1,100

(f) He purchased his ice-cream from a local manufacturer, Floors Ltd. The cost of purchases in the three months to 31 August 20X6 was £6,200, and at 31 August he had sold every item of stock. He still owed £700 to Floors Ltd for unpaid purchases on credit.

(g) One of his credit sale customers has gone bankrupt, owing Jock £250. Jock has decided to write off the debt in full, with no prospect of getting any of the money owed.

(h) He used his own home for his office work. Telephone and postage expenses for the three months to 31 August were £150.

(i) During the period he paid himself £300 per month.

Required

Prepare a trading and profit and loss account for the three months 1 June – 31 August 20X6.

ANSWER

JOCK HEISS
TRADING AND PROFIT AND LOSS ACCOUNT
FOR THE THREE MONTHS ENDED 31 AUGUST 20X6

	£	£
Sales		10,000
Cost of sales		6,200
Gross profit		3,800
Expenses		
Wages	300	
Van rental	1,000	
Van expenses	900	
Bad debt written off	250	
Telephone and postage	150	
Interest charges	75	
		2,675
Net profit (transferred to the balance sheet)		1,125

Note the following points.

(a) The net profit is the profit for the period, and it is transferred to the balance sheet of the business as part of the proprietor's capital.

(b) Drawings are appropriations of profit and not expenses. They must not be included in the profit and loss account. In this example, the payments that Jock Heiss makes to himself (£900) are drawings.

(c) The cost of sales is £6,200, even though £700 of the costs have not yet been paid and Floors Ltd is still a creditor for £700 in the balance sheet.

2.2 What goes in the balance sheet and what goes in the profit and loss account?

You might by now be a little confused about what items appear in a balance sheet and what appears in a profit and loss account. If so, the following activity may help.

Activity 4

(a) Suppose that a business sells goods worth £20,000 (for cash) during one month, and during the same month borrows £10,000 from a money lender. Its total receipts for the month are £30,000.

(b) Suppose that a business spends £15,000 buying some shares of a listed company through the stock market. The company pays a dividend out of its profits, and the business receives a dividend of £1,000 on its investment.

How would these amounts be accounted for in the profit and loss account and/or balance sheet?

The two illustrations above are examples of transactions where it is not necessarily clear whether an item should appear in the balance sheet or the trading, profit and loss

NOTES

account. To try to make a distinction we must now turn our attention to the distinctions between *capital* and *revenue* items.

Capital expenditure and revenue expenditure

Definition

> *Capital expenditure* is expenditure which results in the acquisition of fixed costs, or an improvement in their earning capacity.

(a) Capital expenditure is not charged as an expense in the profit and loss account but a depreciation charge will usually be made to write capital expenditure off over time. Depreciation charges are expenses in the profit and loss account.

(b) Capital expenditure on fixed assets results in the appearance of a fixed asset in the balance sheet of the business.

Definition

> *Revenue expenditure* is expenditure which is incurred in one of the following ways.
>
> (a) For the purpose of the trade of the business, including expenditure classified as selling and distribution expenses, administration expenses and finance charges
>
> (b) To maintain the existing earning capacity of fixed assets

Revenue expenditure is charged to the profit and loss account of a period, provided that it relates to the trading activity and sales of that particular period. For example, if a business buys ten widgets for £200 (£20 each) and sells eight of them during an accounting period, it will have two widgets left in stock at the end of the period. The full £200 is revenue expenditure but only £160 is a cost of goods sold during the period. The remaining £40 (cost of two units) will be included in the balance sheet in the stock of goods held – ie as a current asset valued at £40.

> **Activity 5**
>
> Suppose that a business purchases a building for £30,000. It then adds an extension to the building at a cost of £10,000. The building needs to have a few broken windows mended, its floors polished and some missing roof tiles replaced. These cleaning and maintenance jobs cost £900. Should these three separate amounts be treated as capital or revenue expenditure?

BPP PUBLISHING

Capital income and revenue income

Definition

> *Capital income* is the proceeds from the sale of non-trading assets (ie proceeds from the sale of fixed assets, including fixed asset investments).

The profits (or losses) from the sale of fixed assets are included in the profit and loss account of a business, for the accounting period in which the sale takes place.

Definition

> *Revenue income* is income derived from one of the following items.
>
> (a) The sale of trading assets
>
> (b) Interest and dividends received from investments held by the business

Additional capital, additional loans and the repayment of existing loans

The categorisation of capital and revenue items given above does not mention raising additional capital from the owner(s) of the business, or raising and repaying loans. These are transactions which:

(a) Add to the cash assets of the business, thereby creating a corresponding liability (capital or loan), or

(b) When a loan is repaid, reduce the liabilities (loan) and the assets (cash) of the business

None of these transactions would be reported through the profit and loss account.

Why is the distinction between capital and revenue items important?

Since revenue items and capital items are accounted for in different ways, the correct and consistent calculation of profit for any accounting period depends on the correct and consistent classification of items as revenue or capital.

Activity 6

Complete the missing words to ensure you fully understand the difference between capital and revenue items.

Revenue expenditure results from the purchase of goods and services that will either:

(a)   Be _____ fully in the accounting period in which they are _____ , and so be a cost or expense in the trading, profit and loss account, or

(b)   Result in a _____ asset as at the end of the accounting period (because the goods or services have not yet been consumed or made use of).

Capital expenditure results in the purchase or improvement of _____ assets, which are assets that will provide benefits to the business in more than _____ accounting period, and which are not acquired with a view to being resold in the normal course of trade. The cost of purchased fixed assets is not charged _____ to the trading, profit and loss account of the period in which the purchase occurs. Instead, the fixed asset is gradually _____ over a number of accounting periods.

Activity 7

State whether each of the following items should be classified as 'capital' or 'revenue' expenditure or income for the purpose of preparing the trading, profit and loss account and the balance sheet of the business.

(a)   Purchase of leasehold premises.

(b)   Annual depreciation of leasehold premises.

(c)   Solicitors' fees in connection with the purchase of leasehold premises.

(d)   Costs of adding extra storage capacity to a mainframe computer used by the business.

(e)   Computer repair and maintenance costs.

(f)   Profit on the sale of an office building.

(g)   Revenue from sales by credit card.

(h)   Cost of new machinery.

(i)   Customs duty charged on the machinery when imported into the country.

(j)   'Carriage' costs of transporting the new machinery from the supplier's factory to the premises of the business purchasing the machinery.

(k)   Cost of installing the new machinery in the premises of the business.

(l)   Wages of the machine operators.

Chapter roundup

In this chapter we have built on your understanding of accounts, by looking at the income statement.

- An income statement (called a profit and loss account in the case of an entity trading as a business) shows the revenue generated during a period and the expenditure incurred in earning that revenue. The difference between them is the profit or loss for the period.

- For limited companies, the format of a profit and loss account is defined by the Companies Act 1985. Other organisations have greater flexibility in the way they present their results.

- The correct accounting treatment of an item depends partly on whether it is of a capital or a revenue nature.

The next topic is that of partnerships, which are not incorporated bodies and hence not subject to many of the legal regulations and standard accounting practice requirements which apply to companies.

Quick quiz

1   Explain the distinction between a trading account and a profit and loss account.   (see para 2.1)

2   What are the main categories of expenditure shown in the accounts of a limited company?   (2.1)

3   Where in the profit and loss account do the proprietor's drawings appear?   (2.1)

4   Define capital expenditure and revenue so as to bring out the difference between them clearly.   (2.2)

Answers to activities

1   The profit and loss account shows the profit retained in previous years, plus the profit retained from the current year's activities, giving a total of profits retained as at the end of the period (£64,700). This same total appears as part of the 'Capital' section of the balance sheet. If this is not immediately obvious to you, you should think about it carefully and if necessary refer back to the example of Liza Doolittle to see how profits gradually build up and boost the capital owed by the business to the proprietor(s). (Of course, not every business will earn profits every year – the total can go down as well as up!)

2   A common reason for offering discount is to encourage a higher volume of sales. This is often seen in a retail context ('one ball point pen for 25p or five for £1'), and is common too on a larger scale. For example, a publisher will sell his books to customers, ie bookshops, at a discount level reflecting the purchasing 'clout' of the individual bookshop.

3   You could have thought of some of the following.

    (a)   Salaries of directors, management and office staff

    (b)   Rent and rates

    (c)   Insurance

(d)   Telephone and postage

(e)   Printing and stationery

(f)   Heating and lighting

4   (a)   (i)   The £20,000 of sales appear as sales in the trading, profit and loss account.

(ii)   The £10,000 borrowed will not be shown in the profit and loss account, but will be shown as an asset (cash) and a liability (loan) of £10,000 in the balance sheet.

(b)   (i)   The cost of the shares will not be an expense in the profit and loss account. They will appear as an asset (investment) in the balance sheet.

(ii)   However, the dividend of £1,000 will appear as income of the business in the profit and loss account.

5   The original purchase (£30,000) and the cost of the extension (£10,000) are capital expenditure because they are incurred to acquire and then improve a fixed asset. The other costs of £900 are revenue expenditure, because these merely maintain the building and thus the 'earning capacity' of the building.

6   The missing words are: used; purchased; current; fixed; one; in full; depreciated.

7   (a)   Capital expenditure.

(b)   Depreciation of a fixed asset is revenue expenditure.

(c)   The legal fees associated with the purchase of a property may be added to the purchase price and classified as capital expenditure. The cost of the leasehold premises in the balance sheet of the business will then include the legal fees.

(d)   Capital expenditure (enhancing an existing fixed asset).

(e)   Revenue expenditure.

(f)   Capital income (net of the costs of sale).

(g)   Revenue income.

(h)   Capital expenditure.

(i)   If customs duties are borne by the purchaser of the fixed asset, they may be added to the cost of the machinery and classified as capital expenditure.

(j)   Similarly, if carriage costs are paid for by the purchaser of the fixed asset, they may be included in the cost of the fixed asset and classified as capital expenditure.

(k)   Installation costs of a fixed asset are also added to the fixed asset's cost and classified as capital expenditure.

(l)   Revenue expenditure.

Further question practice

Now try the following practice questions at the end of this text

Multiple choice questions: **37 to 42**

Exam style question: **6**

Chapter 7 :
PARTNERSHIP ACCOUNTS

Introduction

Much of what has been said in earlier chapters relates to the preparation and uses of accounts in general. Although the legal framework which applies particularly to the accounts of limited companies has in places been referred to, we have not tried to take account of the different legal forms under which businesses are conducted.

When building up the picture of a business's transactions we focused on the accounts of a sole trader (Liza Doolittle). We showed how the net assets of such a business would at all times be equal to the proprietor's capital. This capital itself could grow as profits were made, and could reduce if profits were withdrawn from the business (or if losses were made).

All of this applies equally well to businesses conducted under other legal forms. We will now turn, in this chapter and the next, to some aspects of accounting which are peculiar to businesses conducted as partnerships and businesses conducted as limited companies. In this chapter we will concentrate on partnerships.

Your objectives

After completing this chapter you should:

    (a)   Understand the accounting implications of trading as a partnership

    (b)   Understand the main differences between the accounts of a partnership and those of a sole proprietor

1 PARTNERSHIPS

1.1 The characteristics of partnerships

Partnership is defined by the Partnership Act 1890 as the relationship which exists between persons carrying on a business in common with a view of profit. In other words, a partnership is an arrangement between two or more individuals in which they undertake to share the risks and rewards of a joint business operation.

It is usual for a partnership to be established formally by means of a partnership agreement. However, if individuals act as though they are in partnership even though no written agreement exists, then it will be presumed in law that a partnership does exist and that its terms of agreement are the same as those laid down in the Partnership Act 1890.

Activity 1

Try to think of reasons why a business should be conducted as a partnership, rather than:

(a)   As a sole trader

(b)   As a company

The partnership agreement

The partnership agreement is a written agreement in which the terms of the partnership are set out, and in particular the financial arrangements as between partners.

Activity 2

Partnership agreements often cover capital, profit-sharing ratios, interest on capital, salaries and drawings. What sort of matters do you think might be covered under each of these headings?

In the absence of a written partnership agreement, the provisions of the Partnership Act 1890 are presumed to apply between the partners. The Act includes the following provisions relating to financial arrangements.

(a)   Residual profits are shared in equal proportions.

(b)   There are no partners' salaries.

(c)   There is no interest on capital invested by partners.

(d)   If partners advance loans to the business in addition to their agreed capital, they are entitled to interest of 5% per annum on the amount of the loan.

EXAMPLE: PARTNERS' SALARIES AND PROFIT-SHARING

Suppose Bill and Ben are partners sharing profit in the ratio 2:1 and that they agree to pay themselves a salary of £10,000 each. If profits before deducting salaries are £26,000, how much income would each partner receive?

ANSWER

First, the two salaries are deducted from profit, leaving £6,000 (£26,000 – £20,000). This £6,000 has to be distributed between Bill and Ben in the ratio 2:1. In other words, Bill will receive £4,000 and Ben £2,000.

So the final answer to the question is that Bill receives his salary plus £4,000 and Ben his salary plus £2,000. This could be laid out as follows.

	Bill	*Ben*	*Total*
	£	£	£
Salary	10,000	10,000	20,000
Share of residual profits (ratio 2:1)	4,000	2,000	6,000
Gross profit	14,000	12,000	26,000

Activity 3

Tom, Dick and Harry earned total partnership profits of £112,000 in 20X6. They pay themselves salaries of £8,000, £12,000 and £17,000 respectively, and share residual profits in the ratio 7:3:5. Show how much of the total partnership profit would be credited to each.

1.2 How does accounting for partnerships differ from accounting for sole traders?

Activity 4

The following exercise should help clarify the differences in accounting between partnerships and sole tradreships.

Mark the following statements as true or false.

1   The assets of a partnership are like the assets of any other business, and are accounted for in the same way.

2   The net profit of a partnership is calculated in the same way as the net profit of a sole trader.

3   The funds put into the business by each partner are shown differently from the funds put in by a sole trader.

4   The appropriation of profit by the partners is agreed every year.

Funds employed

When a partnership is formed, each partner puts some capital into the business. These initial capital contributions are recorded in a series of *capital accounts*, one for each partner. (Since each partner is ultimately entitled to repayment of his capital it is clearly vital to keep a record of how much is owed to whom.) The precise amount of initial capital contributed by each partner is a matter for general agreement and there is no question of each partner necessarily contributing the same amount, although this does sometimes happen.

In addition to a capital account, each partner normally has a *current account*.

A current account is used to record the *profits retained in the business* by the partner. It is therefore a sort of capital account, which increases in value when the partnership makes profits, and falls in value when the partner whose current account it is makes drawings out of the business.

The main difference between the capital and current account in accounting for partnerships is that:

(a) Whereas the balance on the capital account remains static from year to year (with one or two exceptions)

(b) The current account is continually fluctuating up and down, as the partnership makes profits which are shared out between the partners, and as each partner takes out drawings

A further difference is that when the partnership agreement provides for interest on capital, partners receive interest on the balances in their capital accounts, but *not on the balances in their current accounts*.

The capital side of the partnership balance sheet will therefore consist of:

(a) The capital accounts of each partner

(b) The current accounts of each partner, net of drawings

This will be illustrated in an example later.

Loans by partners

In addition, it is sometimes the case that an existing or previous partner will make a loan to the partnership, in which case he becomes a creditor of the partnership. On the balance sheet, such a loan is not included as partners' funds, but is shown separately as a long-term liability (unless repayable within 12 months, in which case it is a current liability). This is the case whether or not the loan creditor is also an existing partner.

However, *interest on such loans will be credited to the partner's current account (if he is an existing partner)*. This is administratively more convenient, especially when the partner does not particularly want to be paid the loan interest in cash immediately it becomes due. You should bear in mind the following.

(a) Interest on loans from a partner is accounted for as an expense in the profit and loss account, and not as an appropriation of profit, even though the interest is added to the current account of the partner.

(b) If there is no interest rate specified, the Partnership Act 1890 (section 24) provides for interest to be paid at 5% pa on loans by partners.

Appropriation of net profits

The net profit of a partnership is shared out between the partners according to the terms of their agreement. This sharing out is shown in a *profit and loss appropriation account*, which follows on from the profit and loss account itself.

The way in which profit is shared out depends on the terms of the partnership agreement. The steps to take are as follows.

(a) Establish how much the net profit is.

(b) Appropriate interest on capital and salaries first. Both of these items are appropriations of profit and are not expenses in the profit and loss account.

(c) If partners agree to pay interest on their drawings during the year, charge each partner with the amount of interest attributable to him. Then add the total of interest so charged to the pool of residual profits.

(d) The difference between net profits (plus any interest charged on drawings) and appropriations for interest on capital and salaries is the residual profit. This is shared out between partners in the profit-sharing ratio.

(e) Each partner's share of profits is credited to his current account.

Activity 5

The following exercise focuses on the differences between the sole tradership, partnership and company. Fill in the answer to each question for each type of business.

Question	Sole Tradership	Partnership	Company
1 Who is the proprietor?			
2 Which legal regulations is the business subject to?			
3 Is the liability of the owners limited or unlimited?			

EXAMPLE: PARTNERSHIP ACCOUNTS

Locke, Niece and Munster are in partnership with an agreement to share profits in the ratio 3:2:1. They also agree that:

(a) All three should receive interest at 12% on capital

(b) Munster should receive a salary of £6,000 per annum

(c)   Interest will be charged on drawings at the rate of 5% (charged on the end-of-year drawings balances)

(d)   The interest rate on the loan by Locke is 5%

The balance sheet of the partnership as at 31 December 20X5 revealed the following.

	£	£
Capital accounts		
Locke	20,000	
Niece	8,000	
Munster	6,000	
		34,000
Current accounts		
Locke	3,500	
Niece	(700)	
Munster	1,800	
		4,600
Loan account (Locke)		6,000
Capital employed to finance net fixed assets and working capital		44,600

Drawings made during the year to 31 December 20X6 were as follows.

Locke	£6,000
Niece	£4,000
Munster	£7,000

The net profit for the year to 31 December 20X6 was £24,530 before deducting loan interest.

Activity 6   **(15 minutes)**

Before reading on, see if you can work out the interest to be charged on partners' drawings.

EXAMPLE CONTINUED

Required

Show how the 20X6 profit is appropriated between the partners, and draw up the capital side of the partnership balance sheet at 31 December 20X6.

ANSWER

The interest payable to Locke on his loan is:

5% of £6,000 = £300

We can now begin to work out the appropriation of profits.

		£	£
Net profit, less loan interest £(24,530 – 300)			24,230
Add interest on drawings			850
			25,080
Less Munster salary			6,000
			19,080
Less interest on capital			
Locke	(12% of £20,000)	2,400	
Niece	(12% of £8,000)	960	
Munster	(12% of £6,000)	720	
			4,080
			15,000
Residual profits			
Locke	(3)	7,500	
Niece	(2)	5,000	
Munster	(1)	2,500	
			15,000

Make sure you remember what the various interest figures represent and that you understand exactly what has been calculated here.

(a) The partners can take some drawings out of the business, but if they do they will be charged interest on them.

(b) The partners have capital tied up in the business (of course, otherwise there would be no business) and they have agreed to pay themselves interest on whatever capital each has put in.

(c) Once all the necessary adjustments have been made to net profit, £15,000 remains and is divided up between the partners in the ratio 3:2:1.

Now we can calculate the balances on the partners' current accounts at 31 December 20X6.

Current accounts	*Locke*	*Niece*	*Munster*	*Total*
	£	£	£	£
Balances at 31 December 20X5	3,500	(700)	1,800	4,600
Add amounts credited to partners				
Loan interest	300	0	0	300
Interest on capital	2,400	960	720	4,080
Salary	0	0	6,000	6,000
Residual profits	7,500	5,000	2,500	15,000
	13,700	5,260	11,020	29,980
Less amounts charged to partners				
Drawings	(6,000)	(4,000)	(7,000)	(17,000)
Interest on drawings	(300)	(200)	(350)	(850)
Balances at 31 December 20X6	7,400	1,060	3,670	12,130

The capital side of the partnership balance sheet therefore appears as follows at 31 December 20X6.

	£	£
Capital accounts		
Locke	20,000	
Niece	8,000	
Munster	6,000	
		34,000
Current accounts		
Locke	7,400	
Niece	1,060	
Munster	3,670	
		12,130
		46,130

Again, make sure you understand what has happened here.

(a)   The partners' *capital* accounts have not changed. They were brought forward at £20,000, £8,000 and £6,000, and they are just the same in the new balance sheet.

(b)   The partners' *current* accounts have changed. The balances brought forward from last year's balance sheet of £3,500, £(700) and £1,800 have become £7,400, £1,060 and £3,670 in the new balance sheet. How this came about is shown by the movements shown above.

(c)   The events recorded in the current accounts are a reflection of how the partnership has distributed its profit.

Activity 7   **(15 minutes)**

Verify that the net assets side of the partnership balance sheet at 31 December 20X6 is also equal to £46,130.

Hint: think of the business equation.

Chapter roundup

You should have gained a basic understanding of partnership accounts from this chapter.

- Some businesses are run as partnerships, with each partner being a proprietor of the business.

- The financial relations between partners are usually regulated by a written partnership agreement. In the absence of such an agreement, the provisions of the Partnership Act 1890 are presumed to apply.

- Partnership accounts are in principle very similar to those of a sole trader. The main differences are firstly that partners have to appropriate the net profit between themselves, and secondly that the capital side of the balance sheet is displayed differently.

In the next chapter we look at the accounts of limited companies.

Quick quiz

1   Define a partnership.   (see para 1.1)

2   List the financial provisions of the Partnership Act 1890 which are presumed to apply between partners in the absence of any indication to the contrary.   (1.1)

3   How is interest on a partner's loan treated in the accounts of a partnership?   (1.2)

4   Why is it usual to distinguish between capital and current accounts for partners?   (1.2)

Answers to activities

1   (a)   The main problem with trading as a sole trader is the limitation on resources it implies. As the business grows, there will be a need for:

      (i)   Additional capital. Although some capital may be provided by a bank, it would not be desirable to have the business entirely dependent on borrowing

      (ii)   Additional expertise. A sole trader technically competent in his own field may not have, for example, the financial skills that would be needed in a larger business

      (iii) Additional management time. Once a business grows to a certain point, it becomes impossible for one person to look after all aspects of it without help

   (b)   The main disadvantage of incorporating is the regulatory burden faced by limited companies. In addition, there are certain 'businesses' which are not allowed to enjoy limited liability; you may have read about the Lloyd's 'names' who face personal bankruptcy because the option of limited liability was not available to them.

      There are also tax factors to consider, but these are beyond the scope of this book.

2   (a)   *Capital.* Each partner puts in a share of the business capital. If there is to be an agreement on how much each partner should put in and keep in the business, as a minimum fixed amount, this should be stated.

   (b)   *Profit-sharing ratio.* Partners can agree to share profits in any way they choose. For example, if there are three partners in a business, they might agree to share profits equally, but on the other hand, if one partner does a greater share of the work, or has more experience and ability, or puts in more capital, the ratio of profit sharing might be different.

   (c)   *Interest on capital.* Partners might agree to pay themselves interest on the capital they put into the business. If they do so, the agreement will state what rate of interest is to be applied.

   (d)   *Partners' salaries.* Partners might also agree to pay themselves salaries. These are not salaries in the same way that an employee of the business will be paid a wage or salary, because partners' salaries are an appropriation of profit, and not an expense in the profit and loss account of the business. The purpose of paying salaries is to give each partner a satisfactory basic income before the residual profits are shared out.

(e) *Drawings.* Partners may draw out their share of profits from the business. However, they might agree to put a limit on how much they should draw out in any period. If so, this limit should be specified in the partnership agreement. To encourage partners to delay taking drawings out of the business until the financial year has ended, the agreement might also be that partners should be charged interest on their drawings during the year.

3

	£
Total partnership profits	112,000
Less salaries	37,000
Residual profit	75,000

	Tom	Dick	Harry	Total
	£	£	£	£
Salaries	8,000	12,000	17,000	37,000
Residual profits (7:3:5)	35,000	15,000	25,000	75,000
	43,000	27,000	42,000	112,000

4 True:

1. Yes, the assets side of the partnership balance sheet is no different from what has been shown in earlier chapters.

3. Yes, in partnership accounts a capital account is used for each partner.

False:

2. This is largely true except that if a partner makes a loan to the business (as distinct from a capital contribution) then interest on the loan will be an expense in the profit and loss account in the same way as interest on any other loan from a person or organisation who is not a partner.

4. Net profit must be appropriated by the partners in accordance with the partnership agreement which is set up at the beginning of the partnership. Of course it may be amended, but it will remain unchanged from year to year unless a positive decision to amend it is taken.

5

Question		Sole Tradership	Partnership	Company
1	Who is the proprietor?	sole trader	partners	shareholders
2	Which legal regulations is the business subject to?	none	Partnership Act 1890	Companies Acts
3	Is the liability of the owners limited or unlimited?	unlimited	unlimited	limited

Finally, although the liability of partners is generally unlimited, under the Limited Partnership Act 1907, a partnership may have partners whose liability is limited to the amount of capital they have agreed to subscribe. However, limited partners may not take part in the management of the business.

6   The interest payable by each partner on their drawings during the year is:

		£
Locke	5% of £6,000	300
Niece	5% of £4,000	200
Munster	5% of £7,000	350
		850

These amounts are charged against each partner, and the total (£850) added to the pool of residual profit.

7   The business equation states:

$$P = I + D - C_i$$

In this case $C_i = 0$, and the equation can be re-arranged as follows:

$$I = P - D$$

We know that profit for the year is £24,530, and drawings are £17,000. The increase in net assets over the year is therefore £(24,530 − 17,000) = £7,530. The net assets at the beginning of the year were £38,600 (equal to partners' capital accounts £34,000 plus current accounts £4,600); at the end of the year net assets are therefore £(38,600 + 7,530) = £46,130.

Further question practice

Now try the following practice questions at the end of this text

Multiple choice questions: **43 to 50**

Exam style question: **7**

Chapter 8 :

THE ACCOUNTS OF LIMITED COMPANIES

Introduction

So far, this book has dealt mainly with the accounts of businesses in general and, in the last chapter, partnerships in particular. In this chapter we shall turn our attention to the accounts of *limited companies*. As we should expect, the accounting rules and conventions for recording the business transactions of limited companies, and then preparing their final accounts, are much the same as for sole traders. For example, companies will have similar basic accounting records to a sole trader. They also prepare a profit and loss account annually, and a balance sheet at the end of the accounting year.

Your objectives

After completing this chapter you should:

  (a) Understand in more detail the nature of limited liability and the legal safeguards that surround it

  (b) Be aware of the capital structure of limited companies

  (c) Be aware of the main features of the accounts of limited companies

1 LIMITED COMPANIES

1.1 The statutory framework of limited company accounts

There are some differences in the accounts of limited companies compared with unincorporated entities. The legislation governing the activities of limited companies is very extensive. Amongst other things, the Companies Acts define certain minimum accounting records which must be maintained by companies. In addition, a copy of the annual accounts of a limited company must be filed with the Registrar of Companies. This is so that accounts are available for public inspection. Companies legislation also contains detailed requirements on the minimum information which must be disclosed in a company's accounts. Businesses which are not limited companies (non-incorporated businesses) enjoy comparative freedom from statutory regulation and do not have to publish their accounts.

Activity 1

Mark the following statements as true or false.

1   Where there are numerous owners of an enterprise it will always be incorporated.

2   The capital of a company is shown differently from that of a sole trader.

3   Sole traders usually manage their businesses on a day to day basis, unlike shareholders.

4   Shareholders may appropriate profits through drawings.

5   Shareholders receive annual published accounts prepared according to the Companies Acts.

Activity 2

There are other regulatory burdens borne by limited companies which do not apply to unincorporated businesses. Some have been mentioned in earlier chapters of this book. Can you think of at least two?

Limited liability

Sole traders and partnerships are, with some significant exceptions, generally fairly small concerns. The amount of capital involved may be modest, and the proprietors of the business usually participate in managing it. Their liability for the debts of the business is unlimited, which means that if the business runs up debts that it is unable to pay, the proprietors will become personally liable for the unpaid debts, and would be required, if necessary, to sell their private possessions in order to repay them. For example, if a sole trader has some capital in his business, but the business now owes £40,000 which it cannot repay, the trader might have to sell his house to raise the money to pay off his business debts.

NOTES

Activity 3

Fill in the missing words in the following paragraph.

Limited companies offer limited _____ to their _____ . This means that the maximum amount that an owner stands to lose in the event that the company becomes insolvent and cannot pay off its debts, is the _____ in the business. This limited liability is therefore a major _____ of turning a business into a limited company. For example, if a limited company becomes insolvent owing large sums of money to its creditors, the owners of the company will _____ be required to pay the company's debts from their own personal _____ .

As a business grows, it needs more capital to finance its operations, and significantly more than the people currently managing the business can provide themselves. One way of obtaining more capital is to invite investors from outside the business to invest in the ownership or 'equity' of the business. These new co-owners would not usually be expected to help with managing the business. To such investors, limited liability is very attractive. Investments are always risky undertakings, but with limited liability the investor knows the maximum amount that he stands to lose when he puts some capital into a company.

There are two classes of limited company.

(a) *Private companies*. These have the word 'limited' at the end of their name. Being private, they cannot invite members of the public to invest in their equity (ownership).

(b) *Public companies*. These are much fewer in number than private companies, but are generally much larger in size. They have the words 'public limited company,' usually shortened to PLC or plc, at the end of their name. Public companies can invite members of the general public to invest in their equity, and the 'shares' of these companies are usually traded on the Stock Exchange (that is to say, public companies are usually also *listed* companies, though this is not always the case).

Activity 4

If you lent money to a limited company, or supplied goods on credit, how might you try to protect your position?

2 CAPITAL AND RESERVES

2.1 Share capital

The capital of limited companies

The proprietors' capital in a limited company consists of share capital. When a company is set up for the first time, it issues shares, which are paid for by investors, who then

PUBLISHING

become shareholders of the company. Shares are denominated in units of 25p, 50p, £1 or whatever seems appropriate. This 'face value' of the shares is called their *nominal value*.

Activity 5

Fill in the gaps in the following table.

Number of shares	Nominal value	Total value £
100,000		100,000
	50p	100,000
500,000	40p	
	10p	85,000

The nominal value is not the same as the *market value*, which is the price someone is prepared to pay for the share.

A distinction is made between authorised and issued share capital. The *authorised* share capital is the maximum amount of share capital that the company is empowered to issue. *Issued* share capital is the nominal amount of share capital that has been issued to shareholders. This obviously cannot exceed the authorised share capital.

Dividends

Definition

> Profits paid out to shareholders are called *dividends*. Dividends are appropriations of profit after tax.

A company might pay dividends in two stages during the course of its accounting year.

(a) In the middle of the year, after the half-year financial results are known, the company might pay an *interim* dividend.

(b) After the end of the year, the company might pay a further *final* dividend.

The total dividend for the year is the sum of the interim and the final dividend. (Not all companies by any means pay an interim dividend. Interim dividends are, however, commonly paid out by listed companies.)

At the end of an accounting year, a company's directors will have proposed a final dividend payment, but this will not yet have been paid. This means that the final dividend should be appropriated out of profits and shown as a current liability in the balance sheet.

The terminology of dividend payments can be confusing, since they may be expressed either in the form, 'x pence per share' or as 'y per cent'. In the latter case, the meaning is always 'y per cent of the *nominal value* of the shares in issue'. For example, suppose a company's issued share capital consists of 100,000 50p ordinary shares which were issued

BPP
PUBLISHING

at a premium of 10p per share (in other words, investors paid 60p to acquire each share). The company's balance sheet would include the following.

Issued share capital	100,000 50p ordinary shares	£50,000
Share premium account	(100,000 × 10p)	£10,000

If the directors wish to pay a dividend of £5,000, in which two ways may they propose it? Write your answers here.

(a) A dividend of 5p per share (100,000 × 5p = £5,000), or
(b) A dividend of 10% (10% × £50,000 = £5,000).

Ordinary shares and preference shares

At this stage it is relevant to distinguish between the two types of shares most often encountered, preference shares and ordinary shares.

Preference shares carry the right to a final dividend which is expressed as a percentage of their nominal value: for example a 6% £1 preference share carries a right to an annual dividend of 6p. Preference dividends have priority over ordinary dividends. If the directors of a company wish to pay a dividend (which they are not obliged to do) they must pay any preference dividend first. Otherwise, no ordinary dividend may be paid.

Ordinary shares are by far the most common. They carry no right to a fixed dividend but are entitled to all profits left after payment of any preference dividend. Generally however, only a part of such remaining profits is distributed, the rest being kept in reserve (see below). The amount of ordinary dividends fluctuates although there is a general expectation that it will increase from year to year. Should the company be wound up, any surplus is shared between the ordinary shareholders. Ordinary shares normally carry voting rights, and in effect ordinary shareholders are the owners of the company.

Activity 6

The share capital of X Ltd is as follows.

	Authorised	Issued
	£	£
7% preference shares of £1 each	20,000	12,000
Ordinary shares of 20p each	100,000	80,000
	120,000	92,000

The directors declare an ordinary dividend for the year of 12%. How much in total will be paid out by the company in dividends?

2.2 Reserves

Definition

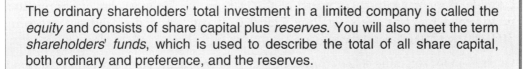
> The ordinary shareholders' total investment in a limited company is called the *equity* and consists of share capital plus *reserves*. You will also meet the term *shareholders' funds*, which is used to describe the total of all share capital, both ordinary and preference, and the reserves.

The important point to note is that all reserves are owned by the ordinary shareholders.

A distinction should be made *between two types of reserves*.

Definition

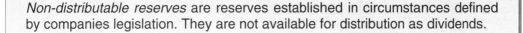
> *Non-distributable reserves* are reserves established in circumstances defined by companies legislation. They are not available for distribution as dividends.

Companies legislation restricts the amounts that companies are allowed to pay out to their shareholders in order to protect the claims of creditors.

Definition

> *Distributable reserves* are reserves consisting of profits which are distributable as dividends, if the company so wishes.

Profit and loss reserve (retained profits)

This is the most significant distributable reserve, and it is described in many different ways, Suggest three possible descriptions. Write your answer here.

Your answer may have included:

    (a)   Revenue reserve

    (b)   Retained profits

    (c)   Retained earnings

    (d)   Undistributed profits

    (e)   Profit and loss account

    (f)   Unappropriated profits

BPP
PUBLISHING

NOTES

These are profits earned by the company and not appropriated by dividends, taxation or transfer to another reserve account. Assuming the company is making profits, this reserve generally increases from year to year, as most companies do not distribute all their profits as dividends. Dividends can be paid from it: even if a loss is made in one particular year, a dividend can be paid from previous years' retained profits. For example, if a company makes a loss of £100,000 in one year, yet has unappropriated profits from previous years totalling £250,000, it can pay a dividend not exceeding £150,000 (ie £250,000 – £100,000).

One reason for retaining some profit each year is to enable the company to pay dividends even when profits are low (or non-existent). Another reason is usually shortage of cash. Very occasionally, you might come across a debit balance (a negative balance) on the profit and loss account. This would indicate that the company has *accumulated losses*.

Other distributable reserves

The company directors may choose to set up other reserves. These may have a specific purpose (for example plant and machinery replacement reserve) or not (for example general reserve). The creation of these reserves usually indicates a general intention not to distribute the profits involved at any future date, although legally any such reserves, being distributable, remain available for the payment of dividends.

Profits are transferred to these reserves by making an appropriation out of profits, usually profits for the year. Typically, you might come across the following.

	£	£
Profit after taxation		100,000
Appropriations of profit		
Dividend	60,000	
Transfer to general reserve	10,000	
		70,000
Retained profits for the year		30,000
Profit and loss reserve brought forward		250,000
Profit and loss reserve carried forward		280,000

There is no real significance about the creation of separate distributable reserves. After all, there is little difference between the following two balance sheet extracts.

			£	£
(a)	Net assets			3,500
	Share capital			2,000
	Reserves:	general (distributable as dividend)	1,000	
		retained profits (distributable)	500	
				1,500
				3,500
(b)	Net assets			3,500
	Share capital			2,000
	Reserves:	general (distributable as dividend)		1,500
				3,500

PUBLISHING

The establishment of a 'plant and machinery replacement reserve' (or something similar) indicates an intention by a company to keep funds in the business to replace its plant and machinery. However, the reserve would still, legally, represent distributable profits, and the existence of such a reserve does not guarantee the company's ability to replace its fixed assets in the future.

The share premium account

There are a number of non-distributable reserves, the most important of which at this stage is the share premium account. A share premium arises when a company sells shares for a price which is higher than their nominal value. By 'premium' is meant the difference between the issue price of the share and its nominal value. When a company is first incorporated (set up) the issue price of its shares will probably be the same as their nominal value and so there would be no share premium. If the company does well, the market value of its shares will increase, but not the nominal value. The price of any new shares issued will be approximately their market value. The difference between cash received by the company and the nominal value of the new shares issued is transferred to the share premium account.

For example, if X Ltd issues 1,000 £1 ordinary shares at £2.60 each how will the £2,600 proceeds be classified in the balance sheet?

Your answer should be:

	£
Share capital	1,000
Share premium	1,600

A share premium account only comes into being when a company issues shares at a price in excess of their nominal value. The market price of the shares, once they have been issued, has no bearing at all on the company's accounts, and so if their market price goes up or down, the share premium account would remain unaltered.

Activity 7

Here are extracts from a company's balance sheet at 30 June 20X5 and 30 June 20X6.

	20X6	20X5
	£	£
Capital reserves		
Issued share capital: 50p ordinary shares	9,000	7,500
Share premium account	3,500	2,000

How many shares were issued during the year, and at what price?

Revaluation reserve

A revaluation reserve must be created when a company revalues one or more of its fixed assets. Revaluations frequently occur with freehold property, as the market value of property rises or falls. The company's directors might wish to show a more 'reasonable' value of the asset in their balance sheet, to avoid giving a misleading impression about the financial position of the company.

When an asset is revalued the revaluation reserve is credited with the difference between the revalued amount of the asset, and its net book value before the revaluation took place. Depreciation is subsequently charged on the *revalued* amount.

EXAMPLE: REVALUATION RESERVE

X Ltd bought freehold land and buildings for £20,000 ten years ago; their net book value (after depreciation of the buildings) is now £19,300. A professional valuation of £390,000 has been given, and the directors wish to reflect this in the accounts.

The revaluation surplus is £390,000 – £19,300 = £370,700. In the balance sheet, this amount will be added to the value of freehold property, so that fixed assets will include a total valuation of £390,000. The £370,700 will also appear on the other side of the balance sheet as a revaluation reserve.

An *unrealised capital profit* (such as the £370,700 above) is generally not distributable, whereas a realised capital profit (ie if the property is actually sold for £390,000) usually is distributable.

The distinction between reserves and provisions

A reserve is an appropriation of distributable profits for a specific purpose (for example plant replacement) while a provision is an amount charged against revenue as an expense. A provision relates either to a diminution in the value of an asset (for example doubtful debtors) or a known liability (for example audit fees), the amount of which cannot be established with any accuracy. Provisions (for depreciation, doubtful debts and so on) are dealt with in company accounts in the same way as in the accounts of other types of business.

Activity 8

The terminology relating to reserves can be confusing. After all, reserves are a part of the owners' capital and appear on the capital side of the balance sheet; yet what is distributed to shareholders (namely cash) appears on the assets side. So in what sense is a reserve 'distributable'? Try to think of this in connection with the revaluation reserve of £370,700 discussed above.

3 THE FINAL ACCOUNTS OF LIMITED COMPANIES

The preparation and publication of the final accounts of limited companies in the UK are governed by the Companies Act 1985. A number of amendments to the provisions of the Companies Act 1985 are contained in the Companies Act 1989. The detailed regulations laid down by these Acts are beyond the scope of this book. However, the general format of the balance sheet and profit and loss account of a limited company will be shown, with some simplifications, in order to introduce certain assets and liabilities which we have not come across before in earlier chapters.

TYPICAL COMPANY LIMITED BALANCE SHEET AS AT .....

Fixed assets	£	£	£
Intangible assets			
Development costs		10,000	
Concessions, patents, licences, trademarks		5,000	
Goodwill		4,000	
			19,000
Tangible assets			
Land and buildings		75,000	
Plant and machinery		24,000	
Fixtures, fittings, tools and equipment		8,000	
Motor vehicles		13,000	
			120,000
Investments			2,500
			141,500
Current assets			
Stocks		6,000	
Debtors and prepayments		8,500	
Investments		1,500	
Cash at bank and in hand		300	
		16,300	
Creditors: amounts falling due within one year			
(ie current liabilities)			
Debenture loans (nearing their redemption date)	4,000		
Bank loans and overdrafts	1,300		
Trade creditors	6,200		
Taxation	2,800		
Accruals	800		
Proposed dividend	1,000		
		16,100	
Net current assets			200
			141,700
Total assets less current liabilities			
Creditors: amounts falling due after more than one year			
Debenture loans			(8,000)
			133,700
Capital and reserves			
Called up share capital		20,000	
Ordinary shares		5,000	
Preference shares			25,000
Reserves			
Share premium account		11,000	
Revaluation reserve		15,000	
Other reserves		6,000	
Profit and loss account (retained profits)		76,700	
			108,700
			133,700

TYPICAL COMPANY LIMITED
PROFIT AND LOSS ACCOUNT FOR THE YEAR ENDED.....

	£	£
Turnover		91,700
Cost of sales		(32,000)
Gross profit		59,700
Distribution costs	17,000	
Administrative expenses	24,000	
		(41,000)
		18,700
Other operating income	1,000	
Income from fixed asset investments	200	
Other interest receivable and similar income	500	
		1,700
		20,400
Interest payable		(3,200)
Profit before taxation		17,200
Tax		(3,500)
Profit after tax		13,700
Dividends: preference	500	
ordinary	1,500	
		(2,000)
Retained profit for the year		11,700
Profit and loss account as at the beginning of the year		65,000
Profit and loss account as at the end of the year		76,700

3.1 Assets and liabilities

Investments

Investments are fixed assets if the company intends to hold on to them for a long time, and current assets if they are only likely to be held for a short time before being sold.

Creditors: amounts falling due within one year

The term 'creditors: amounts falling due within one year' was introduced by the Companies Act 1981 as a phrase meaning 'current liabilities'.

Debenture loans

Limited companies may issue debenture stock ('debentures') or loan stock. These are long-term liabilities described on the balance sheet as loan capital. They are different from share capital.

Activity 9

The following statements concern either shareholders or debenture holders. Mark an 's' or a 'd' beside each.

1   They are members of a company.

2   They may have security against the company's assets.

3   They are creditors of the company.

4   They receive a fixed rate of interest.

5   They receive dividends.

6   Where payment is due and unpaid, they may take legal action against the company.

Interest is calculated on the nominal value of loan capital, regardless of its market value. If a company has £700,000 (nominal value) 12% debentures in issue, interest of £84,000 will be charged in the profit and loss account per year. Interest is usually paid half-yearly. There may be a current liability in the balance sheet for interest due but not yet paid at the year end.

For example, if a company has £700,000 of 12% debentures in issue, pays interest on 30 June and 31 December each year, and ends its accounting year on 30 September, there would be an accrual of three months' unpaid interest ($^3/_{12} \times £84,000 = £21,000$) at the end of each accounting year so long as the debentures are still in issue.

Taxation

Companies pay *corporation tax* on the profits they earn. The charge for corporation tax on profits for the year is shown as a deduction from net profit, before appropriations. In the balance sheet, tax payable to the Government is generally shown as a current liability.

When corporation tax on profits is calculated for the profit and loss account, the calculation is only an estimate of what the company thinks its tax liability will be. In subsequent dealings with the Inland Revenue, a different corporation tax charge might eventually be agreed. Any difference is adjusted in the estimated taxation charge for the following year.

EXAMPLE: TAXATION

Urals Ltd made a profit before tax of £150,000 in the year to 30 September 20X5 and of £180,000 in the following year (to 30 September 20X6).

The estimated corporation tax for the first year was £60,000 and in the second year was £75,000. The actual tax charge in the year to 30 September 20X5 was finally agreed with the Inland Revenue at £55,000.

Required

Compute the charge for taxation in the year to 30 September 20X6.

NOTES

ANSWER

	To 30 September	
	20X5	*20X6*
	£	£
Estimate of tax on profits	60,000	75,000
Actual tax charge	55,000	
Overestimate of tax in 20X5	5,000	(5,000)
Tax charge in year to 30 September 20X6		70,000

The effect of this adjustment will be to increase profits in 20X6 by £5,000, to correct the 'error' in 20X5 when profits were reduced by £5,000 because of the overestimate of the tax charge.

Activity 10

Taxes Ltd estimated its corporation tax charge for the calendar year 20X5 as £170,000; the charge eventually agreed was £178,500. For 20X6, the company estimates its taxation charge on profits for the year as £204,000. What are the amounts of the tax charges appearing in the company's profit and loss accounts for 20X5 and 20X6?

Companies pay tax nine months after their accounting year end. However, the tax on profits in the profit and loss account and the tax payable in the balance sheet are not usually the same amount. The liability still outstanding at the year end, and shown in the balance sheet, will therefore often be less than the total liability for the year shown in the profit and loss account.

EXAMPLE: COMPANY ACCOUNTS PREPARATION

We can now draw together several of the items described in this chapter into an illustrative example. You should study it carefully to ensure that you understand how a company's accounts are compiled.

BPP
PUBLISHING

The accountant of Wislon Ltd has prepared the following trial balance as at 31 December 20X6.

	£'000
50p ordinary shares (fully paid)	350
7% £1 preference shares (fully paid)	100
10% debentures (secured)	200
Retained profit 1 January 20X6	92
General reserve 1 January 20X6	71
Freehold land and buildings 1 January 20X6 (cost)	430
Plant and machinery 1 January 20X6 (cost)	830
Provision for depreciation:	
freehold buildings 1 January 20X6	20
plant and machinery 1 January 20X6	222
Sales	2,695
Cost of sales	2,156
Preference dividend paid	7
Ordinary dividend (interim) paid	8
Debenture interest paid	10
Wages and salaries	274
Light and heat	14
Sundry expenses	107
Suspense account	420
Debtors	179
Creditors	195
Cash	126

Notes

(a) The suspense account is in respect of the following items.

	£'000
Proceeds from the issue of 100,000 ordinary shares	120
Proceeds from the sale of plant	300
	420

(b) The freehold property was acquired some years ago. The buildings element of the cost was estimated at £100,000 and the estimated useful life of the assets was 50 years at the time of purchase. As at 31 December 20X6 the property is to be revalued at £800,000.

(c) The plant which was sold had cost £350,000 and had a net book value of £274,000 as on 1 January 20X6. £36,000 depreciation is to be charged on plant and machinery for 20X6.

(d) The debentures have been in issue for some years. The 50p ordinary shares all rank for dividends at the end of the year.

(e) The directors wish to provide for:

    (i)   Debenture interest due
    (ii)   A final ordinary dividend of 2p per share
    (iii) A transfer to general reserve of £16,000
    (iv) Audit fees of £4,000

(f) Stock as at 31 December 20X6 was valued at £224,000 (cost). The cost of sales has been adjusted for this stock. There was no stock at 1 January 20X6.

(g) Taxation is to be ignored.

NOTES

Required

Prepare the final accounts of Wislon Ltd.

APPROACH AND SUGGESTED SOLUTION

(a) The debenture interest accrued is calculated as follows.

	£'000
Charge needed in P & L account (10% × £200,000)	20
Amount paid so far, as shown in trial balance	10
Accrual – presumably six months' interest now payable	10

(b) Depreciation on the freehold building is calculated as $\dfrac{£100,000}{50} = £2,000$.

The net book value of the freehold property is then £430,000 – £20,000 – £2,000 = £408,000 at the end of the year. When the property is revalued a reserve of £800,000 – £408,000 = £392,000 is then created.

(c) The profit on disposal of plant is calculated as proceeds £300,000 (per suspense account) less net book value £274,000, ie £26,000. The cost of the remaining plant is calculated at £830,000 – £350,000 = £480,000. The depreciation provision at the year end is made up of the following.

	£'000
Balance 1 January 20X6	222
Charge for 20X6	36
Less depreciation on disposals £(350 – 274)	(76)
	182

(d) The other item in the suspense account is dealt with as follows.

	£'000
Proceeds of issue of 100,000 ordinary shares	120
Less nominal value 100,000 × 50p	50
Excess of consideration over nominal value (= share premium)	70

(e) Appropriations of profit must be considered. The final ordinary dividend, shown as a current liability in the balance sheet, is calculated as follows.

$$(700,000 + 100,000 \text{ ordinary shares}) \times 2p = £16,000$$

(f) The transfer to general reserve increases that reserve to £71,000 + £16,000 = £87,000.

BPP
PUBLISHING

WISLON LIMITED
TRADING AND PROFIT AND LOSS ACCOUNT
FOR THE YEAR ENDING 31 DECEMBER 20X6

	£'000	£'000	£'000
Sales			2,695
Less cost of sales			2,156
Gross profit			539
Profit on disposal of plant			26
			565
Less expenses			
Wages and salaries		274	
Sundry expenses		107	
Light and heat		14	
Depreciation: freehold building		2	
plant		36	
Audit fees		4	
Debenture interest		20	
			457
Net profit			108
Appropriations		16	
Transfer to general reserve			
Dividends:			
Preference (paid)			
Ordinary: interim (paid)	7		
final (proposed)	8		
	16		
		31	
			47
Retained profit for the year			61
Retained profit brought forward			92
Retained profit carried forward			153

NOTES

WISLON LIMITED
BALANCE AS AT 31 DECEMBER 20X6

	Cost/val'n £'000	Dep'n £'000	NBV £'000
Fixed assets			
Tangible assets			
Freehold property	800	0	800
Plant and machinery	480	182	298
	1,280	182	1,098
Current assets			
Stock		224	
Debtors		179	
Cash		126	
		529	
Creditors: amounts falling due within one year			
Creditors	195		
Accrued audit fee	4		
Accrued debenture interest	10		
Proposed dividend	16		
		225	
Net current assets			304
Total assets less current liabilities			1,402
Creditors: amounts falling due after more than one year			(200)
10% debentures (secured)			1,202
Capital and reserves			
Called up share capital			
50p ordinary shares		400	
7% £1 preference shares		100	
			500
Reserves			
Share premium		70	
Revaluation reserve		392	
General reserve		87	
Profit and loss account		153	
			702
			1,202

BPP
PUBLISHING

Chapter roundup

You should now understand in more detail the nature of limited liability and how it affects shareholders.

- The shareholders in a limited company enjoy the benefit of limited liability. In return, they must put up with a heavy burden of accounting regulations.

- The net assets side of a company's balance sheet is similar to that of a sole trader. The capital side consists of share capital, and reserves owned by the equity shareholders.

- The items appearing in a limited company's accounts are closely defined by companies legislation.

Quick quiz

1   Who owns a limited company? Who manages its day-to-day activities?
(see para 1.1)

2   A public limited company is the same as a listed company. True or false?
(1.1)

3   Distinguish between the nominal value and the market value of a share.
(2.1)

4   Distinguish between a preference share and an ordinary share.   (2.1)

5   Name two kinds of non-distributable reserve.   (2.2)

6   What is a debenture loan?   (2.2)

Answers to activities

1   True:

   2.   Yes, and similarly the appropriation account of a company is different.

   3.   True. With companies, the owners (shareholders) appoint directors to be responsible for management. However, even if shareholders and directors are the same people there is a legal distinction between the two roles. Where a director receives a salary he is an employee and his salary is an expense; as a shareholder he receives a dividend which is an appropriation.

   5.   True.

   False:

   1.   Generally where there are numerous owners an enterprise will be incorporated, the obvious exception being partnerships.

   4.   Shareholders receive dividends rather than take drawings from the business. Both dividends and drawings are appropriations.

2   The annual accounts of a limited company have to be audited by a qualified person independent of the company. And the activities of listed companies are further regulated by the Stock Exchange's Yellow Book, which requires them, for example, to publish interim results in addition to their annual accounts.

3   The missing words are: liability, owners, capital, advantage, not, resources.

4   The point to be aware of is that suppliers extending credit to the business, or a bank offering loan or overdraft finance, will often be perfectly well aware that the 'company' is little more than a legal fiction and will insist on personal guarantees from the directors/shareholders before putting themselves at risk. If the company's assets become insufficient to meet liabilities, creditors will enforce the personal guarantees and the owners of the company may after all have to sell their houses.

5

Number of shares	Nominal value	Total value £
100,000	£1	100,000
200,000	50p	100,000
500,000	40p	200,000
850,000	10p	85,000

6   To begin with, ignore the figures for authorised capital: dividends are paid only on shares actually in issue.

If an ordinary dividend is proposed, the preference dividends will also have to be paid. The total to be paid is therefore as follows.

		£
Preference dividend	(7% × £12,000)	840
Ordinary dividend	(12% × £80,000)	9,600
		10,440

7   Issued share capital has increased from £7,500 to £9,000; this means that 3,000 shares (nominal value 50p each) have been issued. The amount received for the shares was £1,500 nominal value, plus £1,500 share premium (£3,500 − £2,000), ie £3,000 in total. The issue price was therefore £1 per share.

8   The entire net assets of a company are balanced by shareholders' capital (being share capital plus reserves). When assets are distributed to shareholders (for example in the form of a cash dividend), the amount of net assets reduces and, as the accounting equation makes clear, capital must also reduce.

What is meant by 'distributable reserves' is that the company's assets can be distributed up to the point where the value of such reserves falls to zero. To distribute assets any further would lead to a reduction in non-distributable reserves (and/or share capital), which is generally not permissible.

In the context of a freehold revaluation, the decision to disclose an asset in the balance sheet at a higher value does not generate any funds for the business. However, *selling* the asset at the higher value would be a different matter. It would therefore be quite misleading to say that the cash available for distribution in the case of X Ltd has suddenly risen by £370,700.

9   Shareholders: 1; 5.

Debenture holders: 2; 3; 4; 6.

10   For 20X5, the profit and loss account will include the company's then estimate of its tax charge for the year, namely £170,000.

The charge in 20X6 will comprise the estimated tax (£204,000) on 20X6 profits, plus the amount under-estimated in 20X5 – a total of £212,500.

Further question practice

Now try the following practice questions at the end of this text

Multiple choice questions: **51–58**

Exam style question: **8**

Chapter 9 :
CASH FLOW STATEMENTS

Introduction

In the long run, a profit will result in an increase in the company's cash balance but, as Keynes observed, 'in the long run we are all dead'. In the short run, the making of a profit will not necessarily result in an increased cash balance. The observation leads us to two questions. The first relates to the importance of the distinction between cash and profit. The second is concerned with the usefulness of the information provided by the balance sheet and profit and loss account in the problem of deciding whether the company has, or will be able to generate, sufficient cash to finance its operations.

The importance of the distinction between cash and profit and the scant attention paid to this by the profit and loss account has resulted in the development of *cash flow statements*.

Your objectives

After completing this chapter you should:

(a)   Understand the differences between profits and cash surpluses

(b)   Understand the purpose of cash flow statements and how they are prepared

1 PROFITS AND CASH FLOW

To be successful in business, an enterprise must make a profit. Profits are needed to pay dividends to shareholders (and shareholders expect to receive dividends as a return on their investment in ownership of the business) and to reward partners or proprietors. Some profits are retained within the business as reserves or as proprietor's funds, to finance the development and growth of the business. We can therefore say that although a firm may be able to bear occasional losses, it must be profitable in the long term. A loss means that the value of sales in a period is less than the value of resources used up in making the sales, so that a loss causes a reduction in the overall value of a business. Long-term losses will lead to the eventual collapse of a firm.

In addition to being *profitable* in order to survive and grow, it is also necessary for a firm to 'pay its way': to *pay in cash* for the goods and services and capital equipment it buys, the workforce it employs and the other expenses (such as rent, rates and taxation) that it incurs. If a firm does not pay its bills when they are due, it will first of all lose the goodwill of its suppliers or workforce and may then be driven into liquidation. It is therefore necessary to be not just profitable, but also capable of obtaining cash to meet demand for payment.

Activity 1

Profits and cash surpluses are not the same thing for a number of reasons. For example, cash may be obtained from a transaction which has nothing to do with profit or loss, such as a share issue. Fill in the missing entries in the following table to ensure you understand the impact on cash flow and profit of the items listed.

Item	Effect on cash flow	Effect on profit
Fixed asset purchased 2 years ago		
New issue of shares for cash		
Increase in bank overdraft		
New fixed asset purchased for cash		
Fixed asset sold during year		

The profit and loss account reports the total value of sales in a year. If goods are sold on credit, the cash receipts will differ from the value of sales. The relationship between sales and receipts is as follows, with illustrative figures.

	£
Debtors owing money at the start of the year	20,000
Sales during the year	300,000
Total money due from customers	320,000
Less debtors owing money at the end of the year	30,000
Cash receipts from debtors during the year	290,000

Similarly, the profit and loss account reports the cost of goods sold during the year. However, if materials are bought on credit, the cash payments to suppliers will be different from the value of materials purchased. And in addition, if some materials are bought and added to stocks rather than sold (ie if there is an increase in stocks during the year) total purchases will be different from the materials cost of sales. (In the same way, a firm may decide to run down its stocks and sell goods without making good the stocks used up by purchasing replacement items.)

The relationship between the cost of materials in the materials cost of sales and cash payments for materials purchased is as follows (again with illustrative figures).

	£
Opening stocks (at the start of the year)	3,000
Add purchases during the year	70,000
	73,000
Less closing stocks at the end of the year	5,000
Equals materials cost in the cost of sales	68,000
Payments owed to creditors at the start of the year	6,000
Add purchases during the year	70,000
	76,000
Less payments still owing to creditors at the end of the year	4,000
Equals cash payments to creditors during the year	72,000

Information about cash receipts and payments can add to our understanding of a firm's operations and financial stability. Whereas a profit and loss statement reports on profitability, cash flow statements report on *liquidity*.

Activity 2

Try to think of (a) a transaction which improves cash flow but does not increase profit, (b) a transaction which depresses cash flow but does not reduce profit, (c) a transaction which increases profit but does not contribute to cash flow, (d) a transaction which reduces profit but does not depress cash flow.

---

2 CASH FLOW STATEMENTS

2.1 Cash flow

It can be argued that 'profit' does not always give a useful or meaningful picture of a company's operations. Readers of a company's financial statements might even be misled by a reported profit figure. Shareholders, employees, creditors and management might interpret a company's making a profit in different ways.

(a) Shareholders might believe that if a company makes a profit after tax, of say, £100,000 then this is the amount which it could afford to pay as a dividend. Unless the company has sufficient cash available to stay in business and also to pay a dividend, the shareholders' expectation would be wrong.

(b) Employees might believe that if a company makes profits, it can afford to pay higher wages next year. This opinion may not be correct: the ability to pay wages depends on the availability of cash.

(c) Creditors might consider that a profitable company is a going concern. But this may not be so. For example, if a company builds up large amounts of unsold stocks of goods, their cost would not be chargeable against profits, but cash would have been used up in making them, thus weakening the company's liquid resources.

(d)   Management might suppose that if their company makes a profit, and reinvests some of those profits, then the company must be expanding. This is not the case: in a period of inflation, a company might have insufficient retained profits to prevent the operating capability of the firm from declining.

The survival of a business entity depends not so much on profits as on its ability to pay its debts when they fall due. Such payments might include 'profit and loss' items such as material purchases, wages, interest and taxation, but also capital payments for new fixed assets and the repayment of loan capital when this falls due (for example on the redemption of debentures).

From these examples, it may be apparent that a company's performance and prospects depend not so much on the 'profits' earned in a period, but more realistically on liquidity: cash flows. A cash flow statement goes a long way toward meeting the criticisms of a profit and loss account. FRS 1 (revised) *Cash flow statements* was published in October 1996. You do not need to know the prescribed format in detail, but you should know how to construct a cash flow statement and what its aims are.

The aim of a cash flow statement should be to assist users:

(a)   To assess the enterprise's ability to generate positive net cash flows in the future

(b)   To assess its ability to meet its obligations to service loans, pay dividends and so on

(c)   To assess the reasons for differences between reported profit and cash flows

(d)   To assess the effect on its finances of major transactions in the year

The statement should therefore show changes in cash and cash equivalents rather than in working capital. The opening and closing figures given for cash etc should be those shown in the balance sheet. Receipts and payments should not be netted off. Non-cash transactions should be reported separately by note (for example purchasing an asset with lease finance) and a reconciliation of net income to net cash flow from operating activities should be given.

A cash flow statement can be a historical statement or a forecast. It shows the sources and uses of cash over a period of time, whereas a cash budget shows expected sources and uses of cash daily, weekly or monthly, to help in management of working capital.

Activity 3   **(15 minutes)**

The statement should classify cash receipts and payments as resulting from investing, financing or operating activities. Try classifying the following receipts and payments.

1   Purchase of an asset for cash.

2   Cash repayment of a loan.

3   Issue of shares for cash.

4   Making a loan.

5   Borrowing money.

6   Receipts from customers.

7   Paying dividends.

2.2 FRS 1 *Cash flow statements*

Objective

The FRS begins with the following statement.

The objective of this FRS is to ensure that reporting entities falling within its scope:

- (a) report their cash generation and cash absorption for a period by highlighting the significant components of cash flow in a way that facilitates comparison of the cash flow performance of different businesses; and

- (b) provide information that assists in the assessment of their liquidity, solvency and financial adaptability.

Scope

The FRS applies to all financial statements intended to give a true and fair view of the financial position and profit or loss (or income and expenditure), except those of various exempt bodies in group accounts situations or where the content of the financial statement is governed by other statutes or regulatory regimes. In addition, small entities are excluded as defined by companies legislation.

Format of the cash flow statement

An example is given of the format of a cash flow statement for a single company and this is reproduced below.

A cash flow statement should list its cash flows for the period classified under the following standard headings.

- (a) Operating activities (using either the direct or indirect method)

- (b) Returns on investments and servicing of finance

- (c) Taxation

- (d) Capital expenditure and financial investment

- (e) Acquisitions and disposals

- (f) Equity dividends paid

- (g) Management of liquid resources

- (h) Financing

The last two headings can be shown in a single section provided a subtotal is given for each heading.

Individual categories of inflows and outflows under the standard headings should be disclosed separately either in the cash flow statements or in a note to it unless they are allowed to be shown net. Cash inflows and outflows may be shown net if they relate to the management of liquid resources or financing and the inflows and outflows either:

- (a) Relate in substance to a single financing transaction, or

- (b) Are due to short maturities and high turnover occurring from rollover or reissue (for example, short-term deposits): *see below.

The requirement to show cash inflows and outflows separately does not apply to cash flows relating to operating activities.

Each cash flow should be classified according to the substance of the transaction giving rise to it.

Links to other primary statements

Because the information given by a cash flow statement is best appreciated in the context of the information given by the other primary statements, the FRS requires two reconciliations, between:

    (a)   Operating profit and the net cash flow from operating activities

    (b)   The movement in cash in the period and the movement in net debt

Neither reconciliation forms part of the cash flow statement but each may be given either adjoining the statement or in a separate note.

The *movement in net debt* should identify the following components and reconcile these to the opening and closing balance sheet amount.

    (a)   The cash flows of the entity

    (b)   The acquisition or disposal of subsidiary undertakings (excluding cash balances)

    (c)   Other non-cash changes

    (d)   The recognition of changes in market value and exchange rate movements

2.3   Classification of cash flows by standard heading

Operating activities

Cash flows from operating activities are in general the cash effects of transactions and other events relating to operating or trading activities, normally shown in the profit and loss account in arriving at operating profit. They include cash flows in respect of operating items relating to provisions, whether or not the provision was included in operating profit.

A reconciliation between the operating profit reported in the profit and loss account and the net cash flow from operating activities should be given either adjoining the cash flow statement or as a note. The reconciliation is not part of the cash flow statement: if adjoining the cash flow statement, it should be clearly labelled and kept separate. The reconciliation should disclose separately the movements in stocks, debtors and creditors related to operating activities and other differences between cash flows and profits.

Returns on investments and servicing of finance

These are receipts resulting from the ownership of an investment and payments to providers of finance and non-equity shareholders (for example the holders of preference shares).

Cash inflows from returns on investments and servicing of finance include:

    (a)   Interest received, including any related tax recovered

    (b)   Dividends received, net of any tax credits

Cash outflows from returns on investments and servicing of finance include:

    (a)   Interest paid (even if capitalised), including any tax deducted and paid to the relevant tax authority

(b)   Cash flows that are treated as finance costs (this will include issue costs on debt and non-equity share capital)

(c)   The interest element of finance lease rental payments

(d)   Dividends paid on non-equity shares of the entity

Taxation

These are cash flows to or from taxation authorities in respect of the reporting entity's revenue and capital profits. VAT and other sales taxes are discussed below.

Taxation cash inflows include cash receipts from the relevant tax authority of tax rebates, claims or returns of overpayments.

Taxation cash outflows include cash payments of tax to the relevant tax authority.

Capital expenditure and financial investment

These cash flows are those related to the acquisition or disposal of any fixed asset other than one required to be classified under 'acquisitions and disposals' (discussed below), and any current asset investment not included in liquid resources (also dealt with below). If no cash flows relating to financial investment fall to be included under this heading the caption may be reduced to 'capital expenditure'.

The cash inflows here include:

(a)   Receipts from sales or disposals of property, plant or equipment

(b)   Receipts from the repayment of the reporting entity's loans to other entities

Cash outflows in this category include:

(a)   Payments to acquire property, plant or equipment

(b)   Loans made by the reporting entity

Acquisitions and disposals

These cash flows are related to the acquisition or disposal of any trade or business, or of an investment in an entity that is either an associate, a joint venture, or a subsidiary undertaking (these group matters are beyond the scope of your syllabus).

Cash inflows here include receipts from sales of trades or businesses.

Cash outflows here include payments to acquire trades or businesses.

Equity dividends paid

The cash outflows are dividends paid on the reporting entity's equity shares, excluding any advance corporation tax.

Management of liquid resources

This section should include cash flows in respect of liquid resources as defined above. Each entity should explain what it includes as liquid resources and any changes in its policy. The cash flows in this section can be shown in a single section with those under 'financing' provided that separate subtotals for each are given.

Cash inflows include:

(a)   Withdrawals from short-term deposits not qualifying as cash in so far as not netted under *above

(b)   Inflows from disposal or redemption of any other investments held as liquid resources

Cash outflows include:

(a)   Payments into short-term deposits not qualifying as cash in so far as not netted under *above

(b)   Outflows to acquire any other investments held as liquid resources

Financing

Financing cash flows comprise receipts or repayments of principal from or to external providers of finance. The cash flows in this section can be shown in a single section with those under 'management of liquid resources' provided that separate subtotals for each are given.

Financing cash inflows include:

(a)   Receipts from issuing shares or other equity instruments

(b)   Receipts from issuing debentures, loans and from other long-term and short-term borrowings (other than overdrafts)

Financing cash outflows include:

(a)   Repayments of amounts borrowed (other than overdrafts)

(b)   The capital element of finance lease rental payments

(c)   Payments to reacquire or redeem the entity's shares

(d)   Payments of expenses or commission on any issue of equity shares

---

EXAMPLE: SINGLE COMPANY

The following example is provided by the standard for a single company.

XYZ LIMITED

CASH FLOW STATEMENT FOR THE YEAR ENDED 31 DECEMBER 20X6

Reconciliation of operating profit to net cash inflow from operating activities

	£'000
Operating profit	6,022
Depreciation charges	899
Increase in stocks	(194)
Increase in debtors	(72)
Increase in creditors	234
Net cash inflow from operating activities	6,899

BPP
PUBLISHING

NOTES

CASH FLOW STATEMENT

	£'000
Net cash inflow from operating activities	6,889
Returns on investments and servicing of finance (note 1)	2,999
Taxation	(2,922)
Capital expenditure	(1,525)
	5,441
Equity dividends paid	(2,417)
	3,024
Management of liquid resources (note 1)	(450)
Financing (note 1)	57
Increase in cash	2,631

Reconciliation of net cash flow to movement in net debt (note 2)

	£'000	£'000
Increase in cash in the period	2,631	
Cash to repurchase debenture	149	
Cash used to increase liquid resources	450	
Change in net debt*		3,230
Net debt at 1.1.X6		(2,903)
Net funds at 31.12.X6		327

*In this example all change in net debt are cash flows.

NOTES TO THE CASH FLOW STATEMENT

	£'000	£'000
1 *Gross cash flows*		
Returns on investments and servicing of finance		
Interest received	3,011	
Interest paid	(12)	
		2,999
Capital expenditure		
Payments to acquire intangible fixed assets	(71)	
Payments to acquire tangible fixed assets	(1,496)	
Receipts from sales of tangible fixed assets	42	
		(1,525)
Management of liquid resources		
Purchase of treasury bills	(650)	
Sale of treasury bills	200	
		(450)
Financing		
Issue of ordinary share capital	211	
Repurchase of debenture loan	(149)	
Expenses paid in connection with share issues	(5)	
		57

BPP PUBLISHING

2   *Analysis of changes in net debt*

	As at 1 Jan 20X6 £'000	Cash flows £'000	Other changes £'000	At 31 Dec 20X6 £'000
Cash in hand, at bank	42	847		889
Overdrafts	(1,784)	1,784		
		2,631		
Debt due within 1 year	(149)	149	(230)	(230)
Debt due after 1 year	(1,262)		230	(1,032)
Current asset investments	250	450		700
Total	(2,903)	3,230	0	327

Activity 4   **(15 minutes)**

The directors of Flail Ltd obtain the following information in respect of projected cash flows for the year to 31 December 20X7.

(a)   Fixed asset purchases for cash will be £3,000.

(b)   Further expenses will be:

   (i)   Purchases from suppliers – £18,750 (£4,125 owed at the year end, £2,550 at start)

   (ii)   Wages and salaries – £11,250 (£600 owed at the year end, £750 at start)

   (iii)   Loan interest – £1,575

(c)   Turnover will be £36,000 (£450 debtors at the year end, £900 debtors at start).

(d)   Interest on bank deposits will be £150.

(e)   A capital repayment of £5,250 will be made on a loan.

(f)   A dividend of £5,000 will be proposed and last year's final dividend of £4,000 paid.

(g)   Corporation tax of £2,300 will be paid in respect of 20X6.

Prepare the cash flow forecast for the year to 31 December 20X7.

2.4   Deriving the figures for a cash flow statement

In studying the example of Flail Ltd, you may have wondered how in practice the figures would have been derived.

The answer is that such figures could only be derived from the accounting records. However, it is possible to prepare a cash flow statement from the figures shown in published accounts (as is always done in preparing a funds flow statement). The two methods are referred to as the *direct method* and the *indirect method*. To arrive at a figure of net cash flow from operating activities we can *either* calculate as follows:

	£
Cash received from customers	12,000
Cash paid to suppliers	(8,100)
Cash paid to and on behalf of employees	(2,300)
Other cash payments	(630)
Net increase in cash	970

Or alternatively as follows (the indirect method):

	£
Operating profit	3,500
Depreciation	470
Increase in stocks	(2,800)
Decrease in debtors	1,000
Decrease in creditors	(1,200)
Net increase in cash	970

Activity 5

The summarised balance sheets of Cash flow Ltd at 30 June 20X5 and 20X6 are given below. Calculate the net cash flow from operating activities, assuming no tax or dividends.

		30 June 20X5	30 June 20X6
		£	£
Fixed assets:	cost	12,000	13,600
	depreciation	6,500	7,800
		5,500	5,800
Stock		4,000	5,200
Debtors		6,000	4,700
Cash		1,800	850
		17,300	16,550
Shareholders' funds		13,000	14,700
Creditors		4,300	1,850
		17,300	16,550

If you have worked through the above activity, you will have seen that the net cash inflow from operating activities is very much less than the profit earned. This is an important point for users of accounts and FRS 1 accordingly requires disclosure of the items reconciling operating profit to net cash flow from operating activities. It is worth looking briefly at the nature of these items.

(a) *Depreciation*. To arrive at our figure of operating profit we would deduct an amount to reflect depreciation of our fixed assets. But although this is correctly shown as a reduction in profit, it is *not* a cash outflow. If cash flows are what we are interested in, we must add back amounts deducted in respect of depreciation. The same goes for a loss on disposal of a fixed asset, which in effect is an extra amount of depreciation charged to reflect the fact that we have under-depreciated the asset in the past. Conversely, a *profit* on disposal would have inflated our profit figure without boosting cash flow, and would therefore have to be *deducted* as part of the reconciliation.

(b) *Increase in debtors*. If our debtors have increased over the year, it means that the value of our sales during the year (amounts invoiced to customers for goods and services provided) has not been matched by cash sums actually received from the customers. This balance outstanding is mounting because their payments are not keeping up with the amounts they are buying from us. The effect of this is that part of the sales revenue which, quite properly, is accounted for in reaching our profit figure has not led to an actual cash inflow. The increase in debtors balances – the excess of sales revenue over cash receipts – needs to be stripped out, and is therefore a deduction in the reconciliation.

The opposite applies, of course, if debtor balances have *reduced* over the year. In this case, cash received from debtors is *greater* than the sales figure might suggest.

(c) *Increase in stocks*. Stock in the balance sheet at the year end represents an asset for which money has been paid, but which has not been charged against profits for the period. To the extent that closing stock exceeds opening stock the profit and loss account therefore understates the amount of cash paid out to suppliers. To compensate for this, the increase in stock over the year is shown as a deduction in reconciling operating profit to net cash flow from operating activities.

Once again, it is obvious that a *decrease* in stock levels over the year would be a *positive* item in the reconciliation.

(d) *Increase in creditors*. The situation here is the reverse of that described under debtors. If the amounts we owe to our suppliers have increased over the year, it means that the payments we have made to them have not kept up with the volume of our purchases from them. To that extent, the amounts charged as cost of sales in the profit and loss account *overstate* the actual cash outflows. An increase in creditors is therefore a positive item in the reconciliation, and a decrease in creditors is a negative item.

Activity 6

Can you detect the simplifying assumption which has been made in the above discussion? Re-read the first sentence under 'Increase in stocks' and see if you can put your finger on it.

Now try to fortify your understanding of this area by working through a fuller example.

EXAMPLE: OUTFLOW LTD

The balance sheets of Outflow Ltd at 30 June 20X5 and 20X6 are set out below.

	20X6		20X5	
	£	£	£	£
Freehold property (revalued in 20X6)		30,000		16,000
Plant and machinery				
Cost at 1 July 20X5	8,000		8,000	
Acquisitions at cost	4,500		0	
Disposals at cost	(2,200)		0	
	10,300		8,000	
Depreciation	2,800		1,900	
		7,500		6,100
		37,500		22,100
Stock	12,000		7,800	
Debtors	7,600		5,900	
Balance at bank	0		850	
		19,600		14,550
		57,100		36,650
Bank overdraft	3,500		0	
Loan	0		1,000	
Creditors	5,250		5,000	
		8,750		6,000
		48,350		30,650
Share capital		10,000		8,500
Share premium account		1,000		0
Revaluation reserve		14,000		0
Profit and loss reserve		23,350		22,150
		48,350		30,650

The machinery disposed of had a net book value of £550 and was sold for £800.

Prepare a cash flow statement for the year ended 30 June 20X6.

BPP
PUBLISHING

ANSWER

OUTFLOW LIMITED
CASH FLOW STATEMENT FOR THE YEAR ENDED 30 JUNE 20X6

	£	£
Net cash outflow from operating activities		(2,150)
Capital expenditure		
Payments to acquire tangible fixed assets	(4,500)	
Receipts from sale of tangible fixed assets	800	
Net cash outflow from investing activities		(3,700)
Net cash flow before financing		(5,850)
Management of liquid resources		
Issue of share capital	2,500	
Repayment of loan	(1,000)	
Net cash outflow from financing		1,500
Decrease in cash		(4,350)

Note to the cash flow statement: reconciliation of operating profit to net cash outflow from operating activities.

	£
Operating profit (£23,350 – £22,150)	1,200
Depreciation (£2,800 – (£1,900 (£1,650))	2,550
Profit on sale of tangible fixed assets	(250)
Increase in stocks	(4,200)
Increase in debtors	(1,700)
Increase in creditors	250
Net cash outflow from operating activities	(2,150)

Activity 7

Check your understanding of the above example. Are you sure you know how the figures were derived for:

(a) Issue of share capital?

(b) Depreciation?

2.5 The advantages of cash flow accounting

Suggest some advantages of cash flow accounting.

The advantages of cash flow accounting are as follows.

(a)   Survival in business depends on the ability to generate cash. Cash flow accounting directs attention towards this critical issue.

(b)   Cash flow is more objective than 'profit', which is dependent on accounting conventions and concepts.

(c)   Creditors (long and short-term) are more interested in an entity's ability to repay them than in its profitability. Whereas 'profits' might indicate that cash is likely to be available, cash flow accounting is more direct with its message.

(d)   Cash flow reporting provides a better means of comparing the results of different companies than traditional profit reporting.

(e)   Cash flow reporting satisfies the needs of all users better.

   (i)   For management, it provides the sort of information on which decisions should be taken (in management accounting, 'relevant costs' to a decision are future cash flows); traditional profit accounting does not help with decision-making.

   (ii)   For shareholders and auditors, cash flow accounting can provide a satisfactory basis for stewardship accounting.

   (iii) As described previously, the information needs of creditors and employees will be better served by cash flow accounting.

(f)   Cash flow forecasts are easier to prepare, as well as more useful, than profit forecasts.

(g)   Cash is an easy, familiar concept for users to understand.

You should give some thought to the possible *disadvantages* of cash flow accounting which are essentially the advantages of accruals accounting. There is also the practical problem that few businesses would otherwise keep historical cash flow information in the form needed to prepare a historical cash flow statement and so extra record keeping is likely to be necessary.

Chapter roundup

Cash is critical to the survival of a business. You should now appreciate the following points.

*   Profits are not the same as cash flows. A company can have healthy profits, but poor cash flow or vice versa.

*   A cash flow statement shows changes in cash (and cash equivalents) over a period.

In the next chapter we draw together the financial statements by interpreting the figures they include.

Quick quiz

1   List four examples of transactions which affect profit differently from their effect on cash flow. (see section 1)

2   Explain the limitations of a profit figure for:

    (a)   Shareholders

    (b)   Employees

    (c)   Creditors

    (d)   Management (2.1)

3   What three categories of cash receipts and payments should be identified in a cash flow statement? (2.2)

4   Describe the direct and the indirect methods of deriving net cash flow from operating activities. (2.4)

Answers to activities

1

Item	Effect on cash flow	Effect on profit
Fixed asset purchased 2 years ago	None	Depreciation charge
New issue of shares for cash	Cash inflow	Possible effect on earnings per share*
Increase in bank overdraft	Cash inflow	Increase in interest charge
New fixed asset purchased for cash	Cash outflow	Depreciation charge
Fixed asset sold during year	Cash inflow	Profit or loss on sale

    * Explained in the next chapter.

2   (a)   A debtor pays the amount he owes; or a bank loan is received; or new capital is injected into the business.

    (b)   Payment is made to a creditor to reduce the amount owing; or a bank loan is repaid; or a fixed asset is purchased (although in due course profits will be reduced by depreciation charges).

    (c)   This is perhaps the trickiest part. The most common examples in practice are probably those concerned with the reduction or elimination of provisions. For example, if too much depreciation was charged against profits in previous years, a business might decide to reduce the accumulated provision in the current year. This improves profits (it is the opposite of a depreciation charge) but does not generate any cash.

    (d)   The simplest example (the reverse of (c) above) is the depreciation charge for the year. Another example would be the write-off of a bad debt.

3   You should have included 1 and 4 as investing activities, 2, 3, 5 and 7 as financing activities and 6 as an operating activity. Operating activities also include payments to employees and suppliers and any other cash flows from transactions not classified as investing or financing.

NOTES

4 FLAIL LIMITED
STATEMENT OF FORECAST CASH FLOWS
FOR THE YEAR ENDING 31 DECEMBER 20X7

	£	£
Operating activities		
Cash received from customers		
(£36,000 + £900 – £450)	36,450	
Cash paid to suppliers		
(£18,750 + £2,550 – £4,125)	(17,175)	
Cash paid to and on behalf of employees		
(£11,250 + £750 –£600)	(11,400)	
Interest paid	(1,575)	
Interest received	150	
Paid to tax authorities on profits	(2,300)	
Cash flow from operating activities		4,150
Capital expenditure	(3,000)	
Purchase of fixed assets	(4,000)	
Equity dividends paid		(7,000)
		(2,850)
Management of liquid resources		
Repayment of medium-term loan		5,250
Cash flow from financing activities		
Forecast net decrease in cash		(8,100)

5

	£
Profit for the year	1,700
Depreciation	1,300
Increase in stock	(1,200)
Decrease in debtors	1,300
Decrease in creditors	(2,450)
	650

6 The point is that stock in the balance sheet at the year end does not, strictly, represent 'an asset for which money has been paid'. In practice, some of the closing stock would not have been paid for; its cost would be included in creditors. In theory, we should isolate this amount and make an appropriate adjustment in our cash flow statement. In practice, it is not thought worthwhile to dig into the accounting records to do this, especially in view of the confusion that would be caused to users of accounts, who would not be able to understand why the figure for 'increase/decrease in stock' in the cash flow statement does not accord with the change in stock levels indicated by the balance sheet.

7 (a) The share capital account has risen from £8,500 to £10,000 over the year. This, however, only reflects the nominal value of the shares issued. It is clear that the amount actually received for the shares exceeded this nominal value by £1,000: that is how the balance on share premium account arose. The total received is therefore £10,000 + £1,000 – £8,500 = £2,500.

(b)		£	£
Accumulated depreciation at 30 June 20X6			1,900
Depreciation eliminated on disposal:			
Cost of asset disposed of		2,200	
Net book value of asset disposed of		550	
Accumulated depreciation on asset disposed of			1,650
			250
Accumulated depreciation at 30 June 20X6			2,800
∴ Depreciation charged for the year			2,550

Further question practice

Now try the following practice question at the end of this text

Exam style question: **9**

Chapter 10 :
INTERPRETATION OF FINANCIAL STATEMENTS

Introduction

So far in this book we have been concerned with the types of entity that prepare accounts and the form and content of the accounts they prepare. But accounting is not merely a mechanical shuffling of debits and credits. The accounts prepared by an organisation can help us to assess profitability and financial stability. In this chapter, we are concerned with *interpreting* accounts, and particularly the accounts of limited companies.

Your objectives

After completing this chapter you should:

(a)   Be aware of the major sources of information for the analysis of company accounts

(b)   Know how to calculate a number of the more important accounting ratios

1 INTERPRETING ACCOUNTS

1.1 Sources of information

What sources of information can help us in the task of interpreting accounts?

- The first point of reference, obviously, is the main accounting statements, the balance sheet and profit and loss account. In this chapter and the next we look at how these statements can contribute to our understanding of an organisation by the use of ratios which enable us to compare one organisation with another, and to identify trends within a single organisation over a period of time.

- There are also other sources of information within a company's accounts which help to supplement the balance sheet and profit and loss account. In Chapter 12 we will look briefly at the information contained in the directors' report, the auditor's report and the chairman's statement.

Activity 1

Our task in this chapter is to show how an examination of a set of accounts can help us to assess the financial position of a business. But for a moment put yourself in the position of an individual investor with an interest in a particular company's performance (perhaps he has bought a few shares in British Telecom). Where, in practice, does he derive his information about how well the company is doing?

1.2 Key accounting ratios

The profit and loss account and the balance sheet are both sources of useful information about the condition of a business. The analysis and interpretation of these statements can be carried out by calculating certain ratios, between one item and another, and then using the ratios for comparison, either:

(a) Between one year and the next for a particular business, in order to identify any trends, or significantly better or worse results than before or

(b) Between one business and another, to establish which business has performed better, and in what ways

There are three principal ratios which can be used to measure how efficiently the operations of a business have been managed. These are:

(a) Profit margin

(b) Asset turnover

(c) Return on capital employed

Definition

Profit margin is the ratio of profit to sales, and may also be called 'profit percentage'.

For example, if a company makes a profit of £20,000 on sales of £100,000 its profit percentage or profit margin is 20%. This also means that its costs are 80% of sales. A high profit margin indicates that *either*:

(a)   Costs are being kept well under control (because if the ratio of costs to sales goes down, the profit margin will automatically go up. For example, if the cost:sales ratio changes from 80% to 75%, the profit margin will go up from 20% to 25%), *or*

(b)   Sales prices are high. For example, if a company sells goods for £100,000 and makes a profit of £16,000 costs would be £84,000 and the profit margin 16%. Now if the company can raise selling prices by 20% without affecting the volume of goods sold or their costs, to give total sales of £120,000, profits would rise by the amount of revenue increase (£20,000) to £36,000 and the profit margin would also rise (from 16% to 30%)

Definition

> Asset turnover is the ratio of sales turnover in a year to the amount of capital employed.

For example, if a company has sales in 20X6 of £720,000 and has assets of £360,000, the asset turnover will be:

$$\frac{£720,000}{£360,000} = 2 \text{ times}$$

This means that for every £1 of assets employed, the company can generate sales turnover of £2 per annum. To use assets more efficiently, managers should try to create a higher volume of sales and a higher asset turnover ratio. For example, suppose that our firm with assets of £360,000 can increase its sales turnover from £720,000 to £900,000 per annum. The asset turnover would improve to:

$$\frac{£900,000}{£360,000} = 2.5 \text{ times}$$

The significance of this improvement is that if a business can create more sales turnover from the same amount of assets it should make larger profits (because of the increase in sales) without having to increase the size of its investment.

Definition

> *Return on capital employed* (ROCE) is the amount of profit as a percentage of capital employed.

If a company makes a profit of £30,000, we do not know how good or bad the result is until we look at the amount of capital which has been invested to achieve the profit. £30,000 might be a good sized profit for a small firm, but it would not be good enough for a 'giant' firm such as Marks and Spencer. For this reason, it is helpful to measure performance by relating profits to capital employed, and because this seems to be the only satisfactory ratio or percentage which judges profits in relation to the size of business, it is sometimes called the *primary ratio* in financial analysis.

Activity 2

You may already have realised that there is a mathematical connection between ROCE, profit margin (PM) and asset turnover (AT). Which of the following statements expresses that relationship?

(a) $AT = PM \times ROCE$

(b) $ROCE = PM \times AT$

(c) $AT = PM/ROCE$

If we accept that ROCE is the single most important measure of business performance, comparing profit with the amount of capital invested, we can go on to say that business performance is dependent on two separate 'subsidiary' factors, each of which contributes to ROCE:

(a)   Profit margin

(b)   Asset turnover

For this reason, just as ROCE is sometimes called the primary ratio, the profit margin and asset turnover ratios are sometimes called the *secondary ratios*.

Activity 3

The implications of this relationship must be understood. The following questions and answers should help clarify it for you.

1   Company A decides to sell its products at a fairly high price, making a profit margin of 10%. It has a target ROCE of 20%. What should its asset turnover be?

2   Company B has cut its prices so that it only makes a $2\frac{1}{2}\%$ margin. Again it has a target ROCE of 20%. What should its asset turnover be?

3   Company C has a target ROCE of 20%. What profit margin does company C require if it has an asset turnover of 2 times?

NOTES

The inter-relationship between profit margin and asset turnover

Activity 4

Mark the following statements as true or false.

1   A higher return on capital employed may be obtained by increasing the profit margin.

2   The only way to increase the profit margin is by increasing prices.

3   If prices are raised it is likely that sales demand will fall, with the possible consequence that asset turnover will also decline.

4   The ROCE always improves with an increase in *profit margin*.

Activity 5

Suppose that Swings and Roundabouts Ltd achieved the following results in 20X6.

Sales	£100,000
Profit	£5,000
Capital employed	£20,000

The company's management wish to decide whether to raise its selling prices. They think that if they do so, they can raise the profit margin to 10% and by introducing extra capital of £55,000, sales turnover could be increased to £150,000.

Calculate ROCE, profit margin and asset turnover achieved in 20X6. What will ROCE, profit margin and asset turnover be in 20X7 if management go ahead with their plans?

Whose return and whose capital employed?

Most of the providers of finance to a business expect some return on their investment.

Activity 6

Fill in the missing entries in the following table to make sure you know what they each receive.

Provider of finance	Return on investment
Trade creditor	
Bank: overdraft	
Debenture holder	
Ordinary shareholder	
Preference shareholder	

PUBLISHING

So when we refer to 'return' we must be clear in our mind about which providers of finance we are concerned with, and we should relate the return earned for those providers of finance to the amount of capital they are providing.

(a) If 'return' is profit after tax, it is return earned by ordinary and preference shareholders. The capital employed by these investors is:

   (i) The nominal value of preference shares

   (ii) The nominal value of ordinary shares

   (iii) The amount in various reserves, because reserves are surpluses or profits retained in a business and 'owned' by the equity investors – ie the ordinary shareholders in a company

(b) If 'return' is profit after tax and preference dividend, the left-over return is for ordinary shareholders, and is called *earnings*. The return on equity capital is:

$$\frac{\text{Earnings}}{\text{Ordinary share capital plus reserves}}$$

(c) If we prefer to consider the business as a whole, then the fixed assets and net current assets are financed by long-term capital which may include loan creditors as well as shareholders. The fund available to satisfy the claims of all these providers of finance is the profit before interest payments and taxation. In this case ROCE may be calculated as:

$$\frac{\text{Profit before intrest and tax (PBIT)}}{\text{Loan capital plus share capital plus reserves}}$$

which equals:

$$\frac{\text{PBIT}}{\text{Fixed assets plus net current assets}}$$

EXAMPLE: DIFFERENT WAYS OF CALCULATING ROCE

Suppose that Draught Ltd reports the following figures.

PROFIT AND LOSS ACCOUNT FOR 20X6 (EXTRACT)

	£
Profit before interest and tax	120,000
Interest	(20,000)
Profit before tax	100,000
Taxation	(40,000)
Profit after tax	60,000
Preference dividend	(1,000)
Profit available for ordinary shareholders (= earnings)	59,000
Ordinary dividend	(49,000)
Retained profits	10,000

BALANCE SHEET AT 31 DECEMBER 20X6

	£	£
Fixed assets: tangible assets		350,000
Current assets	400,000	
Less current liabilities	150,000	
Net current assets		250,000
Total assets less current liabilities		600,000
Creditors: amounts falling due after more than one year		
10% debenture loans		200,000
		400,000
Capital and reserves		
Called up share capital		
5% preference shares	20,000	
£1 ordinary shares	80,000	
		100,000
Profit and loss account		300,000
		400,000

Using the three alternatives described above, ROCE might be calculated in any of the following ways.

(a) *Return on shareholders' capital*

$$\frac{\text{Profit after tax}}{\text{Share capital plus reserves}} = \frac{£60,000}{£400,000} = 15\%$$

(b) *Return on equity capital*

$$\frac{\text{Profit after tax and preference dividend (earnings)}}{\text{Ordinary share capital plus reserves}} = \frac{£59,000}{£380,000} = 15\%$$

(c) *Return on total long-term capital*

$$\frac{\text{Profit before interest and tax}}{\text{Loan capital plus share plus reserves}} = \frac{£120,000}{£600,000} = 20\%$$

Earnings per share

In the previous example it is possible to calculate the return on each ordinary share in the year. This is the earnings per share (EPS). Earnings are profits after tax and preference dividend, which can either be paid out as a dividend to ordinary shareholders or retained in the business. Earnings are the total return for ordinary shareholders, and for Draught Ltd in 20X6 the EPS is:

$$\frac{£59,000}{80,000 \text{ shares}} = 73.75\text{p}$$

In practice, there are usually further complications in calculating the EPS but these are beyond the scope of this book.

The EPS is important because it is used in investment analysis. It is considered on its own and compared with previous years, to ensure it is improving, and with other companies by way of performance comparison. It is also used in the price/earnings (P/E) ratio, another ratio used in investment analysis, which is discussed later in this chapter.

Activity 7

Here are some extracts from the 20X6 accounts of Z plc.

	£'000	£'000
Profit before tax		14,760
Taxation		3,840
Profit after tax		10,920
Preference dividends	60	
Ordinary dividends	140	
		200
Retained profit for the year		10,720
Shareholders' funds		
6% preference shares of £1 each		1,000
Ordinary shares of 50p each		2,500
Reserves		4,200
		7,700

Calculate the earnings per share for 20X6.

Gearing

We have now seen that a company is financed by different types of capital and that each type expects a return in the form of interest or dividend.

Definition

> *Gearing* is a method of comparing how much of the long-term capital of a business is provided by equity (ordinary shares and reserves) and how much is provided by investors who are entitled to interest or dividends before ordinary shareholders can have a dividend themselves.

These sources of capital are loans and preference shares, and are sometimes known collectively as 'prior charge capital'.

The two most usual methods of measuring gearing are:

(a) $\dfrac{\text{Prior charge capital (long–term loans and preference shares)}}{\text{Equity (ordinary shares plus reserves)}} \times 100\%$

    (i)   A business is low-geared if the gearing is less than 100%.

    (ii)   It is neutrally-geared if the gearing is exactly 100%.

    (iii)   It is high-geared if the gearing is more than 100%.

(b) $\dfrac{\text{Prior charge capital (long–term loans and preference shares)}}{\text{Total long–term capital}}$

A business is now low-geared if gearing is less than 50% (calculated under method (b)), neutrally-geared if gearing is exactly 50% and high-geared if it exceeds 50%.

These percentages are only *general guidelines* and will vary with the company and the industry it operates in.

Low gearing means that there is more equity finance in the business than there is prior charge capital. High gearing means the opposite – ie that prior charge capital exceeds the amount of equity.

Activity 8

Refer back to the example of Draught Ltd and calculate the company's gearing ratio at 31 December 20X6 under both methods.

Why is gearing important?

Think of a reason why gearing is important. Write it down here.

Gearing can be important when a company wants to raise extra capital, because if its gearing is already too high, it might find that it has difficulty in raising a loan. Would-be lenders might take the view that ordinary shareholders should provide a fair proportion of the total capital for the business and that at the moment they are not doing so. Unless ordinary shareholders are prepared to put in more money themselves (either by an issue of new shares or by the retention of more profits), the company might be viewed as a bad business risk.

If excessive gearing indicates that more loans should not be made to a company, we must now ask the question 'what is excessive gearing?'

Unfortunately, there is no hard and fast answer to this question. The 'acceptable' level of gearing varies according to the country (for example average gearing is higher among companies in Japan than in Britain), the industry, and the size and status of the individual company within the industry. The more stable the company is, the safer high gearing should be.

The advantages of gearing (ie of using debt capital) are highlighted in the following matching activity.

Activity 10

The following descriptions relate to either share capital or debt capital. The 'reward' is the interest or dividend (and possibly capital growth) paid to investors. Match each to one or the other.

1   The reward is expected to grow.

2   The reward is fixed permanently.

3   The reward is reduced because the investment is relatively less risky.

4   The capital investment usually carries voting rights.

5   The payment of the reward attracts tax relief for the company.

6   The payment of the reward is an appropriation of profit.

(a)   Debt capital is cheaper, because:

    (i)   The reward (interest) is fixed permanently, and therefore diminishes in real terms if there is inflation. Ordinary shareholders, on the other hand, usually expect dividend growth

    (ii)   The reward required by debt holders is usually lower than that required by equity holders, because debt capital is often secured on company assets, whereas ordinary share capital is a more risky investment

    (iii)   Payments of interest attract tax relief, whereas ordinary (or preference) dividends do not

(b)   Debt capital does not normally carry voting rights, but ordinary shares usually do. The issue of debt capital therefore leaves pre-existing voting rights unchanged.

(c)   If profits are rising, ordinary shareholders will benefit from high gearing. This is explained below, along with its converse, which is that if profits are falling, the residue available for ordinary shareholders will be hit hard.

One of the reasons why high gearing might be considered risky for lenders is that the more loan capital a business has, the bigger becomes the size of profit before interest and tax (PBIT) which is necessary to meet demands for interest payments.

EXAMPLE: GEARING AND EARNINGS PER SHARE

A numerical example might help to illustrate this point. Suppose that there are two companies, Nogear Ltd and Highgear Ltd, which have the following long-term capital structures.

	Nogear Ltd	*Highgear Ltd*
	£	£
Ordinary shares of £1	10,000	4,000
10% loans	0	6,000
Total long-term capital	10,000	10,000

Required

Calculate the earnings per share for each company if profits before interest and tax are:

 (a) £500

 (b) £2,000

Assume that taxation on profits (after deducting interest) is 50%.

ANSWER

 (a)

		Nogear Ltd	Highgear Ltd
PBIT = £500		£	£
PBIT		500	500
Interest		0	600
Profit/(loss) before tax		500	(100)
Tax (50%)		250	0
Earnings		250	40
Number of shares		10,000	4,000
Earnings per share		2.5p	Nil

 (b)

		Nogear Ltd	Highgear Ltd
PBIT = £2,000		£	£
PBIT		2,000	2,000
Interest		0	600
Profit/(loss) before tax		2,000	1,400
Tax (50%)		1,000	700
Earnings		1,000	700
Number of shares		10,000	4,000
Earnings per share		10p	17.5p

Activity 10

Continue the example of Nogear Ltd and Highgear Ltd by calculating the earnings per share of each company if profit before interest is £3,000.

In a high-geared company, profits before interest and tax might be insufficient to pay interest charges. However, once profits get larger the earnings per share grow at a much faster rate than in a low-geared company. (The term 'gearing' is derived from this rate of change in earnings per share, which is slow in low-gear and fast in high-gear.)

In our example, when PBIT is £500, Highgear makes a loss, whereas Nogear makes earnings of 2.5p per share. When profits rise to £2,000 before interest and tax, the earnings per share in Highgear overtake those of Nogear. The difference gets bigger as profits go up.

We have now looked at 'risk' implications of gearing. There is a view that as a company's gearing gets bigger and exceeds a certain limit, it becomes a bad risk for more loans, and the company might also be in danger of failing to earn enough to pay the interest charges.

Interest cover

One way of measuring this gearing risk is to look at the interest cover a company provides. This is:

$$\frac{\text{Profit before interest and tax}}{\text{Interest paid in the year}}$$

If this ratio is less than 1, it means that the company has not earned enough to cover its interest charges, and has made a loss. A ratio of not much more than 1 would show that the company was able to make a profit after paying interest, but only just, and it must be regarded as a risky investment. A 'safe' ratio for interest cover is thought to be 3 at the very minimum. If the ratio is less than 3, the company probably has too high a gearing for the size of profits that it makes.

For example, in the earlier example of Draught Ltd, interest cover is:

$$\frac{£120,000}{£20,000} = 6 \text{ times}$$

This would be regarded as 'safe'.

Ratios used in investment analysis

Certain ratios are widely used in investment analysis. They will be illustrated using the following example.

DESMOND LIMITED
PROFIT AND LOSS APPROPRIATION ACCOUNT
FOR THE YEAR ENDING 31 DECEMBER 20X6

		£'000	£'000
Net profit			107
Dividends:	preference (paid)	21	
	ordinary (paid)	50	
		71	
Transfer to general reserve		14	
Total profits appropriated			85
Net profit retained for the year			22

Desmond Ltd has 2,000,000 50p ordinary shares in issue, with a current market value of 94p each.

Price/earnings (P/E) ratio

This is a comparison of the current market value of a share and the earnings per share (EPS). The calculation of EPS has already been illustrated. In Desmond's case, EPS is £(107− 21)/2,000 = 4.3p.

Desmond's P/E ratio is therefore 94p/4.3p = 21.9.

The price/earnings ratio varies from company to company, depending on two factors.

    (a)   Market expectations of particular companies' growth rates. For example, the market may expect a company's profits to grow, and be prepared to pay more for its shares. Therefore such a company will have a higher P/E ratio than one with poor growth prospects.

(b) The area in which the company operates. Retail stores typically have P/E ratios for the most part in the region of 15 to 35. Many construction companies, on the other hand, tend to have lower P/E ratios (in the range 8 to 18).

Dividend yield

This relates dividends (the shareholders' reward) to the market price of the shares.

$$\frac{\text{Dividend per share}}{\text{Market price per share}} = 100\%$$

Desmond's net dividend per share is

$$\frac{£50,000}{2,000,000} = 2.5p$$

Net dividend yield is therefore:

$$\frac{2.5p}{94p} \times 100\% = 2.7\%$$

It follows from the above that changes in the market price cause changes in the dividend yield. If annual dividends are halved and the market price drops by 50%, the dividend yield will remain the same.

Dividend cover

This measures the relationship between profits available for distribution to equity and dividends actually declared:

$$\frac{\text{Profit after interest, taxation and preference dividend}}{\text{Ordinary dividend}}$$

Activity 11

Calculate the dividend cover of Desmond Ltd.

Ordinary dividend cover is generally much lower than interest cover or preference dividend cover. An ordinary dividend cover of 2 is widely considered acceptable, and in cases where dividends are paid from retained profits the cover will be negative.

Chapter roundup

In this chapter, we have looked at the primary accounting ratio, ROCE, and at ratios analysing profitability and asset turnover, and the significance of the ratios has been explained.

- Gearing as a feature of capital structure has also been introduced.

- A number of ratios important to investment analysis have been explained.

In Chapter 11 we will look at the operating cycle and at working capital ratios.

Quick quiz

1	Define profit margin and asset turnover.	(see para 1.2)
2	What is the relationship which links ROCE, profit margin and asset turnover?	(1.2)
3	How is the return on total long-term capital calculated?	(1.2)
4	Describe two methods of calculating a gearing ratio.	(1.2)
5	List three advantages of debt capital over equity capital.	(1.2)
6	Define interest cover.	(1.2)
7	Define price earnings ratio.	(1.2)

Answers to activities

1 In practice, he almost certainly does not perform his own analysis of the company's accounts. For a large company the accounts can be very daunting. He will derive his information largely from comments in the press or on TV, perhaps supplemented by an investment magazine (such as Investor's Chronicle).

2 Statement (b) is correct

$$\frac{\text{Profit}}{\text{Capital employed}} = \frac{\text{Profit}}{\text{Sales}} \times \frac{\text{Sales}}{\text{Capital employed}}$$

3
1. 2 times ($10\% \times 2 = 20\%$)
2. 8 times ($2^1/_2\% \times 8 = 20\%$)
3. 10% ($10\% \times 2 \text{ times} = 20\%$)

4 True:

1. Yes, and it may also be achieved by increasing the asset turnover ratio.

3. This is often true and needs to be borne in mind when pricing products.

False:

2. Although the profit margin may be increased by raising prices, it may also be improved by cutting costs.

4. Not necessarily. If prices are increased, sales may be depressed with the increase in profit margin being offset by the fall in asset turnover. Where profit margin is improved by costs being cut it is much more likely to lead to a better ROCE.

5   For 20X6 we have:

Profit margin   5%

Asset turnover   5 times

ROCE (5% × 5)   25%

With the proposed changes, the profit would be 10% × 150,000 = £15,000, and the asset turnover would be:

$$\frac{£150,000}{£75,000} = 2 \text{ times, so that the ratios would be :}$$

Profit margin   × Asset turnover   = ROCE

$$10\% \quad\quad × 2 \text{ times} \quad\quad = 20\% = \frac{£15,000}{£75,000}$$

In spite of increasing the profit margin and raising the total volume of sales, the extra assets required (£55,000) only raise total profits by £(15,000 − 5,000) = £10,000.

The return on capital employed falls from 25% to 20% because of the sharp fall in asset turnover from 5 times to 2 times.

6

Provider of finance	Return on investment
Trade creditor	Only receives money owed, no additional return
Bank: overdraft	Interest
Debenture holder	Interest
Ordinary shareholder	Dividend
Preference shareholder	Dividend at fixed percentage rate of nominal value

Although ordinary shareholders expect a dividend, any retained profits kept in the business also represent funds owned by them.

7   Earnings are the profits available for ordinary shareholders, namely the profit after tax (£10,920,000) less the preference dividend (£60,000), ie £10,860,000.

There are 5,000,000 ordinary shares of 50p each in issue.

EPS is therefore £10,860,000/5,000,000 = 217.2p

8   (a) $\dfrac{\text{Debenture loans + preference shares}}{\text{Ordinary shares + reserves}} = \dfrac{200,000 + 20,000}{80,000 + 300,000} = 57.9\%$

    (b) $\dfrac{\text{Debenture loans + preference shares}}{\text{Total long – term capital}} = \dfrac{200,000 + 20,000}{400,000 + 200,000} = 36.7\%$

9   Share capital: 1; 4; 6.

Debt capital: 2; 3; 5.

10	*PBIT = £3,000*	£	£
	PBIT	3,000	3,000
	Interest	0	600
	Profit before tax	3,000	2,400
	Tax (50%)	(1,500)	(1,200)
	Earnings	1,500	1,200
	Number of shares	10,000	4,000
	Earnings per share	15p	30p

11   The dividend cover of Desmond Ltd is $\dfrac{107,000 - 21,000}{50,000} = 1.72$

Further question practice

Now try the following practice questions at the end of this text

Multiple choice questions: **59 to 66**

Exam style question: **10**

Chapter 11 :

THE OPERATING CYCLE AND WORKING CAPITAL RATIO

Introduction

This chapter continues the subject of the interpretation of financial statements begun in the previous chapter.

Working capital is the difference between current assets (mainly stocks, debtors and cash) and current liabilities (such as trade creditors and a bank overdraft).

(a)   Current assets are items which are either cash already, or which will soon lead to the receipt of cash. Stocks will be sold to customers and create debtors; and debtors will soon pay in cash for their purchases.

(b)   Current liabilities are items which will soon have to be paid for with cash. Trade creditors will have to be paid and a bank overdraft is usually regarded as a short-term borrowing which may need to be repaid fairly quickly.

In published balance sheets, the word 'current' is applied to stocks, debtors, short-term investments and cash (current assets), and amounts due for payment within one year (current liabilities).

Your objectives

After completing this chapter you should:

(a)   Understand the cycle of transactions by which stock is converted to debtors and then to cash

(b)   Understand the importance of working capital to the operations of a business

(c)   Know how to calculate ratios to assess the working capital position of a business

1 THE OPERATING CYCLE

1.1 Working capital and trading operations

Current assets and current liabilities are a necessary feature of a firm's trading operations. There is a repeated cycle of buying and selling which is carried on all the time. For example, suppose that on 1 April a firm has the following items.

	£
Stocks	3,000
Debtors	0
Cash	2,000
	5,000
Creditors	0
Working capital	5,000

It might sell all the stocks on credit for £4,500, and at the same time obtain more stock from suppliers (on credit) at a cost of £3,500. The balance sheet items would now include:

	£
Stocks	3,500
Debtors	4,500
Cash	2,000
	10,000
Creditors	3,500
Working capital	6,500

(The increase in working capital to £6,500 from £5,000 is caused by the profit of £1,500 on the sale of the stocks.)

The debtors for £4,500 will eventually pay in cash and the creditors for £3,500 must also be paid. This would give us:

	£
Stocks	3,500
Debtors	0
Cash (2,000 + 4,500 − 3,500)	3,000
	6,500
Creditors	0
Working capital	6,500

Activity 1

Suppose the stocks are sold on credit for £5,500 and further purchases of stock costing £6,000 are made on credit. What will the firm's working capital position be?

The Working Capital Cycle

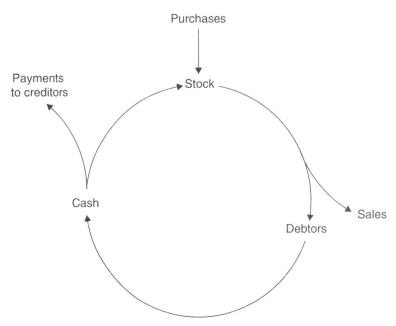

Figure 11.1 Working capital cycle

From this basic example you should be able to see that working capital items are part of a continuous flow of trading operations. Purchases add to stocks and creditors at the same time, creditors must be paid and debtors will pay for their goods. The cycle of operations always eventually comes back to cash receipts and cash payments.

Definition

> The *operating cycle* (or cash cycle) is a term used to describe the connection between working capital and cash movements in and out. The cycle is usually measured in days or months.

A firm buys raw materials, probably on credit. The raw materials might be held for some time in stores before being issued to the production department and turned into an item of finished goods. The finished goods might be kept in a warehouse for some time before they are eventually sold to customers. By this time, the firm will probably have paid for the raw materials purchased. If customers buy the goods on credit, it will be some time before the cash from the sales is eventually received.

The cash cycle, or operating cycle, measures the period of time:

(a) Between the purchase of raw materials and the receipt of cash from debtors for goods sold, and

(b) Between the time cash is paid out for raw materials and the time cash is received in from debtors.

This cycle of repeating events may be shown as follows.

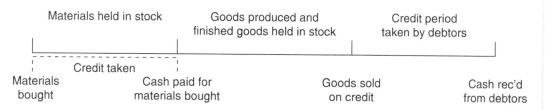

Figure 11.2 Linear cash cycle

The horizontal line represents the passage of time. The operating cycle starts with the purchase of materials and ends with the receipt of cash from debtors. Cash is not paid when materials are bought because credit is taken from suppliers.

Suppose that a firm buys raw materials on 1½ months' credit, holds them in store for one month and then issues them to the production department. The production cycle is very short, but finished goods are held for one month before they are sold. Debtors take two months' credit. The cash cycle would be:

	Months
Raw material stock turnover period	1.0
Less credit taken from suppliers	(1.5)
Finished goods stock turnover period	1.0
Debtors' payment period	2.0
Cash cycle	2.5

There would be a gap of 2½ months between paying cash for raw materials and receiving cash (including profits) from debtors.

A few dates might clarify this point. Suppose the firm purchases its raw materials on 1 January. The sequence of events would then be as follows.

	Date
Purchase of raw materials	1 Jan
Issue of materials to production (one month after purchase)	1 Feb
Payment made to suppliers (1½ months after purchase)	15 Feb
Sale of finished goods (one month after production begins)	1 Mar
Receipt of cash from debtors (two months after sale)	1 May

The cash cycle is the period of 2½ months from 15 February, when payment is made to suppliers, until 1 May, when cash is received from debtors.

Activity 2

A firm buys raw materials on four weeks' credit. Materials purchased are issued to production on average two weeks after they come into stock. The production cycle is approximately four weeks, after which goods are sold immediately. Debtors take an average of six weeks before they pay their debts.

What is the length of the cash cycle in weeks?

PUBLISHING

2   WORKING CAPITAL RATIOS

A 'turnover' period is an (average) length of time.

    (a)   In the case of *stock turnover*, it is the length of time an item of stock is held in stores before it is used.

        (i)   A raw materials *stock turnover* period is the length of time raw materials are held before being issued to the production department.

        (ii)   A work in progress turnover period is the length of time it takes to turn raw materials into finished goods in the factory.

        (iii)   A finished goods stock turnover period is the length of time that finished goods are held in a warehouse before they are sold.

        (iv)   When a firm buys goods and re-sells them at a profit, the stock turnover period is the time between their purchase and their resale.

    (b)   The *debtor's turnover* period, or debt collection period, is the length of the credit period taken by customers – ie it is the time between the sale of an item and the receipt of cash for the sale from the customer.

    (c)   Similarly, the *creditor's turnover* period, or period of credit taken from suppliers, is the length of time between the purchase of materials and the payment to suppliers.

Turnover periods can be calculated from information in a firm's profit and loss account and balance sheet.

Stock turnover periods are calculated as follows.

    (a)   Raw materials:

$$\frac{\text{(Average) raw material stocks held}}{\text{Total raw materials consumed in one year}} \times 12 \text{ months}$$

    (b)   Work in progress (the length of the production period):

$$\frac{\text{(Average) finished goods held in stock}}{\text{Total cost of production in the year}} \times 12 \text{ months}$$

    (c)   Finished goods:

$$\frac{\text{(Average) stocks}}{\text{Total cost of production in the year}} \times 12 \text{ months}$$

    (d)   Stocks of items bought for re-sale:

$$\frac{\text{(Average) stocks}}{\text{Total (materials) cost of goods bought and sold in one year}} \times 12 \text{ months}$$

The word 'average' is put in brackets because although it is strictly correct to use average values, it is more common to use the value of stocks shown in a balance sheet – ie at one point in time – to estimate the turnover periods.

For example, if a company buys goods costing £620,000 in one year but uses goods costing £600,000 in production, and the cost of material in stock at 1 January is £100,000, the stock turnover period would be:

$$\frac{\text{\pounds}100,000}{\text{\pounds}600,000} \times 12 \text{ months } = 2 \text{ months}$$

In other words, stocks are bought two months before they are eventually re-sold.

The debt collection period is calculated as:

$$\frac{\text{Average debtors}}{\text{Annual credit sales}} \times 12 \text{ months}$$

For example, if a company sells goods on credit for £1,200,000 per annum, and if debtors in the balance sheet are £150,000, the debt collection period would be:

$$\frac{\text{\pounds}150,000}{\text{\pounds}1,200,000} \times 12 \text{ months} = 1.5 \text{ months}$$

In other words, debtors will on average pay for goods 1½ months after the time of sale.

The period of credit taken from suppliers is calculated as:

$$\frac{\text{Average trade creditors}}{\text{Total purchases in one year}} \times 12 \text{ months} = 1 \text{ month}$$

(Notice that the creditors are compared with materials bought whereas for raw material stock turnover, raw material stocks are compared with materials used in production. This is a small, but significant, difference.)

For example, if a company sells goods for £600,000 and makes a gross profit of 40% on sales, and if the amount of trade creditors in the balance sheet is £30,000, the period of credit taken from the suppliers is:

$$\frac{\text{\pounds}30,000}{\text{\pounds}600,000 \times 60\%} \times 12 \text{ months} = 1 \text{ month}$$

In other words, suppliers are paid in the month following the purchase of goods.

EXAMPLE: CALCULATING THE CASH CYCLE

The profit and loss account of Legion Ltd for the year to 30 June 20X6 and the balance sheet of the company as at 30 June 20X6 are as follows.

PROFIT AND LOSS ACCOUNT

	£	£
Sales		360,000
Cost of sales	180,000	
Wages and salaries	80,000	
Depreciation	20,000	
Other expenses	60,000	
		340,000
Profit		20,000

BALANCE SHEET

	£	£
Fixed assets at cost less depreciation		180,000
Stocks	30,000	
Debtors	75,000	
Cash	10,000	
	115,000	
Trade creditors	45,000	
		70,000
		250,000
Share capital and reserves		250,000

Required

Calculate the length of the cash cycle.

ANSWER

Stock turnover	*Debt collection period*	*Credit taken from suppliers*
$\dfrac{30,000}{180,000} \times 12$	$\dfrac{75,000}{360,000} \times 12$	$\dfrac{45,000}{180,000} \times 12$
= 2 months	= 2.5 months	= 3 months

The cash cycle is as follows	*Months*
Stock turnover period	2.0
Credit taken from suppliers	(3.0)
Debt collection period	2.5
Cash cycle	1.5

In this example, Legion Ltd pays its suppliers one month after the stocks have been sold, since the stock turnover is two months but credit taken is three months.

If the stock turnover period gets longer or if the debt collection period gets longer, the total amount of stocks held or of debtors will increase. Similarly, if the period of credit taken from the suppliers gets shorter, the amount of creditors will become smaller. The effect of these changes would be to increase the size of working capital (exclusive of bank balances or overdrafts).

Suppose that a company has annual sales of £480,000 (in regular monthly quantities, all on credit) and a materials cost of sales of £300,000. (*Note*. A 'materials cost of sales' is the cost of materials in the cost of sales.)

(a)   If the stock turnover period is two months, the debt collection period one month and the period of credit taken from suppliers is two months, the company's working capital (ignoring cash) would be as follows.

		£
Stocks	$(^2/_{12} \times £300,000)$	50,000
Debtors	$(^1/_{12} \times £480,000)$	40,000
		90,000
Creditors	$(^2/_{12} \times £300,000)$	(50,000)
		40,000

The cash cycle would be $(2 + 1 - 2) = 1$ month.

(b)   Now if the stock turnover period is extended to three months and the debt collection period to two months, and if the payment period for purchases from suppliers is reduced to one month, the company's working capital (ignoring cash) would be as follows.

		£
Stocks	$(^3/_{12} \times £300,000)$	75,000
Debtors	$(^2/_{12} \times £480,000)$	80,000
		155,000
Creditors	$(^1/_{12} \times £300,000)$	(25,000)
		130,000

The cash cycle would be $(3 + 2 - 1) = 4$ months.

If we ignore the possible effects on the bank balance or bank overdraft (which are themselves included in working capital) it should be seen that a lengthening of the cash cycle will result in a larger volume of working capital.

If the volume of working capital required by a business varies with the length of the cash cycle, it is worth asking the question: 'Is there an ideal length of cash cycle and an ideal volume of working capital?'

Obviously, stocks, debtors and creditors should be managed efficiently, and the following true /false questions should clarify this.

Activity 3

Mark the following statements as true or false.

1   Sufficient credit should be given to customers to ensure they buy the goods.

2   Stocks should be large enough to meet demand but not excessive.

3   Payment to suppliers should be made as late as possible and where necessary credit periods can be exceeded.

4   Overdue payments from debtors should be chased up regularly.

> ### Activity 4
>
> The ideas we are discussing here have much in common with ideas you encountered in Chapter 9 on cash flow statements. The relationship will become clear later in this chapter, but in the meantime refer back to the cash flow statement and, in particular, the reconciliation of profit with operating cash flows. Think carefully about the implications of this for working capital. In particular, what does it tell us about the effect on liquid funds of a build-up of stocks and debtors?

Another important aspect of the size of working capital, however, is liquidity. The word 'liquid' means 'readily converted into cash' and a firm's liquidity is its ability to convert its assets into cash to meet all demands for payments when they fall due.

The most liquid asset, of course, is cash itself (or a bank balance). The next most liquid assets are short-term investments (stocks and shares) because these can be sold quickly for cash should this be necessary. Debtors are fairly liquid assets because they should be expected to pay their bills in the near future. Stocks are the least liquid current asset because they must first be sold (perhaps on credit) and the customers given a credit period in which to pay before they can be converted into cash.

Current liabilities are items which must be paid for in the near future. When payment becomes due, enough cash must be available. The managers of a business must therefore make sure that a regular supply of cash comes in (from current assets) at all times to meet the regular flow of payments it is necessary to provide for.

2.1 Liquidity ratios

There are two common liquidity ratios.

(a) The current ratio or working capital ratio;

(b) The quick ratio, liquidity ratio or acid test ratio.

The *current ratio* or *working capital ratio* is the more commonly used and is the ratio of current assets to current liabilities.

> ### Activity 5
>
> Refer back to the earlier example of Legion Ltd. What is the company's current ratio at 30 June 20X6?

A 'prudent' current ratio is sometimes said to be 2:1. In other words, current assets should be twice the size of current liabilities. This is a rather simplistic view of the matter, because particular attention needs to be paid to certain matters.

(a) Bank overdrafts are technically repayable on demand, and therefore must be classified as current liabilities. However, many companies have semi-permanent overdrafts, in which case the likelihood of their having to be repaid in the near future is remote. It would also often be relevant to know a company's overdraft limit – this may give a truer indication of liquidity than a current or quick ratio.

(b) The year-end figures may not be typical of the year as a whole. This is particularly relevant in the case of seasonal businesses. For example, many large retail companies choose an accounting year end soon after the January sales and their balance sheets show a higher level of cash than would be usual at any other time in the year.

(c) The nature of a business's operations will very much determine both its current and quick ratios. For example, supermarkets such as Sainsbury's and Tesco will have more than enough working capital on a liquidity ratio of 0.3:1 whereas Tarmac Construction will probably require at least 2:1.

In practice, many businesses operate with a much lower current ratio than 2:1 and in these cases, the best way to judge their liquidity would be to look at the current ratio at different dates over a period. If the trend is towards a lower current ratio, we would judge that the liquidity position is getting steadily worse.

For example, if the current ratios of two firms A and B are as follows.

	1 Jan	*1 Apr*	*1 July*	*1 Oct*
Firm A	2.2 : 1	2.2 : 1	2.2 : 1	2.2 : 1
Firm B	2.3 : 1	2.2 : 1	2.1 : 1	2.0 : 1

We could say that firm A is maintaining a stable liquidity position, whereas firm B's liquidity is deteriorating. We would then begin to question firm B's continuing ability to pay its bills. A bank for instance, would need to think carefully before granting any request from firm B for an extended overdraft facility.

The *quick ratio* is used when we take the view that stocks take a long time to get ready for sale, and then there may be some delay in getting them sold, so that stocks are not particularly liquid assets. If this is the case, a firm's liquidity depends more heavily on the amount of debtors, short-term investments and cash that it has to match its current liabilities. The quick ratio is the ratio of current assets *excluding stocks* to current liabilities.

A 'prudent' quick ratio is 1 : 1. In practice, many businesses have a lower quick ratio (for example 0.5 : 1), and the best way of judging a firm's liquidity would be to look at the trend in the quick ratio over a period. The quick ratio is also known as the *liquidity ratio* and as the *acid test ratio*.

Activity 6

Again go back to Legion Ltd. What is the company's quick ratio at 30 June 20X6?

Increases in working capital tie up cash. An increase in stocks and debtors, or a decrease in creditors, will have the effect of reducing the cash surplus we might otherwise expect. An example will illustrate this point.

EXAMPLE: IMPACT ON CASH SURPLUS

At 1 January, Cottontail Ltd had stocks of £2,000, no debtors or cash, and creditors of £1,000. During the month, stocks costing £15,000 were purchased and goods costing £14,000 were sold for £20,000. At 31 January, creditors were £500, and debtors £3,000.

The gross profit in January was £6,000, as follows:

	£
Sales	20,000
Cost of sales	14,000
Gross profit	6,000

Cottontail should expect a cash surplus of £6,000 from these sales, but the cash balance at 31 January will not be as high as £6,000. This is because Cottontail has increased its investment in the other items of working capital (ie other than cash).

	£
Increase in stocks held (15,000 – 14,000)	1,000
Increase in debtors (3,000 – 0)	3,000
Decrease in creditors (1,000 – 500)	500
Increase in other items of working capital	4,500
Profit in January	6,000
Increase in cash (balance)	1,500

This can be proved as follows.

	£	£
Creditors at 1 January	1,000	
Purchases	15,000	
	16,000	
	(500)	
Payments to creditors in January		15,500
Debtors at 1 January	0	
Sales in January	20,000	
Debtors at 31 January	(3,000)	
Receipts from debtors in January		17,000
Net receipts of cash in January		1,500

This example is intended to illustrate that an increase in stocks and debtors or a decrease in creditors will tie up cash, so that cash receipts over a period will be less than the profits earned. (Similarly, a decrease in stocks and debtors or an increase in creditors will have the opposite effect of releasing cash, so that cash receipts over a period will exceed the profits earned.)

An extended activity now completes this chapter. Attempt your own calculations and analysis before reading the solution.

Activity 7

The cash balance of Wing Ltd has declined significantly over the last 12 months. The following financial information is provided.

Year to 31 December	20X5	20X6
	£	£
Sales	573,000	643,000
Purchases of raw materials	215,000	264,000
Raw materials consumed	210,000	256,400
Cost of goods manufactured	435,000	515,000
Cost of goods sold	420,000	460,000

Balance at 31 December	£	£
Debtors	97,100	121,500
Creditors	23,900	32,500
Stocks: raw materials	22,400	30,000
work in progress	29,000	34,300
finished goods	70,000	125,000

All purchases and sales were made on credit.

Required

(a) Prepare an analysis of the above information, which should include calculations of the cash operating cycle (ie the time lag between making payment to suppliers and collecting cash from customers) for 20X5 and 20X6.

(b) Prepare a brief report on the implications of the changes which have occurred between 20X5 and 20X6.

Notes

(a) Assume a 360 day year for the purpose of your calculations and assume that all transactions take place at an even rate.

(b) All calculations are to be made to the nearest day.

Chapter roundup

In this chapter we have considered working capital.

- The cash cycle is the time which elapses between payment of suppliers for goods purchased and receipt of cash from debtors in respect of those goods.

- The greater the amount of a business's investment in stocks and debtors (less creditors) the less cash it will have available. For this reason, it is unwise to allow the levels of stock and debtors to rise too high and turnover periods should be monitored carefully. At the same time, a business must ensure that it has enough stock on hand to meet customer demands.

- Two important liquidity ratios which should be learnt are:

    (i) The current ratio $= \dfrac{\text{current assets}}{\text{current liabilities}}$

    (ii) The quick ratio $= \dfrac{\text{current assets excluding stocks}}{\text{current liabilities}}$

We will now look at other sources of information which may be useful in interpreting company accounts.

Quick quiz

1 What is the 'cash cycle'?   (see para 1.1)

2 What is:

    (a) A finished goods stock turnover period?

    (b) A debtor's turnover period?

    How are they calculated?   (see section 2)

3 A lengthening of the cash cycle will result in a smaller volume of working capital. True or false?   (section 2)

4 Define:

    (a) The current ratio

    (b) The quick ratio   (2.1)

5 A decrease in creditors has the effect of increasing the cash balance. True or false?   (2.1)

Answers to activities

1

	£
Stocks	6,000
Debtors	5,500
Cash	3,000
	14,500
Creditors	6,000
Working capital (boosted by further profit of £2,000)	8,500

2

	Weeks
Raw materials held in stock	2
Production cycle	4
Debtors payment period	6
	12
Less credit taken from suppliers	4
Length of cash cycle	8

3 True:

2. Yes, stocks should be sufficient to meet demand but not excessive. Where stocks are too large working capital is being tied up, warehousing space is being used and there may be a danger of obsolescence.

4. This is true. The debtors may default on payment but even where this is unlikely the fact that payment is not received promptly costs the business in lost interest.

False:

1. A reasonable credit period should be given, in the light of what is expected in the industry being considered, but excessive credit should not be justified on the grounds of increasing sales. Cash is vital to the survival of the business and delayed receipts may lead to a cash crisis.

3. Whilst it is true that payment need not be made until the end of the credit period granted by suppliers, payments should not be made late. Late payment is likely to harm the relationship with the supplier and may lead to less favourable terms of supply, for example cash on receipt of goods. Also if discounts are given for early settlement, the business may prefer to pay less in return for paying quickly.

4 As is shown later in this chapter, if stocks and debtors are allowed to build up, there will be a corresponding decrease in available cash and bank balances. This is clear from the format of the first part of the cash flow statement. Clearly for any given amount of surplus, the more that is consumed by stock and debtors, the less there will be in the form of cash.

5 The current ratio is £(30,000 + 75,000 + 10,000): £45,000, or 2.56:1.

6 The quick ratio is £(75,000 + 10,000): £45,000, or 1.89:1.

7　(a)　The information should be analysed in as many ways as possible, and you should not omit any important items. The relevant calculations would seem to be as follows.

(i)

	20X5 £	20X6 £
Sales	573,000	643,000
Cost of goods sold	420,000	460,000
Gross profit	153,000	183,000

(ii)　Size of working capital and liquidity ratios, ignoring cash/bank overdrafts.

		£	£
Debtors		97,100	121,500
Stocks:	Raw materials	22,400	30,000
	Work in progress	29,000	34,300
	Finished goods	70,000	125,000
		218,500	310,800
Creditors		23,900	32,500
Working capital (ignoring cash or overdraft)		194,600	278,300
Current ratio		$\frac{218,500}{23,900}$	$\frac{310,800}{32,500}$
		= 9.1:1	= 9.6:1

(iii)　Turnover periods:

		20X5 days		20X6 days
Raw materials in stock	$\frac{22,400}{210,000} \times 360 =$	38	$\frac{30,000}{256,400} \times 360 =$	42
Work in progress	$\frac{29,000}{435,000} \times 360 =$	24	$\frac{34,300}{515,000} \times 360 =$	24
Finished goods stock	$\frac{70,000}{420,000} \times 360 =$	60	$\frac{125,000}{460,000} \times 360 =$	98
Debtors' collection	$\frac{97,100}{537,000} \times 360 =$	61	$\frac{121,500}{643,400} \times 360 =$	68

		20X5 days		20X6 days
Creditors' payment	$\frac{23,900}{215,000} \times 360 =$	(40)	$\frac{32,500}{264,000} \times 360 =$	(44)
Cash cycle		143		188

(b)　Sales were about 12% higher in 20X6 than in 20X5 and the cost of sales was about 10% higher. The investments in stocks and debtors minus creditors rose from £194,600 to £278,300, ie by £83,700 or 43%. This is completely out of proportion to the volume of increase in trade, which indicates that working capital turnover periods are not being properly controlled.

The increase in working capital of £83,700 means that the net cash receipts from profits in 20X6 were £83,700 less than they would have been if there had been no increase at all in stocks and debtors (less creditors) during 20X6. The company might therefore have an unnecessary bank overdraft, although we are not given enough information to comment on this point fully.

Current assets must be financed by a combination of long-term funds and current liabilities. Working capital (current assets minus current liabilities) is the amount of this finance provided by long-term funds. A large and unnecessary increase in working capital will mean that too many long-term funds are invested in current assets (and they are obviously being invested wastefully if trading operations can be sustained with less working capital). A current ratio (ignoring cash and bank overdraft) of over 9:1 would appear excessive, both in 20X5 and 20X6.

The causes of the increase in working capital in 20X6 are:

(i)   The increase in sales, but mainly

(ii)   The increased length of turnover periods

Raw materials stock turnover has risen from 38 to 42 days, although this increase was 'cancelled out' by an extension of the credit taken from suppliers, from 40 to 44 days. Debtors, already allowed 61 days to pay in 20X5, were allowed 68 days in 20X6 and this would seem to be an excessive length of time. The most serious change, however, is the increase in the finished goods stock turnover period from 60 days (two months) to 98 days (over three months) and it is difficult to see an obvious reason why this should have occurred.

Further question practice

Now try the following practice questions at the end of this text

Multiple choice questions: **67 to 73**

Exam style question: **11**

Chapter 12 :

INTERPRETING COMPANY ACCOUNTS: OTHER SOURCES OF INFORMATION

Introduction

This is the final chapter on the interpretation of financial statements.

Much of the information you would use to interpret a company's financial performance and position is of course contained in the main accounting statements produced by the company, particularly the balance sheet, profit and loss account and cash flow statement. But there are other sources of information in the published annual accounts of a company.

One such source, the directors' report, must be published by all companies and must contain, as a minimum, certain items of information prescribed by companies legislation. In addition, the accounts of a limited company must be audited and must contain the report issued by the auditor. Finally, it is common (though not legally required) for listed companies to publish a chairman's statement. All these reports can throw additional light on the information contained in the financial statements.

Your objectives

After completing this chapter you should:

(a)   Be aware of the content and significance of the directors' report, the auditor's report and the chairman's statement

(b)   Be aware of the summary financial statements published by some listed companies

1 FINANCIAL REPORTS

1.1 The directors' report

The things which must be covered in the *directors' report* are as follows.

    (a)   The state of affairs of the company

    (b)   The company's principal activities

    (c)   Post balance sheet events

    (d)   Likely future developments

    (e)   Employee involvement

    (f)   Details of own shares purchased or charged

    (g)   Proposed dividends and transfers to reserves

    (h)   Fixed assets

    (i)   Health and safety of employees and employment of disabled persons

    (j)   Political and charitable contributions

    (k)   Details of directors

    (l)   Research and development activities

    (m)   Creditor payment policy

There is no specified order in which the information should be disclosed, but it may be useful to group the requirements under three headings:

    (a)   General disclosures

    (b)   Specific disclosures

    (c)   Disclosures in respect of directors

Activity 1

Try to obtain the annual accounts published by a large company. (Business libraries often keep some, or you can write to a company or use the annual reports service in the *Financial Times*.) Examine the directors' report and identify where each of the required items of disclosure appears. Are there any disclosures in the report other than those required by statute?

General disclosures

The *state of affairs of the company*: the directors should give 'a fair review of the development of the business of the company and its subsidiaries during the financial year ending with the balance sheet date and of their position at the end of it.'

The *principal activities* of the company and its subsidiaries during the financial year together with any changes therein. Details of any activities in the field of research and development should be included.

Post balance sheet events: the directors should disclose any important events affecting the company or any of its subsidiaries which have occurred since the end of the financial year. Note that an accounting standard (SSAP 17) requires such information to be disclosed in the body of the accounts.

Likely future developments in the business of the company and of its subsidiaries should be disclosed.

Employee involvement: the directors of any company employing on average more than 250 people each week must state in their report what action has been taken during the financial year to introduce, maintain or develop arrangements aimed at the following.

(a) *Employee information*: providing employees systematically with information on matters of concern to them.

(b) *Employee consultation*: consulting employees or their representatives on a regular basis so that the views of employees can be taken into account in making decisions which are likely to affect their interests.

(c) *Employee involvement*: encouraging the involvement of employees in the company's performance through an employees' share scheme or by some other means.

(d) *Achieving common awareness of company performance* on the part of all employees (and of the financial and economic factors affecting the performance of the company).

You should note that these provisions do not mean that any action must be taken. But, if it is taken, it must be disclosed in the directors' report. Moreover, wide discretion is granted to the directors in deciding what needs to be disclosed, since no definition is given of such terms as 'matters of concern to them' or 'decisions which are likely to affect their interests'.

Specific disclosures

Own shares purchased or charged: in those cases where a company is permitted to acquire its own shares directly, or through a nominee, or charges its own shares, or provides financial assistance to purchase its own shares, full details must be given.

Activity 2

There are several reasons why a company might wish to purchase its own shares. Can you think of three?

Fixed assets: the report must show, in respect of:

(a) Fixed assets, any significant changes which have been made by the company or any of its subsidiaries during the financial year

(b) Land held as fixed assets, the difference between book value and market value, where such a difference is significant

Disclosure in the directors' report is necessary in respect of two areas of particular interest to employees.

(a) *Employment of disabled persons*: the directors of companies with an average of more than 250 UK employees per week must include in their report a statement of company policy as to the employment, training, career development and promotion of disabled people.

(b) Arrangements for securing the health, safety and welfare at work of employees, and for protecting other persons against risks to health or safety arising out of or in connection with the activities at work of those employees. (*Note.* Only certain classes of company are affected by this requirement.)

Political and charitable contributions made by the company or group must be disclosed where, if taken together, these exceed £200. Separate totals must be given for each, and in the case of individual political contributions exceeding £200, the amount and name of the recipient or the political party concerned must be stated. (*Note.* This information is not required in respect of wholly-owned subsidiaries of UK companies.)

Disclosures in respect of directors

The following information is required in respect of directors.

(a) The names of any persons who have served as directors at any time during the financial year.

(b) The directors' interests in the shares or debentures of the company or any other company in the group at the financial year end. There must be shown in respect of each director (including nil holdings):

(i) The number held in each body corporate at the beginning of the year, or, if he became a director during the year, at that date

(ii) The number held at the year end

(iii) Details of options granted to or exercised by a director or his immediate family during the year

The CA 1985 allows directors' interests in shares and debentures to be given in the notes to the accounts instead of in the directors' report.

Activity 3

Use the following exercise to check your understanding of some of the items in the directors' report.

Mark the following sentences as true or false.

1. All companies must give details of employee involvement in the directors' report.

2. Where a company has purchased its own shares, full details must be given.

3. Significant changes in fixed assets should be disclosed.

4 Political contributions should be disclosed in full.

5. Only the names of those persons who are directors at the year end should be given.

1.2 The auditors' report

The annual accounts of a limited company must be audited by persons independent of the company. In practice, this means that the members of the company appoint a firm of chartered accountants or certified accountants (members of a recognised supervisory body) to investigate the accounts prepared by the company and report as to whether or not they show a true and fair view of the company's results for the year and its financial position at the end of the year.

When the auditors have completed their work they must prepare a report explaining the work that they have done and the opinion they have formed. In simple cases they will be able to report that they have carried out their work in accordance with approved auditing standards and that, in their opinion, the accounts show a true and fair view and are prepared in accordance with the Companies Act 1985. This is described as an *unqualified* audit report.

Sometimes the auditors may disagree with the directors on a point concerned with the accounts. If they are unable to persuade the directors to change the accounts, and if the item at issue is material, it is the auditors' duty to prepare a *qualified* report, setting out the matter(s) on which they disagrees with the directors.

The financial statements to which the auditors' refer in their report comprise:

(a) The profit and loss account

(b) The balance sheet

(c) The notes to the accounts

In addition they must consider whether the information given in the directors' report is consistent with the audited accounts. If they believe it is not consistent then they must state that fact in their report.

The auditors' report is included as a part of the company's published accounts. It is addressed to the members of the company (not to the directors).

Activity 4

Fill in the missing words to ensure you understand the purpose and significance of the auditors' report.

The annual accounts of a limited company must be audited by persons _____ of it. The _____ investigate the accounts prepared by the company and report as to whether or not they show a _____ and _____ view of the results for the year and financial _____ as at year end. The auditors must form an _____ and report it. A report may be _____ where, for example, the auditors disagree with the directors.

In addition to auditing the primary financial statements and supporting _____, the auditors must consider whether the _____ _____ is _____ with the audited accounts.

Activity 5

In the set of published accounts you obtained for Activity 1, turn to the auditor's report.

(a) Does the report contain any information looking to the future, or is it purely historical in content?

(b) In most cases, the auditor's report is purely historical. How does this limit the usefulness of the report to users of accounts? Try to illustrate your answer by reference to specific cases you have seen reported.

1.3   The chairman's report

Most large companies include a chairman's report in their published financial statements. This is purely voluntary as there is no statutory requirement to do so.

The chairman's review invariably appears as the first item in the annual report and is not subject to any regulations regarding its content. The chairman is therefore free to say exactly what he wishes. His comments will generally cover the following broad areas: an assessment of the year's results; an examination of factors influencing those results, such as the economic and political climate or the effect of strikes; a reference to major developments, such as takeovers or new products; capital expenditure plans; and an assessment of future prospects.

The chairman's message will usually convey a fair amount of optimism, even if the financial facts published later in the report make depressing reading. A strong point in favour of the chairman's review is that it is readable and readily comprehensible to the layman. A major drawback is that, with regard to future prospects, it is based on opinion rather than fact. Nevertheless it is useful background material.

Activity 6

Now turn to the chairman's statement in your set of published accounts. Compare the mood of the statement with the story disclosed by the profit and loss account and the balance sheet. How far do the chairman's remarks appear to be borne out by the accounts figures?

1.4   Summary financial statements

The CA 1989 has amended the CA 1985 so that listed companies need not send all their members their full financial statements but can instead send them *summary financial statements* (SFSs). All members who want to receive full financial statements are still entitled to them, however.

An SFS must:

(a)   State that it is only a summary of information in the company's annual accounts and the directors' report

(b)   Contain a statement by the company's auditors of their opinion as to whether the summary financial statement is consistent with those accounts and that report and complies with the relevant statutory requirements

(c)   State whether the auditors' report on the annual accounts was unqualified or qualified, and if it was qualified set out the report in full together with any further material needed to understand the qualification

SFSs are derived from the company's annual accounts and the directors' report and the form and content are specified by regulations made by the Secretary of State.

The key figures from the full statements must be included along with the review of the business and future developments shown in the directors' report. Comparative figures must be shown.

A listed company has a choice of approaches.

(a)   It may send both the full accounts and the SFS to members, ask which the member wishes to receive in future and take a failure to respond as a preference only to receive the SFS in future.

(b)   It may send full accounts to all members who express no preference, and send SFSs only to members who notify in writing that this is their preference.

Option (a) is more likely to be adopted because listed companies are anxious to reduce the cost of producing annual reports.

A post-paid form or card must accompany an SFS to allow members to apply for full accounts if required.

Many listed companies already produce their annual reports in two parts: a glossy review of the business, which may include photographs, interviews, bar charts and other diagrams, and a more sober document containing the financial statements. It is likely that the former may be adapted to serve as the SFS. British Telecom, for example, has decided to do this and only one in forty members has requested receipt of full accounts in future. Other companies may prefer to produce an SFS which can be reproduced on one sheet of A4 paper or as a small brochure, much as the building societies already do.

Activity 7

By answering the following questions you should consolidate your knowledge of summary financial statements.

1.   Are users likely to confuse the SFS with the full accounts?

2.   Is the SFS audited?

3.   Can information which has not been included in the full report and accounts be included in the SFS?

Chapter roundup

In this chapter we have considered the contents and significance of the directors' report, the auditor's report and the chairman's statement.

- The accounts of limited companies must contain a directors' report (the minimum content of which is defined by statute) and an auditor's report.

- Most large companies voluntarily include a chairman's statement in their published accounts.

- Listed companies are allowed to send a summary financial statement to members who do not wish to receive the full published accounts.

Quick quiz

1   What information in respect of fixed assets must be disclosed in the directors' report?   (see para 1.1)

2   What information in respect of political and charitable contributions must be disclosed in the directors' report?   (1.1)

3   What documents are comprised in the accounts on which the auditor reports?   (1.2)

4   Which companies are eligible to send out summary financial statements?   (1.4)

Answers to activities

2   (a)   A company might lack investment opportunities and use surplus cash to repurchase shares.

(b)   A change in capital structure might be the purpose behind repurchasing preference shares for example and then issuing ordinary shares.

(c)   A dissident shareholder may be bought out without changing the proportions held by other shareholders.

(d)   A company may feel it is likely to be taken over and repurchase shares in order to create a proportionate increase in the shareholdings of some key major investors who wish the company to retain independence.

(e)   Employees may hold shares during their periods of employment but wish to sell them on leaving. The company may repurchase the shares.

3   True:

2.   Yes, and this is also true of charges on its own shares and the provision of financial assistance to purchase its own shares.

3.   True, and where land is held as a fixed asset, the difference between book value and market value, if significant, should be detailed.

False:

1.   Although all companies may give employee involvement details, only those companies employing an average of more than 250 people each week must give such details.

4.   Political and charitable contributions made by the company or group must be disclosed where, if taken together, these exceed £200. Separate totals must be given for each and, in the case of individual political contributions, contributions exceeding £200 should be fully detailed.

5.   The names of those persons who have served as directors at any time during the year should be given.

4   The missing words are: independent; auditors; true; fair; position; opinion; qualified; notes; directors' report; consistent.

5   (a)   Except in cases where a very critical transaction is hanging in the balance at the date of the auditor's report, such reports are entirely historical.

(b)   Many accounting scandals have been reported in the press in recent years. Often it has appeared that the signs of a company's eventual collapse must have been visible well in advance. Examples you might have mentioned include Polly Peck, BCCI and the Maxwell empire.

One result of these disasters is that the Auditing Practices Board requires auditors not just to look at the historical accuracy of the accounts, but to assess whether the company is likely to survive as a going concern for the near future.

7   1.   This should be avoided because the SFS must state that it is only a summary of information in the company's annual accounts and directors' report.

2.   Only in as far as it must contain a statement by the company's auditors as to whether the SFS is consistent with the accounts and complies with the relevant statutory requirements.

3.   No. SFSs are derived from the company's annual accounts and the directors' report.

Further question practice

Now try the following practice questions at the end of this text

Exam style question: **12**

Chapter 13 :
BUSINESS VALUATION

Introduction

If you have ever studied the financial pages of a newspaper, or watched the financial news on television, you will be aware of the interest that is taken in the share prices of companies. Many people have a portion of their capital invested in company shares and the price at which they can buy new shares, or sell the ones they already have, is of great importance to them. In addition, large institutional investors (such as pension funds) have huge sums of money tied up in this kind of investment. Clearly the process by which share prices are arrived at is a vital factor in the economy.

Your objectives

After completing this chapter you should:

(a)   Understand the factors which affect the valuation of a business

(b)   Be aware of some of the main methods of calculating the value of a business

1 SHARE VALUATION

1.1 Reasons for valuation

In the case of listed companies it is not difficult to obtain a share price. The shares of such companies are traded on the Stock Exchange and there may be many transactions each day in which they are bought and sold. Every day, newspapers like the *Financial Times* publish lists of share prices which reflect the most up-to-date information for each company.

But how are these published prices arrive at? And what happens in the case of those companies, by far the majority, whose shares are not listed on the Stock Exchange? What about the problem of valuing a business that is not established in the form of a company, and does not have shares in issue at all?

In this chapter we look at some general considerations which affect the valuation of a business, whether incorporated as a company or not. We also illustrate some of the basic approaches to placing a value on a company's shares.

When we look at each basis of valuation, it will be helpful to remember the reason why a share valuation is being made. Suggest two parties who would need to establish a share price and the factors which will affect how the price is determined.

(a)   A *buyer* of shares is obtaining a share of the profits (earnings) of the business, and will be entitled to income from dividends. The size of profits and dividends he will expect to earn from the shares will have an important bearing on the price he will be prepared to pay.

(b)   A *seller* of shares will be giving up his share of future profits and dividends, and the price offered by the buyer must be good enough to compensate him for this loss. If the buyer doesn't offer enough money, and the would-be seller owns enough shares to force the company into a voluntary liquidation, it might be more profitable to break up the company and sell off its assets individually to various buyers.

For both the buyer and the seller, the value of a share must depend on the income they could get or might lose in the future. However, estimates of future profits and dividends are bound to be uncertain, because it is difficult to foresee the future accurately. A would-be seller is likely to paint a rosy picture of the future to a buyer, whereas the buyer will probably be cautious and conservative. One fairly good way of estimating future profits and dividends is to suppose that what has happened in the past will continue in the future. For this reason, 'historical' profits and dividends are often used for share valuations, although the future is the real concern.

By law, every share must have a *nominal value*. This is its face value. When a share is first issued, its nominal value might well be its market value. For example, if a company issues 100,000 new shares with a nominal value of 50p each for cash, and the issue is at par, then subscribers will have to pay 50p for each share they buy.

On the other hand, if the company issues 100,000 new shares of 50p each, at a cash price of 75p each, the nominal value of the shares would be £50,000 (50p each) but their market value would be £75,000 (75p each). The difference of £25,000 would be recorded in the accounts as a share premium.

The nominal value of shares at all other times is usually completely different from their market value. (If you look at the prices of quoted shares on The Stock Exchange, the difference between nominal values and market values should convince you that this is so.) We must therefore conclude that when a shareholder wants to put a price on his shares, their nominal value will be totally irrelevant to the valuation.

EXAMPLE: SHARE VALUES

Company A issues 100,000 £1 shares at £1.50, and on the first day of trading they are selling at £1.75.

Company B issues 10,000 50p shares at 75p, and on the first day of trading they are selling at 45p.

(a) What is the total nominal value of Company A's and Company B's shares respectively?

(b) Does the nominal value per share differ from the issue price?

(c) What is the total market value of Company A's and Company B's shares respectively?

ANSWER

(a) The total nominal value of Company A's shares is £100,000 (£1 × 100,000); the total nominal value of Company B's shares is £5,000 (50p × 10,000).

(b) Yes, both companies have issued the shares at a premium, 50p for Company A and 25p for Company B. Share premium must be credited to the share premium account, while the nominal value is credited to the share capital account.

(c) The total market values of Company A and Company B are £175,000 and £4,500 respectively. Once shares have been issued the issue price becomes almost irrelevant in market trading. You should note that Company B's shares have fallen below the nominal value. Shares may never be issued at a discount (ie below nominal value) but once they have been issued their price will depend on the market.

1.2 Asset value of shares

There are three ways of putting a value on shares by working out what the assets 'owned' by the shareholders are worth. These three share valuations are:

(a) Book value

(b) Replacement cost value, or 'going concern' asset value

(c) Liquidation (or breakup) value

Book value

The book value of assets is their value in the books of account and in the balance sheet of the business. Not all assets are financed by shareholders so the book value of shares is:

(a) The book value of all assets (fixed and current)

(b) *Minus* the long-term liabilities (such as debenture stock) and current liabilities of the business

The book value of fixed assets is taken as their net book value.

If there are any preference shares, the book value of equity (ordinary shares) is then found by subtracting the nominal value of the preference shares.

Another way of stating the book value of ordinary shares is:

(a)   The nominal value of the shares

(b)   Plus the book value of reserves

The book value of shares is sometimes used to guess at the 'worth' of the assets which the shares own. If a share with a nominal value of £1 has a book value of, say, £20, it might be said to have a high 'asset backing' whereas a £1 share with a book value of only, say, 50p would have a low asset backing. It is possible that shares would sell for a better price if they had a high book value than if they had a low book value.

Activity 1

As a means of valuing a company, the book value of its assets has serious limitations. Try to think of some of the reasons why this is so.

Replacement cost value

Replacement cost value is the cost that would be incurred if the assets of the business had to be replaced at today's prices, in their current condition. For example, if a machine has only one half of its expected life go to and it would now cost £50,000 to replace with a new machine, its replacement cost value would be estimated as one half of £50,000: £25,000.

With occasional exceptions, the replacement cost value of assets is a reasonable estimate of their value to the business, on the assumption that the business is going to continue its operations. Replacement cost value is therefore an estimate of the 'going concern value' of a business.

The replacement cost value of shares is:

		£
Replacement cost of all assets		X
Less:	liabilities	(X)
	nominal value of preference shares	(X)
		X

If a shareholder wants to *sell* some shares, their replacement cost value is of little interest or relevance to him (except in the rare event that he owns all the shares and intends to use the proceeds from the sale of the business to set up an identical business somewhere else). A prospective buyer of shares is also unlikely to be interested in a replacement cost value because he is not proposing to set up in business by purchasing the assets from scratch.

The only method of share valuation based on asset valuation which has an important bearing on negotiating a share price is the liquidation or break-up basis.

Liquidation value (or break-up value)

The liquidation value of shares is the amount of money they would fetch for shareholders if the business were put into liquidation, and the assets 'broken up' and sold off piecemeal to various buyers.

If the liquidation value of shares is higher than the price a would-be buyer is willing to pay for them, the shareholder would prefer to sell off the company's assets in a liquidation than to sell shares at that price. However, individual shareholders cannot put a business into voluntary liquidation unless they have a very substantial shareholding and the option to break up the company rather than sell off the shares to a buyer simply might not exist.

The break-up value of shares is:

		£
Net realisable value of all assets		X
Less:	liabilities	(X)
	liquidation costs	(X)
	preference shares (nominal value) plus arrears of dividend	(X)
		(X)

Points to bear in mind.

(a) Freehold land and buildings should sell for their current market value.

(b) Plant, machinery and other equipment will probably sell for less than their book value because the costs of removal might be high and second-hand machine values might be low.

(c) Most stocks will probably be sold off at a profit.

(d) Debtors might not pay up in full and so allowance should be made for the most likely bad debt rate.

Activity 2

Mark the following sentences as true or false.

1   Book value is usually historical cost less accumulated depreciation, although it may be a 'revalued' amount.

2   Replacement cost is the cost which would be incurred if the assets of the business had to be replaced with new assets.

3   The liquidation value of shares is the amount of money they would fetch if the business were put into liquidation and the assets were sold off piecemeal.

4   Financial accounts are always prepared on an historical cost basis.

1.3   Share valuations based on a price/earnings ratio

Of much more practical significance for the valuation of companies are methods which attempt to quantify the future benefits that will be enjoyed by a purchaser.

(a) A purchaser intending to acquire the whole of a business, or a very substantial part of it, would be interested in the likely future earnings of the business. As a reminder, earnings are the profits left over for ordinary shareholders after all expenses, interest, taxation and preference dividends have been paid.

(b) A purchaser intending to acquire only a small proportion of a business (say a 1% shareholding or even a 10% shareholding) might be more interested in the dividends likely to be paid by the company. Such an investor does not hold a large enough stake in the company to control its earnings, and the benefit he receives will be measured by the proportion of earnings paid out in the form of dividends.

We will begin by looking at the first case. You first of all need to know what is meant by a price/earnings ratio. You have already looked at this in Chapter 10.

As its name suggests, this ratio is calculated by comparing the price of a share with the earnings attributable to the share (ie the earnings per share, EPS).

Activity 3

Here are some extracts from the 20X6 accounts of Nebraska plc.

PROFIT AND LOSS ACCOUNT (EXTRACT)
FOR THE YEAR ENDED 31 DECEMBER 20X6

	£'000	£'000
Profit before tax		2,680
Taxation		1,110
Profit after tax		1,570
Dividends: ordinary	65	
preference	170	
		235
Retained profit for the year		1,335

BALANCE SHEET (EXTRACT) AS AT 31 DECEMBER 20X6

	£'000
Share capital	
6½% preference shares of £1 each	1,000
Ordinary shares of 10p each	1,000
	2,000

The price of Nebraska's ordinary shares is currently 240p. Calculate the price/earnings ratio.

If a company does not have a quotation on the stock market, it does not have a known price. If it does not have a price, it cannot have a price/earnings ratio. Nevertheless, one method of making a share valuation is to *assume what the price/earnings ratio for a share should be*, and having decided on a suitable ratio, to calculate the share's value as:

[Earnings per share] × [Price/earnings ratio]

This is just an arithmetical re-arrangement based on the definition of a P/E ratio.

$$\text{If P/E ratio} = \frac{\text{Price}}{\text{Earnings}}, \text{ then Price} = \text{P/E ratio} \times \text{Earnings}$$

Suppose that New Mexico Ltd is an unlisted company which last year made earnings of £30,000. The company has 100,000 ordinary shares in issue. If Dakota plc has offered to buy the entire share capital of New Mexico on a price/earnings multiple of 5, the offer price per share would be:

Earnings per share	×	Price/earnings ratio
= 30p	×	5
= £1.50		

In order to make a valuation by the price/earnings ratio method, we need to select an appropriate price/earnings ratio. It has already been mentioned that a price/earnings ratio is always known for quoted companies, but not for unquoted companies.

The obvious solution is to select a price/earnings ratio using the ratio of a quoted company in the same industry. If there are several quoted companies in the same industry, an average of their ratios might be used.

The forecast of maintainable earnings is perhaps the most appropriate earnings figure to use in the valuation. In the absence of a reliable forecast, earnings in the most recent year, or possibly an average of earnings over the past two or three years, might be used instead.

Obviously the valuation includes a large measure of subjectivity.

Activity 4

Ohio Ltd is considering whether to make a bid for the entire share capital of Michigan Ltd, a private company which has made annual earnings of about £25,000 a year for the past few years. Ohio Ltd would offer a price for Michigan Ltd's shares on the basis of a valuation by a price/earnings ratio.

The current price/earnings ratios of quoted companies which are in a similar line of business to Michigan Ltd are as follows.

	P/E ratio
Vermont plc	8.2
New Hampshire plc	9.5
Massachusetts plc	9.3

What might be the offer price for the shares of Michigan Ltd?

The serious drawback to using a price/earnings ratio based on those of quoted companies is that unquoted companies' shares are generally seen as less attractive investments. Thus a lower price/earnings ratio would be appropriate for an unquoted company than for a similar quoted company.

Activity 5

Suggest reasons why shares in a quoted company might be considered a better investment than shares in an unquoted company operating in the same business sector.

In Activity 4, a price/earnings ratio of around 9 is higher than the ratio of one quoted company (Vermont plc) and nearly as high as the ratios of the other two. It would not be unreasonable to argue that a price/earnings ratio of less than 8.2 (perhaps 8, 7 or even 6) would be more appropriate for Michigan. On a price/earnings ratio of 7, the share valuation would be: £25,000 × 7 = £175,000.

The choice of 9 or 8 or 7 as a price/earnings ratio is a subjective judgement on the part of the would-be buyer or seller of shares. If the buyer thinks that a P/E ratio of 7 is appropriate, but the seller selects a P/E ratio of 9 for this valuation, the buyer and seller will end up with widely differing valuations. They would then need to negotiate with each other to find out whether they can agree on a price at which to deal.

1.4 Dividend yield basis of valuation

As an alternative to using earnings as a basis for share valuation, we can use dividends. The buyer of a share will be paying money for an expected future income from dividends, right up to the time he decides to sell the share. The seller of a share is receiving money now, and in return is giving up future income from dividends.

Definition

> *Dividend yield* is the ratio of the dividend paid on a share to the price of the share, expressed as a percentage. (At this stage we will ignore taxation.)

For example, if a quoted company pays a dividend of 16p per share, and the market price of the share is £2, the dividend yield would be:

$$\frac{16p}{£2} \times 100\% = 8\%$$

The dividend yield basis of share valuation is as follows:

If dividend yield (as a percentage or proportion) $= \dfrac{\text{Dividend per share}}{\text{Price per share}}$

then price (value) per share $= \dfrac{\text{Dividend per share}}{\text{Dividend yield}}$

Activity 6

California Ltd is a private company which has paid a regular total annual dividend of £24,000 on its 100,000 ordinary shares. A prospective buyer of some of the share capital of California Ltd considers that the dividend yield from an investment of this type should be 12%.

What value should he place on a share of California Ltd by the dividend yield method? Ignore taxation.

How do we obtain a dividend yield for the valuation?

The dividend yield is the ratio of dividend to share price and if we do not know the share price we cannot calculate a dividend yield. The only shares for which we do know the share price and dividend yield are the shares of quoted companies, and once again it might be appropriate to decide on a dividend yield for share valuation by looking at the yields obtained from shares in similar quoted companies.

Dividend yield is usually taken as $\dfrac{\text{Dividend}}{\text{Share price}} \times 100\%$

For example in the share information pages of the *Financial Times*, the dividend yield on shares is worked out on gross dividend.

If a company, Missouri Ltd, pays a dividend of 5p per share and if a shareholder assumes a dividend yield of 10% on his investment in Missouri, the dividend yield valuation would be found as follows.

(a) Dividend per share = 5p

(b) Valuation of a share 5p/10% = 50p

Chapter roundup

You should now understand the factors which affect the valuation of a business and how the value of a business may be calculated.

- There are many different methods of estimating a share's value. They are intended to help a buyer or seller of shares to decide how much money he might expect to pay or receive for the shares in the absence of a quoted price on a stock exchange.

- Some of the valuation methods we have looked at are unsatisfactory, or even irrelevant, to the 'real' value of a share. The most useful methods are:

  (i) *Liquidation value* (but only if the shareholder or shareholders have the power to put the company into liquidation and would be willing to break up the company)

  (ii) Valuation based on *price/earnings ratio*

  (iii) The *dividend yield method*

- These three methods are the most relevant because they try to put a value to future cash flows from the shares.

- Valuation methods do not give us the actual selling price of shares. They guide a seller or buyer of shares towards a price on which they can agree through negotiation.

In Chapter 14 you will be able to develop your understanding of *management accounting* and the important part it plays in decision making.

Quick quiz

1 What is a listed share? (see para 1.1)

2 Of what relevance in a share valuation exercise is the nominal value of a share? (1.1)

3 What are the three methods of asset valuation of shares? Which is the most useful, and why? (1.2)

4 What factors should be taken into account when selecting a suitable P/E ratio for use in valuing shares? (1.3)

5 If a share has a dividend yield of 8% and a dividend of 24p, what is the share price on the dividend yield basis of valuation? (1.4)

NOTES

Answers to activities

1   Book value is only a very rough approximation of the value of assets. For example, land and buildings might be recorded at their original cost, and if property prices have changed since the date of their purchase, their book value would be unrealistic. The book value of plant and machinery is an 'artificial' value because it depends on the firm's depreciation methods.

Furthermore, if there is fairly rapid price inflation, the book values of most assets will probably be out of date and at historical, non-current figures.

Most importantly, though, book value does not reflect future income. A potential buyer of shares is interested in purchasing because of the benefits he hopes to enjoy in the future, and book values provide no measure of such benefit.

2   True:

1.

3.   True. If the liquidation value of shares is higher than the price a would-be buyer is willing to pay for them then shareholders may prefer to liquidate the company and sell off the assets.

False:

2.   No, the replacement cost is based on replacing with assets in their current condition.

4.   Although this is usually so, a modified historical cost basis may be used (ie where some current values are used), or a current cost basis may be used.

3   Earnings   =   £1,570,000 – £65,000
    =   £1,505,000

There are 10,000,000 ordinary shares of 10p each in issue.

Earnings per share therefore equals: $\dfrac{1,505,000}{10,000,000} = 15.05\text{p}$

The price/earnings ratio is: 240p/15.05p, or 15.95.

4   A range of valuations might be considered.

(a)   One valuation might be based on the lowest price/earnings ratio, 8.2.

(b)   Another valuation might be based on the highest price/earnings ratio, 9.5.

(c)   Perhaps more logically, the valuation might be based on the average price/earnings ratio of the three companies.

(a)   Low valuation: £25,000 × 8.2 = £205,000

(b)   High valuation: £25,000 × 9.5 = £237,500

(c)   Valuation based on average price/earnings ratio:

(i)   Average P/E ratio $\dfrac{8.2 + 9.3 + 9.5}{3} = 9.0$

(ii)   Valuation   £25,000 × 9   = £225,000

BPP
PUBLISHING

A range of valuations between £205,000 and £237,500 might provide the most realistic solution. In practice, considerable negotiation takes place before the price is fixed.

5   (a)   Quoted company shares can be sold whenever the shareholder likes because the stock market exists to provide a trade in shares. Unquoted company shares cannot be sold so easily and the seller must first find prospective buyers and then negotiate a price.

    (b)   Quoted companies are often thought to be more 'secure' and less of a business risk because of their size and status. Private companies are often smaller and perhaps more of a 'gamble' for investors.

6   The dividend per share has been 24p in the past and this level of payment is expected to continue in the future. If the expected dividend yield is 12%, then a dividend of 24p represents 12% of the value of a share. The share valuation will be:

$$\frac{\text{Dividend}}{\text{Dividend yield}} = \frac{24\text{p}}{12\%} = £2$$

Chapter 14 :
THE ANALYSIS OF COST

Introduction

In Chapter 1 of this book we explained a distinction between management accounting and financial accounting. You should refer back to page 4 if you need a reminder.

Up until now, most of what we have covered falls into the category of financial accounting. We have looked at the published accounts of limited companies (and the similar financial statements prepared by unincorporated businesses); how they are prepared, what they contain and how we can use them to assess the financial performance of the business.

From now on we will turn our attention to *management accounting*. This is the system by which financial information is prepared for the use of managers within the business. The form in which such information is prepared is entirely at the discretion of management, who can ask for any statements or analyses which they believe will be useful to them in running the business. There are no external bodies laying down rules about content or presentation.

One of the key points that a manager will be interested in is the cost of the resources used in the business: production materials (in a manufacturing business), labour costs such as wages, salaries and bonuses, overheads (such as light and heat, rent and rates), selling and distribution expenses and so on. These costs of course also feature in the financial accounts of a business, but the level of detail and analysis presented there may be much less than managers require for the efficient running of the business.

Your objectives

After completing this chapter you should:

    (a)   Understand why a business needs to analyse its costs

    (b)   Be aware of the main ways in which costs can be classified

1 REASONS FOR ANALYSING COSTS IN MANAGEMENT ACCOUNTS

It is worth thinking about the reasons why managers require a more detailed analysis of cost than is thought appropriate for external users of accounts. There are lots of reasons that might be advanced; suggest three and write your answers here.

1.

2.

3.

Managers need to establish selling prices for their goods and services. Unless they know exactly which costs are attributable to a particular product or service, there is a risk that they may set prices which are too low to earn a profit.

The question of selling prices is part of the more general problem of decision making. Managers are constantly confronted by choices, and their selection of one option rather than another will be at least partly dependent on the costs associated with each.

Managers need to plan ahead, and possibly to prepare financial budgets. To do so, they need to know what costs are incurred by the business and how the level of any particular cost is likely to vary depending on the plans they decide to adopt.

To maximise profitability, managers need to exercise close control over costs. They need to ensure that their plans, whatever they may be, are achieved with the least possible expenditure of resources. This is not to say that the cheapest way of doing something must always be the best; there is of course a danger of sacrificing quality. But the balancing act between cost and quality is impossible unless the nature of the costs involved is known.

Finally, it is necessary for various reasons to be able to value the assets of a business. As we have already seen, the basis of asset valuation is the cost of the asset. In some cases this will not require much calculation – the cost of a delivery van, for example, will be the total shown on the supplier's invoice. But things can be much more complicated than that. For example, to value the stock of finished goods held by a manufacturing business we would need to aggregate:

(a) The costs of all the raw material used in each product

(b) The cost of wages paid to production employees

(c) A share of the cost of overheads

It should be clear from all this that most businesses need a fairly detailed system for analysing their costs. We will now look at some of the ways in which costs can be differentiated and classified.

Activity 1

There are many reasons which could be given to justify the recording and analysing of costs. Some have been given above. Try to think of some other possibilities.

2   METHODS OF CLASSIFYING COSTS

2.1   Direct costs and indirect costs (overheads)

Total costs of a product or service consist of the following costs.

(a)   The cost of materials consumed in making the product or providing the service.

(b)   The cost of the wages and salaries of employees of the organisation, who are directly or indirectly involved in producing the product or providing the service.

(c)   Other expenses, apart from materials and labour costs. These include items such as rent and rates, electricity bills, gas bills, depreciation, interest charges, the cost of contractors' services (for example sub-contractors and office cleaners), telephone bills.

Materials, labour costs and other expenses can be classified as direct costs or as indirect costs.

Definition

> A *direct cost* is a cost that can be traced in full to the product or service (or department and so on) that is being costed.

(a)   Direct materials costs are the costs of materials that are known to have been used in making and selling a product (or providing a service).

(b)   Direct labour costs are the specific costs of the workforce used to make a product or provide a service. Direct labour costs are established by measuring the time taken for a job, or the time taken in 'direct production work'.

(c)   Other direct expenses are expenses other than materials or labour that have been incurred in full as a direct consequence of making a product or providing a service.

The total direct cost is also known as the *prime cost*.

An *indirect* cost or *overhead* is a cost that is incurred in the course of making a product, providing a service or running a department, but which cannot be traced directly and in full to the product, service or department.

Definition

> An *indirect cost* or *overhead* can be defined as 'expenditure on labour, materials or services which cannot be economically identified with a specific saleable cost unit'.

Examples, respectively, might be supervisor's wages, cleaning materials and buildings insurance. (The definition above, like many of those in this and the coming chapters, is taken from the 1996 edition of *Official Terminology* published by the Chartered Institute of Management Accountants, or CIMA.)

2.2 Fixed costs and variable costs

A different way of analysing and classifying costs is into *fixed costs* and *variable costs*. Some items of expenditure are part-fixed and part-variable or 'semi-fixed' costs, but in cost accounting semi-fixed or semi-variable costs are divided into their fixed and variable elements.

The distinction between fixed and variable costs lies in whether the amount of costs incurred will rise as the volume of activity increases, or whether the costs will remain the same, regardless of the volume of activity. Some examples are as follows.

(a) Direct material costs will rise as more units of a product are manufactured, and so they are variable costs that vary with the volume of production.

(b) Sales commission is often a fixed percentage of sales turnover, and so is a variable cost that varies with the level of sales (but not with the level of production).

(c) Telephone call charges are likely to increase if the volume of business expands, and so they are a variable overhead cost, varying with the volume of production and sales.

(d) The rental cost of business premises is a constant amount, at least within a stated time period, and so it is a fixed cost that does not vary with the level of activity conducted on the premises.

Activity 2

Try to think in greater detail about some of the costs listed here, and check whether you agree with the analysis given. For example, is the total amount shown on a telephone bill a variable cost? Is the rent paid by a business on its premises necessarily a fixed cost?

You will examine variable costs and fixed costs more fully in the next chapter. You should be aware at this stage of your studies that costs can be classified as direct costs or overheads, or as fixed or variable costs. These alternative classifications are not mutually exclusive, but are complementary to each other, so that we can find:

(a) Some direct costs that are fixed costs (although most direct costs are variable costs)

(b) Some overhead costs that are fixed, and some overhead costs that are variable

Activity 3

Mark the following sentences as true or false.

1   Material costs are always direct costs.

2   Fixed costs are only fixed within a relevant range of activity.

3   Overhead costs are always fixed costs.

4   The prime cost is the total direct cost.

2.3 Relevant costs and non-relevant costs

Definition

> *Relevant costs* are defined as 'costs appropriate to a specific management decision' (CIMA, *Official Terminology*).

A relevant cost is a future cash flow arising as a direct consequence of the decision under review. Only relevant costs should be considered in decision making, because it is assumed that in the long run future profits will be maximised if the 'cash profits' of the company, ie the cash earned from sales minus the cash expenditures on making and selling the goods, are also maximised.

Activity 4

Which of the following are 'relevant' costs?

1   Past costs or money already spent.

2   Cash overheads incurred (such as the salary of an extra supervisor).

3   Future spending already committed by separate previous decisions.

4   Non-cash costs, for example depreciation, notional rent or notional interest.

5   Income which may be lost depending on the current decision.

6   Future expenditure which will depend on the decision.

The relevant cost of a unit of production is usually the variable cost of that unit plus (or minus) any change in the total expenditure on fixed costs.

The assumption used is that in the end profits earn cash. Reported profits and cash flow are not the same in any period for various reasons, such as the timing differences caused by giving credit and the accounting treatment of depreciation. In the long run, however, a profit that is earned will eventually produce a net inflow of an equal amount of cash. Hence, accounting for decision making looks at cash flow as a means of measuring profits.

Definition

> *Avoidable costs* are defined by the CIMA as 'the specific costs of an activity or sector of a business which would be avoided if that activity or sector did not exist'.

It is sometimes necessary to identify the avoidable costs to decide whether or not to discontinue a product. The only costs which would be saved are the avoidable costs, which are usually the variable costs and sometimes some specific fixed costs. Costs which would be incurred whether or not the product is discontinued are known as *unavoidable costs*.

A *differential cost* is 'the difference in total cost between alternatives'. If option A will cost an extra £300 and option B will cost an extra £360, the differential cost is £60, with option B being more expensive. A differential cost is the difference between the *relevant costs* of each option.

The differential cost of an extra unit of production is the extra cost required to make that unit: it is the difference in cost between making the unit and not making it. This type of cost is also called an *incremental cost*. Incremental costs are relevant costs.

An *opportunity cost* is the benefit forgone by selecting one course of action in preference to the most profitable available alternative. Suppose for example that there are three mutually exclusive options, A, B and C. The net profit from each would be £80, £100 and £70 respectively. Since only one option can be selected, option B would be chosen because it offers the biggest benefit.

	£
Profit from option B	100
Less opportunity cost (ie the benefit from the most profitable alternative, A)	80
Differential benefit of option B	20

The decision to choose option B would not be taken simply because it offers a profit of £100, but because it offers a differential profit of £20 in excess of the next best alternative.

Definition

> The CIMA's *Official Terminology* defines an *opportunity cost* simply as 'the value of the benefit sacrificed when one course of action is chosen, in preference to an alternative.'

The principle underlying decision accounting is that 'bygones are bygones'. What has happened in the past is done, and cannot be undone. Management decisions can only affect the future. In decision making, managers therefore require information about future costs and revenues which would be affected by the decision under review, and they must not be misled by events, costs and revenues in the past, about which they can do nothing. Past expenditures, in decision making terms, are *sunk costs*.

Activity 5

Fill in the missing words to ensure you understand which costs are relevant.

Relevant costs are _____ costs and benefits obtainable by carrying out a particular course of action, and they also include the benefits which could have been _____, but which have been given up, by choosing one option instead of another. _____ costs will never appear in a set of double entry cost accounts, but they often appear in _____ accounting information reports.

NOTES

Activity 6

A manufacturing company has three tons of raw material X in stock. Raw material X is no longer used in the company's operations and is therefore obsolete, except that it could be used in a special one-off job which the company is thinking about undertaking. The stock on hand originally cost £600 per ton, and would nowadays cost £750 per ton. The scrap value, if the company decides not to take on the one-off job, is £150 per ton.

In deciding whether or not to do the one-off job, what is the relevant cost of the three tons of X?

Chapter roundup

The analysis and classification of costs is the basis of management accounting.

- For many reasons, most companies need to record and analyse their costs in detail. In particular, this is important for decision making, planning and control.

- Costs can be analysed in several different ways: direct and indirect, fixed and variable, relevant and non-relevant.

In the next chapter we will develop your knowledge of costing by looking at cost behaviour.

Quick quiz

1   How is an analysis of costs relevant to setting selling prices?

(see section 1)

2   What costs could be included in the valuation of finished goods stock in a manufacturing business? (2.1)

3   Define 'direct materials cost' (2.1)

4   Which of the following is usually a fixed cost?

    (a)   Direct material costs

    (b)   Telephone call charges

    (c)   Rent of premises (2.2)

5   What is an incremental cost? (2.3)

6   What is an opportunity cost? (2.3)

Answers to activities

1   You may have been able to think of reasons from organisations you have worked for or been connected with.

    (a)   Managers might want to know the profitability of a particular department or decision and would seek to know the costs attributable to it.

PUBLISHING

(b) A group of employees might be entitled to a productivity bonus based on keeping the production costs of particular products to a minimum. To calculate the bonus, we need to know the product costs.

2   The total charge on a telephone bill will include a fixed rental charge as well as a variable call charge.

Rent paid for premises is only a fixed cost within certain limits. For example, if business is booming a manufacturer might need to rent a second factory unit, and rental charges might double.

3   True:

2.

4.

False:

1.   Material costs may be either direct or indirect costs.

3.   Overheads generally have a variable and a fixed element.

4   Only 2, 5 and 6 are relevant costs in that they concern future cash flows dependent on the current decision.

5   The missing words are: future; earned; opportunity; decision.

6   The choice faced by the company is either to scrap the material (so earning £450) or to use it for the one-off job. The relevant cost is the £450 scrap value that will be forgone if the job is undertaken. The original cost of £1,800 is not relevant – it has already been incurred and nothing can now be done about it. Nor is the replacement cost relevant, since the company has no intention of buying more X.

Further question practice

Now try the following practice questions at the end of this text

Multiple choice questions: **74 to 76**

Exam style question: **13**

Chapter 15 :
COST BEHAVIOUR

Introduction

We have already seen that an important part of cost and management accounting is the provision of information for management planning and control. To provide useful information for this purpose, the cost accountant is not concerned simply with recording what actual costs were, but also with:

(a) Estimating what costs are expected to be in the future (for budgeting and planning decisions)

(b) Determining what costs should have been (for comparing with actual costs and triggering off any necessary control action)

Your objectives

After completing this chapter you should:

(a) Understand the importance of the 'level of activity' in analysing costs

(b) Be aware of the more important patterns of cost behaviour

(c) Be aware of the factors influencing cost behaviour

1 COST BEHAVIOUR AND LEVELS OF ACTIVITY

To estimate what costs will be, or what costs should have been, the accountant must understand cost behaviour.

Definition

> *Cost behaviour* is 'the variability of input costs with activity undertaken' (CIMA, *Official Terminology*).

1.1 Level of activity

The *level of activity* refers to the amount of work done, or the number of events that have occurred. Depending on circumstances, the level of activity may refer to the volume of production in a period, the number of items sold, the value of items sold, the number of invoices issued, the number of invoices received, the number of units of electricity consumed, the labour turnover and so on.

The basic principle of cost behaviour is that as the level of activity rises, costs will usually rise. For example, it will cost more to produce 2,000 units of output than it will cost to produce 1,000 units; it will usually cost more to make five telephone calls than to make one call.

This principle is common sense. The problem for the accountant, however, is to determine for each item of cost in what way costs rise as the level of activity increases.

For our purposes here, the level of activity for measuring cost will generally be taken to be the volume of production. You should also remember that there are other factors influencing cost behaviour; for example heating costs are affected by the season of the year.

> **Activity 1**
>
> Would it be true to say that it will normally cost twice as much to make 2,000 units of output as to make 1,000?
>
> *Hint.* This anticipates the discussion in this chapter of fixed costs and variable costs.

2 COST BEHAVIOUR

2.1 Cost behaviour patterns

Fixed costs

What do you think a fixed cost is? Write your answer here.

BPP
PUBLISHING

A fixed cost is a cost which tends to be unaffected by increases or decreases in the volume of output. Fixed costs are a period charge, in that they relate to a span of time; as the time span increases, so too will the fixed costs (which are sometimes referred to as *period costs* for this reason).

A sketch graph of a fixed cost would look like this.

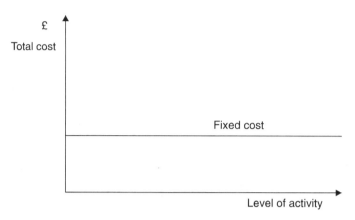

Figure 15.1 Graph of fixed cost

The range over which the fixed cost remains constant is known as the *relevant range*.

Write down two examples of fixed costs.

1.

2.

Examples of a fixed cost could include:

   (a)   The salary of the managing director (per month or per annum)

   (b)   The rent of a single factory building (per month or per annum)

You may have suggested other costs. They will depend upon the business being considered.

Step costs

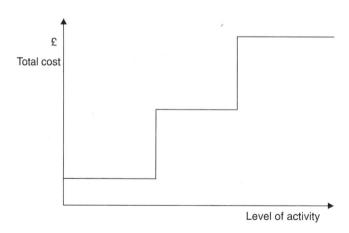

Figure 15.2 Graph of step cost

Many items of cost are fixed within certain levels of activity. For example the depreciation of a machine may be fixed if production remains below 1,000 units per month, but if production exceeds 1,000 units, a second machine may be required, and the cost of depreciation (on two machines) would go up a step. A sketch graph of a step cost would look like this.

Other examples of step costs are:

(a) Rent, where accommodation requirements increase as output levels get higher

(b) Basic wages. Basic pay of employees is nowadays usually fixed, but as output rises, more employees (for example, direct workers, supervisors, managers) are required

Variable costs

A variable cost is a cost which tends to vary directly with the volume of output. The variable cost per unit is the same amount for each unit produced.

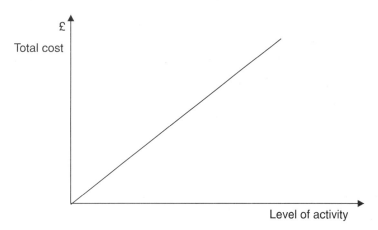

Figure 15.3 Graph of variable cost (1)

A constant variable cost per unit implies that the purchase price per unit of material purchased or cost per labour hour worked is constant, and that the rate of material usage/labour productivity is also constant.

(a) The most important variable cost is the cost of raw materials (where there is no discount for bulk purchasing; bulk purchase discounts reduce the cost of purchases).

(b) Direct labour costs are, for very important reasons, classed as a variable cost even though basic wages are usually fixed.

(c) Sales commission is variable in relation to the volume or value of sales.

Semi-variable costs (or semi-fixed costs or mixed costs)

These are cost items which are part fixed and part variable.

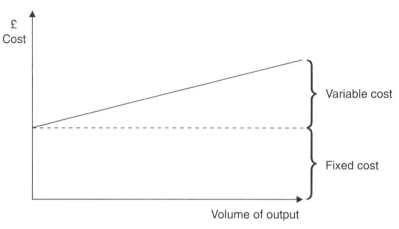

Figure 15.4 Graph of semi-variable costs

Examples of these costs include electricity and gas bills, where there is a standing basic charge plus a variable charge per unit of consumption.

Activity 2

Try to think what kind of cost might be represented by the following graphs.

(a)

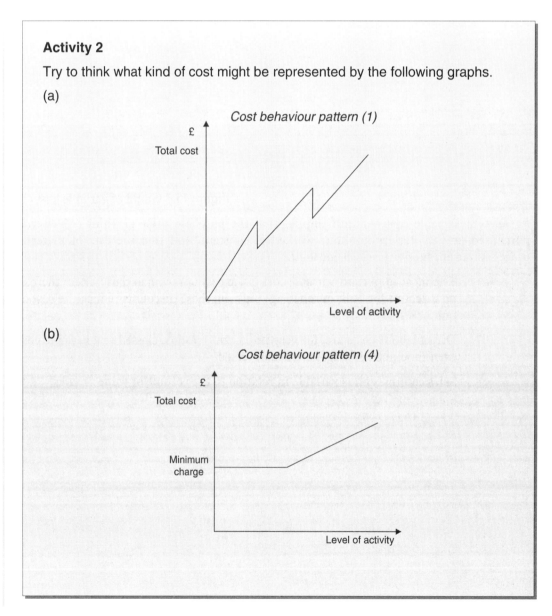

(b)

Determining the fixed and variable elements of semi-variable costs

It is often possible to assume that, within the normal range of output, costs are either variable, fixed or semi-variable. Step costs are fixed within a certain range, and the cost behaviour patterns described earlier are variable or semi-variable within a certain range.

For this reason cost accountants usually treat all costs as fixed or variable, and a semi-variable cost is divided into its variable element and its fixed element. In fact, estimating cost behaviour to derive figures for fixed and variable costs inevitably involves some approximations and assumptions.

There are several ways in which fixed cost elements and variable cost elements within semi-variable costs may be estimated. Each method is only an estimate, and can therefore give differing results from the other methods. The simplest method, illustrated below, is the high/low method.

(a)   To estimate the fixed and variable elements of semi-variable costs, records of cost in previous periods are reviewed and the costs of two periods are selected.

   (i)   The period with the highest volume of output.

   (ii)   The period with the lowest volume of output.

   Note. The periods with the highest/lowest output may not be the periods of highest/lowest cost.

(b)   The difference between the total cost of the high output and the total cost of the low output will be the *variable cost of the difference in output levels* as is shown on the following graph.

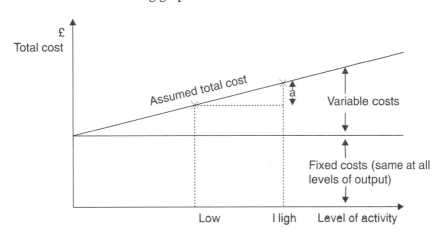

Figure 15.5 Demonstration of high-low method

The difference in cost, £a is seen to consist entirely of variable costs.

(c)   The variable cost per unit may be calculated from this, and the fixed cost may then also be determined.

NOTES

Activity 3

The costs of operating the maintenance department of a computer manufacturer, Sillick and Chips Ltd, for the last four months have been as follows.

Month		£	Production volume Standard hours
	1	110,000	7,000
	2	115,000	8,000
	3	111,000	7,700
	4	97,000	6,000

What costs should be expected in month five when output is expected to be 7,500 standard hours?

Activity 4

Mark the following statements as true or false.

1   The level of activity always refers to the volume of production in a period.

2   The basic principle of cost behaviour is that, as the level of activity rises, costs will usually rise.

3   A fixed cost is one which tends to be unaffected by increases/decreases in the volume of output.

4   The variable cost per unit falls as output rises.

5   The high/low method is used to split semi-variable costs into their variable and fixed elements.

The linear assumption of cost behaviour

The previous paragraphs may be summarised as follows.

(a)   Individual items of cost may have a cost behaviour pattern with an unusual 'shape', but costs are generally considered to be fixed, variable or mixed (semi-fixed, semi-variable) within a normal range of output.

(b)   Departmental costs are assumed to be mixed costs, with a fixed element and a variable cost element. The fixed costs and variable costs per unit may be estimated, with varying degrees of accuracy, by a variety of methods, of which the high-low method is perhaps the simplest to use.

(c)   Departmental costs are therefore assumed to rise in a straight line (linear) fashion as the volume of activity increases.

A worthwhile question to ask at this stage is: are the assumptions in (b) and (c) above correct? In other words, is it true to say that costs may be divided into a fixed element and a variable cost per unit which is the same for every unit produced? There is a good argument that the variable cost per unit changes with the level of output. Because there

PUBLISHING

are growing *economies of scale* up to a certain level, a view put forward in basic economics is that the marginal cost per unit could be graphed as follows.

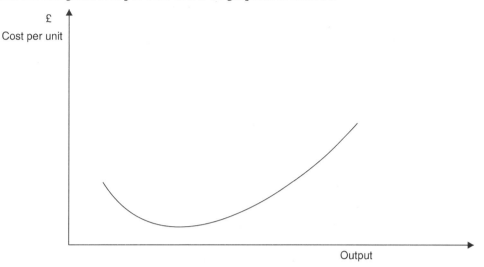

Figure 15.6 Marginal cost per unit

Total costs would therefore appear as a curved line, as follows.

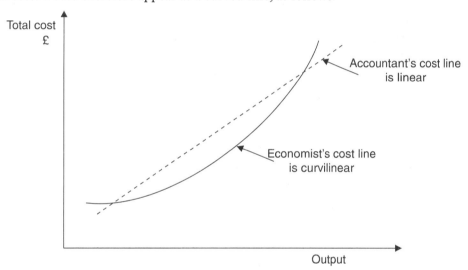

Figure 15.7 Linear versus curvilinear cost lines

It is sufficient at this stage to be aware of the difference of views between the 'accountant' and the 'economist', and to understand that the accountant justifies the linear assumption of cost behaviour for the following reasons.

(a)   It is easier to understand than curvilinear cost behaviour.

(b)   Fixed and variable costs are easier to estimate, and easier to use.

(c)   The assumption of linear costs is only used in practice within normal ranges of output, ie within a 'relevant range of activity'.

(d)   Within this relevant range of activity, the cost estimates of the economist and the accountant would not differ greatly, if at all; therefore linear costs should be used because sufficient accuracy is achieved with less effort (and for less cost).

2.2 Factors influencing cost behaviour

You are by now aware that it is not possible to say that a certain type of cost is always a fixed cost, or that another type is always variable. There are several factors which affect the extent to which a cost is influenced by a change in activity.

(a) *The complexity of production*

Many costs in 1990s manufacturing businesses relate to support activities such as production scheduling, machine set-ups and materials handling. Such costs vary depending upon the number of different varieties of product made rather than the sheer volume of output.

(b) *The make-up of the labour force*

The company's activities will determine whether there is a large production workforce. Where this is the case, a large increase in activity may necessitate hiring of extra workers. In a non-labour intensive industry, increased output may result in a very low increase in costs.

(c) *The attitude of management to the change in activity*

This will depend on the nature of the cost and the management's objectives in the long and short term. Management may have the power to control the amount the cost rises in the case of some indirect costs such as administration and advertising charges.

(d) *The length of time the change in activity is observed*

Changes in cost behaviour may not be noticeable or even occur at all unless a change in activity is sustained.

(e) *The extent to which the company is operating at full capacity*

Where machines were lying idle prior to an increase in activity, the extra demand may be met with a minimal rise in costs.

(f) *The general economic climate*

This may affect the availability of suitable resources and thereby the firm's ability to respond to a change of activity. Also the effects of inflation may be significant; one way of trying to allow for inflation is to use indexation. For example when forecasting cash flows amounts are increased in line with the expected rate of inflation.

(g) *The particular environment of the firm*

This includes the quality of the workforce and industrial relations, and the motivation of the staff.

EXAMPLE: LABOUR COSTS

The following questions and answers will help you to understand when labour costs are regarded as fixed and when they are regarded as variable costs.

(a) Is pay on a piecework basis a fixed or variable cost?

(b) When employees are paid a basic dayrate wage is this a fixed or variable cost?

(c) Why might labour costs be classed as semi-variable?

(d) In an advanced manufacturing environment is the majority of labour cost fixed or variable?

ANSWER

(a) When employees are paid on a piecework basis (ie they are paid according to their level of output) their pay is variable.

(b) When employees are paid a basic dayrate wage, their pay per week is fixed, regardless of the volume of output. The high cost of redundancy payments and the scarcity of skilled labour will usually persuade a company to retain its employees at a basic wage even when output is low.

(c) Because of productivity bonuses, overtime premium, commission and so on, labour costs are often semi-variable.

(d) In advanced manufacturing environments, much labour cost is fixed, as production is automated.

Now try to consolidate your understanding of fixed and variable costs by attempting the following activity.

Activity 5

Hans Bratch Ltd has a fleet of company cars for sales representatives. Running costs have been estimated as follows.

(a) Cars cost £12,000 when new, and have a guaranteed trade-in value of £6,000 at the end of two years. Depreciation is charged on a straight-line basis.

(b) Petrol and oil cost 15p per mile.

(c) Tyres cost £300 per set to replace; replacement occurs after 30,000 miles.

(d) Routine maintenance costs £200 per car (on average) in the first year and £450 in the second year.

(e) Repairs average £400 per car over two years and are thought to vary with mileage. The average car travels 25,000 miles per annum.

(f) Tax, insurance, membership of motoring organisations and so on, cost £400 per annum per car.

What would be the average cost per annum of a car which travels:

(a) 20,000 miles per annum?

(b) 30,000 miles per annum?

NOTES

Chapter roundup

Cost behaviours generally fit one of the fixed, stepped, variable or mixed cost patterns.

- Cost behaviour patterns demonstrate the way in which costs are affected by changes in the level of activity.

- Costs which are not affected by the level of activity are fixed costs or period costs.

- Variable costs increase or decrease with the level of activity, and it is usually assumed that there is a linear relationship between cost and activity.

- Semi-fixed, semi-variable or mixed costs are costs which are part fixed and part variable.

- It is often possible to assume that within the normal range of output, costs are either variable, fixed or semi-variable.

- It is important to establish the time span under consideration in determining cost behaviour patterns. For instance, some fixed costs may become variable in the long run, and in the very short term, costs which are normally considered to be variable may in fact be fixed.

- Even though fixed costs in total remain constant over a range of activity, the cost per unit will tend to reduce with the level of activity because the same fixed cost is being spread over a greater number of units.

We will now look at absorption costing in the next chapter.

Quick quiz

1	Define cost behaviour and level of activity.	(see para 1.1)
2	Give an example of a fixed cost and a step cost.	(2.1)
3	What is meant by 'the relevant range'?	(2.1)
4	Describe the high-low method.	(2.1)
5	Contrast an accountant's and an economist's view of cost behaviour.	(2.2)

Answers to activities

1   No. More commonly, it will cost less than twice as much (ie the unit cost will be lower at the higher level of production). This is because not all the costs incurred in producing the first 1,000 units will be duplicated in producing the second 1,000. For example, consider the production of this book. The printer had to produce plates (by a photographic process) for loading on to his printing press; he also had to incur time in loading the plates; finally he uses a certain amount of paper and ink in producing the printed copies. It is only this last group of costs that will double if the print run is doubled; the other costs remain the same whether he intends to run off a single copy or 10,000 copies.

BPP
PUBLISHING

2   Graph (a) represents a cost which is variable, but which suddenly falls as certain levels are reached. It could represent the purchase price of a raw material for which bulk purchase discounts are available.

Graph (b) represents a cost which is variable with output, subject to a minimum fixed charge.

3

			£
(a)	High output	8,000 hours : total cost	115,000
	Low output	6,000 hours : total cost	97,000
	Variable cost of	2,000 hours =	18,000
	Variable cost per standard hour		£9

(b)   Substituting in either the high or low volume cost.

	High		*Low*
	£		£
Total cost	115,000		97,000
Variable costs			
(8,000 × £9)	72,000	(6,000 × £9)	54,000
Fixed costs	43,000		43,000

(c)   Estimated costs of 7,500 standard hours of output.

	£
Fixed costs	43,000
Variable costs (7,500 × £9)	67,500
Total costs	110,500

4   True:

2.

3.

5.

False:

1.   The level of activity may refer to the volume of production in a period. Alternatively it may refer to the number of times sold, the value of items sold, turnover and so on.

4.   A variable cost is one which varies directly with output. It is the same for each unit produced.

5   Costs may be analysed into fixed, variable and stepped cost items.

(c)

	£ per annum
Fixed costs	
Depreciation £(12,000 − 6,000)/ 2	3,000
Routine maintenance £(200 + 450) / 2	325
Tax, insurance, and so on	400
	3,725

(b)

	Pence per mile
Variable costs	
Petrol and oil	15.0
Repairs (£400 / 50,000 miles)	0.8
	15.8

(c) Step costs are tyre replacement costs, which are £300 at the end of every 30,000 miles.

   (i) If the car travels less than or exactly 30,000 miles in two years, the tyres will not be changed. Average cost of tyres per annum = £0.

   (ii) If a car travels more than 30,000 miles and up to (and including) 60,000 miles in two years, there will be one change of tyres in the period. Annual average cost of tyres = £150.

   (iii) If a car exceeds 60,000 miles in two years (up to 90,000 miles) there will be two tyre changes. Annual average cost of tyres = £300.

The estimated costs per annum of cars travelling 20,000 miles per annum and 30,000 miles per annum would therefore be as follows.

	20,000 miles pa £	30,000 miles pa £
Fixed costs	3,725	3,725
Variable costs (15.8p per mile)	3,160	4,740
Tyres	150	150
Average cost per annum	7,035	8,615

Further question practice

Now try the following practice question at the end of this text

Exam style question: **14**

Chapter 16 :
ABSORPTION COSTING

Introduction

The concept of overheads was introduced in Chapter 15. In this chapter you will look at one particular method of accounting for overheads, absorption costing. This is basically a method of sharing out overheads incurred amongst units produced.

The chapter ends with a brief look at a costing method that might be more appropriate than absorption costing in the current industrial environment – activity based costing. Marginal costing, an alternative method of accounting for overheads, is the topic of the next chapter.

Your objectives

After completing this chapter you should:

    (a)   Understand the purpose of absorption costing

    (b)   Understand the techniques of absorbing costs into products or departments

BPP
PUBLISHING

1 THE PURPOSE OF ABSORPTION COSTING

Definition

> *Absorption costing* is a method of costing which charges a share of all overheads to products whether they be units, jobs or processes.

The most important feature of absorption costing is that the cost of an item is calculated by adding (or 'absorbing') a share of fixed overhead costs as well as variable overheads. (This distinguishes absorption costing from 'marginal costing', under which variable overheads are the only indirect costs included in the cost of an item. Marginal costing is discussed in the next chapter.)

By overheads we mean any or all of the following.

(a) Indirect materials costs.

(b) Indirect labour costs.

(c) Indirect expenses.

In order to determine the fully absorbed (or full) cost attributable to a unit, it is necessary to find out not only its direct cost (the amount of its direct materials cost, direct wages cost and any direct expense) but also its additional indirect cost; that is, the amount of indirect overhead which is deemed to apply to that unit.

The procedure for building up the cost of a unit is as foliows.

(a) Ascertain and charge the items of direct cost.

(b) Add in the appropriate amount of factory overhead.

(c) The sum of (a) and (b) is the factory cost, or full cost of production.

(d) Add in the appropriate amount of administration overhead.

(e) Add in the appropriate amounts of selling and distribution overhead.

(f) The sum of (c), (d) and (e) will be the total cost of sales.

Absorption costing might only go as far as (c). That is, it might apply to production costs only. The full cost of a unit will be:

	£
Direct costs	X
Factory overhead	X
Factory cost	X
Administration overhead	X
Selling overhead	X
Distribution overhead	X
Full cost	X

1.1 Is absorption costing necessary?

Before describing the procedures by which overhead costs are 'recovered' in the cost of production and sales, it may be useful to consider the reasons why absorption costing is commonly used. (Note, incidentally, that the words 'recovery' and 'absorption' are synonymous in this context.)

Suppose that a company makes and sells 100 units of product X each week. The direct cost per unit is £6 and the unit sales price is £10. Production overhead costs £200 per week and administration, selling and distribution overhead costs £150 per week. The weekly profit could be calculated as follows.

	£	£
Sales (100 units × £10)		1,000
Direct costs (100 × £6)	600	
Production overheads	200	
Administration, selling, and distribution costs	150	
		950
Profit		50

In absorption costing, overhead costs will be added to each unit of product manufactured and sold. The example would be dealt with as follows.

	£ per unit
Direct cost per unit	6
Production overhead (£200 per week for 100 units)	2
Full factory cost of product X	8

The weekly profit would be:	£
Sales	1,000
Less factory cost of sales	800
Gross profit	200
Less administration, selling and distribution costs	150
Net profit	50

Sometimes, but not always, the overhead costs of administration, selling and distribution are also added to unit costs, to obtain a full cost of sales.

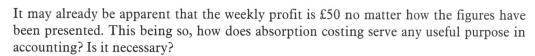

Activity 1

Use the data already provided to calculate the full cost of sales of product X. Show the profit and loss account that would result from this.

It may already be apparent that the weekly profit is £50 no matter how the figures have been presented. This being so, how does absorption costing serve any useful purpose in accounting? Is it necessary?

The reasons for using absorption costing have traditionally been identified as follows.

(a) *Stock valuations*. Stock in hand must be valued both for the balance sheet, and to calculate the cost of stocks used/sold in the period. The valuation of stocks will affect reported profitability during a period.

In our example, closing stocks might be valued at direct cost (£6), but in absorption costing, they would be valued at a fully absorbed factory cost of £8 per unit. (They would not be valued at £9.50, the full cost of sales, because the only costs incurred in producing goods for finished stock are factory costs.)

(b) *Pricing decisions*. Many companies attempt to fix selling prices by calculating the full cost of production or sales of each product, and then adding a margin for profit. In our example, the company might have used a mark up of 25% on factory cost in order to establish the unit sales price of £10. 'Full cost plus pricing' can be particularly useful for companies which do jobbing or contract work, where each job or contract is different, so that a standard unit sales price cannot be fixed.

(c) *Establishing the profitability of different products*. This argument in favour of absorption costing is more contentious, but is worthy of mention here. If a company sells more than one product, it will be difficult to judge how profitable each individual product is, unless overhead costs are shared on a fair basis and charged to the cost of sales of each product.

1.2 Statement of Standard Accounting Practice 9 (SSAP 9)

Of these three arguments, the problem of valuing stocks is perhaps the most significant, because absorption costing is recommended in financial accounting by the *statement of standard accounting practice* on stocks and long-term contracts (SSAP 9). SSAP 9 deals with financial accounting systems and not with cost accounting systems. The cost accountant is (in theory) free to value stocks by whatever method seems best, but where companies integrate their financial accounting and cost accounting systems into a single system of accounting records, the valuation of closing stocks will be determined by SSAP 9.

SSAP 9 states that costs of all stocks should comprise those costs which have been incurred in the normal course of business in bringing the product to its 'present location and condition'. These costs incurred will include all related production overheads, even though these overheads may accrue on a time basis. In other words, in financial accounting, closing stocks should be valued at full factory cost, and it may therefore be convenient and appropriate to value stocks by the same method in the cost accounting system.

Activity 2

To check you understand the meaning and purpose of absorption costing, fill in the missing words in the following paragraph.

Absorption costing is a method of costing which charges a _____ of all _____ to products. A share of both _____ and _____ overheads are absorbed.

Overheads are _____ materials, labour or other costs. Absorption costing is used in valuations and _____ decisions. SSAP 9 requires stocks to be valued on an _____ costing basis.

Activity 3

We are deep in cost and management accounting at the moment, but cast your mind back to the earlier chapters on financial accounting. Who is responsible for issuing FRSs? Are FRSs legally binding?

2 THE TECHNIQUE OF OVERHEAD ABSORPTION

The three stages of calculating the costs of overheads to be charged to manufactured output are allocation, apportionment and absorption. (Absorption costing is the name used since absorption is the ultimate aim of the other two procedures.)

Definition

> *Allocation* is the process of assigning costs to cost centres. A cost centre may be a location (such as a warehouse, or a headquarters office block); or a department (such as a machining department, or an accounts department); or an item of equipment.

Each business will decide on the cost centres it wishes to use. When costs are incurred (for example when a supplier's invoice arrives), they will initially be logged against one or other cost centre.

Definition

> *Apportionment* is the process by which cost items, or cost centre costs, are divided between several other cost centres in a 'fair' proportion.

The reasons for needing apportionment are described later.

Definition

> *Absorbtion* is the process whereby costs of cost centres are added to unit, job or process costs. Overhead absorption is sometimes called 'overhead recovery'.

2.1 Overhead apportionment stage one: share out common costs

Overhead apportionment follows on from overhead allocation. The first stage of overhead apportionment is to identify all overhead costs by function as production department overhead, production service department overhead, administration overhead or selling and distribution overhead. This means that the shared costs (initially allocated to a single cost centre) must now be shared out between the functional cost centres, whose managers are primarily 'responsible' for incurring them.

Activity 4

In the following exercise a list of overheads and possible bases of apportionment are given. Match the most appropriate basis to each overhead.

OVERHEADS

Rent
Depreciation of equipment
Carriage inwards
Personnel office
First aid
Rates
Heating
Lighting
Insurance of equipment
Repairs and depreciation of buildings
Canteen
Welfare
Wages and office costs

BASES

Floor area occupied by each department
Cost of book value of equipment
Number of employees
Labour hours worked in each department
Volume of space occupied by each department
Value of material issues to each cost centre/department

It is important that overhead costs are shared out on a fair basis but this is much more easily said than done. It is rarely possible to use only one method of apportioning costs to the various departments of an organisation.

Activity 5

Portion Ltd incurred the following overhead costs.

	£
Depreciation of factory	1,000
Factory repairs and maintenance	600
Factory office costs (treat as production overhead)	1,500
Depreciation of equipment	800
Insurance of equipment	200
Heating	390
Lighting	100
Canteen	900
	5,490

Activity 5 cont.

Information relating to the production and service departments in the factory is as follows.

	Department			
	Production A	*Production B*	*Service X*	*Service Y*
Floor space (sq. metres)	1,200	1,600	800	400
Volume (cubic metres)	3,000	6,000	2,400	1,600
Number of employees	30	30	15	15
Book value of equipment	£30,000	£20,000	£10,000	£20,000

How should the overhead costs be apportioned between the four departments?

2.2   Stage two: apportioning service costs to production departments

The second stage of overhead apportionment concerns the treatment of service departments. A factory is divided into several production departments and also many service departments, but only the production departments are directly involved in the manufacture of units of output. In order to be able to add production overheads to unit costs, it is necessary to have *all* the overheads charged to (or located in) the production departments. The next stage in overhead costing is, therefore, to apportion the costs of service departments to the production departments.

There are two methods by which the apportionment of service departments costs can be carried out.

(a)   Apportion the costs of each service department to production departments only.

(b)   Apportion the costs of each service department not only to production departments, but also to other service departments which make use of its services, and eventually apportion all costs to the production departments alone by a gradual process of 'repeated distribution'. This can become messy and time-consuming if done by hand, and is not considered any further in this chapter. In practice, large companies use computers to do the apportionment.

Whichever method is used, the basis of apportionment must be fair and a different apportionment basis may be applied for each service department. For example:

Service department	*Possible basis of apportionment*
Stores	Number or cost value of material requisitions.
Maintenance	Hours of maintenance and repair work done for each department.
Production planning	Direct labour hours worked for each production department.

EXAMPLE: OVERHEAD APPORTIONMENT

Reapportion Ltd incurred the following overhead costs.

	Production departments		*Stores department*	*Maintenance department*
	P	*Q*		
	£	£	£	£
Allocated costs	6,000	4,000	1,000	2,000
Apportioned costs	2,000	1,000	1,000	500
	8,000	5,000	2,000	2,500

Production department P worked 5,000 direct labour hours and requisitioned materials to the value of £12,000. Department Q worked 7,500 direct labour hours and requisitioned £8,000 of materials. What are the total production overhead costs of Departments P and Q?

ANSWER

Service department	*Basis of apportionment*	*Total cost*	*Dept P*	*Dept Q*
		£	£	£
Stores	Value of requisitions	2,000	1,200	800
Maintenance	Direct labour hours	2,500	1,000	1,500
		4,500	2,200	2,300
Previously allocated and apportioned costs		13,000	8,000	5,000
Total overhead		17,500	10,200	7,300

2.3 Overhead absorption

Having allocated and/or apportioned all overheads, the next stage in the costing of overheads is to add them to, or *absorb* them into cost units. The cost unit of a business is the thing that it sells. For a pen manufacturer it is a pen, or a box of 100 pens if he only sells them in that quantity. For British Gas it is a unit of gas. For a solicitor it is an hour of his time. For an engineering firm it is one engineering job. There are as many more examples as there are different types of business but this should be enough to give you the general idea.

Overheads are usually added to cost units using a *predetermined overhead absorption rate*, which is calculated from the budget.

Businesses establish their overhead absorption rates for the forthcoming accounting year by:

(a) Estimating the overhead likely to be incurred during the coming year

(b) Estimating the total hours, units, or direct costs or whatever it is upon which the overhead absorption rates are to be based (the *activity level*)

(c) Dividing estimated overhead by the budgeted activity level

The overhead then 'gets into' the cost unit by *applying* the rate that has been calculated to the information already established for the cost unit. If overhead is absorbed at, say, £2 per labour hour, then a cost unit that takes three labour hours to produce absorbs $3 \times £2$ = £6 in overheads.

Activity 6

Suppose total overheads in a business are expected to be £50,000 and total labour hours are expected to be 100,000 hours. The business makes two products, the Abba and the Zorba. Abbas take two labour hours each to make and Zorbas take five. What is the overhead cost per unit for Abbas and Zorbas respectively if overheads are absorbed on the basis of labour hours?

The different bases of absorption which can be used for production overhead are:

(a)   A percentage of direct materials costs

(b)   A percentage of direct labour cost

(c)   A percentage of direct cost

(d)   A rate per machine hour

(e)   A rate per direct labour hour

(f)   A rate per unit

(g)   A percentage of factory cost (for administration overhead)

(h)   A percentage of sales or factory cost (for selling and distribution overhead)

Which basis should be used for production overhead depends largely on the organisation concerned. As with apportionment it is a matter of being fair.

Percentages of materials cost, wages or direct cost should be adopted only where the value of the materials and/or wages is considered for all products to have some relationship with the overhead. For example, it is safe to assume that the indirect costs for producing brass screws are similar to the indirect costs for producing steel screws, but the cost of brass is very much greater than that of steel. Consequently, the overhead charge for brass screws would be too high and that for steel screws too low, if a percentage of cost of materials were to be used. A similar argument applies if a wages based rate is used: a trained mechanic will not use superior quality oily rags to an apprentice!

Note in particular that a rate per unit is effective only if all units are identical and therefore give rise to an identical amount of overhead.

It is for this reason that many factories use the *direct labour hour* rate or *machine hour* rate in preference to a rate based on a percentage of direct materials cost, wages or prime cost. A machine hour rate would be used in departments where production is controlled or dictated by machines. In such a situation, where a small number of workers supervise a process that is performed almost entirely by machine, the distinction between direct and indirect labour may be difficult to identify, and labour costs may not be the principal costs of production. We shall return to this point later in the chapter in our discussion of activity based costing.

The following example will illustrate the application of the different bases of absorption.

NOTES

EXAMPLE: OVERHEAD ABSORPTION

The budgeted production overheads and other budget data of Totalbasis Ltd are as follows.

Budgeted	Production dept A	Production dept B
Overhead cost	£36,000	£5,000
Direct materials cost	£32,000	
Direct labour cost	£40,000	
Machine hours	10,000	
Direct labour hours	18,000	
Units of production		1,000

What would the absorption rate be for each department using the various bases of apportionment?

ANSWER

(a)   For department A:

(i)   Percentage of direct materials cost $= \dfrac{£36,000}{£32,000} \times 100\% = 112.5\%$

(ii)   Percentage of direct labour cost $= \dfrac{£36,000}{£40,000} \times 100\% = 90\%$

(iii)   Percentage of direct cost $= \dfrac{£36,000}{£72,000} \times 100\% = 50\%$

(iv)   Rate per machine hour =

$\dfrac{£36,000}{10,000 \text{ hrs}} = £3.60$ per machine hour

(v)   Rate per direct labour hour =

$\dfrac{£36,000}{18,000 \text{ hrs}} = £2$ per direct labour hour

(b)   For department B absorption rate will be based on units of output:

$\dfrac{£5,000}{1,000 \text{ units}} = £5$ per unit produced

2.4   The aim of absorption costing

Whichever basis of absorption is used in department A in the above example, the intention should be to recover all the overhead costs in the cost of the components produced (so that an adequate selling price is set and stock is properly valued). Whether a percentage of materials cost, labour cost or direct cost, or whether a machine hour or labour hour basis of apportionment is used, provided that the actual cost of materials and labour or the actual labour hours and machine hours are the same as estimated, the total production overheads charged to the cost of production should be £36,000.

EXAMPLE: THE EFFECT ON TOTAL COST OF APPLYING DIFFERENT BASES

The choice of the basis of absorption is significant in determining the cost of individual units, or jobs, produced. Using the previous example, suppose that an individual product has a materials cost of £80, a labour cost of £85, and requires 36 labour hours and 23 machine hours to complete. The overhead cost of the product would vary, depending on the basis of absorption used by the company for overhead recovery. Calculate the overhead cost using the following bases.

   (a)   Percentage of direct material cost

   (b)   Percentage of direct labour cost

   (c)   Percentage of direct cost

ANSWER

   (a)   As a percentage of direct material cost, the overhead cost would be:

         $112.5\% \times £80 = £90.00$.

   (b)   As a percentage of direct labour cost, the overhead cost would be:

         $90\% \times £85 = £76.50$.

   (c)   As a percentage of direct cost, the overhead cost would be:

         $50\% \times £165 = £82.50$.

Activity 7

Now calculate the overhead cost of the product on the following absorption bases.

(a)   Machine hour basis

(b)   Labour hour basis

In theory, each basis of absorption would be possible, but the company should choose a basis for its own costs which seems to be 'fairest'. In our example, this choice will be significant in determining the cost of individual products, as the following summary shows, but the total cost of production overheads is the estimated overhead expenditure, no matter what basis of absorption is selected. It is the relative share of overhead costs borne by individual products and jobs which is affected by the choice of overhead absorption basis.

Summary of product cost, in the previous example

	Basis of overhead recovery				
	Percentage of materials cost	*Percentage of labour cost*	*Percentage of prime cost*	*Machine hours*	*Labour hours*
	£	£	£	£	£
Direct material	80	80.00	80.00	80.00	80
Direct labour	85	85.00	85.00	85.00	85
Production overhead	90	76.50	82.50	82.80	72
Full factory cost	255	241.50	247.50	247.80	237

2.5 The arbitrary nature of absorption costing

Clearly the choice of an appropriate absorption basis is very subjective. This arbitrariness is one of the main criticisms of absorption costing, and if absorption costing is to be used (because of its other virtues) then it is important that the methods used are kept under regular review. Changes in working conditions *should* lead to changes in the way in which work is accounted for, if they are necessary. This is the reason for the development of activity based costing, which we shall explain in a moment.

2.6 Over-absorption and under-absorption of overheads

Suppose that the estimated overhead in a production department is £80,000, and the estimated activity is 40,000 direct labour hours. The overhead recovery rate (using a direct labour hour basis) would be £2 per direct labour hour.

Actual overheads in the period are, say £84,000, and 45,000 direct labour hours are worked.

	£
Overhead incurred (actual)	84,000
Overhead absorbed (45,000 × £2)	90,000
Over-absorption of overhead	6,000

In this example, the cost of produced units or jobs has been charged with £6,000 more than was actually spent. An adjustment to reconcile the overheads charged to the actual overhead incurred is necessary and the over-absorbed overhead will be written as an adjustment to the profit and loss account at the end of the accounting period.

This example shows that the overhead absorption rate is predetermined from estimates of overhead cost and the expected volume of activity.

Activity 8

In which of the following circumstances will there be an under- or over-absorption of overheads?

(a) Budget and actual costs are the same, budget and actual activity differ.

(b) Budget and actual costs differ, budget and actual activity differ.

(c) Budget and actual costs are the same, budget and actual activity are the same.

(d) Budget and actual costs differ, budget and actual activity are the same.

Activity 9

It is easy to get confused about over and under-absorption of overheads. Try to think about the effect on profit if overheads are over- or under-absorbed. For example Soby Ltd budgets to produce 24,000 units. Total overhead is expected to be £72,000. Actual production is as planned but overheads are £75,000. How does this affect the profit statement (assume all units produced are sold)?

2.7 Predetermined rates and actual costs

Using a predetermined overhead absorption rate leads to under- or over-absorption of overheads, because actual output and overhead expenditure will turn out to be different from estimated output and expenditure. You might well wonder why the complications of under or over-absorption are necessary. Surely it would be better to use actual costs and outputs both to avoid under- or over-absorption entirely, and also to obtain more 'accurate' costs of production?

Suppose that a company draws up a budget to make 1,200 units of a product in the first half of 1996. Budgeted production overhead costs, all fixed costs, are £12,000. Owing to seasonal demand for the company's product, the volume of production varies from month to month. Actual overhead costs are £2,000 per month. Actual monthly production in the first half of 1996 is listed below, and total actual production in the period is 1,080 units.

The table below shows the production overhead cost per unit using:

(a) A predetermined absorption rate of $\dfrac{£12,000}{1,200}$ = £10 per unit.

(b) An actual overhead cost per unit each month.

(c) An actual overhead cost per unit based on actual six-monthly expenditure of £12,000 and actual six-monthly output of 1,080 units = £11.11 per unit.

			Overhead cost per unit		
			(a)	*(b)*	*(c)*
					Average actual
			Predetermined	*Actual cost*	*cost in*
	Expenditure	*Output*	*unit rate*	*each month*	*the 6 months*
Month	*(A)*	*(B)*		*(A) ÷ (B)*	
	£	Units	£	£	£
Jan	2,000	100	10	20.00	11.11
Feb	2,000	120	10	16.67	11.11
Mar	2,000	140	10	14.29	11.11
April	2,000	160	10	12.50	11.11
May	2,000	320	10	6.25	11.11
June	2,000	240	10	8.33	11.11
	12,000	1,080			

Methods (a) and (c) give a constant overhead cost per unit each month, regardless of seasonal variations in output. Method (b) gives variable unit overhead costs, depending

NOTES

on the month. For this reason, it is argued that methods (a) or (c) would provide more useful (long-term) costing information.

In addition, if prices are based on full cost with a percentage mark-up for profit, method (b) would give seasonal variations in selling prices, with high prices in low season and low prices in high season. Methods (a) and (c) would give a constant price based on 'cost plus'.

With method (a), overhead costs per unit are known throughout the period, and cost statements can be prepared at any time. This is because predetermined overhead rates are known in advance. With method (c), overhead costs cannot be established until after the end of an accounting period. For example, overhead costs of output in January 20X6 cannot be established until actual costs and output for the period are known, which will be not until after the end of June 20X6.

For the reasons given above, predetermined overhead rates are preferable to actual overhead costs, in spite of being estimates of costs and in spite of the need to write off under- or over-absorbed overhead costs to the profit and loss account.

3   ACTIVITY BASED COSTING

3.1   Direct labour hours and advanced manufacturing technology

A common technique for absorption costing, we have seen, is to discover the number of direct labour hours it takes to make a unit of product, and absorb all overheads on this basis at a predetermined rate per hour, on the grounds that direct labour hours is the best measure of the levels of activity.

This implies that direct labour hours or even direct machine hours are the most significant factor in production cost. However, with advanced manufacturing technology this is not the case. Sometimes only 5% of a product cost is direct labour. Overheads are likely to be the predominant cost.

Some overheads are still determined by volume of activity, as measured by the number of direct labour or machine hours. Other overheads, on the other hand, are not so much related to the volume of *output* as to the *activities* or transactions in the departments where the overhead is incurred.

3.2   Activity based costing and cost drivers

Activity based costing (ABC) is a recent development in cost accounting which attempts to absorb overheads into product costs on a more realistic basis. The basic idea of ABC is that instead of arbitrarily choosing an absorption base for *all* overheads, overhead costs are grouped according to what 'drives' them or causes them to be incurred. These *cost drivers* are then used as an absorption basis. An example is the best way of seeing what ABC is and how it works.

EXAMPLE: ACTIVITY BASED COSTING

A company manufactures two products L and M, using the same equipment and similar processes. An extract from the production data for these products in one period is shown below.

	L	M
Quantity produced (units)	5,000	7,000
Direct labour hours per unit	1	2
Machine hours per unit	3	1
Set-ups in the period	10	40
Orders handled in the period	15	60

	£
Overhead costs	
Relating to machine activity	220,000
Relating to production run set-ups	20,000
Relating to handling of orders	45,000
	285,000

Calculate the production overheads to be absorbed by one unit of each of the products using an activity based costing approach, with suitable cost drivers to trace overheads to products.

ANSWER

		Machine hours
Product L	= 5,000 units × 3 hours	15,000
Product M	= 7,000 units × 1 hour	7,000
		22,000

Using ABC the overhead costs are absorbed according to the *cost drivers*.

Machine-hour driven costs	£220,000 ÷ 22,000 m/c hours	= £10 per m/c hour
Set-up driven costs	£20,000 ÷ 50 set ups	= £400 per set up
Order-driven costs	£45,000 ÷ 75 orders	= £600 per order

Overhead costs are therefore as follows.

	Product L		*Product M*	
		£		£
Machine-driven costs	(15,000 hrs × £10)	150,000	(7,000 hrs × £10)	70,000
Set-up costs	(10 × £400)	4,000	(40 × £400)	16,000
Order handling costs	(15 × £600)	9,000	(60 × £600)	36,000
		163,000		122,000
Units produced		5,000		7,000
Overhead cost per unit		£32.60		£17.43

Activity 10

Now use a traditional costing approach, based on a direct labour rate, to calculate the amount of production overhead to be absorbed into one unit of each product. Compare your result with the figures obtained above.

Activity 11

Check your understanding of ABC with the following exercise.

(a)   What does ABC stand for?

(b)   What is the basic idea behind ABC?

(c)   What is the benefit of ABC?

3.3   Short-term and long-term variable costs

A distinction can be made between *short-term* variable costs and *long-term* variable costs. The latter means costs that are fixed in the short-term (the next year, say) but variable if considered over a longer period. Factory rental in a growing business is a good example. In its first years the business may rent only one factory and rent will stay fixed for this period. In the future however, it will expand and open other factories. Rent therefore *varies* according to the number of factories the business operates. This will remain a *long-term* variable cost because factories cannot be acquired and fitted out or disposed of overnight.

3.4   Cost drivers and cost pools

A cost driver is an activity or transaction that is a significant determinant of costs.

(a)   For short-term variable overhead costs, cost drivers will be *volume* of activity, such as machine hours operated or direct labour hours.

(b)   For long-term variable costs, cost drivers will not be related to output volume. These costs are related to the *transactions* undertaken by the support departments where the costs are incurred. These transactions in the support departments are the appropriate cost drivers to use.

Examples of transaction-based cost drivers are listed below.

Support department costs	*Possible cost driver*
Set up costs	Number of production runs
Production scheduling	Number of production runs
Material handling	Number of production runs
Inspection costs	Number of inspections, inspection hours, or number of production runs
Raw materials inventory handling etc	Number of purchase orders delivered
Finished goods inventory handling and despatch costs	Number of customer orders delivered

All of the costs associated with a particular cost driver would then be grouped into cost *pools*. The main cost pool in the above list is production runs, but there are also three other pools.

Chapter roundup

In this chapter we have looked at the purpose and application of absorption costing.

- Absorption costing charges a share of all overheads to products. It is used for stock valuation, for pricing decisions and to compare the profitability of different products.

- The three stages of absorption costing are allocation, apportionment and absorption.

- Apportionment involves sharing costs out amongst different departments or cost centres.

- Absorption involves adding the costs that have been shared out to the direct cost per unit. This is done according to a predetermined rate found by dividing total estimated overheads by the total quantity of the estimated basis.

- Over-absorption occurs when the estimated absorption rate is too high. Under-absorption occurs when the estimated absorption rate is too low.

- A predetermined rate is used to ensure a constant overhead cost per unit, to avoid fluctuations in selling prices and for administrative convenience.

- Activity based costing is a recent development which appears to be less arbitrary than absorption costing.

We will now consider marginal as opposed to absorption costing. The differences between the two approaches will be discussed.

Quick quiz

1   Describe the reasons for using absorption costing.   (see para 1.1)

2   What is the relevance of SSAP 9 to the choice of costing method used?
                                                                                (1.2)

3   What are the three main stages in absorbing costs into manufactured output?   (2.1)

4   Describe the process by which an absorption rate is calculated.   (2.2)

5   What is the point of using pre-determined absorption rates rather than actual costs and outputs?   (2.7)

6   Describe the basic idea of activity based costing.   (3.1)

Answers to activities

	£ per unit
Direct cost per unit	6.00
Factory overhead cost per unit	2.00
Administration, selling and distribution costs per unit	1.50
Full cost of sales	9.50

The weekly profit would be:

	£
Sales	1,000
Less full cost of sales	950
Profit	50

2   The missing words are: share; overheads; fixed; variable; indirect; stock; pricing; absorption.

3   You will find the answers in Chapter 2. SSAPs were originally issued by the Accounting Standards Committee, though the task of developing new standards (now called financial reporting standards, or FRSs) now falls upon its successor, the Accounting Standards Board. The legal status of these standards is that large companies are required by law to state whether they have complied with them. In the event of a breach, the Financial Reporting Council can apply to the courts, which may direct that revised accounts be prepared.

4   The following table is a suggested answer which shows the most usual bases of apportionment. Your answer may well differ and, providing you can justify your choices, would not be wrong.

Overhead to which the basis applies	Basis
Rent, rates, lighting, repairs and depreciation of buildings	Floor area occupied by each department
Depreciation and insurance of equipment	Cost or book value of equipment
Personnel office, canteen, welfare, wages and office costs, first aid	Number of employees, or labour hours worked in each department
Heating	Volume of space occupied by each department
Carriage inwards (costs paid for the delivery of material supplies)	Value of material issues to each cost centre/department.

5

Item of cost	Basis of apportionment	Total cost £	To Department A £	B £	X £	Y £
Factory depreciation	(floor area)	1,000	300	400	200	100
Factory repairs	(floor area)	600	180	240	120	60
Factory office	(no. of employees)	1,500	500	500	250	250
Equipment depreciation	(book value)	800	300	200	100	200
Equipment insurance	(book value)	200	75	50	25	50
Heating	(volume)	390	90	180	72	48
Lighting	(floor area)	100	30	40	20	10
Canteen	(no. of employees)	900	300	300	150	150
Total		5,490	1,775	1,910	937	868

6   First calculate the absorption rate.

$$\text{Absorption rate} = \frac{\text{Total estimate overhead}}{\text{Total estimated basis}} = \frac{£50,000}{100,000 \text{ hrs}}$$

= 50p per labour hour

Now apply it to the products.

	Abba	*Zorba*
Labour hours per unit	2	5
Absorption rate per labour hour	50p	50p
Overhead absorbed per unit	£1	£2.50

7   Using a machine hour basis, the overhead cost would be 23 hrs × £3.60 = £82.80.

Using a labour hour basis, the overhead cost would be 36 hrs × £2 = £72.00.

8   There will be an under/over absorption in all cases except (c). This is because a variation in either actual costs, or activity or both will lead to a variation from the original estimate.

9   The answer is that profit must be calculated on the basis of actual costs incurred. In respect of overheads, the actual costs are £75,000 and, somehow or other, this is the amount that must be charged in calculating profit, no matter what level of output was achieved.

Where the incorrect forecast of output does have an effect, however, is in the *presentation* of the profit statement. A profit statement prepared under absorption costing principles will show the cost of units produced on the basis of their absorbed costs. In this case, the statement will show 24,000 units produced at an overhead cost of £3 each, totalling £72,000. There will then need to be an extra line in the profit statement showing 'production overhead under-absorbed £3,000'. This £3,000 will be a deduction in computing the actual profit.

10

	Direct labour hours
Product L = 5,000 units × 1 hour	5,000
Product M = 7,000 units × 2 hours	14,000
	19,000

$$\therefore \text{Overhead absorption rate} = \frac{£285,000}{19,000} = £15 \text{ per hour}$$

Overhead absorbed would be as follows.

Product L	1 hour × £15	=	£15 per unit
Product M	2 hours × £15	=	£30 per unit

These figures suggest that product M absorbs an unrealistic amount of overhead using a direct labour hour basis. Overhead absorption should be based on the activities which drive the costs, in this case machine hours, the number of production run set-ups and the number of orders handled for each product. Advocates of ABC argue that the resulting product costs will be more relevant for management planning and decision making.

11 (a) Activity based costing.

(b) The basic idea is that instead of arbitrarily choosing an absorption basis for all overheads, the overheads are grouped according to what drives them. The cost drivers are then used as absorption bases.

(c) ABC attempts to absorb costs on a fair basis, rather than the traditional approach which tends to be more arbitrary and less 'accurate'.

Further question practice

Now try the following practice questions at the end of this text

Multiple choice questions: **77 to 86**

Exam style question: **15**

NOTES

Chapter 17 :

MARGINAL COSTING AND BREAKEVEN ANALYSIS

Introduction

This chapter defines marginal costing and compares it with absorption costing. Whereas absorption costing recognises fixed costs (usually fixed production costs) as part of the cost of a unit of output and hence as product costs, marginal costing treats all fixed costs as period costs. Two such different costing methods obviously each have their supporters and we will be looking at the arguments both in favour of and against each method, as well as their comparative usefulness for reporting to management, for reporting profits and stock values in externally published accounts and for providing decision-making information. Each costing method, because of the different stock valuation used, produces a different profit figure and we will be looking at this particular point in detail. We will also look at the use of marginal costing techniques in breakeven analysis.

Your objectives

After completing this chapter you should:

    (a)   Understand the principles of marginal costing

    (b)   Appreciate the differences between marginal costing and absorption costing in reporting profit

    (c)   Understand the use of marginal costing techniques in breakeven analysis

BPP PUBLISHING

1 MARGINAL COSTING

1.1 The principles of marginal costing

Marginal costing is an alternative method of costing to absorption costing. In marginal costing, it is the task of the accountant to identify the marginal costs of production and sales, ie:

    (a)   The variable cost of production, consisting of direct material cost, direct labour cost (usually), and variable production overhead

    (b)   The variable cost of administration, sales and distribution

Definition

> The CIMA's Official Terminology defines marginal cost as 'the part of the cost of one unit of a product or service which would be avoided if that unit were not produced, or which would increase if one extra unit were produced.'

The marginal production cost per unit of an item usually consists of:

    (a)   Direct materials

    (b)   Direct labour

    (c)   Variable production overheads

The marginal cost of sales usually consists of the marginal cost of production adjusted for stock movements plus the variable selling costs, which would include items such as sales commission, and possibly also some variable distribution costs.

As the definition of marginal cost indicates, it is also possible to identify the marginal cost of an operation or process, or even the marginal cost of a batch of output.

Similar definitions can be developed in respect of service (rather than manufacturing) industries.

Activity 1

Why is it that the cost of a second week's holiday offered by a package operator is invariably less than the cost of the first week?

Definition of marginal costing

In marginal costing, only variable costs are charged as a cost of sale and a contribution is calculated, being the value of sales less the variable cost of sales. Closing stocks of work in progress or finished goods are valued at marginal (variable) production cost.

Fixed costs are treated as a period cost, and are charged in full to the profit and loss account of the accounting period in which they are incurred.

Definition

> *Marginal costing* is defined by the CIMA's *Official Terminology* as 'the accounting system in which variable costs are charged to cost units and fixed costs of the period are written off in full against the aggregate contribution'.

Contribution

Contribution is the difference between sales value and the marginal cost of sales. It is of fundamental importance in marginal costing, and the term 'contribution' is really short for 'contribution towards covering fixed overheads and making a profit'.

Definition

> *Contribution* is defined by the CIMA as 'sales value less variable cost of sales'.

It is a central term in marginal costing, when the contribution per unit is expressed as the difference between its selling price and its marginal cost. In turn this is often related to a key or limiting factor to give a sum required to cover fixed overheads and profit, such as contribution per machine hour, per direct labour hour or per kilo of scarce raw material.

> **Activity 2**
>
> 1   What is a marginal cost?
>
> 2   What is meant by 'contribution' in this context?
>
> 3   How is the contribution often expressed?

> **Activity 3**
>
> Why is it that many hotels offer 'weekend breaks' at prices way below their normal room charges? Are they making a loss in doing so?

Marginal costing principles

The principles of marginal costing are set out below.

    (a)   Since period fixed costs are the same, no matter what the volume of sales and production (provided that the level of activity is within the 'relevant range') it follows that by selling an extra item of product or service the following will happen.

(i) Revenue will increase by the sales value of the item sold.

(ii) Costs will increase only by the variable cost per unit.

(iii) Therefore the increase in profit will equal the sales value minus variable costs, that is, the amount of contribution earned from the item.

(b) Similarly, if the volume of sales falls by one item, the profit will fall by the amount of contribution earned from the item.

(c) Profit measurement should therefore be based on an analysis of total contribution. Since fixed costs relate to a period of time, and do not change with increases or decreases in sales volume, it is misleading to charge units of sale with a share of fixed costs. Absorption costing is therefore misleading, and it is more appropriate to deduct fixed costs from total contribution for the period to derive a profit figure.

(d) When a unit of product is made, the extra costs incurred in its manufacture are the variable production costs. Fixed costs are unaffected, and no extra fixed costs are incurred when output is increased. It is therefore argued that the valuation of closing stocks should be at variable production cost (direct materials, direct labour, direct expenses (if any) and variable production overhead) because these are the only costs properly attributable to the product.

Before explaining marginal costing principles any further, it will be helpful to look at a numerical example.

EXAMPLE: MARGINAL COSTING PRINCIPLES

Rain Until September Ltd makes a product, the Splash, which has a variable production cost of £6 per unit and a sales price of £10 per unit. At the beginning of September 20X5, there were no opening stocks and production during the month was 20,000 units. Fixed costs for the month were £45,000 (production, administration, sales and distribution). There were no variable marketing costs.

Required

Calculate the contribution and profit for September 20X6, using marginal costing principles, if sales were:

(a) 10,000 Splashes

(b) 15,000 Splashes

(c) 20,000 Splashes

ANSWER

The first stage in the profit calculation must be to identify the variable cost of sales, and then the contribution. Fixed costs are deducted from the total contribution to derive the profit. All closing stocks are valued at marginal production cost (£6 per unit).

	10,000 splashes		15,000 splashes		20,000 splashes	
	£	£	£	£	£	£
Sales (at £10)		100,000		150,000		200,000
Opening stock	0		0		0	
Variable						
production cost	120,000		120,000		120,000	
	120,000		120,000		120,000	
Less value of						
closing stock	60,000		30,000		0	
Variable cost of						
sales		60,000		90,000		120,000
Contribution		40,000		60,000		80,000
Less fixed costs		45,000		45,000		45,000
Profit/(loss)		(5,000)		15,000		35,000
Profit (loss)						
per unit		(50p)		£1		£1.75
Contribution						
per unit		£4		£4		£4

The conclusions which may be drawn from this example are as follows.

(a) The profit per unit varies at differing levels of sales, because the average fixed overhead cost per unit changes with the volume of output and sales.

(b) The contribution per unit is constant at all levels of output and sales. Total contribution, which is the contribution per unit multiplied by the number of units sold, increases in direct proportion to the volume of sales.

(c) Since the contribution per unit does not change, the most effective way of calculating the expected profit at any level of output and sales is:

(i) Calculate the total contribution, then

(ii) Deduct fixed costs as a period charge in order to find the profit.

(d) If total contribution exceeds fixed costs, a profit is made.

(e) If total contribution exactly equals fixed costs, no profit and no loss is made; ie breakeven point is reached.

(f) If total contribution is less than the fixed costs, there will be a loss.

Activity 4

Calculate the expected profit from the sale of 17,000 Splashes.

1.2 Marginal costing and absorption costing compared

Marginal costing as a cost accounting system is significantly different from absorption costing. It is an alternative method of accounting for costs and profit, which rejects the principles of absorbing fixed overheads into unit costs.

NOTES

Activity 5

If fixed overheads are not absorbed, does this mean that the manager of a business can ignore them?

(a) *Marginal costing*

  (i) Closing stocks are valued at marginal production cost.

  (ii) Fixed costs are charged in full against the profit of the period in which they are incurred.

  (iii) This method is often used in decision making situations.

(b) *Absorption costing* (sometimes referred to as full costing)

  (i) Closing stocks are valued at full production cost, and include a share of fixed production costs. This means that the cost of sales in a period will include some fixed overheads incurred in a previous period (ie in opening stock values) and will exclude some fixed overhead incurred in the current period but carried forward in closing stock values as a charge to a subsequent accounting period.

  (ii) This method complies with SSAP 9.

In marginal costing, it is necessary to identify variable costs, contribution and fixed costs. In absorption costing it is not necessary to distinguish variable costs from fixed costs (except in preparing the budget, when the overhead absorption rate is based on expected expenditure).

EXAMPLE: ABSORPTION VS MARGINAL COSTING

Rusky Ltd manufactures a single product, the Igor. Information relating to the Igor is as follows.

Opening stock at 1 April 20X6	Nil
Production (in units) during April (budget and actual)	2,000
Sales (in units) during April	1,500
Selling price per unit	£20
Variable production cost per unit	£7
Fixed production costs for April (budget and actual)	£8,000
Other fixed costs for April (budget and actual)	£4,000

Calculate the company's profit for the month of April using:

(a) Absorption costing, and

(b) Marginal costing.

ANSWER

(a) Using absorption costing, fixed costs would be absorbed into units of production at the rate of £6 per unit ((£8,000 + £4,000) ÷ 2,000). The fully absorbed cost per unit would therefore be £(7 + 6) = £13. The profit would be calculated as follows.

PUBLISHING

	£
Sales	30,000
Less cost of sales (1,500 units at £13)	19,500
Profit	10,500

(*Note.* There is no under- or over-absorbed overhead, because budgeted production and costs were equal to the actual outcome.)

(b)   Using marginal costing, the profit calculation would be as follows:

	£
Sales	30,000
Less variable cost of sales (1,500 units at £7)	10,500
Contribution	19,500
Less fixed costs	12,000
Profit	7,500

The difference between the two figures is £6 × 500 units produced but not sold.

Activity 6

In May 20X6, data for Rusky Ltd is exactly the same as for April, except that sales in the month amount to 2,500 units. Calculate the profit for May using both marginal costing and absorption costing principles.

We can draw a number of conclusions from the example of Rusky Ltd.

(a)   Marginal costing and absorption costing are different techniques for assessing profit in a period.

(b)   If there are changes in stocks during a period, so that opening stock or closing stock values are different, marginal costing and absorption costing give different results for profit obtained. This is seen in April 20X6. Because opening stocks (nil) differ from closing stocks (500 units) the two profit figures differ. The amount of the difference (£3,000) is the amount of fixed overhead included in the closing stock valuation under the absorption costing method.

(c)   If the opening and closing stock volumes and values are the same, marginal costing and absorption costing will give the same profit figure. This is because the total cost of sales during the period would be the same, no matter how calculated. This is seen in the two month period April–May 20X6. Total profits for the two months are equal under both methods, because opening and closing stocks for the two month period are the same (nil).

In the long run, total profit for a company will be the same whether marginal costing or absorption costing is used, because total costs will be the same by either method of accounting. Different accounting conventions merely affect the profit of individual accounting periods.

Marginal costing versus absorption costing – which is better?

There are accountants who favour each costing method.

(a) Arguments in favour of absorption costing include the following.

(i) Fixed production costs are incurred in order to make output; it is therefore 'fair' to charge all output with a share of these costs.

(ii) Closing stock values, by including a share of fixed production overhead, will be valued on the principle required for the financial accounting valuation of stocks SSAP 9. The explanatory notes to SSAP 9 state that:

in order to match costs and revenue, 'costs' of stocks and work in progress should comprise that expenditure which has been incurred in the normal course of business in bringing the product or service to its present location and condition. Such costs will include all related production overheads, even though these may accrue on a time basis.

(iii) A problem with calculating the contribution of various products made by a company is that it may not be clear whether the contribution earned by each product is enough to cover fixed costs, whereas by charging fixed overhead to a product we can decide whether it is profitable or not.

(b) Arguments in favour of marginal costing include the following.

(i) Fixed costs will be the same regardless of the volume of output, because they are period costs. It makes sense, therefore, to charge them in full as a cost to the period.

(ii) The cost to produce an extra unit is the variable production cost. It is realistic to value closing stock items at this directly attributable cost.

(iii) As we have seen, the size of total contribution varies directly with sales volume at a constant rate per unit. For management purposes, better information about expected profit is obtained from the use of variable costs and contribution in the accounting system.

(iv) It is also argued that absorption costing gives managers the wrong signals. Goods are produced, not to meet market demand, but to absorb allocated overheads. Production in excess of demand in fact increases the overheads (for example warehousing) that the organisation must bear.

2 BREAKEVEN ANALYSIS

Cost and management accounting is concerned not just with recording historical costs, and with budgetary control, but also with the provision of information which will help managers to make decisions for the future. To forecast costs, accountants must know about the cost behaviour of all cost items.

One way of providing information about expected future costs and revenues for management decision making is breakeven analysis. Breakeven analysis is an application of marginal costing techniques which is often used in budget planning, by marketing managers as well as by accountants.

You should now understand that by using marginal costing techniques, it is possible to ascertain the contribution per unit. The total contribution from all sales during a period is then compared with the fixed costs for that period; any excess or deficiency of contribution over fixed costs represents the profit or loss respectively for the period.

	£
Sales	X
Less variable costs	X
Contribution	X
Less fixed costs	X
Profit	X

The management of an organisation usually wishes to know not only the profit likely to be made if the aimed-for production and sales for the year are achieved, but also the point at which neither profit nor loss occurs (the *breakeven point*) and the amount by which actual sales can fall below anticipated sales without a loss being incurred.

The breakeven point can be calculated arithmetically. The number of units needed to be sold in order to break even will be the total fixed costs divided by the contribution per unit. This is because the contribution required to break even must be an amount which exactly equals the amount of fixed costs.

$$\text{Breakeven point (BEP)} = \frac{\text{Total fixed costs}}{\text{Contribution}} = \frac{\text{Required contribution to breakeven}}{\text{Contribution per unit}}$$

$$= \text{Number of units of sale required to break even.}$$

Activity 7

Expected sales	10,000 units at £8 = £80,000
Variable cost	£5 per unit
Fixed costs	£21,000

Compute the breakeven point.

2.1 The margin of safety

In budgeting, the *margin of safety* is a measure by which the budgeted volume of sales is compared with the volume of sales required to break even.

Definition

The *margin of safety* is the difference in units between the budgeted sales volume and the breakeven sales volume and it is sometimes expressed as a percentage of the budgeted sales volume. (It may also be expressed as the difference between the budgeted sales revenue and breakeven sales revenue, expressed as a percentage of the budgeted sales revenue.)

EXAMPLE: MARGIN OF SAFETY

Mal de Mer Ltd makes and sells a product which has a variable cost of £30 and which sells for £40. Budgeted fixed costs are £70,000 and budgeted sales are 8,000 units.

What is the breakeven point and what is the margin of safety?

ANSWER

(a)   Breakeven point $= \dfrac{\text{Fixed costs (required contribution)}}{\text{Contribution per unit}}$

$$= \dfrac{£70,000}{£(40-30)} = £7,000 \text{ units}$$

(b)   Margin of safety $= 8,000 - 7,000 \text{ units} = 1,000 \text{ units}$

which may be expressed as $\dfrac{1,000 \text{ units}}{8,000 \text{ units}} \times 100\% = 12\frac{1}{2}\%$ of budget

(c)   The margin of safety indicates to management that actual sales can fall short of budget by 1,000 units or 12½% before the breakeven point is reached and no profit at all is made.

2.2   Breakeven arithmetic

At the breakeven point, sales revenue equals total costs and there is no profit.

$$S = V + F$$

where S = Sales revenue
V = Total variable costs
F = Total fixed costs

Subtracting V from each side of the equation, we get:

$S - V = F$, ie total contribution = fixed costs.

A similar formula may be applied where a company wishes to achieve a certain profit during a period. To achieve this profit, sales must cover all costs and leave the required profit, ie:

$$S = V + F + P, \text{ where}$$
$$P = \text{required profit}$$

Subtracting V from each side of the equation, we get:

$$S - V = F + P, \text{ ie}$$

Total contribution required = F + P.

Activity 8

R Ltd's product sells for £30 a unit. Fixed costs are £68,000 a year, and variable costs per unit are as follows.

	£
Direct materials	10
Direct labour	8
Variable production overhead	4
Variable sales overhead	2
	24

What level of sales will give an annual profit of £16,000?

Activity 9

Which of the following will lead to an increase in total contribution and which will lead to a decrease in total contribution?

1 Costs increase, sales remain stable.

2 Price increases, sales remain stable.

3 Price increases, sales deteriorate significantly.

4 Costs remain stable, sales increase.

5 Costs fall, sales remain stable.

2.3 Sales price and sales volume

It may be clear by now that, given no change in fixed costs, total profit is maximised when the total contribution is at its maximum. Total contribution in turn depends on the unit contribution and on the sales volume.

An increase in the sales price will increase unit contribution, but sales volume is likely to fall because fewer customers will be prepared to pay the higher price. A decrease in sales price will reduce the unit contribution, but sales volume may increase because the goods on offer are now cheaper. The optimum combination of sales price and sales volume is arguably the one which maximises total contribution.

EXAMPLE: PROFIT MAXIMISATION

Cymbeline Ltd has developed a new product which is about to be launched on to the market. The variable cost of selling the product is £12 per unit. The marketing department has estimated that at a sales price of £20, annual demand would be 10,000 units.

However, if the sales price is set above £20, sales demand would fall by 500 units for each 50p increase above £20. Similarly, if the price is set below £20, demand would increase by 500 units for each 50p stepped reduction in price below £20.

NOTES

What is the price which would maximise Cymbeline Ltd's profit in the next year?

ANSWER

At a price of £20 per unit, the unit contribution would be £(20 – 12) = £8. Each 50p increase (or decrease) in price would raise (or lower) the unit contribution by 50p. The total contribution is calculated at each sales price by multiplying the unit contribution by the expected sales volume.

	Unit price	Unit contribution	Sales volume	Total contribution
	£	£	Units	£
	20.00	8.00	10,000	80,000
Reduce price	19.50	7.50	10,500	78,750
	19.00	7.00	11,000	77,000
Increase price	20.50	8.50	9,500	80,750
	21.00	9.00	9,000	81,000
	21.50	9.50	8,500	80,750
	22.00	10.00	8,000	80,000
	22.50	10.50	7,500	78,750

The total contribution would be maximised, and therefore profit maximised, at a sales price of £21 per unit, and sales demand of 9,000 units.

Activity 10

Those of you with a mathematical background should attempt a solution by the use of calculus. You will find that your answer agrees with the solution above.

2.4 Breakeven charts

The breakeven point can also be determined graphically. A breakeven chart is prepared showing on the horizontal axis the sales/output (in units or in value) and on the vertical axis values for sales revenue and costs. The following lines are then drawn.

(a)   The *sales line*, which starts at the origin (zero sales volume = zero sales revenue) and ends at the point which signifies the expected sales.

(b)   The *fixed costs line* which runs above and parallel to the horizontal axis, at a point on the vertical axis denoting the total fixed costs.

(c)   The *total costs line*, which starts at the point where the fixed costs line meets the vertical axis (at zero output), and ends at the point which represents, on the horizontal axis, the anticipated sales in units, and on the vertical axis the sum of the total variable cost of those units plus the total fixed costs.

The breakeven point is the intersection of the sales line and the total costs line. By projecting the lines horizontally and vertically from this point to the appropriate axes, it is possible to read off the breakeven point in sales units and sales value.

The number of units represented on the chart by the distance between the breakeven point and the expected (or budgeted) sales, in units, indicates the margin of safety.

EXAMPLE: A BREAKEVEN CHART

The budgeted annual output of a factory is 120,000 units. The fixed overhead amounts to £40,000 and the variable costs are 50p per unit. The average sales price is £1 per unit.

Construct a breakeven chart showing the current breakeven point and profit earned up to the present maximum capacity.

ANSWER

	£
Sales (120,000 units)	120,000
Variable costs	60,000
Contribution	60,000
Fixed costs	40,000
Profit	20,000

The chart is drawn as follows.

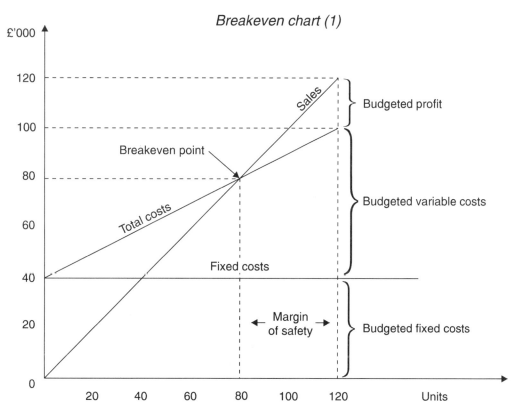

Breakeven chart (1)

(a) The y axis represents money (costs and revenue) and the x axis represents the level of activity (production and sales).

(b) The fixed costs are a straight line parallel to the x axis (in our example, at £40,000).

(c) The variable costs are added 'on top' of fixed costs, to give total costs. To draw the straight line of total costs, only two points need to be plotted and joined up. Perhaps the two most convenient points to plot are total costs at zero output, and total costs at the budgeted output and sales.

    (i) At zero output, costs are equal to the amount of fixed costs only, £40,000, since there are no variable costs.

    (ii) At the budgeted output of 120,000 units, costs are £100,000.

	£
Fixed costs	40,000
Variable costs (120,000 × 50p)	60,000
Total costs	100,000

(d) The revenue 'line' is also drawn by plotting two points and joining them up.

    (i) At zero sales, revenue is nil.

    (ii) At the budgeted output and sales of 120,000 units, revenue is £120,000.

The breakeven point is where total costs are matched exactly by total revenue. From the chart, this can be seen to occur at output and sales of 80,000 units, when revenue and costs are both £80,000.

Activity 11

Check this conclusion by means of the arithmetical method used earlier in the chapter.

The margin of safety can be seen on the chart as the difference between the budgeted level of activity and the breakeven level.

2.5 Limitations of breakeven analysis

Breakeven charts and breakeven arithmetic should be used carefully. The major limitations of breakeven analysis are as follows.

(a) A breakeven chart can only apply to one single product or a single mix (fixed proportions) of a group of products. This restricts its usefulness.

(b) It is assumed that fixed costs are the same in total, and variable costs are the same per unit, at all levels of output. This assumption is a great simplification.

    (i) Fixed costs will change if output falls or increases substantially (most fixed costs are step costs).

    (ii) The variable cost per unit will decrease where economies of scale are made at higher output volumes, and the variable cost per unit will also eventually rise where diseconomies of scale begin to appear at higher volumes of output (for example the extra cost of labour in overtime working).

It is important to remember that, although a breakeven chart is drawn on the assumption that fixed costs and the variable cost per unit are constant, this is only correct within a normal range or relevant range of output. It is generally assumed that both the budgeted output and also the breakeven point of sales lie within this relevant range.

(c)   It is assumed that sales prices will be constant at all levels of activity. This may not be true, especially at higher volumes of output, where the price may have to be reduced to win the extra sales.

(d)   Production and sales are assumed to be the same, therefore the consequences of any increase in stock levels (when production volumes exceed sales) or 'de-stocking' (when sales volumes exceed production levels) are ignored.

(e)   Uncertainty in the estimates of fixed costs and unit variable costs is often ignored in breakeven analysis, and some costs (for example mixed costs and step costs) are not always easily categorised or divided into fixed and 'variable'.

In spite of limitations, however, breakeven analysis is a useful technique for managers in planning sales prices, the desired sales mix and profitability.

Chapter roundup

You should now be aware of both absorption and marginal costing and understand their differences and their relative advantages/disadvantages.

- Marginal costing is a technique based on a comparison of sales value with the variable cost of sales. The difference between these two values is the contribution.

- Marginal costing differs from absorption costing in that it values stocks at their variable production cost only. Fixed production costs are written off as a period cost, not absorbed into the cost of production units.

- One consequence of the difference is that, in periods when stock levels fluctuate, the profit calculated under marginal costing principles will not be the same as that calculated under absorption costing principles.

- One application of marginal costing is the technique of breakeven analysis.

In the next chapter we will look at budgets, why they are necessary and how they are prepared.

Quick quiz

1   Define marginal cost.   (see para 1.1)

2   What is meant by 'contribution'? Contribution to what?   (1.1)

3   In the long run, total profits calculated under marginal costing will be the same as total profits calculated under absorption costing. True or false?
                                                                        (1.2)

4   List three arguments for preferring the use of absorption costing, and three in favour of marginal costing.   (1.2)

5   Define 'breakeven point'.   (section 2)

6   Define 'margin of safety'.   (2.1)

7   List four limitations on the technique of breakeven analysis.   (2.5)

Answers to activities

1   Because the cost to the tour operator of offering the second week is less than for the first week. For one thing, he doesn't have the cost of flying you to your destination – you are already there.

2   1.   The marginal cost of production plus the marginal cost of administration, sales and distribution.

     2.   Contribution is sales value less the marginal cost ie it is the contribution to fixed costs and profit.

     3.   It is often related to a key or limiting factor, such as contribution per machine hour or per direct labour hour.

3   In the absence of business travel, conferences and so on the hotels are unable to fill their rooms. They save the marginal costs of letting the empty rooms (the cost of laundering sheets for example), but lose valuable revenue. To overcome this, they offer discounted prices. The prices need cover only the marginal costs of letting the room in order to earn a contribution, which will help towards covering overheads. This example may suggest to you that a marginal costing approach leads to better decision making than an absorption costing approach. If hoteliers calculated the cost of letting rooms on a fully absorbed basis, they might conclude that they could not 'afford' to offer discounted prices. By taking that decision, they would forfeit valuable contribution.

4   The expected profit from the sale of 17,000 Splashes would be as follows.

	£
Total contribution (17,000 ÷ £4)	68,000
Less fixed costs	45,000
Profit	23,000

5   No: cash must still be found to pay fixed overheads, and for accounting purposes they are simply deducted in full each period when computing profits.

6   (a)   *Absorption costing*

	£
Sales	50,000
Less cost of sales (2,500 units at £13)	32,500
Profit	17,500

     (b)   *Marginal costing*

	£
Sales	50,000
Less variable cost of sales (2,500 units at £7)	17,500
Contribution	32,500
Less fixed costs	12,000
Profit	20,500

7   The contribution per unit is £(8 – 5) = £3
    Contribution required to break even = fixed costs = £21,000
    Breakeven point (BEP)   =   £21,000 ÷ £3
                                   =   7,000 units
    In revenue, BEP   =   (7,000 × £8) = £56,000

    Check   *7,000 units*
                                                        £
    Revenue   56,000
    Less variable costs   35,000
    Contribution   21,000
    Less fixed costs   21,000
    Profit   0

8   Required contribution = fixed costs + profit = £68,000 + £16,000 = £84,000

    Required sales can be calculated as follows:

    $$\frac{\text{Required contribution}}{\text{Contribution per unit}} = \frac{£84,000}{£(30 - 24)}$$

    = 14,000 units, or £420,000 in revenue

9   Decrease total contribution: 1; 3.

    Increase total contribution: 2; 4; 5.

10 Unit contribution = (P – 1,200) pence

    $$\text{Demand (D)} = 10,000 + \frac{500}{50}(2,000 - P)$$

    Total contribution (C) = (P – 1,200) × D
                           = $10P^2 + 42,000P - 36,000,000$

    $\frac{dC}{dP} = -20P + 42,000$ and the answer follows at once.

11 Required contribution – $\dfrac{\text{Fixed costs}}{\text{Contributions per unit}}$

                           = $\dfrac{£40,000}{50p}$ = 80,000 units

Further question practice

Now try the following practice questions at the end of this text

Multiple choice questions: **87 to 96**

Exam style question: **16**

Chapter 18 :
MANAGERIAL CONTROL: THE USE OF BUDGETS

Introduction

This chapter begins by explaining why an organisation might prepare a budget and goes on to detail the steps in the preparation of a budget. The method of preparing and the relationship between the various functional budgets is then set out. The chapter then considers the construction of cash budgets and budgeted profit and loss accounts and balance sheets, the three components of what is known as a *master budget*. It includes an explanation of why budgeted profit/loss for a period will probably not be the same as the budgeted cash flow for the period.

We then look at flexible budgets, a vital management planning and control tool. This part of the chapter relies on your understanding of cost behaviour covered in Chapter 15.

This ends our study of budgeting. You will, however, come across variances, which are mentioned in this chapter in relation to flexible budgets, in Chapter 19, which considers the use of standard costing.

Your objectives

After completing this chapter you should:

(a)   Understand the purposes of preparing budgets

(b)   Be aware of the main steps in budget preparation

(c)   Understand how budgets are adjusted ('flexed') in the light of changing circumstances

(d)   Understand how budgets are used in controlling the costs of a business

1   THE PURPOSE AND ADMINISTRATION OF BUDGETS

A budget is a financial and/or quantitative plan of operations for a forthcoming accounting period. Many *functional budgets* (a budget of income or expenditure for individual functions of a business, such as the sales budget, production budget or direct labour budgets) are summarised and incorporated into a *master budget* (or a *summary budget*).

Definition

> A *budget* is defined as 'a quantitative statement, for a defined period of time, which may include planned revenues, assets, liabilities and cash flows' (CIMA, *Official Terminology*).

1.1   The purposes of a budget

Why do you think budgets are used? Think of two reasons. Write your answer here.

1.

2.

The purposes of a budget are as follows.

(a)   To *co-ordinate* the activities of all the different departments of an organisation into a single master plan; in addition, through participation by employees in preparing a budget, it may be possible to motivate them to raise their targets and standards and to achieve better results.

(b)   To *communicate* the policies and targets to every manager in the organisation responsible for carrying out a part of that plan.

(c)   To establish a system of *control* by having a plan against which actual results can be progressively compared.

(d)   To *compel planning*. By having a formal budgeting procedure, management is forced to look to the future instead of 'living hand-to-mouth' without any clear idea of purpose.

The budget period is the time period to which the budget relates. Except for capital expenditure budgets, the budget period is commonly the accounting year (sub-divided into 12 or 13 control periods).

1.2   The budget manual

The budget manual is a collection of instructions governing the responsibilities of persons and the procedures, forms and records relating to the preparation and use of budgetary data.

A budget manual may contain the following.

    (a)   An explanation of the objectives of the budgetary process including:

        (i)   The purpose of budgetary planning and control

        (ii)   The objectives of the various stages of the budgetary process

        (iii)   The importance of budgets in the long-term planning and administration of the enterprise

    (b)   Organisational structures, including:

        (i)   An organisation chart

        (ii)   A list of individuals holding budget responsibilities

    (c)   An outline of the principal budgets and the relationships between them.

    (d)   Administrative details of budget preparation, for example:

        (i)   Membership, and terms of reference of the budget committee

        (ii)   The sequence in which budgets are to be prepared

        (iii)   A timetable

    (e)   Procedural matters, for example:

        (i)   Specimen forms and instructions for completing them

        (ii)   Specimen reports

        (iii)   Account codes (or a chart of accounts)

        (iv)   The name of the budget officer to whom enquiries must be sent

1.3   The formulation of budgets

Managers responsible for preparing budgets should ideally be the managers (and their subordinates) who are responsible for carrying out the budget, selling goods and authorising expenditure. Each manager should prepare appropriate budgets for the areas within his control.

Activity 1

You might think it strange that most of the input to the budgetary process comes not from accountants, but from departmental managers who may have little familiarity with accounting methods. Try to think of reasons why budgets are prepared in this way.

The procedures in the preparation of a master budget will differ from organisation to organisation, but a step-by-step approach will be described in this chapter. The preparation of a budget may take weeks or months, and the budget committee may meet several times before the master budget is finally agreed. Functional budgets and cost centre budgets prepared in draft may need to be amended many times over as a consequence of discussions between departments, changes in market conditions, reversals of decisions by management, and so on during the course of budget preparation.

1.4 The principal budget factor

In practice the purpose of budgeting is a concerted effort on the part of the staff from all sections of a business. The first task is to identify the *principal budget factor*.

Definition

> The *principal budget factor*, also known as the *key budget factor* or *limiting budget factor*, is the factor which 'will limit the activities of an undertaking and which is often the starting point in budget preparation' (CIMA, *Official Terminology*).

For example, a company's sales department might estimate that it could sell 1,000 units of product X, which would require 5,000 hours of grade A labour to produce. If there are no units of product X already in stock, and only 4,000 hours of grade A labour available in the budget period, then the company would be unable to sell 1,000 units of X because of the shortage of labour hours. Grade A labour would be a limiting budget factor, and the company's management must decide on the appropriate action to take.

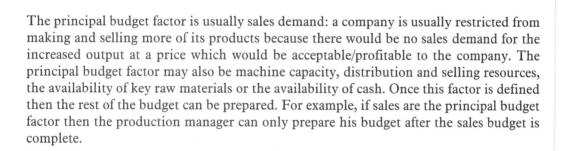

Activity 2

What options are open to management in such a case?

The principal budget factor is usually sales demand: a company is usually restricted from making and selling more of its products because there would be no sales demand for the increased output at a price which would be acceptable/profitable to the company. The principal budget factor may also be machine capacity, distribution and selling resources, the availability of key raw materials or the availability of cash. Once this factor is defined then the rest of the budget can be prepared. For example, if sales are the principal budget factor then the production manager can only prepare his budget after the sales budget is complete.

1.5 The sequence of budget preparation

Although some functional budgets and cost centre budgets can be prepared at the same time as others, there is a rough sequence of preparation, as follows.

(a)   A budgeted profit and loss account will be prepared, comprising the following functional budgets and cost centre budgets.

    (i)   The sales budget (in units of each product and also in sales value).

    (ii)   Finished goods stock budget (this budget decides the planned increase or decrease in finished goods stock levels).

    (iii)   Production budget (the sales budget in units plus the budgeted increase in finished goods stocks or minus the budgeted decrease in finished goods stocks. Goods may be produced for stock or sold out of stock, therefore planned production and sales volumes are not necessarily the same amount). The production budget is stated in units of each product.

NOTES

(iv) The budgets of resources for production.

(1) Materials usage budget (all types of materials, direct and indirect). This budget is stated in quantities and perhaps cost, for each type of material used.

(2) Machine utilisation budget (the operating hours required on each machine or group of machines).

(3) The labour budget, or wages budget (of all grades of labour, direct and indirect. For hourly paid staff, the budget will be expressed in hours for each grade of labour and the wages cost).

(v) During the preparation of the sales and production budgets, the managers of the cost centres of the organisation will prepare their draft budgets for the (department) overhead costs. There will be cost centres for each type of overhead.

(1) Production overheads (for example repairs and maintenance, stores, production control, factory supervision).

(2) Administration overheads (for example budgeted costs of the accounting department, personnel department, computer department, corporate planning).

(3) Selling and distribution overheads, or marketing overheads (for example budgeted costs for advertising and sales promotion, perhaps for each product group, budgeted costs of the sales force, distribution cost budgets).

(4) Research and development department overheads.

(vi) A raw materials stock budget must be prepared, to decide the planned increase or decrease of the level of stocks held by the storekeeper.

(vii) Once the raw material usage requirements and the raw materials stock budget are known, the purchasing department can prepare a raw material purchases budget, in quantities and value for each type of material purchased.

(viii) Once the production volumes are planned, and the overhead cost centre budgets prepared, the cost accountant can prepare an overheads analysis in order to decide the overhead absorption rate to use in the next budget period (year). This work is only required where a system of absorption costing is in operation. It will not be required if a company uses a marginal costing system.

(b) In addition to the budgeted profit and loss account, there is a requirement for several other budgets.

(i) Fixed assets purchase budget, or the capital budget (this usually covers a long time span, say three to ten years). Assets to be purchased in the next 12 months will give rise to a depreciation charge in the appropriate cost centre budget for the profit and loss account.

(ii) Working capital budget; that is, budgeted increases or decreases in the level of debtors and creditors (as well as stocks).

(iii) Cash budget; this is described more fully later in this chapter. A business relying on credit sales will need a debtors budget and this together with a creditors budget will be a part of the final cash budget.

(iv) Budgeted concluding balance sheet.

2 PREPARING A BUDGET

To illustrate the basic process of budget preparation, we will look at examples of:

(a) A production budget and direct labour budget

(b) A materials purchases budget

EXAMPLE: THE PREPARATION OF THE PRODUCTION BUDGET AND DIRECT LABOUR BUDGET

Landslide Ltd manufactures two products, A and B, and is preparing its budget for 20X7. Both products are made by the same grade of labour, grade Q. The company currently holds 800 units of A and 1,200 units of B in stock, but 250 of these units of B have just been discovered to have deteriorated in quality, and must therefore be scrapped. Budgeted sales of A are 3,000 units and of B 4,000 units, provided that the company maintains finished goods stocks at a level equal to three months' sales.

Grade Q labour was originally expected to produce one unit of A in two hours and one unit of B in three hours, at an hourly rate of £2.50. However, in discussions with trade union negotiators, it has been agreed that the hourly wage rate should be raised by 50p, provided that the times to produce A and B are reduced by 20%.

Required

Prepare the production budget and direct labour budget for 20X7.

ANSWER

The expected time to produce a unit of A will now be 80% of 2 hours = 1.6 hours, and the time for a unit of B will be 2.4 hours. The hourly wage rate will be £3, so that the direct labour cost will be £4.80 for A and £7.20 for B (thus achieving a saving for the company of 20p per unit of A produced and 30p per unit of B).

(a) *Production budget*

	Product A		Product B	
	Units	Units	Units	Units
Budgeted sales		3,000		4,000
Closing stocks				
(3/12 of 3,000)	750		1,000*	
Opening stocks				
(minus stocks scrapped)	800		950	
Increase/(decrease) in stocks		(50)		50
Production		2,950		4,050

(b) *Direct labour budget*

	Grade Q hours	Cost £
2,950 units of product A	4,720	14,160
4,050 units of product B	9,720	29,160
Total	14,440	43,320

It is assumed that there will be no idle time among grade Q labour which, if it existed, would have to be paid for at the rate of £3 per hour.

*(3/12 of 4,000)

2.1 The standard hour

A useful concept in budgeting for labour requirements is the standard hour (or standard minute) which is the quantity of work achievable at standard performance, expressed in terms of a standard unit of work done in a standard period of time. For example, budgeted output of various different products or jobs in a period could be converted into standard hours of production, and a labour budget constructed accordingly.

Standard hours are particularly useful when management wants to monitor the production levels of a variety of dissimilar units. For example product A may take five hours to produce and product B, seven hours. If four units of each product are produced, instead of saying that total output is eight units, we could state the production level as (4 × 5) + (4 × 7) standard hours = 48 standard hours.

The concept of the standard hour is used in standard costing, which is described in Chapter 19. You might also come across it in a situation where standard costing is not used. Study the following example.

EXAMPLE: DIRECT LABOUR BUDGET BASED ON STANDARD HOURS

Thankless Task Ltd manufactures a single product, Q, with a single grade of labour. Its sales budget and finished goods stock budget for period 3 of 20X7 are as follows.

Sales	700 units
Opening stocks, finished goods	50 units
Closing stocks, finished goods	70 units

The goods are inspected only when production work is completed, and it is budgeted that 10% of finished work will be scrapped.

The standard direct labour hour content of product Q is three hours. The budgeted productivity ratio for direct labour is only 80%.

The company employs 18 direct operatives, who are expected to average 144 working hours each in period 3.

Required

    (a)   Prepare a production budget.

    (b)   Prepare a direct labour budget.

    (c)   Comment on the problem that your direct labour budget reveals, and suggest how this problem might be overcome.

ANSWER

Production budget	Units
Sales	700
Add closing stock	70
	770
Less opening stock	50
Production required of 'good' output	720
Wastage rate	10%

(assumed to be 10% of total production, not 10% of good production)

Total production required $\qquad 720 \times \dfrac{100}{90} \star = 800$ units

($\star$ Note that the required adjustment is 100/90, not 110/100)

Direct labour budget

Standard hours per unit = 3

Total standard hours required = 800 units $\times$ 3 hours = 2,400 hours

Productivity ratio = 80%

Actual hours required = $2,400 \times \dfrac{100}{80}$ = 3,000 hours

Problem

	Hours
Budgeted hours available = 18 operatives $\times$ 144 hours =	2,592
Actual hours required	3,000
Shortfall in labour hours below amount required	408

The (draft) budget indicates that there will not be enough direct labour hours to meet the production requirements. This problem might be overcome in one, or a combination, of the following ways.

(a) Reduce the closing stock requirement below 70 units. This would reduce the number of production units required.

(b) Persuade the workforce to do some overtime working.

(c) Perhaps recruit more direct labour, if long-term prospects are for higher production volumes.

(d) Discuss with the workforce (or their union representatives) the possibility of:

   (i) Improving the productivity ratio, and so reducing the number of hours required to produce the output

   (ii) If possible, reducing the wastage rate below 10%

EXAMPLE OF A MATERIAL PURCHASES BUDGET

Earthquake Ltd manufactures two products, S and T, which use the same raw materials, D and E. One unit of S uses 3 litres of D and 4 kilograms of E. One unit of T uses 5 litres of D and 2 kilograms of E. A litre of D is expected to cost £3 and a kilogram of E £7.

Budgeted sales for 20X7 are 8,000 units of S and 6,000 units of T; finished goods in stock at 1 January 20X7 are 1,500 units of S and 300 units of T, and the company plans to hold stocks of 600 units of each product at 31 December 20X7.

Stocks of raw material are 6,000 litres of D and 2,800 kilograms of E at 1 January, and the company plans to hold 5,000 litres and 3,500 kilograms respectively at 31 December 20X7.

The warehouse and stores managers have suggested that a provision should be made for damages and deterioration of items held in store, as follows.

PUBLISHING

NOTES

Product S : loss of 50 units
Product T : loss of 100 units
Material D : loss of 500 litres
Material E : loss of 200 kilograms

Required

Prepare a materials purchases budget for the year 20X7.

ANSWER

To calculate material purchase requirements, it is first of all necessary to calculate the budgeted production volumes and material usage requirements.

	Product S		*Product T*	
	Units	Units	Units	Units
Sales		8,000		6,000
Provision for losses		50		100
Closing stock	600		600	
Opening stock	1,500		300	
Increase/(decrease) in stock		(900)		300
Production budget		7,150		6,400

	Material D		*Material E*	
	litres	litres	kg	kg
Usage requirements				
To produce 7,150 units of S		21,450		28,600
To produce 6,400 units of T		32,000		12,800
Usage budget		53,450		41,400
Provision for losses		500		200
		53,950		41,600
Closing stock	5,000		3,500	
Opening stock	6,000		2,800	
Increase/(decrease) in stock		(1,000)		700
Material purchases budget		52,950		42,300
Cost per unit		£3 per litre		£7 per kg
Cost of material purchases		£158,850		£296,100
Total purchases cost		£454,950		

2.2 Cash budgets

A cash budget is prepared to show the expected receipts of cash and payments of cash during the next year. The annual cash budget will be divided into smaller time periods (or control periods), commonly of one month or four weeks.

Receipts of cash may be from cash sales, payments by debtors, the sale of fixed assets, the issue of new shares or loan stock, the receipt of interest and dividend from investments outside the business.

Not all of these are profit and loss account items. The following activity illustrates this.

> **Activity 3**
>
> Tick all those receipts and payments which are not profit and loss account items.
>
> 1 Profit on the sale of a fixed asset.
>
> 2 Cash payment for a new vehicle.
>
> 3 The issue of shares or loan stock.
>
> 4 Depreciation of vehicles.
>
> 5 Cash received from the sale of a fixed asset.

The issue of new shares or loan stock is a balance sheet item.

The cash received from selling an asset affects the balance sheet; the profit or loss on the sale of the asset, which appears in the P & L account, is not the cash received but the difference between the cash received and the written-down value of the asset.

Cash paid for a new vehicle does not affect the profit and loss account, but depreciation of the vehicle does.

Payments of cash may be for purchase of stocks, payment of wages or other expenses, the purchase of capital items, the payment of interest, dividends, or taxation. Not all payments are profit and loss account items (for example the purchase of capital equipment or the payment of VAT).

It may be seen from the above exercise that receipts and payments are not the same as sales and cost of sales for the following reasons.

(a) Not all receipts affect profit and loss account income.

(b) Not all payments affect profit and loss account costs.

(c) Some costs in the profit and loss account such as loss or profit on sale of assets and depreciation are not cash items but are 'costs' derived from accounting conventions.

(d) The timing of receipts and payments does not coincide with the profit and loss accounting period. This is an important point, which is illustrated by the following example.

EXAMPLE: TIMING OF CASH FLOWS

Two Brass Farthings Ltd operates a retail business. Purchases are sold at cost plus $33^{1}/_{3}\%$.

(a)

	Budgeted sales £	*Labour cost* £	*Expenses incurred* £
January	40,000	3,000	4,000
February	60,000	3,000	6,000
March	160,000	5,000	7,000
April	120,000	4,000	7,000

(b) It is management policy to have sufficient stock in hand at the end of each month to meet sales demand in the next half month.

(c) Creditors for materials and expenses are paid in the month after the purchases are made.

(d) Expenses include a monthly depreciation charge of £2,000.

(e) (i) 75% of sales are for cash.

(ii) 25% of sales are on one month's interest-free credit.

(f) The company will buy equipment for cash costing £18,000 in February and will pay a dividend of £20,000 in March. The opening cash balance at 1 February is £1,000.

Required

(a) A profit and loss account for February and March.

(b) A cash budget for February and March.

ANSWER

(a) PROFIT AND LOSS ACCOUNT

	February		*March*		*Total*	
	£	£	£	£	£	£
Sales		60,000		160,000		220,000
Cost of purchases (75%)		45,000		120,000		165,000
Gross profit		15,000		40,000		55,000
Less: labour	3,000		5,000		8,000	
expenses	6,000		7,000			
					13,000	
		9,000		12,000		21,000
		6,000		28,000		34,000

(b) *Workings*

					£
(i)	Receipts:	February	75% of Feb sales		
			(75% × £60,000)		45,000
			+25% of Jan sales		
			(25% × £40,000)		10,000
					55,000
		March	75% of Mar sales		
			(75% × £160,000)		120,000
			+25% of Feb sales		
			(25% × £60,000)		15,000
					135,000

(ii) *Purchases*

	January £		February £
For Jan sales			
(50% of £30,000)	15,000		
For Feb sales			
(50% of £45,000)	22,500	(50% of £45,000)	22,500
For Mar sales	0	(50% of £120,000)	60,000
	37,500		82,500

These purchases are paid for in February and March.

(iii) Expenses: cash expenses in January (£4,000 – £2,000) and February (£6,000 – £2,000) are paid for in February and March respectively. Depreciation is not a cash item.

CASH BUDGET

	February £	March £	Total £
Receipts from sales	55,000	135,000	190,000
Payments			
Trade creditors	37,500	82,500	120,000
Expenses creditors	2,000	4,000	6,000
Labour	3,000	5,000	8,000
Equipment purchase	18,000	0	18,000
Dividend	0	20,000	20,000
Total payments	60,500	111,500	172,000
Receipts less payments	(5,500)	23,500	18,000
Opening cash balance b/f	1,000	* (4,500)	1,000
Closing cash balance c/f	* (4,500)	19,000	19,000

Notes

1   *The cash balance at the end of February is carried forward as the opening cash balance for March.

2   The profit in February and March does not mean that there is sufficient cash to operate the business as planned.

3   Steps should be taken either to ensure that an overdraft facility is available for the cash shortage at the end of February, or to defer certain payments so that the overdraft is avoided.

2.3   A comparison of profit and cash flows

You might notice in the example above (Two Brass Farthings) that the total profit of £34,000 differs from the total of receipts less payments (£18,000). Profit and cash flows during a period need not be the same amount and indeed, will not usually be the same.

The reasons for the difference between profit and cash flow might be familiar to you from your study of cash flow statements. The differences are as follows.

(a)   There are some items in the profit and loss account which are not cash flow items. For example, depreciation is a charge against profit, but is not a cash flow.

(b)   There are some sources of cash income which are not fully reported, or not reported at all, in the P & L account. These include funds from a new issue of shares or a loan, or the cash earned from the sale of fixed assets.

(c)   There are some payments which are not reported fully, or at all, in the P & L account, such as the payment for new capital equipment (fixed assets), the payment of dividends and taxation, and the repayment of loans.

(d)   Increases in the volume of working capital tie up funds and reduce the cash inflow. For example an increase in debtors represents sales on credit (and so profit) without cash income yet having been received.

2.4   Cash budgets and an opening balance sheet

You might be given a cash budget question in which you are required to analyse an opening balance sheet to decide how many outstanding debtors will pay what they owe in the first few months of the cash budget period, and how many outstanding creditors must be paid.

EXAMPLE

A balance sheet as at 31 December 20X6 shows that a company has the following debtors and creditors.

Debtors   £150,000
Trade creditors   £60,000

You are informed of the following.

(a)   Debtors are allowed two months to pay.

(b)   1½ months' credit is taken from trade creditors.

(c)   Sales and materials purchases were both made at an even monthly rate throughout 20X6.

Required

In which months of 20X7 will the debtors eventually pay and the creditors be paid?

ANSWER

(a)   Since debtors take two months to pay, the £150,000 of debtors in the balance sheet represent credit sales in November and December 20X6, who will pay in January and February 20X7 respectively. Since sales in 20X6 were at an equal monthly rate, the cash budget should plan for receipts of £75,000 each month in January and February from the debtors in the opening balance sheet.

(b)   Similarly, since creditors are paid after $1\frac{1}{2}$ months, the balance sheet creditors will be paid in January and the first half of February 20X7, which means that budgeted payments will be as follows.

	£
In January (purchases in second half of November and first half of December 20X6)	40,000
In February (purchases in second half of December 20X6)	20,000
Total creditors in the balance sheet	60,000

(The balance sheet creditors of £60,000 represent 1½ months' purchases, so that purchases in 20X6 must be £40,000 per month, which is £20,000 per half month.)

Students are expected to be capable of dealing with fairly detailed cash budget problems in examinations, and a final example is therefore included for careful study.

EXAMPLE: A MONTH BY MONTH CASH BUDGET

From the following information which relates to George and Zola Ltd you are required to prepare a month by month cash budget for the second half of 20X7 and to append such brief comments as you consider might be helpful to management.

(a) The company's only product, a calfskin vest, sells at £40 and has a variable cost of £26 made up as follows.

   Material £20   Labour £4   Overhead £2

(b) Fixed costs of £6,000 per month are paid on the 28th of each month.

(c) Quantities sold/to be sold on credit

May	June	July	Aug	Sept	Oct	Nov	Dec
1,000	1,200	1,400	1,600	1,800	2,000	2,200	2,600

(d) Production quantities

May	June	July	Aug	Sept	Oct	Nov	Dec
1,200	1,400	1,600	2,000	2,400	2,600	2,400	2,200

(e) Cash sales at a discount of 5% are expected to average 100 units a month.

(f) Customers are expected to settle their accounts by the end of the second month following sale.

(g) Suppliers of material are paid two months after the material is used in production.

(h) Wages are paid in the same month as they are incurred.

(i) 70% of the variable overhead is paid in the month of production, the remainder in the following month.

(j) Corporation tax of £18,000 is to be paid in October.

(k) A new delivery vehicle was bought in June, the cost of which, £8,000, is to be paid in August. The old vehicle was sold for £600, the buyer undertaking to pay in July.

(l) The company is expected to be £3,000 overdrawn at the bank at 30 June 20X7.

(m) The opening and closing stocks of raw materials, work in progress and finished goods are budgeted to be the same.

NOTES

ANSWER

CASH BUDGET FOR 1 JULY TO 31 DECEMBER 20X7

	July £	Aug £	Sept £	Oct £	Nov £	Dec £	Total £
Receipt							
Credit sales	40,000	48,000	56,000	64,000	72,000	80,000	360,000
Cash sales	3,800	3,800	3,800	3,800	3,800	3,800	22,800
Sale of vehicles	600						600
	44,400	51,800	59,800	67,800	75,800	83,800	383,400

	July £	Aug £	Sept £	Oct £	Nov £	Dec £	Total £
Payments							
Materials	24,000	28,000	32,000	40,000	48,000	52,000	224,000
Labour	6,400	8,000	9,600	10,400	9,600	8,800	52,800
Variable o'head (W1)	3,080	3,760	4,560	5,080	4,920	4,520	25,920
Fixed costs	6,000	6,000	6,000	6,000	6,000	6,000	36,000
Corporation tax				18,000			18,000
Purchase of vehicle		8,000					8,000
	39,480	53,760	52,160	79,480	68,520	71,320	364,720
Excess of receipts over payments	4,920	(1,960)	7,640	(11,680)	7,280	12,480	18,680
Balance b/f	(3,000)	1,920	(40)	7,600	(4,080)	3,200	(3,000)
Balance c/f	1,920	(40)	7,600	(4,080)	3,200	15,680	15,680

Working: variable overhead

	June £	July £	Aug £	Sept £	Oct £	Nov £	Dec £
Variable overhead production cost	2,800	3,200	4,000	4,800	5,200	4,800	4,400
70% paid in month		2,240	2,800	3,360	3,640	3,360	3,080
30% in following month		840	960	1,200	1,440	1,560	1,440
		3,080	3,760	4,560	5,080	4,920	4,520

Comments

(a) There will be a small overdraft at the end of August but a much larger one at the end of October. It may be possible to delay payments to suppliers for longer than two months or to reduce purchases of materials or reduce the volume of production by running down existing stock levels.

(b) If neither of these courses is possible, the company may need to negotiate overdraft facilities with its bank.

(c) The cash deficit is only temporary and by the end of December there will be a comfortable surplus. The use to which this cash will be put should ideally be planned in advance.

2.5 Other budgeting systems

So far our discussion has been based on the traditional method of building up a master budget by assembling its 'components', the detailed budgets for different departments, functions or cost centres. But it is useful to consider some other methods of preparing budgets. These methods include:

(a) Rolling budgets

(b) Zero base budgeting

2.6 Rolling budgets

These are also called *continuous budgets*. A rolling budget is a 12-month budget which is prepared several times each year (say, once each quarter). The purpose of a rolling budget is to give management the chance to revise its plans, but more importantly, to make more accurate forecasts and plans for the next few months. For example, if a company prepares a rolling budget every quarter, and has an accounting year which ends on 31 December, there will be four annual budgets each year. The first three months will be planned in meticulous detail, and over this relatively short period, forecasts of sales, labour wage rates, material prices and so on should be reasonably accurate. The remaining nine months need not be quite as accurate, because the budget for these months will be reviewed in at least one other following budget. Study the following table to ensure you understand this.

Year	Rolling budget prepared	Period covered
20X6	1 January	January to March 20X6 in detail
		April to December 20X6 in less detail
20X6	1 April	April to June 20X6 in detail
		July 20X6 to March 20X7 in less detail
20X6	1 July	July to September 20X6 in detail
		October 20X6 to June 20X7 in less detail
20X6	1 October	October to December 20X6 in detail
		January to September 20X7 in less detail

Rolling budgets are relatively expensive to produce, so how can this be justified?

Where rolling budgets are used, the extra administrative costs (and effort) of producing several budgets each year, instead of just one, should be compensated by more accurate forecasting and planning. Management are continually forced to think 12 months ahead and the resulting budgets are more up to date and relevant for control purposes.

2.7 Zero base budgeting

This is a technique to eliminate wastefulness and inefficiency in budget cost estimates, and also to allocate scarce resources (for example the limited amounts of funds and cash available) between different departments and activities. In practice, zero base budgeting can be fairly complex to operate but its basic principles are as follows.

(a) When the functional budgets and cost centre budgets are prepared for the master budget, the managers responsible must evaluate every activity and item of spending in their department. Budgets may not be prepared by simply adding an amount to the previous year's expenditure.

(b) Every activity has a cost and there must be quantifiable benefits to justify the spending. Any activity which costs more than it is worth must be eliminated.

(c) Some activities can be carried out in several ways, or with a varying thoroughness. Zero base budgeting expects managers to choose the best method of getting a job done, on a cost-benefit comparison.

(d) Since the company may not have enough money to do every worthwhile activity budgeted for by individual managers, it is also necessary to rank activities in order of priority. Individual managers must rank activities in their department in an order of priority, so that if insufficient funds are available, the activities with the lowest priority can be abandoned.

Zero base budgeting is most appropriate when budgeting for *discretionary* costs. Central and local government in particular have a large number of such costs, for instance, the cost of services which they are not legally obliged to provide, such as recreation facilities and cultural activities. This does not necessarily mean that ZBB is not appropriate for profit-oriented organisations. Although such organisations must incur a large proportion of their expenditure merely to stay in existence, some expenditure items are discretionary and lend themselves to a ZBB exercise, for example advertising, entertainment and research and development. Such costs are sometimes called *programmed* costs.

3   FLEXIBLE BUDGETS

The master budgets so far described are known as *fixed budgets*. By the term 'fixed', we do not mean that the budget is kept unchanged. Revisions to a fixed master budget will be made if the situation so demands. The term 'fixed' means the following.

(a) The budget is prepared on the basis of an estimated volume of production and an estimated volume of sales, but no plans are made for the event that actual volumes of production and sales may differ from budgeted volumes.

(b) When actual volumes of production and sales during a control period (month or four weeks) are achieved, a fixed budget is not adjusted (in retrospect) to the new levels of activity.

A *flexible budget* recognises the difference in behaviour between fixed and variable costs in relation to fluctuations in output, turnover, or other variable factors and is designed to change appropriately with such fluctuations. Flexible budgets may be used in one of two ways.

(a) *At the planning stage*. For example, suppose that a company expects to sell 10,000 units of output during the next year. A master budget (the fixed budget) would be prepared on the basis of these expected volumes. However, if the company thinks that output and sales might be as low as 8,000 units or as high as 12,000 units, it may prepare contingency flexible budgets, at volumes of, say 8,000, 9,000, 11,000 and 12,000 units.

(b)   Flexible budgets are used *retrospectively* at the end of each month (control period) or year, to compare actual results achieved with what results should have been under the circumstances. Flexible budgets are an essential factor in budgetary control.

Activity 4

Try to think precisely about this last sentence. Why exactly are flexible budgets, rather than fixed budgets, the appropriate tool to use in budgetary control?

3.1   Flexible budgets, cost behaviour and marginal costing

In order to prepare a flexible budget it is first necessary to determine the cost behaviour patterns. Variable costs must be separately identified from fixed costs so that it is possible to determine which costs will change as the activity level changes and which costs will remain fixed.

Flexible budgets are often prepared on a marginal costing basis, which means that the contribution is highlighted. The flexing of budgets is simplified if they are prepared in this format because the fixed costs will be clearly segregated from the variable costs.

EXAMPLE: FIXED AND FLEXIBLE BUDGETS

Suppose that Lodestone Ltd expects production and sales during the next year to be 90% of the company's output capacity, ie 9,000 units of a single product. Cost estimates will be made using the high/low technique and the following historic records of cost.

Units of output/sales	Cost of sales
9,800	£44,400
7,700	£38,100

The company's management is not certain that the estimate of sales is correct, and has asked for flexible budgets to be prepared at output and sales levels of 8,000 and 10,000 units. The sales price per unit has been fixed at £5.

ANSWER

If we assume that within the range 8,000 to 10,000 units of sales, all costs are fixed, variable or semi-variable (ie there are no stepped costs, material discounts, overtime premiums, bonus payments and so on) the fixed and flexible budgets would be based on the estimate of fixed and variable cost.

	£
Total cost of 9,800 units	44,400
Total cost of 7,700 units	38,100
Variable cost of 2,100 units	6,300

The variable cost per unit is £3.

	£
Total cost of 9,800 units	44,400
Variable cost of 9,800 units (9,800 × £3)	29,400
Fixed costs (all levels of output and sales)	15,000

The fixed budgets and flexible budgets might now be prepared as follows.

	Flexible budget 8,000 units	Master budget 9,000 units	Flexible budget 10,000 units
	£	£	£
Sales (× £5)	40,000	45,000	50,000
Variable costs (× £3)	24,000	27,000	30,000
Contribution	16,000	18,000	20,000
Fixed costs	15,000	15,000	15,000
Profit	1,000	3,000	5,000

These budgets have not been prepared using the principles of absorption costing, but have used instead the principles of marginal costing. Absorption costing systems will use the same sort of ideas in flexible budgeting, but it is also necessary to deal with absorption rates for fixed overheads, and any under- or over-absorption of overheads at differing levels of output.

3.2 Why are flexible budgets necessary?

We have seen that flexible budgets may be prepared in order to plan for variations in the level of activity above or below the level set in the fixed budget. It has been suggested however, that since many cost items in modern industry are fixed costs, the value of flexible budgets in planning is dwindling.

(a)   In many manufacturing industries, plant costs (such as depreciation or rent) are a very large proportion of total costs, and these tend to be fixed costs.

(b)   Wage costs also tend to be fixed, because employees are generally guaranteed a basic wage for a working week of an agreed number of hours.

(c)   With the growth of service industries, labour (wages or fixed salaries) and overheads will account for most of the costs of a business, and direct materials will be a relatively small proportion of total costs.

Flexible budgets are nevertheless necessary, and even if they are not used at the planning stage, they must be used for budgetary control variance analysis.

(a)   Material costs are variable costs.

(b)   Labour costs, although often fixed, are treated as variable costs in order to measure efficiency of working (productivity) for control purposes.

4   BUDGETARY CONTROL

Budgetary control is the practice of establishing budgets which identify areas of responsibility for individual managers (for example production managers or purchasing managers) and of regularly comparing actual results against expected results. The most important method of budgetary control is *variance analysis*, which involves the comparison of actual results achieved during a control period (a month, or four weeks)

with a flexible budget. The differences between actual results and expected results are called variances and these are used to provide a guideline for control action by individual managers (or a guideline for altering the master budget in the light of actual events).

Definition

> The CIMA *Official Terminology* describes *budgetary control* as 'the establishment of budgets relating the responsibilities of executives to the requirements of a policy, and the continuous comparison of actual with budgeted results, either to secure by individual action the objective of that policy or to provide a basis for its revision'.

You should notice from this definition that individual managers are held responsible for investigating differences between budgeted and actual results, and are then expected to take corrective action or amend the plan in the light of actual events.

4.1 The wrong approach to budgetary control

The wrong approach to budgetary control is to compare actual results against a fixed budget. Consider the following illustration.

Sidewinder Ltd manufactures a single product, the varmint. Budgeted results and actual results for June 20X6 are shown below.

	Budget	Actual results	Variance
Production and sales of the varmint (units)	2,000	3,000	
	£	£	£
Sales revenue (a)	20,000	30,000	10,000 (F)
Direct materials	6,000	8,500	2,500 (A)
Direct labour	4,000	4,500	500 (A)
Maintenance	1,000	1,400	400 (A)
Depreciation	2,000	2,200	200 (A)
Rent and rates	1,500	1,600	100 (A)
Other costs	3,600	5,000	1,400 (A)
Total costs (b)	18,100	23,200	5,100
Profit (a) – (b)	1,900	6,800	4,900 (F)

Note. (F) denotes a favourable variance and (A) an adverse or unfavourable variance. Adverse variances are sometimes denoted as (U) for unfavourable.

Why are the variances shown above misleading? Jot down some ideas below.

(a)   In this example, the variances are meaningless for purposes of control. Costs were higher than budget because the volume of output was also higher; variable costs would be expected to increase above the budgeted costs in the fixed budget. There is no information to show whether control action is needed for any aspect of costs or revenues.

(b)   For control purposes, it is necessary to know the following.

   (i)   Whether actual costs were higher than they should have been to produce and sell 3,000 units of varmint.

   (ii)   Whether actual revenue was satisfactory from the sale of 3,000 units of varmint.

   (iii)   Whether the volume of units made and sold has varied from the budget favourably or adversely.

4.2   The correct approach to budgetary control

The correct approach to budgetary control is to identify fixed and variable costs and produce a flexible budget. It is preferable to use marginal costing techniques, and keep fixed costs at the same amount in the flexed budget as in the original master budget.

In the previous example of Sidewinder Ltd, let us suppose that we have the following estimates of cost behaviour.

(a)   Direct materials and maintenance costs are variable.

(b)   Although basic wages are a fixed cost, direct labour is regarded as variable in order to measure efficiency/productivity.

(c)   Rent and rates and depreciation are fixed costs.

(d)   Other costs consist of fixed costs of £1,600 plus a variable cost of £1 per unit made and sold.

Now that the cost behaviour patterns are known, a *budget cost allowance* can be calculated for each item of expenditure. This allowance is shown in a flexible budget as the expected expenditure on each item for the relevant level of activity. The budget cost allowances are calculated as follows.

(a)   Variable cost allowances   =   original budget × (3,000 units/2,000 units)

        eg material cost allowance   =   £6,000 × 3/2 = £9,000

(b)   Fixed cost allowance   =   as original budget

(c)   Semi-fixed cost allowances =   original budgeted fixed costs plus
                                         (3,000 units × variable cost per unit)

        eg Other costs allowances   =   £1,600 + (3,000 × £1) = £4,600

The budgetary control (variance) analysis should look like this.

	Fixed budget (a)	Flexible budget (b)	Actual results (c)	Variance (b) – (c)
Production and sales (units)	2,000	3,000	3,000	
	£	£	£	£
Sales revenue	20,000	30,000	30,000	0
Variable costs				
Direct materials (i)	6,000	9,000	8,500	500 (F)
Direct labour (ii)	4,000	6,000	4,500	1,500 (F)
Maintenance (iii)	1,000	1,500	1,400	100 (F)
Semi-variable costs				
Other costs (iv)	3,600	4,600	5,000	400 (A)
Fixed costs				
Depreciation (v)	2,000	2,000	2,200	200 (A)
Rent and rates (v)	1,500	1,500	1,600	100 (A)
Total costs	18,100	24,600	23,200	1,400 (F)
Profit	1,900	5,400	6,800	1,400 (F)

Analysis

In selling 3,000 units, the expected profit should have been, not the fixed budget profit of £1,900 but the flexible budget profit of £5,400. Instead, actual profit was £6,800, ie £1,400 more than we should have expected. One of the reasons for the improvement is that, given output and sales of 3,000 units, costs are lower than expected (and sales revenue exactly as expected).

		£
(i)	Direct materials cost variance	500 (F)
(ii)	Direct labour cost variance	1,500 (F)
(iii)	Maintenance cost variance	100 (F)
(iv)	'Other costs' cost variance	400 (A)
(v)	Fixed cost expenditure variances	
	Rent and rates	100 (A)
	Depreciation	200 (A)
		1,400 (F)

Activity 5

The analysis above explains the difference between actual profit and the profit shown in the flexed budget. What about the difference between the profit shown in the flexed budget and that shown in the original fixed budget? Using your knowledge of variable costing, show how this difference can be explained.

Investigation of the variances, with a view to deciding whether control action is required, will be carried out for those variances which seem significantly large, by the

PUBLISHING

manager responsible for the area of operations concerned. Large favourable variances should be checked, as well as adverse variances, in order to find out what has happened and why. In our example, the sales manager may be asked to check why sales were 50% higher than budgeted and the production manager may be asked to explain the large favourable variance in labour costs. The adverse variances are probably insufficiently large, in this example, to warrant an investigation. This is known as *management* by *exception* and allows managers to focus on areas which are not performing in line with expectations.

4.3 Cost control and cost reduction

Budgetary control is the basis of a cost control system which requires managers to be held responsible for aspects of a budget or plan. They are also responsible for differences between the actual results and the budget or plan. The reporting system provides management with information to enable them to identify which costs and revenues are in need of management action to keep them under control.

Cost reduction, in contrast, is concerned with bringing down expenditure levels and spending less than before without reducing the quality of the products or service. Cost reduction implies 'cuts' whereas cost control implies keeping costs within planned and acceptable limits. Do not make the common error of confusing these two techniques.

4.4 Controllable costs

Budgetary control reporting systems must report costs to the managers who are accountable for them and the concept of the *controllable or managed cost* is an important one. This is a cost, which can be influenced by its budget holder. It is not always possible to pre-determine responsibility, because the reason for deviation from expected performance may only become evident later. For example, excessive scrap may arise from inadequate supervision or from a latent defect in purchase material.

In contrast, a non-controllable cost is a cost over which the manager of a cost or budget centre has no control. It would be incorrect to attempt to hold the manager responsible for any variance occurring on such a cost.

4.5 Responsibility accounting

Responsibility accounting is the term used to describe decentralisation of authority, with performance of the decentralised units measured in terms of accounting results. 'Responsibility accounting, profitability accounting or activity accounting systems recognise various decision centres throughout an organisation and trace costs (and revenues, assets and liabilities where pertinent) to the individual managers who are primarily responsible for making decisions about the costs in question.'

Definition

> *Responsibility accounting* may be defined as a system of accounting that segregates revenues and costs into areas of personal responsibility in order to assess the performance attained by persons to whom authority has been assigned.

Responsibility accounting aims to provide accounting reports, so that all managers are made aware of all the items which are within their area of authority so that they are in a position to explain them.

Definition

> A *responsibility centre* is 'a department or organisational function whose performance is the direct responsibility of a specific manager' (CIMA, *Official Terminology*).

Remember that it is important to hold managers responsible only for those areas over which they can exercise control.

4.6 Different methods of budgetary control

There are different ways in which variance analysis can be done, but the basic principles are the same for each. Basically, the different methods are as follows.

(a) To compare actual results in one period against *standard costs*. This is the ideal method, because standard costs should be carefully prepared budget estimates. Standard costs are described more fully in the next chapter.

(b) To compare actual results in one period against the budget for that period, without resorting to standard costs.

(c) To compare actual results in one period against actual results in a previous corresponding period (for example last month, or last year). This is the worst type of budgetary control, because the previous period is used as a 'budget' even though actual results in the previous period may not have been at all satisfactory. A true measure of current efficiency is not obtainable, although a measure of the improvement or worsening of results as compared with an earlier period is found.

4.7 The problems in constructing budgets

This chapter on budgets might seem to have concerned itself mainly with computational work. Most of the practical problems in budgeting are, however, not so much the computations themselves, but rather other factors. Suggest three non-computational issues which may hinder preparation of budgets.

1.

2.

3.

You could have included some of the following points.

(a) It might be difficult to forecast sales with any accuracy.

(b) The availability of resources, especially skilled labour and cash, might be difficult to predict, and so it might be difficult to identify the principal budget factor.

(c) Because of inflation, it might be difficult to estimate future price levels for materials, expenses, wages and salaries.

(d) Managers might be reluctant to budget accurately.

  (i) They may overstate their expected expenses, so that by having a larger-than-necessary budget, they will be unlikely to overspend their budget allowance (they will then not be held accountable in control reports for excess spending). Excess expenditure built into a budget is known as *slack* and zero base budgeting is an attempt to eliminate this.

  (ii) They may compete with other departments for the available resources, by trying to expand their budgeted expenditure. Budget planning might well intensify inter-departmental rivalry and the problems of 'empire building'.

(e) Inter-departmental rivalries and self-interests might ruin the efforts towards co-ordination in a budget.

(f) Employees might resist budget plans either because the plans are not properly communicated to them, or because they feel that the budget puts them 'under pressure' from senior managers to achieve better results.

Chapter roundup

Planning and control of costs are important in all organisations. The most efficient method is to co-ordinate effort by preparing budgets in advance and then comparing the actual results against the budget. Any differences revealed by this comparison will then trigger the appropriate management control action.

- Budgets are prepared to co-ordinate activities, to communicate policies and targets, to establish a system of control and to compel planning.

- It is common to prepare a master budget for the organisation by combining the information in departmental or functional budgets.

- For purposes of control, a fixed budget is inadequate. Instead, managers should examine variances between a flexed budget and actual outcomes.

In the final chapter of this text you will develop your understanding of budgets by concentrating on the compilation of standard costs, the calculation of variances and how they may be used as a tool of managerial control.

Quick quiz

1	Define a budget.	(see para 1.1)
2	What is meant by the principal budget factor?	(1.4)
3	What is a rolling budget?	(2.6)
4	Describe the principles of zero base budgeting.	(2.7)
5	What is meant by a flexible budget?	(section 3)
6	Define budgetary control.	(section 4)
7	Why is the use of a fixed budget inadequate for purposes of budgetary control?	(4.1)
8	Distinguish between cost control and cost reduction.	(4.3)
9	Define a controllable cost.	(4.4)
10	What is meant by responsibility accounting?	(4.5)

Answers to activities

1 Many reasons might be put forward, including the following.

 (a) Although it is expressed in monetary terms, a budget is more than an accounting statement. It is an expression of the strategic and operational plans of an enterprise.

 (b) Much of what goes into a budget is dependent on the planning decisions taken by functional managers rather than by the accounts department.

 (c) In due course, functional managers will be held responsible for any failure to achieve targets expressed in the budget. This would be quite unfair if they had no say in setting the targets.

 Of course, none of this means that managers are prohibited from using the services of the accounts department in order to translate their plans and projections into monetary terms.

2 (a) They could accept the limitation on grade A labour as insuperable and reduce their sales target by 20%.

 (b) They could try to increase the availability of grade A labour, by recruitment or overtime working.

 (c) They could try to sub-contract the production of 1,000 units to another manufacturer, but still profit on the transaction.

3 Numbers 2, 3 and 5 are not profit and loss account items.

4 (a) Management needs to be informed about how good or bad actual performance has been. To provide a measure of performance, there must be a yardstick (budget or standard) against which actual performance can be measured.

 (b) Every business is dynamic, and actual volumes of output cannot be expected to conform exactly to the fixed budget. Comparing actual costs directly with the fixed budget costs may be highly misleading.

 (c) For useful control information, it is necessary to compare actual results at the actual level of activity achieved against the results that should have been expected at this level of activity (the flexible budget).

Our answers take the conventional stance on this question. In practice in the 1990s many businesses have sufficient control over their production processes and sufficient understanding of their market for 'budget' and 'actual' to be virtually synonymous.

5   The contribution earned for every unit sold is as follows.

		£	£
Sales value			10.00
Variable costs:	direct materials	3.00	
	direct labour	2.00	
	maintenance	0.50	
	other	1.00	
			6.50
Contribution			3.50

The extra contribution earned is 1,000 units at £3.50 per unit, ie £3,500, which is the difference between the two profit figures (£1,900 and £5,400).

Further question practice

Now try the following practice questions at the end of this text

Multiple choice questions: **97 to 105**

Chapter 19 :

MANAGERIAL CONTROL: STANDARD COSTING AND VARIANCE ANALYSIS

Introduction

Just as there are standards for most things in our daily lives (cleanliness in hamburger restaurants, educational achievement for nine year olds, number of tubes on the Circle line running on time), there are standards for the costs of units of products and units of services rendered. Moreover, just as the standards in our daily lives are not always met, the standards for the costs of units of products and services rendered are not always met. We will not, however, be considering the cleanliness of hamburger restaurants in this chapter but we will be looking at *standard costs* and *standard costing*.

The actual results achieved by an organisation during a reporting period (week, month, quarter, year) will more than likely be different from the expected results (the expected results being the standards costs and revenues). Such differences may occur between individual items, such as the cost of labour and the volume of sales, and between the total expected profit/contribution and the total actual profit/contribution.

Management will have spent considerable time and trouble setting standards. Actual results have differed from the standards. Have costs been controlled? What does the wise manager do? Ignore the difference and continue trying to attain the standards? Hopefully not. The wise manager will consider the differences that have occurred and use the results of his considerations to assist him in his attempt to attain the standards. The wise manager will use *variance analysis* as a method of cost control.

This chapter examines variance analysis and sets out the method of calculating material cost variances, labour cost variance and the total overhead variance.

Your objectives

After completing this chapter you should:

(a)   Understand what is meant by a standard cost, and how a standard cost is calculated

(b)   Be aware of some of the main variances and how they are calculated

(c)   Understand the way in which standard costs and variances are used as a tool of managerial control

1   STANDARD COSTS

A standard cost is an estimated unit cost, prepared in advance and calculated from management's expectations of:

    (a)   Efficiency levels in the use of materials and labour

    (b)   The expected price of materials, labour and expenses

    (c)   Budgeted overhead costs and budgeted volumes of activity

It is a planned cost (the cost that should be incurred in making the unit, if everything goes according to plan).

Standard costing is the preparation of standard costs:

    (a)   For use in cost accounting as a means of valuing stocks and the cost of production

    (b)   For use in budgetary control (variance analysis)

The CIMA's *Official Terminology* stresses the control and variance analysis aspect of standard costing.

Definitions

>   (a)   *Standard*: 'a benchmark measurement of resource usage, set in defined conditions'.
>
>   (b)   *Standard cost*: 'the planned unit cost of the products, components or services produced in a period. The main uses of standard costs are in performance measurement, control, stock valuation and in the establishment of selling prices'.
>
>   (c)   *Standard costing*: 'a control technique which compares standard costs and revenues with actual results to obtain variances which are used to stimulate improved performance'.

Standard costing may be used as a system of absorption costing or as a system of marginal costing. Initially, we shall describe standard costs in absorption costing systems.

When standard costs are fully absorbed costs, the absorption rate of fixed production overheads will be pre-determined, usually each year when the budget is prepared, and based in the usual manner on budgeted fixed production cost expenditure and budgeted production. It is common for the absorption rate to be on a direct labour hours basis, so that the standard fixed production overhead cost per unit will be calculated as follows.

        Standard hours per unit × absorption rate per hour

1.1   The standard cost card

A standard cost card (or standard cost sheet) will be prepared for each product. The card will normally show the quantity and price of each direct material to be consumed, the time and rate of each grade of direct labour required, the overhead recovery and the full cost. The standard selling price and the standard profit per unit may also be shown.

The overhead portion of the standard cost should distinguish between the following overhead costs.

(a) Fixed and variable overhead costs of production unless variable overheads are insignificant in value, and all production overheads are therefore regarded as fixed costs.

(b) Production overhead and other overheads (administration and marketing). In many costing systems, administration and marketing overheads are excluded from the standard unit cost, so that the standard cost is simply a standard production cost.

A standard cost card might therefore consist of the following items.

STANDARD COST CARD – PRODUCT 1234

	£	£
Direct materials		
Material X – 3 kg at £4 per kg	12	
Material Y – 9 litre at £2 per litre	18	
		30
Direct labour		
Grade A – 6 hours at £1.50 per hour	9	
Grade B – 8 hours at £2 per hour	16	
		25
Standard prime (direct) cost		55
Variable production overhead – 14 hours at 50p per hour		7
Standard variable cost of production		62
Fixed production overhead – 14 hours at £4.50 per hour		63
Standard full production cost		125
Administration and marketing overhead		15
Standard cost of sale		140
Standard profit		20
Standard sales price		160

Activity 1

It is Monday morning. You have had the most horrendous weekend. Your Some of the features of standard costing and variance analysis are brought out very clearly in the context of manufacturing companies, and for that reason this chapter concentrates on manufacturing. But these techniques are used in service industries too.

Try to imagine what items might appear on the standard cost card for:

(a) A bed provided for a patient in a public sector hospital

(b) An episode of *Coronation Street*

1.2 Standard costs and budgetary control

Standard costing and budgetary control are interlinked. When standard costs have been determined it is relatively easy to compute budgets for production costs and sales. On the other hand, in determining standard costs it is necessary to ascertain the budgeted level of output for the period in order to prepare a standard fixed production overhead cost per unit.

When actual costs differ from standard costs we call these differences cost variances. Similarly, we get sales variances when actual sales are different from budgeted sales either due to the number sold (volume variance) or to a different price (price variance). These variances will affect our budgeted profit because our budgeted profit is based on standard costs and standard selling prices.

1.3 Determining standards and performance

The responsibility for setting standard costs should be shared between managers able to provide the necessary levels of expected efficiency, prices and overhead costs.

It is common for standard costs to be revised once a year to allow for changes in prices, wage rates and any expected alterations in such factors as volume of output, efficiency levels and standard practices.

When there is a sudden change in economic circumstances, or in technology or production methods, the standard cost will no longer be accurate. In practice, changing standards frequently is an expensive operation and can cause confusion. For this reason standard cost revisions are usually only made once a year. From the point of view of providing a target, however, an out-of-date standard is useless and some revision may be necessary.

Activity 2

Think about the impact of inflation on standards expressed in monetary terms. In a period of high inflation what are the pros and cons of frequent adjustments to standards?

It is also necessary to estimate the materials required to make each product (material usage) and also the labour hours required (labour efficiency).

Technical specifications must be prepared for each product by production experts (either in the production department or the work study department).

Standards are averages. Even under ideal working conditions, it would be unrealistic to expect every unit of activity or production to take exactly the same time, using exactly the same amount of materials, and at exactly the same cost. Some variations are inevitable, but for a reasonably large volume of activity, it would be fair to expect that on average, standard results should be achieved.

A further problem arises in standard setting because there are four types of performance standard, ideal, attainable, current and basic. Briefly explain what you think is meant by each of these. Write your answer down here.

(a)   *Ideal standards.* These are based on the most favourable operating conditions, with no wastage, no inefficiencies, no idle time and no breakdowns. Variances from ideal standards are useful for pinpointing areas where a close examination may result in large savings, but they are likely to have an unfavourable motivational impact. Employees will often feel that the goals are unattainable and not work so hard.

(b)   *Attainable standards.* These are based on the hope that a standard amount of work will be carried out efficiently, machines properly operated or materials properly used. Some allowance is made for wastage and inefficiencies. If well-set they provide a useful psychological incentive, and for this reason they should be introduced whenever possible. The consent and co-operation of employees involved in improving the standard are required.

(c)   *Current standards.* These are standards based on current working conditions (current wastage, current inefficiencies). The disadvantage of current standards is that they do not attempt to improve on current levels of efficiency, which may be poor and capable of significant improvement.

(d)   *Basic standards.* These are standards which are kept unaltered over a long period and may be out-of-date. These are used to show changes in efficiency or performance over a long period of time. Basic standards are perhaps the least useful and least common type of standard in use.

A standard cost, when established, is an *average expected unit cost*. Because it is only an average, actual results will vary to some extent above and below the average. Variances should only be reported where the difference between actual and standard is significant, ie the principle of *reporting by exception* should be used.

You will have realised that when setting standards, managers must be aware of two requirements: the need to establish a useful control measure; and the need to set a standard that will have the desired motivational effect. These two requirements are often conflicting, so that the final standard cost might be a compromise between the two.

Activity 3

Mark the following statements as true or false.

1   A standard cost is an estimated unit cost, prepared in advance and calculated from management expectations.

2   Standard costing is only used as a means of valuing stock and the cost of production.

3   Standard costs are generally prepared by one member of management.

4   Performance standards used in standard costing may be ideal, attainable, current or basic.

5   All variances produced by the standard costing control system should be investigated.

6   All businesses would benefit from the introduction of a standard costing system.

2   THE NATURE OF VARIANCES

Variances explain the difference between actual results and expected results. Expected results are the standard cost and standard revenue.

It is possible to analyse variances in great detail, sub-dividing the principal ones into their components. Such analysis is beyond the scope of this book. However, you do need to get a flavour of what is involved in the process in order to understand how variance analysis is used as a tool of managerial control.

To begin with, we will list some of the main variances with a brief description of each. Complete the following activity, which lists some variances and their description.

Activity 4

Match the correct description to each variance.

Variances

Sales price variance

Sales volume variance

Materials price variance

Materials usage variance

Labour rate variance

Labour efficiency variance

Overhead efficiency variance

Descriptions

Arises when more or less is spent on overheads than was budgeted.

Analogous to materials price variance – employees are paid more or less per hour than budgeted.

Arises when raw materials cost more or less per unit than budgeted.

Analogous to materials usage variance – each unit of finished product requires more or less labour than budgeted.

Arises when the number of units sold differs from budget.

Arises when products are sold at prices different from those budgeted.

Arises when more or less raw material than budgeted is used per unit of finished product.

To illustrate the calculations involved, we will look at an example of materials price and usage variances.

EXAMPLE: MATERIALS PRICE AND USAGE VARIANCES

Product A has a standard material cost of 5 kilograms of material M @ £2 per kg = £10 per unit of A.

In April 20X6, 100 units of A are manufactured, using 520 kilograms of material M, which cost £1,025.

Calculate the materials usage and materials price variances for April 20X6.

PUBLISHING

ANSWER

If everything had gone according to plan, our 100 units of A should have used up 500 kilograms of material M, which would have cost £1,000. In fact, our 100 units of A have cost us £1,025 in raw materials – an adverse variance of £25. This can be analysed as follows.

			£	£
Materials usage variance				
100 units of A should use	500	units of M		
100 units of A did use	520	units of M		
Adverse variance at standard price	20	units of M		(40)
Material price variance				
520 units of M should cost			1,040	
520 units of M did cost			1,025	
Favourable variance				15
Net variance (adverse)				(25)

Activity 5

Now test yourself on this type of calculation. Product B has a standard direct labour cost as follows: three hours of grade Y labour at £4.20 per hour. In April 20X6, it took 120 hours of grade Y labour, at a cost of £516, to produce 45 units of product B. Calculate the labour efficiency variance, the labour rate variance, and hence the total variance.

2.1   The reasons for cost variances

There are many possible reasons for cost variances arising, including efficiencies and inefficiencies of operations, errors in standard setting and changes in exchange rates. Here is a table of possible reasons for the variances.

Variance		Favourable	Adverse
(a)	Material price	Unforeseen discounts received	Price increase
		Greater care taken in purchasing	Careless purchasing
		Change in material standard	Change in material standard
(b)	Material usage	Material used of higher quality than standard	Defective material
			Excessive waste
		More effective use made of material	Theft
			Stricter quality control
		Errors in allocating material to jobs	Errors in allocating material to jobs
(c)	Overhead expenditure	Savings in costs incurred	Increase in cost of services used
		More economical use of services	Excessive use of services
			Change in type of services used

Activity 6

Attempt a similar analysis of the possible causes of labour rate and labour efficiency variances.

2.2 Interdependence between variances

The cause of one variance may be wholly or partly explained by the cause of another variance. Examples could be as follows.

(a) If the purchasing department buys a cheaper material which is poorer in quality than the expected standard, the material price variance will be favourable, but this may cause material wastage and an adverse usage variance.

(b) Similarly, if employees used to doing some work are highly experienced, they may be paid a higher rate than the standard wage per hour, but they should do the work more efficiently than employees of 'average' skill, ie an adverse rate variance may be compensated for by a favourable efficiency variance.

(c) An increase in sales price may result in a fall in sales volume below budgeted levels, ie a favourable sales price variance may result in an adverse sales volume variance.

Chapter roundup

In this chapter you have been introduced to standard costing and variance analysis. In practice, when all relevant variances are calculated, analysis may become complex. However, when used in an appropriate environment, standard costing is a useful managerial tool.

- Managers will sometimes attempt to build up standard cost (and revenue) information for a unit of production. These are the costs that will be incurred, and the revenue that will be earned, on a standard unit of production if everything goes according to plan.

- By comparing actual results with standard data it is possible to highlight variances.

- As part of their control function, managers examine variances and try to discover what caused them. This analysis may help to identify remedial action and improvements in procedures.

You have now reached the end of this text and should have a good basic understanding of financial and management accounting. If you found any areas particularly difficult try to revise the relevant chapters and make use of the recommended reading list.

Quick quiz

1   Define standard cost. Define standard costing.   (see section 1)

2   Describe the build-up of items on a standard cost card.   (1.1)

3   Why do standards need to be revised from time to time?   (1.3)

4   Name four types of performance standard and give a brief description of each.   (1.3)

5   What is meant by reporting by exception?   (1.3)

6   Describe what is meant by:

(a)   Materials price variance

(b)   Labour efficiency variance   (2.1)

7   Explain how a materials price variance and a materials usage variance may be interdependent.   (2.2)

Answers to activities

1   (a)   The standard cost per day of providing a hospital bed for a patient might include, for example:

(i)   The cost of washing the sheets

(ii)   A depreciation cost on the bed itself, and perhaps on the visitor's chair and the bedside cupboard that go with it

(iii)   A proportion of the salaries of nursing staff tending the occupant of the bed

(iv)   A notional rent charge for the physical space occupied by the bed

You could easily think of other costs.

The revenue side is more difficult, in that the hospital does not 'sell' the use of the bed to the patient. Nevertheless, at least some of the income granted to the hospital from NHS funds is based on the number of beds in the hospital, and it would not be impossible to work out a daily figure of revenue per bed.

(b)   The costs of an episode of Coronation Street include:

(i)   Payments made to the actors and production staff

(ii)   The cost of consumable supplies, such as costumes

(iii)   The cost of physically broadcasting the episode

and many more.

On the revenue side, you might include:

(i)   Revenue from advertisers booking space in the interval of the programme

(ii)   Revenue from selling the rights to broadcast the programme in other countries

2   At times of rapid price inflation, many managers have felt that the high level of inflation forced them to change price and wage rate standards continually. This, however, leads to a reduction in the value of the standard as a yardstick. At the other extreme is the adoption of 'basic' standards which will remain unchanged for many years. They provide a

constant base for comparison, but this is hardly satisfactory when there is technological change in working procedures and conditions.

3   True:

1.   Yes, management's expectations of efficiency levels, costs and volumes of activity will all affect the standard cost.

4.

False:

2.   Although a standard cost may be used in stock valuation and in determining the cost of production, it is primarily a control technique. Standard costs and revenues are compared with actual results to obtain variances which are then used to stimulate improved performance.

3.   It is not good practice to allow one individual to take sole responsibility for setting standard costs since he/she may not have the variety of experience and knowledge needed. The responsibility for setting standard costs should be shared between managers able to provide the necessary levels of expected efficiency, prices and overhead costs.

5.   No, variances should only be investigated where the difference between actual and standard is significant ie the principle of management by exception should be used.

6.   This is not always so. The typical business that will benefit most from a standard costing system will tend to be a larger organisation which will enjoy long production runs. Standard costing systems are expensive to install, and there is the cost of investigating variances to consider.

4

Variance	Description
Sales price variance	Arises when products are sold at prices different from those budgeted
Sales volume variance	Arises when the number of units sold differs from budget
Materials price variance	Arises when raw materials cost more or less per unit than budgeted
Materials usage variance	Arises when more or less raw material than budgeted is used per unit of finished product
Labour rate variance	Analogous to materials price variance – employees are paid more or less per hour than budgeted
Labour efficiency variance	Analogous to materials usage variance – each unit of finished product requires more or less labour than budgeted
Overhead expenditure	Arises when more or less is spent on overheads variance than was budgeted.

5   We would expect 45 units of product B to cost $45 \times 3 \times £4.20 = £567$. Instead they have been produced for only £516, a favourable variance of £51.

NOTES

This can be analysed as follows.

		£	£
Labour efficiency variance			
45 units of B should take	135 hours		
45 units of B did take	120 hours		
Favourable variance at standard price £4.20	15 hours		63
Labour rate variance			
120 hours of grade Y labour should cost		504	
120 hours of grade Y labour did cost		516	
Adverse variance			(12)
Total variance (favourable)			51

6	Variance	Favourable	Adverse
(a)	Labour rate	Use of apprentices or other workers at a rate of pay lower than standard	Wage rate increase
(b)	Labour efficiency	Output produced more quickly than expected, ie actual output in excess of standard output set for same number of hours because of work motivation, better quality of equipment or materials Errors in allocating time to jobs	Lost time in excess of standard allowed Output lower than standard set because of deliberate restriction lack of training, or sub-standard, materials used Errors in allocating time to jobs

Further question practice

Now try the following practice questions at the end of this text

Multiple choice questions: **106 to 114**

MULTIPLE CHOICE QUESTIONS

Chapter 1

1   What is *The corporate report*?

A	A discussion paper published by the Accounting Standards Committee
B	A statement of recommended practice published by the Accounting Standards Committee
C	A statement of standard accounting practice published by the Accounting Standards
D	A proposed revision of the law relating to company accounts published by the Government

A   B   C   D

2   *The corporate report* identifies seven categories of people having a right to financial information about companies. Which one of the following is *not* included in the list?

A	Trade contacts
B	Financial analysts
C	The general public
D	Managers of the company

A   B   C   D

Chapter 2

3   Which one of the following accounting concepts is *not* one of the fundamental concepts identified in SSAP 2?

A	The going concern concept
B	The consistency concept
C	The prudence concept
D	The entity concept

A   B   C   D

4   A company owns an item of stock which cost £4 and has a net realisable value of £3. The company accountant is unsure which of these valuations to use in preparing a balance sheet. Which of the following concepts should dictate his choice?

A	The going concern concept
B	The accruals concept
C	The prudence concept
D	The money measurement concept

A   B   C   D

5   Mr Bod has paid rent of £2,400 for the period 1 January 20X8 to 31 December 20X8. His first accounts are drawn up for the nine months ended 30 September 20X8.

His first accounts should show:

A   Only a rent expense of £2,400

B   A rent expense of £1,800 and a pre-payment of £600

C   A rent expense of £1,800 and accrued income of £600

D   A rent expense of £2,400, with an explanatory note that this is the usual charge for 12 months

A   B   C   D

6   At 1 January 20X8 the accounts of a trader show accrued rent payable of £250. During the year he pays rent bills totalling £1,275, including one bill for £375 in respect of the quarter ending 31 January 20X9.

What is the profit and loss charge for rent payable for the year ended 31 December 20X8?

A   £900

B   £1,150

C   £1,400

D   £1,650

A   B   C   D

Data for questions 7 – 10

A company has made the following payments in respect of rent and telephone expenses.

	Date paid	Amount £
Rent (payable quarterly in advance)		
Quarter ended 31 January 20X5	2.1.X5	480
Quarter ended 30 April 20X5	28.1.X5	480
Quarter ended 31 July 20X5	31.4.X5	810
Quarter ended 31 October 20X5	30.7.X5	810
Quarter ended 31 January 20X6	1.11.X5	810
Telephone (payable quarterly in arrears)		
Quarter ended 30 November 20X4	1.2.X5	630
Quarter ended 28 February 20X5	1.4.X5	570
Quarter ended 31 May 20X5	17.7.X5	710
Quarter ended 31 August 20X5	12.10.X5	650
Quarter ended 30 November 20X5	1.2.X6	840
Quarter ended 28 February 20X6	2.4.X6	720

The company maintains a full double entry accounting system and has a calendar year end. All invoices for rent and telephone expenses were received on the due dates.

BPP

PUBLISHING

7   What balance should have been brought forward on the rent account at 1 January 20X5?

    A   £160 debit
    B   £160 credit
    C   £320 debit
    D   £320 credit

    A   B   C   D

8   What balance should have been brought forward on the telephone expenses account at 1 January 20X5?

    A   £190 credit
    B   £380 credit
    C   £570 credit
    D   £820 credit

    A   B   C   D

9   What balance should be carried forward on the rent payable account at 31 December 20X5?

    A   £270 debit
    B   £270 credit
    C   £540 debit
    D   £540 credit

    A   B   C   D

10 What balance should be carried forward on the telephone expenses account at 31 December 20X5?

    A   £240 credit
    B   £480 credit
    C   £720 credit
    D   £1,080 credit

    A   B   C   D

Chapter 3

11 Andy starts a business and introduces capital of £10,000. He also obtains a loan of £6,000 to purchase fixed assets.

    The amount of his opening net assets is:

    A   £4,000
    B   £6,000
    C   £10,000
    D   £16,000

    A   B   C   D

12   A trader's net profit for the year may be computed by using which of the following formulae?

    A   Opening capital + drawings – capital introduced – closing capital

    B   Closing capital + drawings – capital introduced – opening capital

    C   Opening capital – drawings + capital introduced – closing capital

    D   Closing capital – drawings + capital introduced – opening capital

A   B   C   D

13   The profit earned by a business in 20X7 was £72,500. The proprietor injected new capital of £8,000 during the year and withdrew goods for his private use which had cost £2,200.

If net assets at the beginning of 20X7 were £101,700, what were the closing net assets?

    A   £35,000

    B   £39,400

    C   £168,400

    D   £180,000

A   B   C   D

14   The profit made by a business in 20X7 was £35,400. The proprietor injected new capital of £10,200 during the year and withdrew a monthly salary of £500.

If net assets at the end of 20X7 were £95,100, what was the proprietor's capital at the beginning of the year?

    A   £50,000

    B   £55,500

    C   £63,900

    D   £134,700

A   B   C   D

15   A business had net assets of £32,500 at 1 January 20X9. The net profit, after proprietor's drawings, for the year ended 31 December 20X9 was £13,250. Drawings were made at the rate of £750 per month in cash. The proprietor also withdrew for his own use goods costing £340 and with a selling price of £800. No new capital was introduced during the year.

What were the net assets at 31 December 20X9?

    A   £35,950

    B   £36,410

    C   £45,750

    D   £64,430

A   B   C   D

16   A business had net assets at 1 January and 31 December 20X9 of £75,600 and £73,800 respectively. During the year, the proprietor introduced additional capital of £17,700 and withdrew cash and goods to the value of £16,300.

What profit or loss was made by the business in 20X9?

   A   £3,200 loss

   B   £400 loss

   C   £400 profit

   D   £3,200 profit

A B C D

17   A business had net assets at 1 January and 31 December 20X9 of £47,100 and £54,200 respectively. During the year the proprietor introduced additional capital of £22,000 and made drawings of £200 per week.

What profit or loss was made by the business in 20X9?

   A   £18,700 loss

   B   £4,500 loss

   C   £4,500 profit

   D   £18,700 profit

A B C D

Chapter 4

18   A business purchased a machine at a cost of £8,300 including £200 carriage from the supplier's premises and £300 installation costs. After two months in operation the machine broke down and cost £450 to repair. In the balance sheet at the year end the asset's cost would appear as:

   A   £8,000

   B   £8,100

   C   £8,300

   D   £8,750

A B C D

19   Which one of the following assets may be classified as an intangible fixed asset in the accounts of a business?

   A   Leasehold premises

   B   Trade investment

   C   Goodwill

   D   Preliminary expenses of incorporation

A B C D

20   Which one of the following would *not* be classified amongst current liabilities in the accounts of a business?

   A   A provision for doubtful debts

   B   Accrued interest charges

   C   Bank overdraft

   D   Corporation tax payable

A B C D

NOTES

21   What is the purpose of charging depreciation in accounts?

A   To allocate the cost of a fixed asset over the accounting periods expected to benefit from its use

B   To ensure that funds are available for the eventual replacement of the asset

C   To reduce the cost of the asset in the balance sheet to its estimated market value

D   To comply with the prudence concept

A   B   C   D

22   The net book value of a fixed asset represents

A   Its undepreciated cost

B   Its market value on a going concern basis

C   Its realisable value in a forced sale

D   The amount still to be written off over its remaining life

A   B   C   D

Chapter 5

23   Which one of the following records is often maintained on an imprest system?

A   Cash book

B   Petty cash book

C   Journal

D   Sales day book

A   B   C   D

24   Which one of the following records might form part of a business's double entry accounting system?

A   Sales ledger

B   Sales day book

C   Sales returns day book

D   Journal

A   B   C   D

25   The extract below is taken from a book of prime entry.

Date	Narrative	Folio	Total £	Discounts allowed £	Sales ledger £	Sundry £
1.5.20X9	M James & Co	SL12	140.00	10.00	140.00	0

Which book of prime entry is represented here?

A	Sales day book
B	Purchase day book
C	Journal
D	Cash book

A   B   C   D

26   What ledger entries would be made to record the purchase of an item of machinery on credit?

A	Debit machinery, credit cash
B	Debit machinery, credit creditors
C	Debit purchases, credit creditors
D	Debit creditors, credit machinery

A   B   C   D

27   What transaction is represented by the entries: debit bank, credit M Smith?

A	Sale of goods to Smith for cash
B	Purchase of goods from Smith for cash
C	Receipt of cash from Smith
D	Payment of cash to Smith

A   B   C   D

28   What ledger entries would be made to record cash withdrawn by the business proprietor for his personal use?

A	Debit capital, credit drawings
B	Debit cash, credit drawings
C	Debit drawings, credit capital
D	Debit drawings, credit cash

A   B   C   D

29   What transaction is represented by the entries: debit rent, credit landlord?

A	The receipt of rental income by the business
B	The issue of an invoice for rent to a tenant
C	The payment of rent by the business
D	The receipt of a bill for rent payable by the business

A   B   C   D

30   What ledger entries would be made to record goods withdrawn by the business proprietor for his personal use?

A	Debit drawings, credit purchases
B	Debit purchases, credit drawings
C	Debit capital, credit drawings
D	Debit purchases, credit sales

A   B   C   D

31 Which one of the following occurrences could *not* account for a credit balance on a trade debtor's account?

   A   A sales invoice has been paid twice

   B   A sales invoice has been posted to another customer's account in error

   C   Returns outwards have not been taken into account

   D   A cheque from the customer was made out in the wrong account

A B C D

32 Customer Ltd receives goods from Supplier Ltd on credit. Subsequently, payment is made by cheque. It then becomes apparent that the goods are faulty. This is discovered just in time for Customer Ltd to cancel the cheque before it can be cashed.

What entries should be made by Customer Ltd to record the cancellation of the cheque?

   A   Debit returns outwards, credit creditors

   B   Debit creditors, credit returns outwards

   C   Debit creditors, credit bank

   D   Debit bank, credit creditors

A B C D

33 What transaction is represented by the entries: debit bank, credit cash?

   A   Topping up of the petty cash imprest balance

   B   Payment of bank charges

   C   Receipt from credit customer paying by cash

   D   Lodgement of cash in the bank

A B C D

34 The returns outwards book is totalled at convenient intervals and the total must be entered into appropriate ledger accounts. Which one of the following postings would be acceptable?

   A   Debit returns outwards, credit creditors

   B   Debit creditors, credit purchases

   C   Debit returns outwards, credit debtors

   D   Debit sales, credit debtors

A B C D

35 Expenses recorded in the petty cash book are posted:

   A   To the credit of the suppliers' personal accounts

   B   To the credit of the nominal ledger expense accounts

   C   To the debit of the nominal ledger expense accounts

   D   To the debit of the main cash book

A B C D

36 Which one of the following occurrences might explain the existence of a credit balance on an individual debtor's account?

    A   The bookkeeper failed to make a posting from the returns inwards book to the debtors ledger

    B   The debtor took advantage of a settlement discount and paid less than the full amount invoiced

    C   The bookkeeper failed to post an invoice for the sales day book to the debtors ledger

    D   The bookkeeper posted a total from the returns inwards book to the debtors control account twice by mistake

A B C D

Chapter 6

37 Which one of the following costs would be classified as capital expenditure in the accounts of a business?

    A   The annual depreciation charge on freehold premises

    B   The cost of redecorating freehold premises

    C   The cost of roof repairs on freehold premises

    D   Solicitors' fees in connection with the acquisition of freehold premises

A B C D

38 Which one of the following items should be treated as capital expenditure in the accounts of a sole trader?

    A   £2,000 spent on purchasing a micro-computer for re-sale?

    B   £700 drawings to buy a new television for the proprietor

    C   £200 spent on purchasing a new typewriter to replace his secretary's old one

    D   £150 paid to a painter in respect of office decoration

A B C D

39 Which one of the following costs would be classified as revenue expenditure on the invoice for a new company car?

    A   Road tax

    B   Number plates

    C   Fitted stereo radio

    D   Delivery costs

A B C D

40   Which one of the following formulae may be used to calculate gross profit?

A   Net profit plus expenses

B   Cost of goods sold less purchases

C   Sales plus cost of goods sold

D   Opening stock plus purchases less closing stock

A   B   C   D

41   The following information is available in respect of a sole trader:

	£
Net profit for the year	7,000
Drawings	9,000
Capital at end of the year	31,000

There were no new injections of capital during the year.

What was the trader's opening capital?

A   £16,000

B   £29,000

C   £33,000

D   £47,000

A   B   C   D

42   Mr Harmon does not keep full accounting records, but the following information is available in respect of his accounting year ended 31 December 20X9.

	£
Cash purchases in year	3,900
Cash paid for goods supplied on credit	27,850
Creditors at 1 January 20X9	970
Creditors at 31 December 20X9	720

In his trading account for 20X9, what will be Harmon's figure for purchases?

A   £27,600

B   £31,500

C   £31,750

D   £32,000

A   B   C   D

Chapter 7

43   A partnership employs an inexperienced bookkeeper. He has written up the current account of one of the partners as follows.

CURRENT ACCOUNT

	£		£
Interest on capital	2,800	Balance b/f	270
Salary	1,500	Drawings	6,200
Balance c/f	10,870	Net profit	8,700
	15,170		15,170

The balance brought forward is entered correctly and the other entries are all correct in amount. However, the bookkeeper is not very sure of the difference between debits and creditors.

What is the corrected balance carried forward?

A   A debit balance of £1,530

B   A debit balance of £6,530

C   A credit balance of £7,070

D   A credit balance of £16,470

A   B   C   D

44   A partner's private petrol bills have been treated as part of the partnership's motor vehicle expenses. Which of the following entries is necessary to correct the error?

A   *Debit*   Drawings account
     Credit   Motor vehicle expenses account

B   *Debit*   Motor vehicles expenses account
     Credit   Drawings account

C   *Debit*   Motor vehicles expenses account
     Credit   Capital account

D   *Debit*   Capital account
     Credit   Motor vehicle expenses account

A   B   C   D

45   What double entry is necessary to reflect interest earned on partners' capital account balances?

A   *Debit*   Partners' current accounts
     Credit   Profit and loss appropriation account

B   *Debit*   Profit and loss appropriation account
     Credit   Partners' current accounts

C   *Debit*   Profit and loss appropriation account
     Credit   Cash

D   *Debit*   Profit and loss appropriation account
     Credit   Partners' capital accounts

A   B   C   D

46   What double entry is necessary to reflect interest payable on partners' drawings?

A   Debit   Partners' drawings accounts
     Credit   Partners' current accounts

B   Debit   Profit and loss appropriation account
     Credit   Partners' drawings accounts

C   Debit   Partners' drawings accounts
     Credit   Interest payable account

D   Debit   Partners' current accounts
     Credit   Profit and loss appropriation account

A   B   C   D

> *Data for questions 47 – 48*
>
> Faith, Hope and Charity are partners sharing residual profits in the ratio 3:2:1. The partnership agreement provides for interest on capital at the rate of 8% per annum and for a salary for Hope of £8,000 per annum. Net profit for 20X5 was £84,000 and the balances on partners' capital accounts during the year were: Faith £20,000; Hope £15,000; Charity £12,000.

47   Calculate Charity's share of residual profits for 20X5.

   A   £12,040

   B   £12,667

   C   £13,000

   D   £14,000

   A   B   C   D

48   Calculate the total of the appropriations credited to Hope's account in 20X5.

   A   £24,080

   B   £28,000

   C   £33,280

   D   £33,333

   A   B   C   D

> *Data for questions 49 – 50*
>
> Publysh and Bedamd are partners in a bookshop business. They share residual profits in the ratio 3:2 after interest on partners' capital of 6% per annum and interest on partners' drawings of 10% per annum. Their capital balances throughout 20X6 were £8,000 and £6,000 respectively, and the average balances on their drawings accounts were £12,000 and £15,000. Net trading profit for 20X6 was £32,000.

49   Calculate the balance of residual profits available for appropriation in profit sharing ratio.

   A   £30,140

   B   £31,160

   C   £33,860

   D   £34,700

   A   B   C   D

50   Calculate the net amount of all sums transferred from the appropriation account to the current account of Publysh.

   A   £19,116

   B   £19,596

   C   £20,316

   D   £20,796

   A   B   C   D

Chapter 8

51   What is the meaning of the word 'limited' in the name of a limited company?

    A   The number of shareholders is limited to 50

    B   The liability of the company for its own debts is limited

    C   The liability of shareholders for the company's debts is limited

    D   There is a limit on the amount of debts that the company can contract

A   B   C   D

52   What is the meaning of a company's 'authorised capital'?

    A   The total amount of share capital it is allowed to issue

    B   The amount of share capital it has issued

    C   The amount of share capital for which payment has been received from subscribers

    D   The maximum amount of loan capital prescribed by its articles of association

A   B   C   D

53   Company law defines certain accounting and other records that a limited company must maintain. Which one of the following is not required to be maintained by a limited company in the retail trade?

    A   A register of shareholders' 5% interests in the company

    B   A register of debenture holders

    C   A record of day-to-day cash inflows and outflows

    D   A statement of stocks held at the year end

A   B   C   D

54   Which one of the following items would not appear in the appropriation account of a limited company?

    A   Ordinary dividend payable

    B   Preference dividend payable

    C   Debenture interest payable

    D   Transfer to general reserve

A   B   C   D

55   A company has an authorised share capital of £1,000,000 consisting of 25p ordinary shares. Its issued share capital consists of 500,000 shares.

A dividend of 2p per share is declared. The cash payable to the shareholders amounts to:

A   £10,000

B   £20,000

C   £40,000

D   £80,000

A B C D

56   A company has an authorised capital of 1,000,000 10p ordinary shares of which 800,000 are in issue. It is proposed to pay a dividend totalling £40,000. Which of the following expressions correctly describes the amount of the dividend?

A   An ordinary dividend of 4%

B   An ordinary dividend of 4p per share

C   An ordinary dividend of 5%

D   An ordinary dividend of 5p per share

A B C D

57   A company's authorised capital consists of 4,000,000 50p ordinary shares. The company pays a dividend of 3% and the total sum received by shareholders is £45,000. What is the figure of called up share capital appearing in the company's balance sheet?

A   £1,500,000

B   £2,000,000

C   £3,000, 000

D   £4,000,000

A B C D

58   A company's share capital consists of 40,000 20p ordinary shares, which were all issued at a premium of 25%. The market value of the shares is currently 50p each. The figure for ordinary share capital appearing in the company's balance sheet would be:

A   £8,000

B   £10,000

C   £18,000

D   £20,000

A B C D

Chapter 10

The company's profit before interest and tax for 20X3 was £37,000. Tax on the year's

<table>
<tr><td colspan="2">*Data for questions 59 – 65*</td></tr>
<tr><td colspan="2">Extracts below are taken from the balance sheet of Barney Ltd at 31 December 20X3.</td></tr>
<tr><td></td><td>£</td></tr>
<tr><td>*Total assets less current liabilities*</td><td>114,000</td></tr>
<tr><td>*Creditors: amounts falling due after more than one year*</td><td></td></tr>
<tr><td>10% debentures 20X9</td><td>(20,000)</td></tr>
<tr><td></td><td>94,000</td></tr>
<tr><td>*Capital and reserves*</td><td></td></tr>
<tr><td>Called-up share capital</td><td></td></tr>
<tr><td>   Ordinary shares of 25p each</td><td>50,000</td></tr>
<tr><td>   12% preference shares of £1 each</td><td>10,000</td></tr>
<tr><td>Reserves</td><td>34,000</td></tr>
<tr><td></td><td>94,000</td></tr>
</table>

profits has been estimated as £9,000.

59   Calculate the return on total long-term capital employed earned by Barney Ltd in 20X3.

    A   24.6%

    B   27.7%   **A B C D**

    C   32.5%

    D   39.4%

60   Calculate the return on shareholders' capital earned by Barney Ltd in 20X3.

    A   27.7%

    B   29.8%   **A B C D**

    C   31.0%

    D   43.3%

61   Calculate the return on equity capital earned by Barney Ltd in 20X3.

    A   26.4%

    B   29.5%   **A B C D**

    C   31.9%

    D   49.6%

62   Calculate the gearing ratio of Barney Ltd at 31 December 20X3.

   A   17.5%

   B   26.3%

   C   31.9%

   D   50.0%

   A   B   C   D

63   Calculate Barney Ltd's earnings per share for 20X3.

   A   12.4p

   B   13.0p

   C   18.5p

   D   49.6p

   A   B   C   D

64   Calculate the interest cover of Barney Ltd.

   A   11.6 times

   B   13.0 times

   C   17.5 times

   D   18.5 times

   A   B   C   D

65   Calculate the preference dividend cover of Barney Ltd.

   A   20.7 times

   B   21.7 times

   C   29.2 times

   D   30.8 times

   A   B   C   D

66   Which one of the following formulae correctly expresses the relationship between return on capital employed (ROCE), profit margin (PM) and asset turnover (AT)?

   A $PM = \dfrac{AT}{ROCE}$

   B $ROCE = \dfrac{PM}{AT}$

   C $AT = PM \times ROCE$

   D $PM = \dfrac{ROCE}{AT}$

   A   B   C   D

Chapter 11

67   During a year a business sold stock which had cost £60,000. The stock held at the beginning of the year was £6,000 and at the end of the year £10,000.

What was the annual rate of stock turnover?

A   6 times

B   7 times

C   7.5 times

D   10 times

A   B   C   D

Data for questions 68 – 73

The trading account of Bruno Ltd for the year ended 30 June 20X6 is set out below.

	£	£
Sales		860,000
Opening stock	100,000	
Purchases	625,000	
	725,000	
Closing stock	76,000	
Cost of sales		649,000
Gross profit		211,000

The following amounts have been extracted from the company's balance sheet at 30 June 20X6.

	£
Trade debtors	120,000
Prepayments	8,000
Cash in hand	12,000
Bank overdraft	16,000
Trade creditors	80,000
Accruals	6,000
Proposed dividend	10,000

In the questions that follow you should assume a year of 365 days. Ignore VAT.

---

68   Calculate the stock turnover period of Bruno Ltd in days.

A   33 days

B   37 days

C   49 days

D   51 days

A   B   C   D

69   Calculate the debtors collection period of Bruno Ltd in days.

    A   51 days

    B   54 days

    C   67 days

    D   72 days

    A   B   C   D

70   Calculate the creditors payment period of Bruno Ltd in days.

    A   45 days

    B   47 days

    C   50 days

    D   78 days

    A   B   C   D

71   Calculate the current ratio of Bruno Ltd at 30 June 20X6.

    A   1.25:1

    B   1.93:1

    C   2.04:1

    D   2.12:1

    A   B   C   D

72   Calculate the quick ratio (or acid test ratio) of Bruno Ltd at 30 June 20X6.

    A   1.25:1

    B   1.28:1

    C   1.37:1

    D   1.50:1

    A   B   C   D

73   Calculate the length of Bruno Ltd's cash cycle in days.

    A   2 days

    B   4 days

    C   53 days

    D   100 days

    A   B   C   D

Chapter 14

74   Gross wages incurred in Department 1 in June were £54,000. The wages analysis shows the following summary breakdown of the gross pay.

	Paid to direct labour £	Paid to indirect labour £
Ordinary time	25,185	11,900
Overtime – basic pay	5,440	3,500
– premium	1,360	875
Shift allowance	2,700	1,360
Sick pay	1,380	300
	36,065	17,935

What is the direct wages cost for Department 1 in June?

A	£25,185
B	£30,625
C	£34,685
D	£36,065

A   B   C   D

75   Grant Leeve is an assembly worker in the main assembly plant of Gonnaway Ltd. Details of his gross pay for the week are as follows.

	£
Basic pay for normal hours worked: 38 hours at £5 per hour	190
Overtime: 8 hours at time-and-a-half	60
Group bonus payment	12
Gross pay	262

Although paid for normal hours in full, Grant had been idle for 10 hours during the week because of the absence of any output from the machining department.

The *indirect* labour costs of his total gross pay of £262 are

A	£70
B	£72
C	£82
D	£110

A   B   C   D

Data for question 76

The cost items which relate to operating a fleet of transport vehicles operated by Jagger Naughton Ltd are as follows.

Item

1   Vehicle depreciation (based on straight line method)

2   Drivers' wages (one driver per vehicle)

3   Employer's National Insurance contributions

4   Fuel

5   Oil

6   Holiday pay

7   Rent and running costs for garage and compound

8   Management salaries

9   Mechanic's wages

10   Replacement parts (vary with miles travelled)

11   Road fund licences

12   Security costs

13   Tyre replacements (once every three months per vehicle regardless of mileage)

14   Vehicle insurance

---

76   The items to include in the calculation of the direct costs (variable costs) per mile travelled would be

A   Items 1, 2, 3, 4, 5, 6, 10 and 13 only

B   Items 2, 3, 4, 5, 6, 10 and 13 only

C   Items 4, 5, 10 and 13 only

D   Items 4, 5 and 10 only

A   B   C   D

Chapter 16

Data for questions 77 – 79

Budgeted information relating to two departments in Rydons Tables Limited for the next period is as follows.

Department	Production overhead £	Direct material cost £	Direct labour cost £	Direct labour hours	Machine hours
1	27,000	67,500	13,500	2,700	45,000
2	18,000	36,000	100,000	25,000	300

Individual direct labour workers within each department earn differing rates of pay, according to their skills, grade and experience.

---

77   What is the most appropriate production overhead absorption rate for Department 1?

   A   40% of direct material cost

   B   200% of direct labour cost

   C   £10 per direct labour hour   **A   B   C   D**

   D   60p per machine hour

78   What is the most appropriate production overhead absorption rate for Department 2?

   A   50% of direct material cost

   B   18% of direct labour cost

   C   72p per direct labour hour   **A   B   C   D**

   D   £60 per machine hour

79   During the period, job number 9287 is carried out by Rydons Tables Limited. Production data is as follows.

Direct material cost		£40
Direct labour	– dept 1	4 hours at £5 per hour
	– dept 2	9 hours at £4 per hour
Machine hours	– dept 1	65 hours
	– dept 2	1 hour

   What is the total production cost of job 9287 using overhead absorption rates based on your selection in questions 77 and 78?

   A   £141.48

   B   £142.48   **A   B   C   D**

   C   £195.00

   D   £201.48

80   What is cost apportionment?

   A   The charging of discrete identifiable items of cost to cost centres or cost units

   B   The collection of costs attributable to cost centres and cost units using the costing method, principles and techniques prescribed for a particular business entity

   C   The process of establishing the costs of cost   **A   B   C   D**
       centres or cost units

   D   The spread of costs amongst two or more cost units or centres in proportion to the estimated benefit received, using an appropriate basis, eg square feet

81   Tumbil and Faull Limited has been using an overhead absorption rate of £5.60 per machine hour in its machining department throughout the year. During the year the overhead expenditure amounted to £275,000 and 48,000 machine hours were used. Which one of the following statements is correct?

A   Overhead was under-absorbed by £6,200

B   Overhead was under-absorbed by £7,600

C   Overhead was over-absorbed by £6,200

D   Overhead was over-absorbed by £7,600

A B C D

82   The following budgeted and actual data relate to production activity and overhead cost in Severn Windows of the World Ltd.

	Budget	Actual
Production overhead:		
fixed	£36,000	£39,000
variable	£9,000	£12,000
Direct labour hours	18,000	20,000

The company uses an absorption costing system and production overheads are absorbed on a direct labour hour basis.

Production overhead during the period was

A   Under-absorbed by £1,000

B   Over-absorbed by £1,000

C   Under-absorbed by £5,000

D   Under-absorbed by £6,000

A B C D

Data for questions 83 – 85

The annual costs listed below have been budgeted for Isabel Ringing Ltd, a company which manufactures fire alarm equipment.

	£'000
Energy and water costs (for the building as a whole)	10
Electricity for machines	5
Building rental and rates	90
Building repairs and maintenance	10
Machine repairs and maintenance	8
Direct materials	350
Direct wages	171
Machinery depreciation	52
Security	30
Carriage inwards for raw materials	30
Carriage outwards	70
Indirect production wages and salaries	50
Sales staff's salaries and expenses	76
General administration and management	38
Advertising	30

	Area occupied: square metres
Production	6,000
Sales and distribution	1,000
Administration	3,000

Costs related to the building are apportioned between production, sales and administration overheads on the basis of floor area.

83   The budgeted total of allocated and apportioned production overhead costs for the year is

    A   £199,000

    B   £229,000

    C   £255,000

    D   £299,000

A B C D

84   Sales and distribution overheads are absorbed into the cost of sales as a percentage of sales value. Given budgeted sales of £4,000,000, the sales and distribution overhead absorption rate for the year will be

    A   3.00% of sales value

    B   4.00% of sales value

    C   4.75% of sales value

    D   5.45% of sales value

A B C D

85   Administration overheads are absorbed into the cost of sales as a percentage of full production cost. The administration overhead absorption rate for the year will be (to one decimal place)

    A   10.7% of full production cost

    B   11.1% of full production cost

    C   14.5% of full production cost

    D   14.7% of full production cost

A B C D

86   The budgeted absorption rate for variable production overhead in Department X of Wiggipen Ltd's factory is £2.50 per direct labour hour and for fixed overhead is £4 per direct labour hour. Actual direct labour hours worked fell short of budget by 1,000 hours. If expenditures were as expected for variable and fixed overheads, the total under-absorbed overhead for the period would be

    A   £0

    B   £2,500

    C   £4,000

    D   £6,500

A B C D

NOTES

Chapter 17

Data for questions 87 – 88

The accountant of Katten Mousse plc has calculated the company's breakeven point from the following data.

	£
Selling price per unit	6.00
Variable production cost per unit	1.20
Variable selling cost per unit	0.40
Fixed production costs per unit, based on a budgeted 10,000 units pa	4.00
Fixed selling costs per unit, based on budgeted 10,000 units pa	0.80

87   What is the company's breakeven point?

    A   8,333 units

    B   9,091 units

    C   10,000 units   A   B   C   D

    D   10,909 units

88   It is now expected that the variable production cost per unit and the selling price per unit will each increase by 10%, and fixed production costs will rise by 25%.

    What will the breakeven point now be, to the nearest whole unit?

    A   9,470 units

    B   11,885 units

    C   12,295 units   A   B   C   D

    D   12,397 units

89   The following is a graph of cost against volume of output.

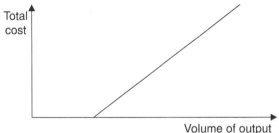

To which of the following costs does the graph correspond?

    A   Electricity bills made up of a standing charge and a variable charge

    B   Bonus payments to employees when production reaches a certain level

    C   Salesmen's commissions payable per unit up to a maximum amount of commission   A   B   C   D

    D   Bulk discounts on purchases, the discount being given on all units purchased

PUBLISHING

90

Which of the following does the graph illustrate?

A   Fixed cost per unit

B   Variable cost per unit

C   Full cost of production per unit

D   Full cost of sales per unit

A   B   C   D

91   Ian Tyrol Hats Limited has recorded the following data in the two most recent periods.

Total costs of production £	*Volume of production* Units
13,500	700
18,300	1,100

What is the best estimate of the company's fixed costs per period?

A   £4,800

B   £5,100

C   £9,900

D   £13,500

A   B   C   D

Data for questions 92 – 95

Danzig plc sells one product for which data is given below.

	£
Selling price per unit	10
Variable cost per unit	6
Fixed cost per unit	2

The fixed costs are based on a budgeted level of activity of 5,000 units for the period.

---

92   What is Danzig plc's breakeven point in £ of sales revenue?

A   2,500

B   5,000

C   25,000

D   50,000

A   B   C   D

93   How many units must be sold if Danzig wishes to earn a profit of £6,000 for the period?

   A   2,000
   B   4,000
   C   6,000   A B C D
   D   8,000

94   What is Danzig's margin of safety for the budget period if fixed costs prove to be 20% higher than budgeted?

   A   60%
   B   40%
   C $33^1/_3\%$ A B C D
   D   20%

95   If the selling price and variable cost increase by 20% and 12% respectively by how much must sales volume change compared with the original budgeted level in order to achieve the original budgeted profit for the period?

   A   24.2% decrease
   B   24.2% increase
   C   37.9% decrease   A B C D
   D   37.9% increase

96   Hans Bratch Ltd is a manufacturing company that employs a marginal batch costing system in its cost accounts. Which of the following cost items will be included in the company's marginal production costs of finished output?

   Item
   1   Marginal cost of products scrapped at routine final inspection
   2   Carriage inwards
   3   Set-up costs (variable with each batch produced)
   4   Salesmen's travelling expenses

   A   Items 1, 2, 3 and 4
   B   Items 1, 2 and 3 only
   C   Items 1 and 2 only   A B C D
   D   Items 2 and 3 only

Chapter 18

97   Which of the following is not a functional budget?

    A   Research and development

    B   Purchasing budget

    C   Cash budget

    D   Direct labour cost budget

A B C D

98   For a company that does not have any production resource limitations, in what sequence would the following budgets be prepared?

Budget
1   Cash budget
2   Sales budget
3   Stocks budget
4   Production budget
5   Purchases budget

    A   Sequence 2, 3, 4, 5, 1

    B   Sequence 2, 3, 4, 1, 5

    C   Sequence 2, 4, 3, 5, 1

    D   Sequence 4, 3, 2, 1, 5

A B C D

99   Each unit of product Alpha requires 3 kg of raw material. Next month's production budget for product Alpha is as follows.

Opening stocks:
        raw materials   15,000 kg
        finished units of Alpha   2,000 units
Budgeted sales of Alpha   60,000 units
Planned closing stocks:
        raw materials   7,000 kg
        finished units of Alpha   3,000 units

The number of kilograms of raw materials that should be purchased next month is

    A   172,000

    B   175,000

    C   183,000

    D   191,000

A B C D

100   The following information is available about budgets for next year of Roger Handout Ltd.

	Opening stocks £	Closing stocks £
Raw materials	23,200	17,300
Work in progress	4,700	8,200
Finished goods	16,600	18,800
Raw materials purchases budget	£140,000	
Direct labour hours budget (30,000 hrs)	£120,000	
Production overhead absorption rate	£5 per direct labour hour	
Administration overhead	£80,000	
Sales and distribution overhead	£120,000	
Sales budget	£620,000	

What is the company's budgeted profit for the year?

A   £6,300

B   £7,600

C   £9,800   **A   B   C   D**

D   £10,200

101   Sayles Tork Ltd is preparing next year's budget, using the current year's figures as a basis for forecasting next year's results.

Current year data includes:

Sales volume: 100,000 units

Price of raw materials: £2 per kg

There is a wastage rate of 20% of output produced, so that each unit of output requires 1.2 kg of materials input.

Data for next year

A reduction in selling price for the finished product is expected to increase sales volume by 25%.

The wastage rate on materials is expected to be reduced to 10% of output produced. The price of raw materials will go up by 10%, but a bulk purchase discount of 5% should be obtained, whereas none was obtained in the current year.

There are expected to be no opening and no closing stocks of raw materials, work in progress or finished goods.

What is the raw materials purchase budget for next year?

A   £256,500

B   £280,500   **A   B   C   D**

C   £287,375

D   £288,750

Data for questions 102 – 104

Extracts from next year's budget for Millstone Ltd are shown below.
Product X

Sales	37,500 units. Selling price £20 per unit
Opening stock	4,000 units, value £16 per unit
Budgeted closing stock	2,500 units

	£
Direct material cost per unit	4
Direct labour cost per unit (two hours)	8

Budgeted annual overheads	£
Variable production overheads	28,080
Fixed production overheads	140,400
Other overheads (administration, selling etc)	120,000

The company operates a full absorption costing system using a direct labour hour absorption rate and prices stock issues on the FIFO basis of valuation.

Production is budgeted to occur evenly throughout the year, but monthly sales are expected to vary. Budgeted sales of Product X in month 1 are 5,000 units. Overhead expenses will occur at an even monthly rate.

---

102   What is the budgeted value of closing stocks of Product X at the end of month 1?

    A   £32,640

    B   £33,360

    C   £40,800

    D   £41,700

                                             A   B   C   D

103   What is the budgeted profit for month 1?

    A   £8,600

    B   £9,320

    C   £18,600

    D   £19,320

                                             A   B   C   D

104   The effect on budgeted profit in month 1, if actual results are as predicted, except that actual production of Product X is 50 units higher than the budget, would be an increase in profit over budget by

    A   £180

    B   £195

    C   £216

    D   £234

                                             A   B   C   D

105   What is the name given to the method of budgeting whereby all activities are re-evaluated each time a budget is prepared, and the incremental cost of activities compared with their incremental benefits?

    A   Incremental budgeting

    B   Rolling budgets

    C   Zero base budgeting

    D   Flexible budgets

A   B   C   D

Chapter 19

106   Hake and Legge Ltd manufactures Product T and uses a standard costing system. Closing stocks of direct materials are valued at actual cost. Data for the production of product T in June include the following.

Direct materials used:	21,600 kg of material V
Cost of direct materials used	£128,304
Direct materials price variance (material V)	£1,296 (F)
Direct materials usage variance (material V)	£2,880 (A)

4,800 units of Product T were manufactured in June.

What is the standard direct materials cost of Product T?

    A   4.6 kg of V at £5.88 per kg

    B   4.5 kg of V at £5.94 per kg

    C   4.5 kg of V at £6.00 per kg

    D   4.4 kg of V at £6.00 per kg

A   B   C   D

107   A manufacturing company revises its standard costs at the beginning of each year. Because of inflation, it sets it standard price for materials at the estimated price level for the middle of the year. During one control period early in the year, a fairly large favourable direct materials price variance was reported. Which one of the following would not help to explain this variance?

    A   The control period was early in the year

    B   Direct materials were purchased in greater bulk than normal

    C   An alternative source of supply for materials was found and used

    D   Discounts were taken from suppliers for early settlement of invoices

A   B   C   D

108   Which one of the following would *not* help to explain a favourable direct materials usage variance?

> A   Using a higher quality of materials than specified in the standard
>
> B   Achieving a lower output volume than budgeted
>
> C   A reduction in quality control checking standards
>
> D   A reduction in materials wastage rates

A   B   C   D

109   Paul Damstring Ltd manufactures Product W. It employs a standard costing system, and the standard direct labour cost for Product W is two hours per unit at £3.60 per hour = £7.20.

In July, 5,000 units of W were manufactured. The direct labour costs totalled £36,400, and of the 9,700 direct labour hours worked in July, 200 hours were in overtime.

What were the direct labour rate variance and the direct labour efficiency variance in July?

	Rate variance	Efficiency variance
A	£400 (A)	£1,080 (F)
B	£400 (A)	£1,800 (F)
C	£1,480 (A)	£1,080 (F)
D	£1,480 (A)	£1,800 (F)

A   B   C   D

110   Which one of the following would not explain an adverse direct labour efficiency variance?

> A   Poor scheduling of direct labour workers
>
> B   Setting standard efficiency at a level that is too low
>
> C   Unusually lengthy machine breakdowns
>
> D   A reduction in direct labour training

A   B   C   D

111   Good Elf Insurance Ltd uses standard costing for its insurance-selling operations. Its 20X1 budget was to sell 8,000 policies. Labour costs of underwriting staff were budgeted at £56,000, and these are regarded as direct costs that vary with activity. Actual results in 20X1 were to sell 6,250 policies, and underwriting staff costs were £51,700. The underwriting staff would have been paid exactly at the budgeted rate, except that they received a pay award of 10% which was back-dated to 1 January, but had not been included in the budget.

Taking the original budget as the basis for comparison, what were the underwriting staff rate variance and the underwriting staff efficiency variance in 20X1?

	Rate variance	Efficiency variance
A	£4,700 (A)	£3,250 (A)
B	£4,700 (A)	£7,950 (A)
C	£5,170 (A)	£2,780 (A)
D	£5,170 (A)	£7,950 (A)

A B C D

Data for questions 112-114

Ed Lice Ltd manufactures a single product, Product F, for which the standard production overhead cost is four hours per unit at £6 per hour = £24 per unit.

This standard overhead cost is based on a budgeted absorption rate per direct labour hour. All production overheads are fixed costs.

Data for the year's operations are as follows.

Actual production of F:	4,500 units
Actual production overhead expenditure	£126,000
Budgeted production of F:	4,800 units
Direct labour hours worked	18,800 hrs

---

112 What was the production overhead expenditure variance for the year?

A £7,200 (A)

B £10,800 (A)

C £13,200 (A)

D £18,000 (A)

A B C D

113 What was the production overhead efficiency variance for the year?

A £4,800 (A)

B Nil

C £2,400 (F)

D £4,800 (F)

A B C D

114 What was the production overhead volume variance for the year? (This variance is sometimes known as the fixed overhead capacity variance.)

A £18,000 (A)

B £4,800 (A)

C £2,400 (A)

D £2,400 (F)

A B C D

EXAM STYLE QUESTIONS

Chapter 1

1   Users of accounting statements

It has been suggested that, apart from owners/investors, there are six separate user groups of published accounting statements: the loan creditor group, the employee group, the analyst-advisor group, the business contact group, the Government and the public.

Required

(a)   Taking any four of these six user groups, explain the information they are likely to want from published accounting statements.

(b)   Are there any difficulties in satisfying the requirements of all four of your chosen groups, given the requirements of other users?

Chapter 2

2   SSAP 2

SSAP 2 *Disclosure of accounting policies*, issued in 1971, distinguishes between fundamental concepts, accounting bases and accounting policies. Part of Paragraph 14 of the SSAP defines the four suggested 'fundamental concepts'.

Required

(a)   Explain and distinguish between:

    (i)   Fundamental concepts

    (ii)   Accounting bases

    (iii)   Accounting policies

    as the terms are used in SSAP 2.

(b)   Explain and give an example of the effect on a set of published financial statements of a company if the going concern convention is held not to apply.

Chapter 3

3   The accounting and business equations

Dave has given you some numbers extracted from the financial statements of an enterprise. He has heard of two 'equations' in which these numbers can be used: the accounting equation; and the business equation.

(a)   Profit is £1,051
Capital introduced is £100
There is an increase in net assets of £733

    What are drawings?

(b)   The increase in net assets is £173
Drawings are £77
Capital introduced is £45

    What is the net profit for the year?

NOTES

(c)   Liabilities of a business are £153 whereas assets are £174.

      How much capital is in the business?

(d)   Capital introduced is £50
      Profits brought forward at the beginning of the year amount to £100
      Liabilities are £70
      Assets are £90

      What is the retained profit for the year?

Chapter 4

4   Terminology

A friend has bought some shares in a quoted United Kingdom company and has received the latest accounts. There is one page he is having difficulty in understanding.

Required

Briefly, but clearly, answer his questions.

(a)   What is a balance sheet?

(b)   What is an asset?

(c)   What is a liability?

(d)   Why does the balance sheet balance?

(e)   To what extent does the balance sheet value my investment?

Chapter 5

5   Opening balance sheet

You are given the following information about a sole trader.

TRIAL BALANCE 31 DECEMBER 20X8

	£'000	£'000
Bank	53	
Capital		300
Land and buildings	320	
Plant and machinery: cost	200	
depreciation		80
Closing stock	100	
Sales		1,000
Cost of sales	600	
Operating expenses (including depreciation of £20,000)	140	
Bad debt written off	2	
Debtors	100	
Accruals		5
Creditors		130
	1,515	1,515

	£'000
Cash receipts (year to 31 December 20X8)	
Sales	950
Cash payments (year to 31 December 20X8)	
Purchases	560
Plant (1 January 20X8)	90
Operating items	130
Drawings	20

The creditors figure has doubled since 1 January 20X8.

Required

Open appropriate T accounts to enable you to calculate the items in the opening balance sheet at 1 January 20X8. Submit the summarised 1 January 20X8 balance sheet and all workings.

Chapter 6

6   Account preparation

The following trial balance has been extracted from the ledger of Mr Yousef, a sole trader.

TRIAL BALANCE AS AT 31 MAY 20X6

	Dr	Cr
	£	£
Sales		138,078
Purchases	82,350	
Carriage	5,144	
Drawings	7,800	
Rent, rates and insurance	6,622	
Postage and stationery	3,001	
Advertising	1,330	
Salaries and wages	26,420	
Bad debts	877	
Provision for doubtful debts		130
Debtors	12,120	
Creditors		6,471
Cash on hand	177	
Cash at bank	1,002	
Stock as at 1 June 20X5	11,927	
Equipment		
at cost	58,000	
accumulated depreciation		19,000
Capital		53,091
	216,770	216,770

The following additional information as at 31 May 20X6 is available.

(a)   Rent is accrued by £210.

(b)   Rates have been prepaid by £880.

(c)   £2,211 of carriage represents carriage inwards on purchases.

(d)   Equipment is to be depreciated at 15% per annum using the straight line method.

(e)   The provision for bad debts to be increased by £40.

(f)   Stock at the close of business has been valued at £13,551.

Required

Prepare a trading and profit and loss account for the year ended 31 May 20X6 and a balance sheet as at that date.

Chapter 7

7   **Partnership accounts**

A, B and C have been in partnership for many years, sharing profits equally. Their trial balance at 1 January 20X6 is as follows.

			£'000	£'000
A	Capital			30
	Current			2
B	Capital			28
	Current			4
C	Capital			32
	Current		4	
Land and buildings:	cost		70	
Plant and machinery:	cost		100	
	depreciation			66
Stock			40	
Trade debtors			30	
Bank			3	
Creditors:	trade			40
	operating expenses			5
Loan from D, at 10% per annum				40
			247	247

With effect from 1 January 20X6, the partnership agreement is changed. Profits are to be shared A : B : C – 3 : 2: 1.

At 1 January 20X6, the partnership goodwill is agreed at £60,000 but a ledger account for goodwill is not to be maintained in the accounting records. The land and buildings are agreed to be worth £100,000 and this figure is to be recorded in the accounting records.

At the end of each year each partner is to be allowed interest of 10% on the opening net balance on capital and current accounts (ie on the given balances before any adjustments).

The following information relating to 20X6 should be taken into account as necessary.

(a) The cash book summary for 20X6 is as follows.

	£'000			£'000
Opening balance	3	To trade suppliers		110
Received from customers	172	For operating expenses		30
From sale of old plant	10	For new plant		50
Balance c/d	38	Drawings	A	10
			B	11
			C	12
	223			223

(b) At 31 December 20X6 £10,000 is prepaid for rent, and £2,000 is to be accrued for electricity. Rent and electricity are both included in operating expenses.

(c) All plant and machinery is depreciated at 10% pa straight-line basis, assuming no scrap value, and with a full year's depreciation in the year of purchase and none in the year of sale. The old plant sold in 20X6 had been bought in June 20W8 at a cost of £60,000.

(d) At 31 December 20X6 trade creditors were £35,000. Trade debtors, after deducting £4,000 of bad debts, were £40,000. Gross profit is consistently 50% of cost of sales.

Required

Prepare trading, profit and loss and appropriation accounts for 20X6 for the partnership, and a summary balance sheet at 31 December 20X6. Submit all workings, which must be clear and legible. Ignore taxation.

Chapter 8

8 Limited companies' accounts

The trial balance of Zed Ltd at 1 January 20X3 contains the following items.

		£'000
Bank overdraft		7
Building:	cost	80
	depreciation	5
Creditors:	trade	28
	operating expenses	2
16% debentures		50
Debtors		24
Land at valuation		125
Machinery:	cost	90
	depreciation	43
Ordinary shares, £1 each		100
10% preference shares, £1 each		40
Profit and loss account		34
Revaluation reserve		45
Stocks		35

Summarised transactions and events for the year to 31 December 20X3 are as follows.

(a)

	£'000
Sales	920
Purchases	500
Bad debts written off	5
Contras between debtors and creditors accounts	8
Operating expenses paid	360

(b) 30,000 £1 ordinary shares were issued at £2.00 per share on 1 January 20X3; this transaction was not reflected in the trial balance above.

(c) Debenture interest and the preference dividend for the year were all paid on 31 December. An ordinary dividend of 20p per share was paid on 31 December.

(d) The land is revalued at 31 December 20X3 at £130,000. The machinery is to be depreciated at 10% on cost and the buildings are to be depreciated on the straight line basis over 80 years.

(e) At 31 December 20X3:

	£'000
Additional operating expenses owing are	10
Closing stock is	40
Closing debtors are	35
Closing trade creditors are	25

Required

Prepare the balance sheet at 31 December 20X3 and the profit and loss account for the year ended 31 December 20X3. These statements do not need to comply with Companies Act disclosure requirements, but should be presented in a format which is generally accepted and which presents the information helpful to the reader. Submit all workings. Ignore taxation.

Chapter 9

9 Cash flow statements

Set out below are the balance sheets of Cat Ltd as at 30 June 20X1 and 20X2.

CAT LIMITED
BALANCE SHEET AS AT 30 JUNE

	20X1	20X2
	£'000	£'000
Fixed assets		
Cost	85,000	119,000
Depreciation	26,000	37,000
	59,000	82,000
Current assets and liabilities		
Stocks	34,000	40,000
Debtors	26,000	24,000
Cash at bank	10,000	13,500
Trade creditors	15,000	23,000
Taxation	12,000	15,000
Dividend	13,000	17,000
	30,000	22,500
Long-term liabilities		
10% debentures	20,000	10,000
	69,000	94,500
Share capital and reserves		
Ordinary shares of £1 each	26,000	28,000
Share premium	12,000	13,000
Profit and loss account	31,000	53,500
	69,000	94,500

Notes

(a)   No fixed assets were disposed of during the year.

(b)   Of the 10% debentures, £10m was redeemed on 31 December 20X1.

Required

Prepare a cash flow statement for the year to 30 June 20X2, using the format specified in FRS 1.

Chapter 10

10 Company capital and interpretation

(a)   In the context of limited companies explain the following terms. Avoid using further technical expressions as far as possible, and explain any that you do have to use.

(i)   Shares (do not discuss different types of share)
(ii)   Reserves
(iii) Debentures
(iv) Shareholders' equity

NOTES

(v)   Capital employed

(b)   Define return on capital employed, and explain (without numerical illustration) how 'return' is calculated for this purpose. To whom is this ratio likely to give useful information, and why?

Chapter 11

11   **Working capital ratios**

You are given summarised results of an electrical engineering business, as follows.

PROFIT AND LOSS ACCOUNT

	Year ended	
	31.12.X5	31.12.X6
	£'000	£'000
Turnover	60,000	50,000
Cost of sales	42,000	34,000
Gross profit	18,000	16,000
Operating expenses	15,500	13,000
	2,500	3,000
Interest payable	2,200	1,300
Profit before taxation	300	1,700
Taxation	350	600
(Loss) profit after taxation	(50)	1,100
Dividends	600	600
Transfer (from) to reserves	(650)	500

BALANCE SHEET	£'000	£'000
Fixed assets		
Intangible	850	0
Tangible	12,000	11,000
	12,850	11,000
Current assets		
Stocks	14,000	13,000
Debtors	16,000	15,000
Bank and cash	500	500
	30,500	28,500
Creditors due within one year	24,000	20,000
Net current assets	6,500	8,500
Total assets less current liabilities	19,350	19,500
Creditors due after one year	6,000	5,500
	13,350	14,000
Capital and reserves		
Share capital	1,300	1,300
Share premium	3,300	3,300
Revaluation reserve	2,000	2,000
Profit and loss	6,750	7,400
	13,350	14,000

PUBLISHING

Required

(a)   Prepare a table of the following 12 ratios, calculated for both years, clearly showing the figures used in the calculations.

Current ratio
Quick assets ratio
Stock turnover in days
Debtors turnover in days
Creditors turnover in days
Gross profit %
Net profit % (before taxation)
Interest cover
Dividend cover
ROOE (before taxation)
ROCE
Gearing

(b)   Making full use of the information given in the question, of your table of ratios, and your common sense, comment on the apparent position of the business and on the actions of the management.

Chapter 12

12   Interpreting company accounts

Examine the arguments for and against the proposition that all limited liability companies, of whatever size, should be legally required to have an independent audit.

Chapter 14

13   Classifying costs

Your company is considering installing a costing system and is examining ways in which different classifications of cost can assist management.

Required

Prepare a report for your finance director which outlines the following.

(a)   How costs can be classified

(b)   How the different classifications can assist management

Chapter 15

14   Cost behaviour

(a)   Evaluate whether the assumption that costs are readily identifiable as either fixed or variable throughout a range of production is realistic.

Give examples of any alternative classification.

(b)   Production labour has traditionally been regarded as a directly variable cost.

Required

Discuss the factors or circumstances which would make this treatment inappropriate. You may draw on your own experience in answering.

Chapter 16

15 Absorption costing

Towers of Ilium Ltd has two production departments (machining and assembly) and two service departments (maintenance and stores).

The budgeted overheads for period 2 were – machining £18,000; assembly £15,000.

The machining department uses a machine hour rate basis for overhead absorption (budget 720 machine hours) and the assembly department a direct labour hour rate (budget 4,800 direct labour hours).

In budgeting production department overheads, service department overheads were dealt with as follows.

Maintenance department:	70% to machining department
	20% to assembly department
	10% to stores department

Stores department:	40% to machining department
	30% to assembly department
	30% to maintenance department

During period 2 the machining department worked for 703 machine hours and the direct labour hours recorded in the assembly department were 5,256.

Overhead incurred was as follows.

	Machining	*Assembly*	*Maintenance*	*Stores*
	£	£	£	£
Directly allocated:				
Materials	2,400	3,600	4,200	800
Labour	1,400	1,800	6,000	2,300
Other items	1,700	1,500	600	400
	5,500	6,900	10,800	3,500
Apportioned	2,200	3,100	1,700	1,000
	7,700	10,000	12,500	4,500

Required

(a) Write up the overhead account for each production department.

(b) Explain how the under-/over-absorption occurred for each department.

Chapter 17

16 Marginal costing

(a)   What are the most important features which distinguish marginal costing from absorption costing?

(b)   To help decision making during budget preparation, Costain Baddley Ltd has prepared the following estimates of sales revenue and cost behaviour for a one-year period, relating to a product item called Allergic.

Activity	60%	100%
Sales and production (thousands of units)	36	60
	£'000	£'000
Sales	432	720
Production costs:		
Variable and fixed	366	510
Sales, distribution and administration costs:		
Variable and fixed	126	150

The normal level of activity for the current year is 60,000 units, and fixed costs are incurred evenly throughout the year.

There were no stocks of Allergic at the start of the quarter, in which 16,500 units were made and 13,500 units were sold. Actual fixed costs were the same as budgeted.

Required

(i)   Using absorption costing, calculate the following.

(1)   The amount of fixed production costs absorbed by Allergic

(2)   The over-/under-absorption of fixed product costs

(3)   The profit for the quarter

(ii)   Using marginal costing, calculate the net profit or loss for the quarter.

You may assume that sales revenue and variable costs per unit are as budgeted.

ANSWERS TO MULTIPLE CHOICE QUESTIONS

Chapter 1

1   A   Strictly, the discussion paper was published by the Accounting Standards Steering Committee, now the Accounting Standards Board.

2   D

Chapter 2

3   D   The fourth concept in SSAP 2 is the accruals concept.

4   C   Stock would normally be valued at cost, but where realisable value is less than cost prudence requires that the lower value is taken.

5   B

6   A   The ledger account looks like this.

RENT PAYABLE

20X8		£	20X8		£
31 Dec	Bank – paid in year	1,275	1 Jan	Balance b/f	250
			31 Dec	Balance c/f (prepaid:	
				$1/3 \times £375$)	125
				P&L account	900
		1,275			1,275

7   D   The company should have accrued an amount in respect of the

months of November and December 20X4 – $2/3 \times £480 = £320$ credit.

8   A   The bill for the quarter ended 30 November 20X4 had not been paid by 31 December 20X4 but would have been credited to the supplier's account in the purchase ledger. The credit (liability) on the telephone expenses account is just one third of the bill for the quarter ended 28 February 20X5 should have been accrued. The amount is therefore $(1/3 \times £570) = £190$.

9   A   The bill for the quarter ended 31 January 20X6 was paid in 20X5. Only two thirds of this bill (November and December) related to 20X5; the balance $(1/3 \times £810 = £270)$ is a pre-payment at 31 December 20X5.

10   A   One third of the bill for the quarter ended 28 February 20X6 should be accrued. The amount is therefore $(1/3 \times £720) = £240$.

Chapter 3

11   C   The accounting equation states that:

Capital + Liabilities = Assets

or

Capital = Assets – Liabilities (= net assets)

Andy's capital is £10,000 and his net assets are therefore also £10,000. Total assets are £16,000, but net assets are only £10,000.

12   B   Closing capital – opening capital = increase (I) in net assets. This means that option B is equivalent to:

$$P = I + D - C_i$$

This is the correct form of the business equation.

BPP
PUBLISHING

NOTES

13   D $I = P + C_i - D$

$= \pounds(72{,}500 + 8{,}000 - 2{,}200)$

$= \pounds78{,}300$

∴ Closing net assets $= \pounds(101{,}700 + 78{,}300) = \pounds180{,}000$.

14   B $I = P + C_i - D$

$= \pounds(35{,}400 - 6{,}000 + 10{,}200)$

$= \pounds39{,}600$

∴ Opening capital $=$ opening net assets $= \pounds(95{,}100 - 39{,}600) = \pounds55{,}500$.

15   C $I = P - D + C_i$

We are told that C_i is zero, and that $(P - D)$ (ie profit after drawings) is £13,250. Therefore $I = \pounds13{,}250$ and closing net assets are $\pounds(32{,}500 + 13{,}250) = \pounds45{,}750$.

16   A $P = I + D - C_i$

$= -\pounds1{,}800 + \pounds16{,}300 - \pounds17{,}700$

$= -\pounds3{,}200$

17   B $P = I + D - C_i$

$= \pounds7{,}100 + \pounds10{,}400 - \pounds22{,}000$

$= -\pounds4{,}500$

Chapter 4

18   C   Purchase price, carriage and installation are all parts of the capital costs of acquiring the machine. The £450 spent on repairs is charged against revenue.

19   C   Leasehold premises are shown under tangible assets; trade investments are shown under fixed asset investments (or possibly current asset investments); preliminary expenses must not be treated as an asset at all.

20   A   A provision for doubtful debts is disclosed as a deduction from debtors.

21   A

22   A   Options B and C are wrong because NBV (despite its name) is not a measure of value. Option D might sometimes be true, but in most cases would not. For example, there may be an estimated residual value which it is not intended to write off; or the reducing balance method may be in use, under which cost is never fully written off.

Chapter 5

23   B   Imprest system is a term that describes the process by which a petty cash balance is periodically 'topped up' to a predetermined amount.

24   A   In the case of a business with no total debtor's account in its nominal ledger, the sales ledger would be an integral part of the double entry system. The other records are books of prime entry, which could never be part of the system.

25   D   The extract records a cash receipt of £140.00 from a credit customer, who is also entitled to a discount of £10.00.

26   B   The purchase of a fixed asset is recorded by debiting the asset account. Because the purchase is on credit, the credit entry must be in the creditor's account rather than in the bank account.

27   C   A debit in the bank account represents a receipt of cash, presumably

because goods have earlier been sold to Smith on credit. Option A is incorrect, because a cash sale (as opposed to a credit sale) would be indicated by the entries: debit bank, credit sales.

28   D   Because cash leaves the business, there must be a credit to the bank account. The debit would initially be made in the drawings account, though the balance on that account might eventually be transferred to the capital account.

29   D   Options A and B are ruled out because they relate to rental income, which would be a credit (not a debit) in a rent account. Option C is ruled out because there is no entry made in the bank account and therefore no payment can yet have been made.

30   A   The goods would have been debited to the purchases account when they were originally acquired. Now that they have been removed from the business that debit entry must be reversed by crediting purchases. Since it is the proprietor who has taken the goods the debit must be to his drawings account.

31   C   Returns outwards relate to purchases and creditors, and could not affect a debtor's account in any way.

32   D   When the cheque was originally made out, the entries were: credit bank, debit creditors. These entries must be reversed now that the cheque is being cancelled.

33   D   Because the cash account is credited, it means that cash (ie notes and coins) has been paid out. Because the bank account is debited, it means that funds have been received in the bank. The entries for the other transactions would be:

         A   Debit cash, credit bank

         B   Debit bank charges, credit bank

         C   Debit cash, credit debtors

34   B   Returning goods to suppliers means that liabilities are reduced (debit creditors). The credit entry could either be in a returns outwards account or, more directly, in the purchases account.

35   C   Payments of expenses are credit entries in the petty cash book, and so must be posted to the debit of some other account. This rules out A and B. D is ruled out because a debit in the main cash book would record a receipt of funds into the bank account.

36   C   The situation in option C is that cash may be received from the debtor (a credit entry in his account) without there being any matching debit entry (because the relevant invoice has not been posted). Options A and B work the opposite way, while option D affects the debtors control account rather than the individual debtor's account.

PUBLISHING

Chapter 6

37   D   The cost of freehold premises (including any incidental costs of acquisition, such as solicitors' fees) is a capital item. Depreciation is an annual charge against revenue; repairs and decoration are also revenue items.

38   C   A new typewriter would be capitalised as office equipment.

39   A   Number plates, radio and delivery costs are included in the capital cost of acquiring the car. Road tax is an annual charge against revenue.

40   A   Gross profit – expenses = net profit. Therefore gross profit = net profit plus expenses. Option B gives a figure of no particular significance, being the difference between opening and closing stock levels. Option C is wrong because gross profit = sales minus cost of goods sold. Option D is the formula for cost of goods sold.

41   C   This is a reminder of the business equation:

$$I = P + C_i - D$$
$$= £(7{,}000 + 0 - 9{,}000)$$
$$= -£2{,}000$$

In other words, net assets (= capital) have fallen over the year by £2,000 and must therefore have been £33,000 to begin with.

42   B   Harmon's cash purchases for the year are £3,900. His credit purchases are £(27,850 + 720 – 970) = £27,600. Total purchases amount to £(3,900 + 27,600) = £31,500. One way of showing this is to construct a total creditors account.

TOTAL CREDITORS ACCOUNT

	£		£
Cash paid in year:		Balance b/f	970
For cash purchases	3,900	∴ Total purchases	31,500
To credit suppliers	27,850		
Balance c/f	720		
	32,470		32,470

The term 'total creditor's account' is misleading, because it includes cash purchases as well as credit purchases. Even so, the term is common and the technique is a useful one in incomplete records problems.

Chapter 7

43   C   The corrected account looks like this.

CURRENT ACCOUNT

	£		£
Interest on capital	6,200	Balance b/f	270
Balance c/f	7,070	Interest on capital	2,800
		Salary	1,500
		Net profit	8,700
	13,270		13,270

44   A   The petrol bills have been debited to motor vehicle expenses. This is incorrect and should be revised (so credit motor vehicle expenses). Because

NOTES

they are private expenses of the partner they should be debited to his drawings account.

45 B Interest on partners' capital is an appropriation of profit (debit appropriation account). Since partners have earned the money by their investment in the business, their current accounts should be credited with it. (Option D would be theoretically possible, but most firms maintain current accounts separately from capital accounts in order to record such items.)

46 D Interest payable by partners increases the amounts of profits available for appropriation (credit appropriation account). It must be charged against the partners (debit partners' current accounts).

47 A The appropriations earned by each partner are as follows.
and
48 C

	Faith £	Hope £	Charity £	Total £
Interest on capital	1,600	1,200	960	3,760
Salary		8,000		8,000
	1,600	9,200	960	11,760
Residual profit (3:2:1)	36,120	24,080	12,040	72,240
	37,720	33,280	13,000	84,000

49 C

	£
Net profit from trading	32,000
Add interest on drawings (10% × £(12,000 + 15,000))	2,700
	34,700
Less interest on capital (6% × £(8,000 + 6,000))	840
Residual profit	33,860

50 B

	£
Interest on capital (6% × £8,000)	480
Share of residual profit (3/5 × £33,860)	20,316
	20,796
Less interest on drawings (10% × £12,000)	1,200
Net transfers from appropriation account	19,596

Chapter 8

51 C A company can enter into trading obligations without limit. Its own liability to meet those obligations from its own assets is unlimited. However, if its own assets are insufficient, shareholders will not in general be called on to make up the deficiency; their personal liability is limited.

52 A Option B is the company's issued share capital; option C is the company's *paid-up* share capital. Option D refers to *borrowings* rather than to share capital.

53 B Companies are required to maintain a register of charges on company assets, but not of debenture holders.

54   C   Debenture interest is paid to debenture holders, who are creditors of the company and do not share in its ownership. Such interest is therefore a charge against revenue in arriving at the profit figure; it is *not* an appropriation of profit.

55   A   Dividends are paid in respect of *issued* shares only. Here there are 500,000 shares in issue and the dividend payable is 2p per share. The total amount is therefore $500,000 \times 2p = £10,000$.

56   D   Issued share capital consists of 800,000 shares with a nominal value of £80,000. £40,000 represents either a dividend of 50% (not given as an option) or a dividend of 5p per share (option D).

57   A   £45,000 represents 3% of the nominal value of the company's share capital. The full nominal value must therefore be $£45,000 \times 100/3 = £1,500,000$.

58   A   The nominal value of the issued shares is simply $40,000 \times 20p = £8,000$.

Chapter 10

59   C   Total long-term capital includes debentures as well as share capital and

reserves, ie it amounts to £114,000. The profits available to meet the claims of debenture holders and shareholders are the profits before interest and tax, ie £37,000. The ROCE is therefore £37,000/£114,000 or 32.5%.

60   A

	£
Profit before interest and tax	37,000
Debenture interest	2,000
Profit before tax	35,000
Taxation	9,000
Profit after tax	26,000

This is the amount available for shareholders. Their total capital amounts to £94,000, and so the return on shareholders' capital is £26,000/£94,000 or 27.7%.

61   B

	£
Profit after tax (see 60 above)	26,000
Preference dividend	1,200
Profits available for equity shareholders	24,800

Equity shareholders' capital consists of share capital (£50,000) plus reserves (£34,000), £84,000 in total. The return on equity shareholders' capital is therefore £24,800/£84,000 = 29.5%.

62   B   Gearing is defined as the ratio of prior charge capital (here debentures £20,000 plus preference shares £10,000) to total long-term capital (here £114,000). The ratio is therefore £30,000/£114,000 or 26.3%.

63   A   Earnings are the profits after tax and preference dividends, ie the profits available to ordinary shareholders. The earnings of Barney Ltd amount to £24,800 (see 61 above). The number of shares in issue is $50,000 \times 100/25 = 200,000$. Earnings per share are therefore £24,800/200,000 = 12.4p.

64   D   Interest cover measures the extent to which profits before interest and tax are sufficient to meet interest payments owed to loan creditors. Here Barney

Ltd has profits before interest and tax of £37,000 and loan interest payable is only £2,000. Interest payments are therefore covered 18½ times (£37,000/£2,000).

65 B Preference dividend cover measures the extent to which profit after tax

is sufficient to meet dividend payments due to preference shareholders. Here Barney Ltd has a profit after tax of £26,000 (see 60 above) and preference dividends payable are only £1,200. Preference dividends are therefore covered 21.7 times (£26,000/£1,200).

66 D $ROCE = \dfrac{Profit}{Capital\ employed}$

$PM = \dfrac{Profit}{Sales}$

$AT = \dfrac{Sales}{Capital\ employed}$

It follows that ROCE = PM × AT, which can be re-arranged to the form given in option D.

Chapter 11

67 C $\dfrac{Cos\ of\ goods\ sold}{Average\ stock} = \dfrac{£60,000}{£8,000} = 7.5\ times$

68 C The stock turnover period in days is given by the formula:

$\dfrac{Average\ stock}{Cost\ of\ goods\ sold} \times 365\ days$

Here: $\dfrac{£88,000}{£649,000} \times 365\ days = 49\ days$

69 A We do not know the average level of debtors during the year because

the opening balance is not given. In these circumstances it is necessary to use the closing debtors figure.

The calculation is: $\dfrac{Closing\ debtors}{Sales} \times 365\ days = 51\ days$

70 B Again, we must base our calculations on the closing figure for creditors rather than the average figure.

$\dfrac{Closing\ creditors}{Sales} \times 365\ days = 47\ days$

BPP
PUBLISHING

71 B

	Current assets £	Current liabilities £
Stock	76,000	
Trade debtors/creditors	120,000	80,000
Prepayments/accruals	8,000	6,000
Cash in hand/overdraft	12,000	16,000
Proposed dividends		10,000
	216,000	112,000

The current ratio is 216:112 = 1.93:1.

72 A The quick ratio is calculated in the same way as the current ratio, except that stock is excluded from the total of current assets. The ratio is therefore 140:112 = 1.25:1.

73 C

	Days
Stock turnover period (question 68)	49
Debtors collection period (question 69)	51
	100
Less creditors payment period (question 70)	47
Length of cash cycle	53

Chapter 14

74 B £25,185 + £5,440 = £30,625. The only direct costs are the wages paid to direct workers for ordinary time, plus the basic pay for overtime. Overtime premium and shift allowances are usually treated as overheads. However, if and when overtime and shiftwork are incurred specifically for a particular cost unit, they are classified as direct costs of that cost unit. Sick pay is treated as an overhead and is therefore classified as an indirect cost.

75 A

	£	£
Cost of normal hours actively worked		
(38 hours – 10 hours + 8 hours) × £5		180
Group bonus		12
Direct cost		192
Idle time: 10 hours × £5	50	
Overtime premium: 8 hours × £2.5	20	
Indirect cost		70
Total cost		262

76 D The direct cost or variable cost per mile

(1) Fuel and oil, because their consumption varies with vehicle usage.

(2) Replacement parts, because the question states that they vary with mileage.

Tyre replacements might sometimes be considered as variable with mileage, but the question states that tyres are replaced every three months, regardless of mileage. Drivers' wages do not vary with mileage, nor does vehicle depreciation: these are direct costs per *vehicle*, but not direct costs *per mile travelled*.

Chapter 16

77   D   All of the suggested overhead absorption rates could be acceptable.

However, a time-based method should be used whenever possible because most items of overhead expenditure tend to increase with time. A direct labour cost percentage is to an extent time based, but if differential wage rates exist this can lead to inequitable overhead absorption. Since department 1 appears to be primarily for machine work, a machine hour rate should be used.

78   C   For the same reasons as for question 77, a time-based method should be used. Since department 1 appears to be labour intensive, a direct labour hour rate is the most appropriate.

79   A   The overhead absorption rates from questions 77 and 78 are (£27,000 ÷ 45,000) = 60p per machine hour in department 1 and (£1,800 ÷ 25,000) = 72p per direct labour in department 2. The total production cost can be calculated as follows:

	£
Direct material	40.00
Direct labour	
– department 1: 4 hours × £5	20.00
– department 2: 9 hours × £4	36.00
Overhead	
– department 1: 65 machine hours × 60p	39.00
– department 2: 9 labour hours × 72p	6.48
	141.48

The machine hour in department 2 is not relevant to the calculation, because the overhead absorption is based on labour hours. If you included one machine hour at £60 in your calculation, you would have answered D, which is incorrect.

80   D   Definitions A, B and D are all taken from a previous edition of the CIMA *Official Terminology*.

A is the definition of cost allocation, which is part of cost attribution.

B is the definition of cost ascertainment.

Cost apportionment is also part of cost attribution.

81   A

	£
Overhead absorbed = 48,000 × £5.60	268,000
Overhead incurred	275,000
Overhead under-absorbed	6,200

Overhead was under-absorbed because absorbed overhead is less than actual costs incurred.

BPP
PUBLISHING

82   A

	£
Budget absorption rate per hour	
Fixed (£36,000 ÷ 18,000 hours)	2.0
Variable (£9,000 ÷ 18,000)	0.5
Total	2.5
Overheads absorbed 20,000 hours × £2.50 per hour	50,000
Overheads incurred (£39,000 fixed + £12,000 variable)	51,000
Under-absorbed overhead	1,000

83   A

	Production	Overheads Admin	Sales & dist'n	Total
	£000	£000	£000	£000
Energy and water (6:3:1)	6	3	1	10
Electricity for machines	5			5
Building rental (6:3:1)	54	27	9	90
Building repairs (6:3:1)	6	3	1	10
Machine repairs	8			8
Machinery depreciation	52			52
Security (6:3:1)	18	9	3	30
Carriage outwards			70	70
Indirect production wages	50			50
Salesmen's costs			76	76
General admin		38		38
Advertising			30	30
	199	80	190	469

Notes. The costs relating to the building must be apportioned between production, administration and sales. Carriage inwards costs are added to the cost of the materials, and are not an overhead. Carriage outwards is a distribution cost.

Total budgeted production overhead costs = £199,000.

84   C   Budgeted sales and distribution overheads £190,000

Budgeted sales   £4,000,000

Absorption rate = 4.75% of sales value

85   A

	£000
Budgeted full production	
Direct materials	350
Direct labour	171
Carriage inwards	30
Production inwards	199
	750

Budgeted administration overheads   £80,000

Absorption rate for admin overheads (80 ÷ 750) = 10.7% of full production cost

86 C When expenditures are as budgeted, but actual and budgeted production activity levels are different, only fixed overhead can be under- or over-absorbed.

Under-absorbed overhead = 1,000 hours × £4 = £4,000

Variable overhead absorbed would be (1,000 × £2.50) £2,500 less than budgeted in the fixed budget, but variable incurred would be £2,500 less as well, leaving neither under- nor over-absorbed variable overheads.

Chapter 17

87 D Budgeted fixed costs (10,000 × £4) + (10,000 + 80p) £48,000

Unit contribution £(6 – 1.2 – 0.4) £4.40

Breakeven point (£48,000 ÷ £4.4) 10,909 units

88 B Selling costs are unchanged (both variable and fixed)

	£
New sales price (£6 × 1.1)	6.60
New variable cost per unit (£1.2 × 1.1) + 0.4	1.72
New unit contribution	4.88
New fixed costs (£40,000 × 1.25) + 8,000	£58,000
New breakeven point (58,000 × 4.88)	11,885 units

89 B The graph shows a variable cost which only starts to be incurred *beyond* a certain volume of output. Only B fits this description of cost behaviour.

90 B The cost per unit is the same for each additional unit produced. This is a variable cost. In contrast, although the *total* fixed cost is constant at all levels of output, the fixed cost *per unit* falls as output increases. Because the fixed costs per unit declines with increasing output, the full cost of production per unit and the full cost of sale per unit also declines.

91 B The high-low method of estimating fixed and variable costs is used.

	£
Total cost of 1,100 units	18,300
Total cost of 700 units	13,500
Variable cost of 400 units	4,800
Variable cost per unit (÷ 400)	£12
	£
Total cost of 1,100 units	18,300
Variable cost of 1,100 units (× £12)	13,200
Fixed costs	5,100

92 C Budgeted fixed costs (5,000 × £2) £10,000

Contribution per unit (£10 – 6) £4

Units required to break even (£10,000 ÷ 4) 2,500 units

Sales revenue needed to break even (2,500 × £10) £25,000

93   B

	£
Target profit	6,000
Fixed costs	10,000
Target contribution	16,000
Contribution per unit	£4
Units required to achieve target profit	4,000

94   B

Fixed costs (£10,000 × 120%)	£12,000
Units required now to break even (÷ 4)	3,000
Budgeted units of sales	5,000
Margin of safety (5,000 – 3,000)	2,000

In % terms, MOS $= \dfrac{2,000}{5,000} \times 100\% = 40\%$

95   A   Original budgeted profit:

	£
Contribution (5,000 units × £4)	20,000
Fixed costs	10,000
Profit	10,000

	£
New sales price (£10 × 120%)	12.00
New variable cost (£6 × 1.12%)	6.72
New unit contribution	5.28
Contribution required	£20,000
Sales volume now needed (÷ £5.28)	3,788 units

This is 1,212 units or 24.24% less than the original budgeted level of 5,000 units of sales.

96   B   Item 4 is a selling cost, not a production cost. All the other three items are variable with the number of batches produced, and so would be included in the marginal production cost per batch of finished output.

Chapter 18

97   C   A functional budget (or department budget) is a budget applicable to a

particular function or department. Items A, C and D are examples, but a cash budget is not.

98   A   A sales budget and budgeted changes in finished goods stock are needed to prepare a production budget. The production budget and budgeted changes in raw materials stocks are needed to prepare a purchases budget for raw materials. A purchases budget is needed to prepare a cash budget.

99   B

Increase in finished goods stock required	1,000 units
Budgeted sales of product Alpha	60,000 units
Production required	61,000 units
Raw materials usage budget (× 3 kg)	183,000 kg
Decrease in raw materials stock budgeted	8,000 kg
Raw materials purchase budget	175,000 kg

100   C

	£	£
Raw materials opening stock		23,200
Purchases		140,000
Raw materials closing stock		(17,300)
Raw materials usage budget		145,900
Direct labour budget		120,000
Production overhead (30,000 hrs × £5)		150,000
Production budget		415,900
WIP Opening stock	4,700	
Closing stock	8,200	
		(3,500)
Budgeted output to finished goods (completed production)		412,400
Finished goods opening stock		16,600
Finished goods closing stock		(18,800)
Production cost of goods sold		410,200
Administration overhead		80,000
Sales and distribution overhead		120,000
Total cost of sales		610,200
Sales		620,000
Budgeted profit		9,800

101   B

Production budget (= sales budget)	125,000 units
Raw materials usage (× 1.1 kg)	137,500 units
	£
Cost of raw materials (before discount) × £2.2	302,500
less bulk purchase discount (5%)	15,125
Purchase budget	287,375

102   B

	Unit cost of production
	£
Direct material	4.00
Direct labour	8.00
Variable production overhead (28,080 ÷ 36,000)	0.78
Fixed production overhead (140,400 ÷ 36,000)	3.90
	16.68

103 B *Month 1*

	£	£
Sales (5,000 × £20)		100,000
Production cost of sales		
Opening stock	64,000	
Production costs (3,000 units × £16.68)	50,040	
	114,040	
Closing stock (2,000 units × £16.68)	33,360	
		80,680
Gross profit		19,320
Other overheads (120,000 ÷ 12)		10,000
Net profit		9,320

104 B If actual production is 50 units higher than budgeted, but sales remain 5,000 units, there will be over-absorbed *fixed* overhead in the month of 50 × £3.90 = £195, which will add to profit.

(Variable costs *per unit*, including variable overhead, will be as in the budget for the year as a whole and so the only effect on profit would be the over-absorbed fixed overhead.)

105 C Incremental budgeting is a term used to describe budgets prepared on the basis of last year's costs plus an extra percentage, for inflation etc. Rolling budgets describe the continuous preparation of budgets, such as annual budgets prepared monthly, with one extra month added at the end and so the 'old' first month, now ended, taken off the beginning, each time a budget is prepared. Rolling budgets (or continuous budgets) are likely to be more accurate than 'traditional' budgets, especially in a period of high inflation.

Chapter 19

106 D Since stocks are valued at actual cost, the raw materials price variance is calculated on materials quantities used (rather than quantities purchased).

	£
21,600 kg of V did cost	128,304
Price variance	1,296 (F)
21,600 kg of V should cost	129,600

Standard cost per kg of V = £6.

Usage variance is £2,880 (A).

	Kg
Usage variance in kg (£2,880 ÷ £6)	480 (A)
4,800 units of T did use	21,600
4,800 units of T should use	21,120
Standard usage per unit of T	4.4 kg

107 D Early settlement discounts (item D) are a financial matter and do not affect the actual purchase price of materials. In a period of inflation, and with a mid-year standard price, reported price variances in the early part of the year (item A) ought to be favourable. Item B refers to the possibility of bulk purchase discounts. With item C, an alternative supplier might offer a lower price perhaps in order to win new business.

108   B   Variations in output volume (item B) should not affect usage of materials *per unit* produced. A high quality of material (item A) might reduce waste or scrap levels (item D) which would in turn improve the materials usage rate. With lower quality control standards (item C), there should be fewer rejected items, a higher proportion of successfully-completed items, and so an improvement in materials usage.

109   C

	£
9,700 hours worked should cost (× £3.6)	34,920
did cost	36,400
Rate variance	1,480 (A)

5,000 units of W should take (× 2 hrs)	10,000 hrs
did take	9,700 hrs
Efficiency variance in hours	300 hrs (F)
Standard rate per hour	3.6
Efficiency variance in £	1,080 (F)

(Standard direct labour cost of 5,000 units of W = 5,000 × £7.20 = £36,000. Actual cost = £36,400. Total direct labour cost variance = £400 (A) which is the sum of the rate variance and the efficiency variance.)

110   B   If the standard efficiency level is too *low*, efficiency variances will be favourable (item B). Poor work scheduling (item A), and machine breakdowns (item C) create abnormal amounts of idle time. Idle time is a form of efficiency (or inefficiency) variance. Less training (item D) will often make staff less efficient in doing their work.

111   A   The only cause of the rate variance was the back-dated pay rise of 10%, which must be 10/110 or 1/11 of the actual amount paid. The rate variance is therefore £51,700 ÷ 11 = £4,700 (A).

Actual pay at the 'old' pay rate was therefore £51,700 – £4,700 = £47,000. At the old pay rate, 6,250 policies should cost

$$\frac{6,250}{8,000} \times £56,000 = £43,750$$

Since they did cost £47,000, there is an adverse variance of £3,250, which must be an efficiency variance, since the rate variance has already been taken out of the figure.

	£	£
Budgeted standard cost of 6,250 policies		43,750
Rate variance	4,700 (A)	
Efficiency variance	3,250 (A)	
		7,950 (A)
Actual cost		51,700

112   B   The fixed overhead expenditure variance is the difference between budgeted and actual fixed overhead expenditure.

113   A

	£	
Budgeted expenditure (4,800 × £24)	115,200	
Actual expenditure	126,000	
Expenditure variance	10,800	(A)
4,500 units should take (× 4 hrs)	18,000	hrs
did take	18,800	hrs
Efficiency variance in hours	800	hrs (A)
Fixed overhead absorption rate per hour	£6	
Fixed overhead efficiency variance	4,800	(A)
Budgeted hours (4,800 × 4)	19,200	hrs
Actual hours	18,800	hrs
Volume/capacity variance	400	hrs (A)
	× £6	per hr
	2,400	(A)

Note. 4,500 units were produced, and the standard fixed overhead cost of these units is (× £24) £108,000.

	£	
Standard fixed overhead cost of units produced (4,500 × £24)	108,000	
Fixed overhead efficiency variance	4,800	(A)
Fixed overhead volume/capacity variance	2,400	(A)
Budgeted fixed overhead expenditure	115,200	
Fixed overhead expenditure variance	10,800	(A)
Actual fixed overhead expenditure	126,000	

114   C   The three variances together explain the total under-absorbed fixed overhead of (£126,000 – £108,000) £18,000.

ANSWERS TO EXAM STYLE QUESTIONS

Chapter 1

1   Users of accounting statements

(a)   (i)   *Loan creditors*

Lenders are concerned that an enterprise is able to pay back any borrowings. Cash and borrowing positions are therefore quite useful information for them in the short term. In the long term they are interested in the overall health and operational viability of the enterprise.

(ii)   *The employee group*

Employees are interested in financial statements for a number of reasons. Job security is one concern, as the long-term financial viability of a company is indicated in the accounts. Also, the profit information might be a basis for judging pay claims. Employees would also be interested in social accounting.

(iii) *Analysts and advisors*

Analysts and advisors are interested in the operating performance of an enterprise as they aim to identify investment opportunities. Their information requirements are quite complex, with an emphasis on profit performance and estimates of future operations.

(iv)   *Business contacts (eg suppliers and customers)*

Suppliers are interested in the long term health of a company, to assess whether orders will be continued. They are also interested in an enterprise's liquidity position, to assess whether they will get paid. Customers need to know whether products will still be available. Competitors are also interested, to compare performance.

(v)   *The Government*

Government departments have an interest in published financial statements. The most obvious examples are the Inland Revenue and the Customs and Excise, for the collection of taxes and duties. Published financial information is used by central and local government in other ways: economic statistics, information for regional policy making, and so forth.

(vi)   *The public*

The general public has an interest in financial statements on three counts. Firstly, the activities of any enterprise have social consequences. For example, proponents of 'social accounting' have supported the introduction of statistics of industrial injuries into published financial statements: apart from humanitarian considerations, the cost of treating industrial injuries in the National Health Service is a cost to the tax payer caused by poor safety procedures or dangerous work. Issues related to the environment are also of interest. This expands the scope of purely financial statements to include social issues and social costs. Secondly, in many cases members of the public are potential investors. Thirdly, the public has an interest, as customers, in the activities of an enterprise.

(b)   Section (a) demonstrates that different users can have valid uses of the same information, with differences of emphasis. Owners and investors and the analysts who advise them will concentrate in more detail on the financial performance of an enterprise than on information related to more public concerns (for example the environment).

Chapter 2

2 SSAP 2

(a) (i) Fundamental accounting concepts are the broad basic assumptions underlying all financial statements. They are as follows.

    (1) *Going concern*. The entity preparing statements is assumed to be continuing in existence for the foreseeable future.

    (2) *Accruals/matching*. Revenue and expenses which are related to each other are matched, so as to be dealt with in the same accounting period, without regard to when the cash is actually received or paid.

    (3) *Prudence*. Revenues and profits are recognised only when realised, losses and liabilities are recognised as soon as they are foreseen. (The prudence concept overrides the accruals concept if the two are in conflict.)

    (4) *Consistency*. Accounting treatments should not be altered from one period to another without good cause. Similar items should be treated alike within each accounting period.

(ii) Accounting bases are methods which have been developed for applying fundamental accounting concepts to financial transactions. They include the following.

    (1) *Depreciation*. A variety of depreciation methods is possible, including the straight line, reducing balance and sum-of-the-digits method. Each has the same aim of expensing the cost of a fixed asset over its useful life.

    (2) *Stock valuation*. Methods such as FIFO, historical cost and average cost all aim at determining the cost of stock items in the accounts.

(iii) Accounting policies are the accounting bases adopted by a business entity as the most appropriate for its circumstances. The entity should disclose material accounting policies in a note to its accounts.

Accounting concepts, bases and policies are thus linked together as follows. Accounting concepts are the fundamental approaches to accounting, accounting bases apply these approaches to particular problems and accounting policies are the bases selected by a particular company.

(b) The going concern concept is that an enterprise will continue in operational existence for the foreseeable future. This means that the financial statements of an enterprise are prepared on the assumption that the enterprise will continue trading. If this were not the case, various adjustments would have to be made to the accounts: provisions for losses; revaluation of assets to their possible market value and so forth.

Unless it can be assumed that the business is a going concern, the other three fundamental accounting concepts cannot apply. This can be seen by considering each concept in turn as follows.

Consistency

It is meaningless to speak of consistency from one accounting period to the next when this is the final accounting period.

Accruals

The accruals or matching concept states that revenue and expenses which are related to each other are matched, so as to be dealt with in the same accounting period, without regard to when the cash is actually paid or received. This is particularly relevant to the purchase of fixed assets. The cost of a fixed asset is spread over the accounting periods expected to benefit from it, thus matching costs and revenues. In the absence of the going concern convention, this cannot happen, as an example will illustrate.

Suppose a company has a machine which cost £10,000 two years ago and now has a net book value of £6,000. The machine can be used for another three years, but as it is obsolete, there is no possibility of selling it, and so it has no market value.

If the going concern concept applies, the machine will be shown at cost less depreciation in the accounts, as it still has a part to play in the continued life of the enterprise. However, if the assumption cannot be applied the machine will be given a nil value and other assets and liabilities will be revalued on the basis of winding down the company's operations.

Prudence

The prudence concept as we normally understand it cannot apply if the business is no longer a going concern. A more drastic approach than mere caution is required when it is known that the business must cease trading.

Chapter 3

3   **The accounting and business equations**

    (a)   Profit £1,051 = Drawings + £733 – £100

          £1,051 – £733 + £100   = Drawings = £418

    (b)   Profit = Drawings + increase in net assets – capital introduced

          £205 = £77 + £173 – £45

    (c)   Capital + liabilities = Assets

          Capital + £153 = £174

          ∴ Capital = £21.

    (d)   Capital = Assets – Liabilities

          £50 + £100 + profit for the year = £90 – £70

          £150 + profit for the year = £20

          ∴ the profit for the year is in fact a loss of £130.

Chapter 4

4   Terminology

(a)   A *balance sheet* is a statement of the assets, liabilities and capital of a business as at a stated date. It is laid out to show either total assets as equivalent to total liabilities and capital or net assets as equivalent to capital. Other formats are also possible but the top half (or left hand) total will always equal the bottom half (or right hand) total. Some balance sheets are laid out vertically and others horizontally.

(b)   An *asset* is owned by a business and is expected to be of some future benefit. Its value is determined as the historical cost of producing or obtaining it (unless an attempt is being made to reflect rising prices in the accounts, in which case a replacement cost might be used). Examples of assets are:

   (i)   Plant, machinery, land and other long-term or fixed assets

   (ii)   Current assets such as stocks, cash and debts owed to the business with reasonable assurance of recovery: these are assets which are not intended to be held on a continuing basis in the business

(c)   A *liability* is an amount owed by a business, other than the amount owed to its proprietors (ie capital). Examples of liabilities are:

   (i)   Amounts owed to the Government (VAT or other taxes)

   (ii)   Amounts owed to suppliers

   (iii) Bank overdraft

   (iv)   Long-term loans from banks or investors

   It is usual to differentiate between 'current' and 'long-term' liabilities. The former fall due within a year of the balance sheet date.

(d)   Balance sheets do not always balance on the first attempt, as all accountants know! However, once errors are corrected, all balance sheets balance. This is because in double entry bookkeeping every transaction recorded has a dual effect. Assets are always equal to liabilities plus capital and so capital is always equal to assets less liabilities. This makes sense as the owners of the business are entitled to the net assets of the business as representing their capital plus accumulated surpluses (or less accumulated deficit).

(e)   The balance sheet is not intended as a statement of a business's worth at a given point in time. This is because, except where some attempt is made to adjust for the effects of rising prices, assets and liabilities are recorded at historical cost and on a prudent basis. For example, if there is any doubt about the recoverability of a debt, then the value in the accounts must be reduced to the likely recoverable amount. In addition, where fixed assets have a finite useful life, their cost is gradually written off to reflect the use being made of them.

   Sometimes fixed assets are *revalued* to their market value but this revaluation then goes out of date as few assets are revalued every year.

   The balance sheet figure for capital and reserves therefore bears no relationship to the market value of shares. Market values are the product of a large number of factors, including general economic conditions, alternative investment returns (for example interest rates), likely future profits and dividends and, not least, market sentiment.

Chapter 5

5   Opening balance sheet

BALANCE SHEET AS AT 1 JANUARY 20X8

		£'000	£'000
Fixed assets			
Land and buildings (given)			320
Plant and machinery:	cost (W1)	110	
	depreciation (W2)	60	
			50
			370
Current assets			
Stock (W4)		75	
Debtors (W5)		52	
		127	
Current liabilities			
Bank overdraft (W6)		97	
Creditors (W3)		65	
Accruals (W7)		15	
		177	
Net current liabilities			(50)
			320
Capital (W8)			320

Workings

1   PLANT AND MACHINERY – COST

	£'000		£'000
∴ Balance b/d	110	Balance c/d	200
Bank	90		
	200		200

2   PLANT AND MACHINERY – DEPRECIATION

	£'000		£'000
Balance c/d	80	∴ Balance b/d	60
		Charge for the year	20
	80		80

3   CREDITORS

	£'000		£'000
Bank	560	Balance b/d (2 × £45,000)	65
Balance c/d	130	∴ Purchases	625
	690		690

4   COST OF SALES

	£'000		£'000
∴ Opening stock	75	Closing stock	100
Purchases (W3)	625	P&L account	600
	700		700

5   DEBTORS

	£'000		£'000
∴ Balance b/d	52	Bank	950
Sales	1,000	Bad debts written off	2
		Balance c/d	100
	1,052		1,052

6   BANK

	£'000		£'000
Debtors	950	Opening balance	97
		Creditors	560
		Plant and machinery	
		– cost	90
		Operating expenses	130
		Drawings	20
		Balance c/d	53
	950		950

7   OPERATING EXPENSES

	£'000		£'000
Bank	130	∴ Accruals b/d	15
Accruals c/d	5	P&L account	120
	135		135

8   Capital

As no drawings account is shown on the trial balance, you must assume that drawings during the year have been debited to the capital account.

∴ Opening balance = £300,000 + £20,000 = £320,000.

Chapter 6

6   Accounts preparation

MR YOUSEF
PROFIT AND LOSS ACCOUNT FOR THE YEAR ENDED 31 MAY 20X6

	£	£
Sales		138,078
Opening stock	11,927	
Purchases (W1)	84,561	
	96,488	
Less closing stock	(13,551)	
Cost of goods sold		(82,937)
Gross profit		55,141
Carriage out (W2)	2,933	
Rent, rates and insurance (W3)	5,952	
Postage and stationery	3,001	
Advertising	1,330	
Salaries and wages	26,420	
Bad debts	877	
Depreciation charge (W4)	8,700	
Increase in provision for bad debts	40	
		(49,253)
Net profit		5,888

MR YOUSEF
BALANCE SHEET AS AT 31 MAY 20X6

	Cost £	Accumulated depreciation £	NBV £
Fixed assets			
Equipment	58,000	27,700	30,300
Current assets			
Stock		13,551	
Debtors	12,120		
Less provision for bad debts	(170)		
		11,950	
Prepayment		880	
Cash		177	
Bank		1,002	
		27,560	
Current liabilities			
Creditors		6,471	
Accrual		210	
		6,681	
Net current assets			20,879
			51,179
Capital			
At 1 June 20X5			53,091
Profit for year			5,888
			58,974
Drawings			(7,800)
At 31 May 20X6			51,179

Workings

1   Purchases

	£
Per trial balance	82,350
Add carriage inwards	2,211
Per P & L a/c	84,561

2   Carriage out = £5,144 – £2,211 = £2,933.

3   Rent, rates and insurance

	£
Per trial balance	6,622
Add rent accrual	210
Less rates prepayment	(880)
Per P & L a/c	5,952

4   Depreciation charge = 15% × £58,000 = £8,700

Chapter 7

7   **Partnership accounts**

A, B & C TRADING, PROFIT AND LOSS ACCOUNT
FOR THE YEAR TO 31 DECEMBER 20X6

	£	£
Sales (W1)		186,000
Cost of sales		
Opening stock	40,000	
Purchases (W2)	105,000	
	145,000	
Closing stock (bal fig)	(21,000)	
		(124,000)
Gross profit $186 \times {}^{50}/_{150}$		62,000
Expenses		
Operating expenses (W3)	17,000	
Depreciation (W5)	9,000	
Loss on the sale of plant (W4)	2,000	
Bad debt	4,000	
Loan interest 40 × 1%	4,000	
		(36,000)
Net profit		26,000

A, B & C APPROPRIATION ACCOUNT
FOR THE YEAR TO 31 DECEMBER 20X6

		£	£
Net profit			26,000
Interest on capital	A	3,200	
	B	3,200	
	C	2,800	
			(9,200)
			16,800
Profit for appropriation			
A $^3/_6$		8,400	
B $^2/_6$		5,600	
C $^1/_6$		2,800	
			16,800

A, B & C SUMMARY BALANCE SHEET AS AT 31 DECEMBER 20X6

		£	£	£
Fixed assets				
Land and buildings				100,000
Plant and machinery (W5)		90,000	27,000	63,000
				163,000
Current assets				
Stock			21,000	
Debtors			40,000	
Prepayments			10,000	
			71,000	
Current liabilities				
Creditors		35,000		
Accruals		2,000		
Loan interest (not paid)		4,000		
Bank overdraft		38,000		
			(79,000)	
Net current liabilities				(8,000)
Total assets less current liabilities				155,000
Loan				(40,000)
				115,000
Capital accounts	A	30,000		
(W6)	B	38,000		
	C	52,000		
				(120,000)
Current accounts	A	3,600		
	B	1,800		
	C	(10,400)		
				(5,000)
				115,000

Workings

1   *Sales*

DEBTORS CONTROL ACCOUNT

	£'000		£'000
Balance b/d	30	Bank	172
Sales (bal fig)	186	Bad debts	4
		Balance c/d	40
	216		216

2   *Purchases*

CREDITORS CONTROL ACCOUNT

	£'000		£'000
Bank	110	Balance b/d	40
Balance c/d	35	Purchases (bal fig)	105
	145		145

3   *Operating expenses*

OPERATING EXPENSES

	£'000		£'000
Electricity accrual c/d	2	Balance b/f	5
Bank	30	Rent prepaid c/d	10
		Charge for year (bal fig)	17
	32		32

4   *Loss on the sale of plant*

PLANT DISPOSALS

	£'000		£'000
Plant (cost)	60	Plant (depn provn)	48
		Proceeds	10
		Loss on disposal	2
	60		60

5   *Plant and machinery*

PLANT AND MACHINERY (COST)

	£'000		£'000
Balance b/d	100	Disposals	60
Additions (bank)	50	Balance c/d	90
	150		150

PLANT AND MACHINERY (DEPN PROVN)

	£'000		£'000
Disposals	48	Balance b/d	66
Balance c/d	27	Charge for year ($10\% \times 90$)	9
	75		75

6   *Capital and current accounts*

CAPITAL ACCOUNTS

	A	B	C	A	B	C
	£'000	£'000	£'000	£'000	£'000	£'000
Balance b/d				30	28	32
Goodwill	30	20	10	20	20	20
Revaluation				10	10	10
Balance c/d	30	38	52			
	60	58	62	60	58	62

CURRENT ACCOUNTS

	A	B	C	A	B	C
	£'000	£'000	£'000	£'000	£'000	£'000
Balance b/d			4.0	2.0	4.0	
Interest (W7)				3.2	3.2	2.8
Drawings	10.0	11.0	12.0			
Profit				8.4	5.6	2.8
Balance c/d	3.6	1.8				10.4
	13.6	12.8	16.0	13.6	12.8	16.0

7   *Interest on capital and current accounts*

	Capital	*Current*	*Total*	*Interest @ 10%*
A	30,000	2,000	32,000	3,200
B	28,000	4,000	32,000	3,200
C	32,000	(4,000)	28,000	2,800

BPP PUBLISHING

Chapter 8

8   Limited companies' accounts

ZED LIMITED
TRADING, PROFIT AND LOSS ACCOUNT FOR THE YEAR ENDED 31 DECEMBER 20X3

	£'000	£'000
Sales		920
Cost of sales		
Opening stock	35	
Purchases	500	
	535	
Closing stock	40	
		(495)
Gross profit		425
Operating expenses (W4)	368	
Depreciation: machinery	9	
building	1	
Bad debts	5	
		(383)
Operating profit		42
Debenture interest		8
Net profit		34
Dividends: preference	4	
ordinary	26	
		30
Retained profit for the year		4

ZED LIMITED
BALANCE SHEET AS AT 31 DECEMBER 20X3

	£'000	£'000	£'000
Fixed assets			
Land at valuation			130
Building	80	6	74
Machinery	90	52	38
			242
Current assets			
Stock		40	
Debtors		35	
Bank (W1)		56	
		131	
Creditors (25 + 10)		(35)	
Net current assets			96
			338
Debentures			(50)
			288
Capital and reserves			
Ordinary shares of £1 each			130
Preference shares			40
Share premium			30
Revaluation reserve (45 + 5)			50
Profit and loss account (34 + 4)			38
			288

Workings

1   *Bank balance*

BANK A/C

	£'000		£'000
Debtors (W2)	896	Balance b/d	7
Share issue	60	Creditors (W3)	495
		Dividends: ordinary	26
		preference	4
		Debenture interest	8
		Operating expenses	360
		Balance c/d	56
	956		956

2   *Receipts from debtors*

DEBTORS CONTROL A/C

	£'000		£'000
Balance b/d	24	Bad debts	5
Sales	920	Contra	8
		Bank (bal. fig)	896
		Balance c/f	35
	944		944

3   *Payments to creditors*

CREDITORS CONTROL A/C

	£'000		£'000
Contra	8	Balance b/d	28
Bank (bal fig)	495	Purchases	500
Balance c/f	25		
	528		528

4   *Operating expenses*

	£'000
Owed 1.1.X3	(2)
Paid during year	360
Owed 31.12.X3	10
P & L charge	368

Chapter 9

9   Cash flow statements

CAT LIMITED
CASH FLOW STATEMENT FOR THE YEAR ENDED 30 JUNE 20X2

	£'000	£'000
Net cash inflow from operating activities		71,000
Returns on investment and servicing of finance		
Interest paid	1,500	
Net cash outflow for returns on investment and servicing of finance		(1,500)
		69,500
Taxation		
Corporation tax paid (W3)	12,000	
Tax paid		(12,000)
Capital expenditure		57,500
Payments to acquire tangible fixed assets (W4)	34,000	
Net cash outflow from investing activities		(34,000)
Net cash outflow before financing		23,500
Equity dividends paid		(13,000)
Financing		10,500
Issue of ordinary share capital	3,000	
Redemption of debentures	(10,000)	
		(7,000)
Increase in cash		3,500

NOTES TO THE CASH FLOW STATEMENT

1   *Reconciliation of operating profit to net cash inflow from operating activities*

	£'000
Operating profit (W1)	56,000
Depreciation	11,000
Increase in stocks	(6,000)
Decrease in debtors	2,000
Increase in creditors	8,000
Net cash inflow from operating activities	71,000

2   *Analysis of changes in cash and cash equivalents during the year*

	£'000
Balance at 1 July 20X1	10,000
Net cash inflow	3,500
Balance at 30 June 20X2	13,500

BPP PUBLISHING

3   *Analysis of the balances of cash and cash equivalents as shown in the balance sheet*

	20X1	20X2	*Change in year*
	£'000	£'000	£'000
Cash at bank	10,000	13,500	3,500

4   *Analysis of changes in financing during the year*

	Share capital	*Share premium*	*10% debentures*
	£'000	£'000	£'000
Balance at 1 July 20X1	26,000	12,000	20,000
Cash inflow (outflow) from financing	2,000	1,000	(10,000)
Balance at 30 June 20X2	28,000	13,000	10,000

Workings

1   *Operating profit*

PROFIT AND LOSS ACCOUNT

	£'000		£'000
Taxation	15,000	Balance b/f 1.7.X1	31,000
		Profit for the year	
Dividends	17,000	(bal fig)	54,500
Balance c/f 30.6.X2	53,500		
	85,500		85,500

Profit for the year is after charging debenture interest of 10% × 10,000 for 12 months and 10% × 10,000 for 6 months. Therefore operating profit for Note 1 to the cash flow statement is 54,500 + 1,500 = 56,000.

2   *Dividends*

DIVIDENDS

	£'000		£'000
Dividends paid	13,000	Balance b/f 1.7.X1	13,000
Balance c/f 30.6.X2	17,000	Profit and loss account	17,000
	30,000		30,000

3   *Tax paid*

TAXATION

	£'000		£'000
Tax paid*	12,000	Balance b/f 1.7.X1	12,000
Balance c/f 30.6.X2	15,000	Profit and loss a/c	15,000
	27,000		27,000

*Note. The tax paid will be last year's year-end provision

397

4   *Fixed assets*

FIXED ASSETS

	£'000		£'000
Balance b/f 1.7.X1	85,000	Balance c/f 30.6.X2	119,000
Purchases (bal fig)	34,000		
	119,000		119,000

Chapter 10

10   Company capital and interpretation

(a) (i)   Shares are the units through which investors take up the capital of a company. They are designated a fixed nominal value and together represent the share capital of the company.

(ii) Reserves represent the remainder of shareholders' funds excluding share capital. They are the additional amount to which the shareholders would be entitled on a winding up after all other claims had been met and the nominal value of the shares repaid. There are many different types of reserve, both revenue and capital, distributable and non-distributable.

(iii) A debenture is a long-term loan to the company written under deed and usually secured on the assets of the company. Debentures earn a fixed rate of interest and usually have a fixed redemption date.

(iv) Shareholders' equity comprises share capital and reserves as described above.

(v)   Capital employed comprises shareholders' equity and long term loans.

(b) Return on capital employed is a profitability ratio which states the profits as a percentage of the capital used to earn it.

The return is calculated by dividing profit on ordinary activities before interest and tax by the total of shareholders' funds and long-term liabilities.

The ratio is useful to management and of interest to financial analysts on a comparative basis. It has its limitations, however, not least the fact that it is calculated on out-of-date historical cost figures for assets.

Chapter 11

11 Working capital ratios

(a)

	20X5		20X6	
Current ratio	$\dfrac{30,500}{24,000}$	= 1.27	$\dfrac{28,500}{20,000}$	= 1.43
Quick assets ratio	$\dfrac{16,500}{24,000}$	= 0.69	$\dfrac{15,500}{20,000}$	= 0.78
Stock (number of days held)	$\dfrac{14,000}{42,000}$	× 365 = 122 days	$\dfrac{13,000}{34,000}$	× 365 = 140 days
Debtors (number of days outstanding)	$\dfrac{16,000}{60,000}$	× 365 = 97 days	$\dfrac{15,000}{50,000}$	× 365 = 109 days
Creditors (number of days outstanding)	$\dfrac{24,000}{42,000}$	× 365 = 209 days	$\dfrac{30,000}{34,000}$	× 365 = 215 days
Gross profit	$\dfrac{18,000}{60,000}$	= 30%	$\dfrac{16,000}{50,000}$	= 32%
Net profit % (before taxation)	$\dfrac{300}{60,000}$	= 0.5%	$\dfrac{1,700}{50,000}$	= 3.4%
Interest cover	$\dfrac{2,500}{2,200}$	=1.14	$\dfrac{3,000}{1,300}$	= 2.31
Dividend cover	$\dfrac{(50)}{600}$	= (0.08)	$\dfrac{1,100}{600}$	= 1.83
ROOE (before taxation)	$\dfrac{300}{13,350}$	= 2.2%	$\dfrac{1,700}{14,000}$	= 12%
ROCE	$\dfrac{2,500}{19,350}$	= 13%	$\dfrac{3,000}{19,500}$	= 15%
Gearing	$\dfrac{6,000}{19,350}$	= 31%	$\dfrac{5,500}{19,500}$	= 28%

(b)   Turnover has increased by 20%, but cost of sales has increased at a faster rate (23%) with the result that gross profit percentage has fallen by 2%. This trend may well be due to forces beyond the company's control such as the recession and the actions of suppliers and competitors.

Interest expense has increased significantly, and this is one of the main factors contributing to the after tax loss shown in 20X6. In view of the loss it was perhaps imprudent of the company to maintain the dividend at its 20X5 level although this may be a deliberate device to maintain shareholder confidence. Borrowing has increased, leading to a worsening of the gearing ratio. Interest cover is too low for comfort.

As regards current assets, there is a welcome improvement in stock, debtors and creditors turnover which have all fallen. This is linked to a fall in the current and quick ratios neither of which, however, appears dangerously low.

An encouraging sign is that the company has invested in fixed assets which, it is to be hoped, will pay off in future years.

Chapter 12

12 **Interpreting company accounts**

The case for retaining the small company audit rests on the value of the statutory audit to those who have an interest in audited accounts, ie the users of accounts. Examples include the following.

(a) Shareholders not involved in management need the reassurance given by audited accounts. Furthermore, the existence of the audit deters the directors from treating the company's assets as their own to the detriment of minority shareholders or, more importantly, the creditors.

Audited financial statements are invaluable in arriving at a fair valuation of the shares in an unquoted company either for taxation or other purposes.

(b) Banks rely on accounts for the purposes of making loans and reviewing the value of their security.

(c) The Inland Revenue and Customs and Excise rely on accounts for computing corporation tax and checking VAT returns.

(d) Audit is the price to be paid for limited liability, regardless of the size of the company.

The case in favour of abolition is as follows.

(a) In an owner-managed company where the directors are the shareholders there is no need for an independent check on the directors' stewardship to be carried out on behalf of the shareholders.

(b) The audit fee represents a substantial sum to a small company. The benefits of a small company audit are less than the cost.

(c) Many accounting standards do not apply to small companies, or are excessive.

(d) The argument that the audit is the price to be paid for limited liability carries less weight when, as is often the case with, for example, small companies and banks, the latter often obtain personal guarantees from directors.

(e) There is no evidence that the Inland Revenue, Customs and Excise or the banks value audited accounts more than unaudited accounts.

Chapter 14

13   Classifying costs

REPORT

To: Finance Director
From: Cost Accountant
Date: 1 January 20X1
Subject: Cost classification

(a)   Costs can be classified in the following ways.

   (i)   Direct and indirect cost

   (ii)   By function (manufacturing, administration, marketing)

   (iii)   By element of cost

   (iv)   Fixed and variable cost

(b)   Cost classification assists management in decision making, planning and control.

   (i)   Direct and indirect cost classification is especially useful for decision making and for control purposes. For example, if managers know the direct cost of a unit they can assess its individual profitability and the direct cost of a cost centre can help in judging the efficiency and effectiveness of the centre. This type of classification also allows the identification of overheads and their subsequent apportionment and absorption.

   (ii)   Collecting costs by function allows the cost accountant to cost a product or service.

   (iii)   Classification by element will improve control because management will be able to allocate responsibilities more effectively and then be able to concentrate on the more important and significant elements of cost.

   (iv)   If managers know which costs are fixed and which are variable they can plan to achieve a desired level of profit and can determine the breakeven point. A knowledge of cost behaviour will also help them to understand the effect on cost of any proposed change in activity levels and it will assist in various ad hoc decisions such as dropping a product line and make or buy decisions.

Chapter 15

14   Cost behaviour

(a)   It is an over-simplification to say that costs are readily identifiable as either fixed or variable throughout a range of production.

While many variable costs approximate to a linear behaviour pattern (rise in a straight line fashion as the volume of activity increases), some variable costs are in fact curvilinear, becoming either more expensive or cheaper per unit as activity levels change. A unit variable cost which might increase as activity increases is direct labour. Bonus payments might be paid progressively as certain levels of production are reached. An example of a variable cost becoming progressively cheaper per unit as activity increases is direct materials. Discounts are sometimes available when larger quantities are purchased.

Fixed costs do not necessarily remain fixed. While many fixed costs do remain constant within the relevant range of activity, there are likely to be steps or changes in the fixed cost if activity extends beyond this range. For example, it may be possible to operate with one salaried supervisor at a certain level of activity, but once this activity level is exceeded more supervisors are required and there is a resulting step in the fixed cost. This is known as step cost behaviour.

A lot of costs are actually semi-fixed (or semi-variable or mixed). The increasing labour cost described above has a flat fixed rate and a variable bonus element and a telephone bill will have a fixed cost for rental and a variable cost depending on the number of calls made. Other cost patterns include step costs (supervisor, as described above, and rent, where accommodation requirements increase as output levels get higher) and patterns appropriate to certain items (such as where a bulk purchase discount applies retrospectively to all units purchased or where a discount applies only to units purchased in excess of a certain quantity).

(b) A directly variable cost is a cost which increases or decreases in direct proportion to the level of activity. Production labour has traditionally been regarded as a directly variable cost. Any of the following factors or circumstances could make this treatment inappropriate.

(i) *The existence of guaranteed daily or weekly wages.* These are payable regardless of the level of activity. Production labour would then be a fixed or a semi-variable cost.

(ii) *Negotiated permanent manning levels.* This would mean that employees would still be paid even if there was no work available in a slack period.

(iii) *Differential bonus or piecework rates.* These would cause the labour cost per unit to increase for higher levels of output.

(iv) *A high degree of mechanisation.* This could mean that the labour input has little effect on the volume of output.

Chapter 16

15 **Absorption costing**

(a) The actual overhead may be apportioned to the production departments from the service departments by means of the repeated distribution method calculation.

	Machining £	Assembly £	Maintenance £	Stores £
Actual overhead	7,700	10,000	12,500	4,500
Apportion maintenance	8,750	2,500	(12,500)	1,250
			0	5,750
Apportion stores	2,300	1,725	1,725	(5,750)
			1,725	0
Apportion maintenance	1,208	345	(1,725)	172
			0	172
Apportion stores	69	52	51	(172)
			51	0
Apportion maintenance	36	10	(51)	5
Apportion stores (say)	3	2		(5)
	20,066	14,634		

The total overheads of £34,700 are therefore apportioned as shown to become 'actual' overheads of the two production departments.

Absorbed overhead	*Machining*	*Assembly*
Budgeted overhead	£18,000	£15,000
Budgeted activity	720 machine hours	4,800 direct labour hours
Absorption rate	£25 per machine hour	£3.125 per direct labour hour
Actual activity	703 machine hours	5,256 direct labour hours
Absorbed overhead	£17,575	£16,425

MACHINING DEPARTMENT OVERHEAD ACCOUNT

	£		£
Overhead incurred	20,066	Work in progress (machining department)	17,575
		Under-absorbed overhead account	2,491
	20,066		20,066

ASSEMBLY DEPARTMENT OVERHEAD ACCOUNT

	£		£
Overhead incurred	14,634	Work in progress	16,425
Over-absorbed overhead a/c	1,791	(assembly department)	
	16,425		16,425

(b)   In the machining department, the under-absorbed overhead occurred because actual expenditure was in excess of budgeted expenditure, and actual activity was below the budget of 720 machine hours. The excess spending and under-capacity should be investigated to learn their cause.

In the assembly department, the over-absorption of overhead was due to the extra capacity (the number of direct labour hours worked was in excess of budget) and also because actual expenditure was below the budget of £15,000.

Chapter 17

16   Marginal costing

(a)   The features which distinguish marginal costing from absorption costing are as follows.

(i)   In absorption costing, items of stock are costed to include a 'fair share' of fixed production overhead, whereas in marginal costing, stocks are valued at variable production cost only. Closing stocks will therefore be valued more highly in absorption costing than in marginal costing.

(ii)   As a consequence of carrying forward an element of fixed production overheads in closing stock values, the cost of sales used to determine profit in absorption costing will:

(1)   Include some fixed production overhead costs incurred in a previous period but carried forward into opening stock values of the current period

(2)   Exclude some fixed production overhead costs incurred in the current period by including them in closing stock values

In contrast marginal costing charges the actual fixed costs of a period in full into the profit and loss account of the period. (Marginal costing is therefore sometimes known as period costing.)

(iii) In absorption costing, 'actual' fully absorbed unit costs are reduced by producing in greater quantities, whereas in marginal costing, unit variable costs are unaffected by the volume of production (that is, provided that variable costs per unit remain unaltered at the changed level of production activity). Profit in any period can be affected by the actual volume of production in absorption costing; this is not the case in marginal costing.

(iv)   In marginal costing, the identification of variable costs and of contribution enables management to use cost information more easily for decision-making purposes (such as in budget decision making). It is easy to decide by how much contribution (and therefore profit) will be affected by changes in sales volume. (Profit would be unaffected by changes in production volume.)

In absorption costing, however, the effect on profit in a period of changes in both:

(1)   Production volume, and

(2)   Sales volume

is not easily seen, because behaviour is not analysed and incremental costs are not used in the calculation of actual profit.

BPP
PUBLISHING

(b)   *Working*

	Production costs £	Sales etc costs £
Total costs of 60,000 units (fixed plus variable)	510,000	150,000
Total costs of 36,000 units (fixed plus variable)	(366,000)	(126,000)
Difference = variable costs of 24,000 units	144,000	24,000
Variable costs per unit	£6	£1

It therefore follows that:

	£	£
Total costs of 60,000 units	510,000	150,000
Variable costs of 60,000 units	(360,000)	(60,000)
Fixed costs	150,000	90,000

The rate of absorption of fixed production overheads will therefore be:

$$\frac{£150,000}{60,000} = £2.50 \text{ per unit}$$

(i)   (1)   The fixed production overhead absorbed by Allergic would be 16,500 units produced × £2.50 = £41,250.

	£
(2) Budgeted annual fixed production overhead	150,000
Budgeted = actual quarterly overhead	37,500
Absorbed into production (see (1) above)	(41,250)
Over-absorption of fixed production costs	3,750

(3)   Profit for the quarter, using absorption costing

	£	£
Sales (13,500 × £12)		162,000
Costs of production (no opening stocks)		
Value of stocks produced (16,500 × £8.50)	140,250	
Less value of closing stocks		
(3,000 units × full production cost £8.50)	(25,500)	
Production cost of sales	114,750	

Sales etc costs	£	
Variable (13,500 × £1)	13,500	
Fixed ($\frac{1}{4}$ of £90,000)	22,500	
	36,000	
Total cost of sales	150,750	
Less over-absorbed production overhead	(3,750)	
		(147,000)
Profit		15,000

(*Tutorial note.* Several alternative methods of presenting the profit statement would be acceptable. Students are advised, however, that an absorption costing statement should include the overheads absorbed in production costs and the adjustment for under-/over-absorption of overhead.)

(ii)   Profit statement using marginal costing

	£	£
Sales		162,000
Variable costs of production (16,500 × £6)	99,000	
Less value of closing stocks (3,000 × £6)	18,000	
Variable production cost of sales	81,000	
Variable sales etc costs	13,500	
Total variable cost of sales (13,500 × £7)		94,500
Contribution (13,500 × £5)		67,500
Fixed costs: production	37,500	
sales etc	22,500	
		60,000
Profit		7,500

(*Tutorial note*. The difference between the profit in (i) and (ii) of £7,500 is caused by the difference in closing stock values, which amounts to the fixed overhead absorbed on the 3,000 units at £2.50 per unit. Had there been any opening stocks, the difference in their valuation would also have affected the comparative figures.)

GLOSSARY

Absorption costing/Full costing A method of costing which includes in the total cost of a product an appropriate share of an organisation's total overhead.

Account A record in the bookkeeping ledger in which is kept details of all the financial transactions relating to one individual supplier, customer, asset, liability or type of expense or receipt.

Accounting The recording of financial transactions and the preparation of accounting reports and financial statements from bookkeeping records in accordance with acknowledged methods and conventions.

Accounting equation Assets = Capital + Liabilities.

Accrual Expense (usually) or revenue outstanding at the end of a trading period which needs to be *accrued* for inclusion with the accounting records for the period.

Accruals concept Revenue and costs are accrued, that is, recognised as they are earned or incurred, not as money is received or paid, matched with one another so far as their relationship can be established or justifiably assumed and dealt with in the profit and loss account of the period to which they relate (SSAP 2).

Acid test ratio Also known as *quick ratio*. This is a measure of a company's ability to meet its short term debts. It is a more stringent test of liquidity than the *current ratio*, because it assumes that stocks cannot necessarily be readily converted into liquid funds.

$$\text{Acid test ratio} = \frac{\text{Current assets} - \text{stock}}{\text{Current liabilities}}$$

Activity based costing (ABC) An alternative to the more traditional absorption costing. Involves the identification of the factors which cause the costs of an organisation's major activities. Support overheads are charged to products on the basis of their usage of an activity.

Amortisation This is similar to *depreciation*, but is generally applied either to leasehold buildings, or to intangible fixed assets such as *research and development* or *goodwill*, rather than to machinery and equipment.

Appropriation account The record of how the profit or loss has been allocated to distributions or reserves.

Asset Resource *owned* by a business and of value to that business. Assets are classified as *fixed* or *current*.

Asset turnover The ratio of sales in a year to the amount of net assets (capital employed).

Audit A systematic examination of the activities and status of an entity, based primarily on investigation and analysis of its systems, controls, and records (CIMA *Official Terminology*). It is important to distinguish between *internal audit* and *external audit*.

Auditors' report The formal document in which the auditors express an opinion as to whether the financial statements of an entity:

(a) Show a true and fair view of:

    (i) Its position at a given date, and

(ii)   The results of its operations for the accounting period ended on that date, and

(b)   Have been properly prepared in accordance with the relevant statutory requirements.

OR

Any report by auditors in accordance with their terms of appointment. (CIMA *Official Terminology*, adapted)

Average cost A materials pricing and stock valuation method which bases values/prices on the average for a given period.

Bad debt A debtor who fails to pay his outstanding debt to a company within a reasonable time, after which the balance is written off.

Balance The difference between the totals of the debit and credit entries in an account.

Balance sheet A statement of the *liabilities*, *capital* and *assets* of a business at a given moment. It is like a 'snapshot' photograph since it captures on paper a still image of something which is constantly changing.

Bank reconciliation A comparison of a bank statement with the cash book. Differences between the balance on the bank statement and the balance in the cash book will be errors or timing differences, and they should be identified and explored.

Bookkeeping The recording of monetary transactions.

Business entity concept The concept that financial accounting information relates only to the activities of the business entity and not to the activities of its owner(s). (CIMA *Official Terminology*)

Business equation $P = I + D - C_i$

    where   P   represents profit

                I   represents the increase in net assets after drawings have been taken out by the proprietor

                D   represents drawings

                C_i represents the amount of extra capital introduced into the business during the period.

Capital employed The total funds invested in a business made up of shareholders' funds and loan capital. It is equivalent in value to a company's net assets.

Capital expenditure Expenditure on fixed assets, the net cost of which is to be 'capitalised' and depreciated over the anticipated useful working life of the assets.

Capital Money put into a business by its owner(s) with the intention of earning a profit.

Cash account A record of receipts and payments of cash or cheques.

Cash cycle See *operating cycle*.

Cash flow The amount of money flowing into and out of a business during a period. It does not necessarily equate to costs and revenues over the same period.

Cash flow statement A statement produced either for management or for external reporting purposes showing, by broad category, cash receipts and payments in a period. The term may also refer to a forecast for future period.

Chairman's report A voluntary report often produced by large companies giving a (generally favourable) overview of the state of the business.

Company A company is a business which is a separate legal entity formed by registration under the Companies Act.

Consistency concept The principle that there is uniformity of accounting treatment of like items within each accounting period and from one period to the next. (SSAP 2)

Contribution Sales value less variable cost of sales.

Corporate report A comprehensive package of information which describes an organisation's economic activities.

Cost accounting An internal reporting system for an organisation's own management.

Cost behaviour The variability of input costs with activity undertaken.

Cost centre Acts as a collecting place for certain costs before they are analysed further.

Cost classification The grouping of costs having regard to their nature and purpose.

Cost driver Factor which causes the costs of an activity. Used in activity based costing.

Cost pool A group of all costs that are associated with the same activity or cost driver.

Credit An entry recorded on the right hand side of the account which represents a decrease in the value of a company's assets or expenses or an increase in the value of its liabilities or revenues.

Creditor A person to whom a business owes money. A trade creditor is a person to whom a business owes money for debts incurred in the course of trading operations.

Creditors' turnover period This is the period of credit taken from suppliers. It is the length of time between the purchase of materials and the payment to suppliers. It may be calculated as:

$$\frac{\text{Average (or year-end) trade creditors}}{\text{Purchases}} \times 365$$

Current asset Current assets are either:

(a) Items owned by the business with the intention of turning them into cash within one year, or

(b) Cash, including money in the bank, owned by the business.

These assets are current in the sense that they are continually flowing through the business.

Current cost accounting (CCA) A method of accounting in which profit is defined as the surplus after allowing for price changes on the funds needed to continue the existing business and to maintain its operating capability, whether financed by shares or borrowing. A CCA balance sheet shows the effect of physical capital maintenance. (CIMA *Official Terminology*)

Current liabilities Debts of the business which must be paid within a fairly short period, by convention one year.

Current purchasing power (CPP) A way of accounting for inflation in which the values of the non-monetary items in the historical cost accounts are adjusted using a general price index to show the change in the general purchasing power of money. The CPP balance sheet shows the effect of financial capital maintenance.

Current ratio A ratio which measures a company's liquidity by comparing its short term liabilities with the current assets out of which these liabilities will be met.

$$\text{Current ratio} = \frac{\text{current assets}}{\text{current liabilities}}$$

Debenture The written acknowledgement of a debt by a company, usually given under its seal, and normally containing provisions as to payment of interest and the terms of repayment of principal. A debenture may be secured on some or all of the assets of the company or its subsidiaries. (CIMA *Official Terminology*)

Debit An entry made on the left hand side of the account which represents an increase in the value of a business' assets or expenses or a decrease in the value of its liabilities or revenue.

Debt collection period The length of the credit period taken by the customer: the time between the sale of an item and the receipt of cash from the customer. It may be calculated as:

$$\frac{\text{Average debtors (or year-end debtors)}}{\text{Credit sales}} \times 365$$

Debtor A person who owes the business money. A trade debtor is a customer who buys goods without paying cash for them straight away.

Debtors' turnover See *debt collection period*.

Depreciation The measure of the wearing out, consumption or other loss of value of a fixed asset whether arising from use, effluxion of time, or obsolescence through technology and market changes. (FRS 15)

Direct cost A cost that can be traced in full to the product, service or department that is being costed.

Directors' report A report contained in the annual report which gives a fair review of the development of the business during the year and of its position at the end of it. (CA 1985, adapted)

Distribution cost The cost of warehousing products for sale and of delivering them to customers.

Dividend A distribution to shareholders out of profits, usually in the form of cash, in proportion to the number of shares that they hold in the business.

Double entry (bookkeeping) The method by which a business records financial transactions. An account is maintained for every supplier, customer, asset, liability, and income and expense. Every transaction is recorded twice so that every *debit* is balanced by a *credit*.

Doubtful debts An amount charged against profit which allows for the fact that a proportion of debts may not be recovered. The amount is also deducted from debtors.

External audit A periodic examination of the books of account and records of an entity carried out by an independent third party (the auditor) to ensure that they have been properly maintained, are accurate and comply with established concepts, principles, accounting standards, legal requirements and give a true and fair view of the financial state of the entity. (CIMA *Official Terminology*)

Financial accounting The classification and recording of the monetary transactions of an entity in accordance with established concepts, principles, accounting standards and legal requirements and their presentation, by means of profit and loss accounts, balance sheets and cash flow statements, during and at the end of an accounting period. (CIMA *Official Terminology*)

Financial Reporting Standard (FRS) An accounting standard produced by the Accounting Standards Board (ASB).

Financial statements Summaries of accounts to provide information for interested parties. The most common financial statements are:

(a)   Trading and profit and loss account

(b)   Profit and loss appropriation account

(c)   Balance sheet

(d)   Cash flow statement

(e)   Auditor's report (CIMA *Official Terminology*, adapted)

First in first out (FIFO) A method of stock valuation in which it is assumed that the first goods into stock will be the first to be issued for use or sale. Compare LIFO and *average cost*.

Fixed asset An asset acquired for continuing use within the business with a view to earning income or making profits from its use either directly or indirectly. A fixed asset is not acquired for sale to a customer.

Fixed cost/period cost Cost which tends to be unaffected by increases or decreases in the volume of output. It is a period charge and so as the time span increases, so too will the cost.

Fundamental accounting concepts The basic assumptions which underlie the periodic financial accounts of an entity.

Gearing The proportion of a company's capital employed that is tied up in loan capital. There are various ways of calculating the ratio, which may be found in Chapter 10.

Going concern concept The assumption that the entity will continue in operational existence for the foreseeable future. (SSAP 2)

Historical cost accounting A system of accounting in which all values are based on the historical costs incurred. This is the basis prescribed in the Companies Act for published accounts. (Note: the Companies Act also contains Alternative Accounting Rules which enable certain assets to be stated at revalued amounts. (CIMA *Official Terminology*)

Imprest system A method of controlling cash or stock. When the cash or stock has been reduced by disbursements or issues it is restored to its original level.

Indirect cost/overhead Cost incurred in the course of making a product, providing a service or running a department, but which cannot be traced directly and in full to the product, service or department.

Intangible assets Assets which do not have a physical identity (such as *goodwill*, patents, trade marks unamortised research and development costs). They are classified as fixed assets because they cannot readily be converted into cash.

Last in first out (LIFO) A method of stock valuation which is the opposite of *FIFO*. Materials are charged to production in the reverse order of their receipt.

Ledger A collection of accounts, for example a collection of suppliers' accounts is the purchase ledger.

Liabilities An amount owed to a business.

Limiting factor A resource which limits an organisation's activities. An organisation should attempt to maximise the benefit it can obtain from the resource.

Loan capital Money that has been loaned to the company on a long-term basis at a pre-agreed rate of interest. The lenders of loan capital do not (normally) share in the profits of a business.

Long term liabilities Debts which are not payable within the *short term* and so any liability which is not current must be long-term.

Management accounting A management information system which analyses data to provide information as a basis for management action. The concern of a management accountant is to present accounting information in the form most helpful to management.

Marginal cost The part of the cost of one unit of product or service which would be avoided if the unit were not produced, or which would increase if one extra unit were produced.

Marginal costing A method of costing in which only variable costs are charged as a cost of sale. Closing stocks of work in progress and finished goods are valued at marginal (variable) production cost. Fixed costs are treated as a period cost, and are charged in full to the profit and loss account of the accounting period in which they are incurred.

Mark-up The addition to the cost of goods to arrive at a selling price. Mark-up is often expressed as a percentage.

Materiality concept The principle that financial statements should separately disclose terms which are significant enough to affect evaluation or decisions.

Net assets The value of a company's total assets less its current liabilities, equivalent in value to its *capital employed*.

Net book value The historical cost of an asset less accumulated depreciation or other write down.

Net realisable value The price at which goods in stock could be currently sold less any costs which would be incurred to complete the sale. (SSAP 9)

Operating cycle A term used to describe the connection between working capital and cash movements in and out. The cycle is usually measured in days or months. It is also called the *cash cycle*.

Overhead See indirect cost.

Overhead absorption rate Used to attribute overhead to a product or service. Can be based on, for example, direct labour hours or direct machine hours.

Partnership The relationship which exists between persons carrying on businesses in common with a view to profit. (Partnership Act 1890)

Period cost See fixed cost.

Prepayments Amounts of money already paid by the business for benefits which have not yet been enjoyed but will be enjoyed within the next accounting period.

Profit and loss account A record of income earned and expenditure incurred over a given period.

Profit margin This is ratio of profit to sales and may also be called profit percentage. For example, if a company makes a profit of £20,000 on sales of £100,000 its profit margin is 20%.

Prudence concept The principle that revenue and profits are not anticipated, but are included in the profit and loss account only when realised in the form either of cash or of other assets, the ultimate cash realisation of which can be assessed with reasonable certainty; provision is made for all known liabilities (expense and losses) whether the amount of these is known with certainty or is a best estimate in the light of the information available. (SSAP 2)

Reserves Profit which has been re-invested in the business.

Return on capital employed (ROCE) The amount of profit as a percentage of capital employed. In your CIMA examination it should be calculated as:

$$\frac{\text{Net profit before tax and interest}}{\text{Average capital employed}}$$

Revenue expenditure Expenditure incurred for the purpose of the trade of the business or to maintain the existing earning capacity of fixed assets.

Semi-fixed cost See semi-variable cost.

Semi-variable/semi-fixed/mixed cost A cost containing both a fixed component and a variable component. It is therefore partly affected by changes in the volume of output.

Share capital The amount of money invested in a company by its risk-taking shareholders.

Share premium The excess of the share price over the nominal value of the share.

Shareholders' funds The amount of part of a company's capital owned by its shareholders. It is made up of share capital plus profits not distributed by the business.

Short term investments Stocks and shares of other businesses currently owned but with the intention of selling them in the near future.

Sole trader A person who carries on a business with sole legal responsibility. A sole trader's business is not a separate *legal* entity from the owner, but it is a separate accounting entity.

Step cost A cost which is fixed in nature but only within certain levels of activity.

Stock turnover The time an item is held in stores before it is used. It may be calculated as:

$$\frac{\text{Average stocks held (or year end stocks held)}}{\text{Cost of sales}}$$

Suspense account A temporary account opened for a number of reasons of which the most common are:

(a) The trial balance does not balance

(b) The bookkeeper of a business does not know where to post one side of a transaction

Tangible asset An asset having a physical identity, for example plant and machinery.

Trial balance A list of all the balances in a company's ledger accounts. Such a listing is generally used as the first step in the preparation of the final accounts and is used to prove that the total of all the debit balances is equal to the total of all the credit balances.

True and fair view Accounts will not be true and fair unless the information they contain is sufficient in quantity and quality to satisfy the reasonable expectations of the readers to whom they are addressed. (Legal Opinion)

Under-/over-absorbed overhead The difference between the overhead absorbed in a period and the overhead incurred.

Variable cost Cost which tends to vary directly with the volume of output.

Work-in-progress Any material component, product or contract at an intermediate stage of completion.

Working capital The difference between current assets and current liabilities.

BPP
PUBLISHING

INDEX

ORDER FORM

Any books from our Business Basics range can be ordered in one of the following ways:

- Telephone us on **020 8740 2211**

- Send this page to our **Freepost** address

- Fax this page on **020 8740 1184**

- Email us at **publishing@bpp.com**

- Go to our website: **www.bpp.com**

We aim to deliver to all UK addresses inside 5 working days. Orders to all EU addresses should be delivered within 6 working days. All other orders to overseas addresses should be delivered within 8 working days.

BPP Publishing Ltd
Aldine House
Aldine Place
London W12 8AW
Tel: 020 8740 2211
Fax: 020 8740 1184
Email: publishing@bpp.com

Full name: _____

Day-time delivery address: _____

_____

_____ Postcode _____

Day-time telephone (for queries only): _____

Please send me the following quantities of books:

	No. of copies	Price	Total
Accounting		£13.95	
Law		£13.95	
Quantitative Methods		£13.95	
Information Technology		£13.95	
Economics		£13.95	
Marketing		£13.95	
Human Resource Management		£13.95	
Organisational Behaviour		£13.95	

Sub Total	£	

Postage & Packaging

UK : £3.00 for first plus £2.00 for each extra	£
Europe : (inc. ROI) £5.00 for first plus £4.00 for each extra	£
Rest of the world : £20.00 for first plus £10.00 for each extra	£

Grand Total	£

I enclose a cheque for £_____ (cheque to BPP Publishing Ltd) or charge to Access/VISA/Switch

Card number: ☐☐☐☐☐☐☐☐☐☐☐☐☐☐☐☐☐☐☐

Issues number (Switch only): _____

Start date: _____ Expiry date: _____

Signature _____

REVIEW FORM & FREE PRIZE DRAW

We are constantly reviewing, updating and improving our publications. We would be grateful for any comments or thoughts you have on this book. Cut out and send this page to our Freepost address and you will be automatically entered in a £50 prize draw.

Jed Cope
Business Basics Range Manager
BPP Publishing Ltd, FREEPOST, London W12 8BR

Full name: _____

Address: _____

_____

_____ Postcode _____

Where are you studying?

Where did you find out about BPP books?

Why did you decide to buy this book?

Have you used our texts any other BPP books in your studies?

What thoughts do you have on our:

- Introductory pages

- Topic coverage

- Summary diagrams, icons, chapter roundups and quick quizzes

- Activities, case studies and questions

The other side of this form is left blank for any further comments you wish to make.

Please give any further comments and suggestions (with page number if necessary) below.

FREE PRIZE DRAW RULES

1   Closing date for 31 January 2001 draw is 31 December 2000. Closing date for 31 July 2001 draw is 30 June 2001.

2   Restricted to entries with UK and Eire addresses only. BPP employees, their families and business associates are excluded.

3   No purchase necessary. Entry forms are available upon request from BPP Publishing. No more than one entry per title, per person. Draw restricted to persons aged 16 and over.

4   Winners will be notified by post and receive their cheques not later than 6 weeks after the relevant draw date.

5   The decision of the promoter in all matters is final and binding. No correspondence will be entered into.